GEORGE JOFFÉ
editor

Jordan in Transition

T0333139

HURST & COMPANY, LONDON

First published in the United Kingdom by
C. Hurst & Co. (Publishers) Ltd.,
38 King Street, London WC2E 8JZ
Copyright © C. Hurst & Co. (Publishers) Ltd, 2002
All rights reserved.
Typeset by Discript, London WC2
Printed in Scotland

ISBNs
1-85065-483-2 *cased*
1-85065-488-3 *paperback*

ACKNOWLEDGEMENTS

This book is a collective work by an international group of scholars, brought together in July 2000 by the Amman branch of the Centre d'Etudes et de Recherches sur le Moyen-Orient Contemporain (CER-MOC) and the Konrad Adenauer Foundation (KAF) Jordan office. Both the editor and the contributors would like to express their thanks to both organisations and their staffs for their unfailing and generous support at Amman and subsequently in organising the production of this book. Particular thanks are due to Dr Jean-Pierre Cassarino who was responsible for initially bringing the conference together and for shepherding its participants through their deliberations.

CONTENTS

TABLES AND FIGURES

THE CONTRIBUTORS

Ala al-Haharmaneh is at the University of Mainz, Germany.

Nassim Barham is at the University of Jordan in Amman.

Markus Bouillon is at St. Antony's College, Oxford University.

Françoise de Bel Air is at CERMOC in Jordan.

Renate Dietrich is at the University of Bonn, Germany.

Hamed el-Said teaches in the University of Manchester, England.

Eugenia Ferragina is at the University of Naples, Italy.

Matthew Gray is at the Australian National University in Canberra.

Waleed Hazbun is at Massachusetts Institute of Technology in Cambridge, MA.

George Joffé is affiliated to the Centre for International Studies at the University of Cambridge, England.

Christine Jungen is at the University of Nanterre, Paris.

Ali Kassay is an analyst based in Jordan.

Irene Maffi is at the University of Lausanne, Switzerland.

David Mednicoff teaches at the University of Massachusetts (in the USA).

Maen Nsour is Director of the Economic Aid Coordination Unit in the Ministry of Planning, Amman.

Oliver Schlumberger is at the University of Tübingen, Germany.

Ranjit Singh is at the University of Virginia.

Rateb Sweis is at the Jordan Institute of Diplomacy, Amman.

Quintin Wiktorowicz is at Chippensburg University (in the USA).

Introduction

JORDAN IN TRANSITION

George Joffé

The purpose of this book is to investigate the way in which Jordan is handling the transition from the long reign of King Hussain, who died in 1999 after ruling his kingdom for forty-eight tumultuous years, to the new circumstances that face his son, King Abdullah. It is also designed to investigate how Jordan will confront the external realities of economic globalisation and its domestic realities of political and social change, in an environment rendered particularly sensitive by the difficulties of the Middle East peace process between the Arab world and Israel.

Contemporary Jordan undoubtedly poses many serious questions of interpretation and analysis, particularly for the decade of the 1990s. The decade opened with the end of the Cold War and, for Jordan, the difficult issues of how to respond to the economic crisis which emerged in the wake of the Ma'an riots, provoked by the IMF-sponsored economic reform programme which began in 1989, as well as the problems arising from its close alliance with Iraq in the light of the Saddam Hussain regime's decision to annex Kuwait in August 1990. Jordan responded with the twin policies of domestic political liberalisation and peace with Israel in 1994, both initiatives being designed, in part, to recover the Western support that had been lost as a result of the Second Gulf War. Behind both lay the assumption that appropriate political and economic initiatives would enable Jordan to attract foreign aid and investment and preserve its socio-political structures upon which the survival of the monarchy depended. Indeed, in some cases, the real objectives of policy ran counter to its declared intent – this was certainly the case with political liberalisation – and in others, one policy was designed to substitute for another, once the latter had served its purpose – a development that, in part, lay behind the 1994 peace treaty with Israel and the subsequent (and consequent) stagnation in domestic political liberalisation.

Behind these considerations lie deeper questions. To what extent, for example, did the Hashemite monarchy really seek the restructuring of the domestic political scene after 1989, or was its objective merely to reformulate its traditional neo-patrimonial discourse, based on tribal support? Indeed, how capable would Jordanian society have been of undertaking such political and social transformations, given the persistence of patriarchal social structures within a neo-patriarchal political system? To what extent does the reinvention and reformulation of tribal values vitiate the assumptions behind participatory political life, whether in the form of political liberalisation or democratisation? Indeed, is democratisation really possible in a society of the kind found in Jordan and what is the real role played within it by civil society and non-governmental organisations? And what is Jordan's economic potential, given its massive resource constraints, particularly in the water sector? Is there sufficient entrepreneurial spirit, is the environment appropriate and do Jordanian entrepreneurs understand their limitations? And, finally, what will be the future role of Jordan's Palestinian majority within the future Jordanian state, whatever the outcome of the Middle East peace process? Many of these questions have no clear answers yet, although trends have already begun to emerge.

The international arena

The conventional interpretation of Jordan's strategy in foreign policy is based on the role of the national economic structure as a rentier economy.[1] In other words, its deficiencies in terms of resources and economic efficiency are countered by access to remittance, aid and other rents and its foreign policy is designed to maximise these returns. Markus Bouillon, however, argues that this is only part of the story and that the real key to foreign policy strategy is based in regime survival. One aspect of this process is ensuring access to sufficient capital inflows and the peace treaty with Israel can be seen in this context, quite apart from the long-standing Hashemite policy of seeking accommodation with its Israeli neighbour. However, the dominant concern is domestic stability and here the monarchy has been prepared to exploit foreign policy objectives, even when this has had adverse consequences in the international arena. Thus, during the Second Gulf War, King Hussain was at least as anxious to pacify domestic opinion as he was to avoid Western and Gulf Arab condemnation for the policies he followed. Subsequently, despite tilts against Iraq and towards Israel, often for financial benefit – the peace treaty in 1994 also generated a \$900 million debt forgiveness windfall from the United States – the king nevertheless kept his options with Iraq open and his successor has done the same.

A somewhat different approach has been adopted by Maen Nsour who argues that the fundamental tenor of Jordan's international environment has changed so that national security policy, which was originally concerned with geo-political threat, has been amplified by growing anxieties over geo-economic survival. In a sense, the underlying principle remains the same – regime and national survival – but the means by which it is articulated has changed. Geo-political dangers still remain, of course, particularly in the form of Israel despite the 1994 peace treaty. Furthermore, any expansion of the Middle East peace process to include Syria or the Palestinians could further marginalise Jordan's regional stature. However, the new challenge of economic globalisation requires the mobilisation of new policies designed to strengthen the domestic economy through regional economic integration and domestic economic restructuring.

Both concerns come together in the context of Jordan's participation in the Barcelona Process, more correctly the Euro-Mediterranean Partnership – the European Union's own, holistic policy towards the countries of the Southern Mediterranean basin which seeks to create a zone of 'shared peace, prosperity and stability', to quote the November 1995 Barcelona Declaration which introduced the Partnership. Jordan's inclusion in the Process – it is, after all, not a Mediterranean state – reflected European perceptions of the country's key importance in the Middle East peace process and its long tradition as a moderate Arab state in the context of the Arab-Israeli conflict. It also recalled European awareness of Jordan's economic status within the region, as a result of work already undertaken in the multilateral part of the Middle East peace process, through the Regional Economic Development Working Group (REDWG), which the Union had chaired. In that context, Jordan had a key role to play in regional economic integration alongside Israel, as it did in the MENA Economic Forum initiative, which sought to encourage regional and international private sector cooperation in the Middle East. Indeed, the economic provisions of the Barcelona Process have enabled Jordan, which depends on its ability to purchase from Europe as its leading import source, to sign a bilateral free trade area agreement with Europe that is designed both to galvanise the economic reform process inside Jordan as a precursor to increased private direct investment flows and to encourage regional economic integration after 2010.

The Barcelona Process, however, was far more than simply an economic initiative from Europe, as the dominant economic partner for Southern countries, such as Jordan (see Table[2]). It also involved

JORDAN'S IMPORTS AND EXPORTS, 1995–9

	1999	1998	1997	1996	1995
	%	%	%	%	%
Import source					
European Union	31.6	32.8	32.6	31.6	33.2
Arab world	22.1	19.2	23.5	25.0	23.5
United States	9.8	9.5	9.5	9.7	9.3
Export destination					
European Union	6.1	6.6	7.3	8.3	6.3
Arab world	41.2	44.6	51.9	46.6	45.0
United States	0.9	0.5	0.5	1.3	1.5

Source: Jordanian Government: *International Trade Statistics 2000*, Amman; http://www.nic.gov.jo

security, political, cultural and social provisions. These included co-operative security within the Mediterranean basin – a provision obviously dependent on a prior settlement of the Middle East peace process but which encouraged peace between Jordan and Israel as a first step – and requirements for good governance and respect for human rights – which ran counter to the stagnation in the political liberalisation agenda in Jordan. Insofar as these measures were designed to promote peace and stability, they would, if put properly into effect, also remove regime survival as the priority for Jordan's foreign policy and would protect Jordan against the dangers of economic globalisation. Indeed, the Barcelona Process would provide a solution to Jordan's growing awareness of the future geo-economic agenda in its security perspectives.

The economic agenda

In one respect, Jordan has already taken steps to adjust to this reality, even before the economic measures of the Barcelona Process begin to affect the Jordanian economy. Jordan's membership of the World Trade Organisation does, as Rateb Sweis points out, respond to the implications of economic globalisation, even though it is extremely difficult to anticipate what the likely outcomes may be as there are no documented accounts of how developing economies have responded to the conditions that membership imposes. There will be undoubted adverse short-term consequences, for the Jordanian economy, despite years of economic adjustment, is still dependent on rent and suffers from the engrained behavioural problems that typify Middle Eastern economies, as Oliver Schlumberger argues. He points out that

patronage and its concomitants are disincentives for economic efficiency and that, until institutional culture changes, institutional
change in itself cannot transform the economy. This is certainly important as far as the Barcelona Process is concerned, for, given the
preponderant role of the European Union in Jordan's imports, the
eventual removal of tariff barriers and the exposure of the Jordanian
private sector to unrestrained competition with European industry
will have initially calamitous effects on the Jordanian private sector
which will be worsened by 'patrimonial capitalism'.

In any case, Jordan's environmental situation is parlous, as Eugenia Ferragina describes. Without a dramatic improvement in water
supply and greater care and innovation over its use, Jordan faces the
unpleasant possibility of being unable to satisfy the demands to be
placed on this scarce resource in future. This is, in large measure, a
cultural concern, for the perception of water is often in opposition to
the constraints implied by reform to overcome water deficit. Thus
the social dynamics of water management will have a major part to
play in resolving this tension and the institutions introduced to
achieve reform must be seen to be both economically efficient and socially equitable. Unless this is achieved, there will be no social adaptive capacity to adjust to the situation of water scarcity.

Hamid El-Said is more sanguine. He points out that economic reform and restructuring in Jordan began in the late 1980s with IMF
and World Bank help but under the economic conditionalities normally imposed on fiscal deficits and balance of payments. Jordan responded to these demands but economic restructuring was painfully
slow until 1998, largely for domestic political reasons. Thereafter,
just as the political transition process in Jordan began, the restructuring process speeded up for the two processes were linked. Not
only was there a change in economic direction as regimes changed –
and, of course, King Hussain had to delegate power for some
months before his death – but there was a realisation that the promised 'peace dividend' from the peace treaty with Israel had been an
illusion. The question now is what the outcome of economic restructuring will be.

Nassim Barham is also more optimistic for he believes that Jordanian entrepreneurs can rise to the challenge. Even though most Jordanian entrepreneurs are still constrained by size constraints and
problems over investment access, as well as family ties and patron-
client strategies, so that they tend to be risk-averse, some sectors are
beginning to respond to the new challenges implicit in the contemporary economic environment. One such sector is tourism, seen in the
wake of the peace treaty with Israel as a powerful opportunity for

employment and wealth creation, as well as regional economic integration. Its overall effects on the domestic scene in Jordan will depend on the outcome of the economic liberalisation process, Matthew Gray argues, and on the 'peace dividend', should it materialise. It is thus an initiative that is also fraught with risk and, because of its political implications of closer association with Israel, it is an option that faces growing opposition.

These are themes that are analysed by Waleed Hazbun who points out that, in the context of the 1994 peace treaty, tourism was seen as key to the promotion of open borders and economic cooperation that would both strengthen peace and produce prosperity. There was, indeed, a short-term boom that, in turn, led the Jordanian state to encourage major investment in the sector. However, the necessary management skills were lacking and the centralised direction of the expansion of tourist facilities undermined initiatives towards integration with regional and global tourism strategies. Enclaves in the economy did benefit and rent-seeking opportunities were maximised but the subsequent stagnation of the expansion initiative meant that the state eventually bore the overall costs of failure.

The political dimension

Relative economic stagnation and disappointments such as the failure of tourist expansion were paralleled by other abortive initiatives, too, particularly in the political field. As Ranjit Singh points out, during the 1990s Jordan manifested – in comparison to Tunisia and Egypt – the contradiction of an illiberal state policy persisting within a context of formal liberalism. Although the parliamentary process was revived after 1989 and despite the formal agreements over the legitimate liberalised political arena contained in the 1991 National Charter, there has been little real progress and the Jordanian legislature is essentially marginalised by the monarchy – as was demonstrated by the 1993 Press Law, the imposition of the 1994 peace treaty with Israel and the high-handed official treatment of the *Hamas* leadership in Jordan in 1999 when four leading members were expelled to Qatar despite outraged public protest. In effect, the monarchy's general treatment of those dissenting from its policies seems to suggest that, despite liberalisation, the king still considers himself above the political process.

In many respects, the current situation recalls that of the Nabulsi government in 1956–7, for it was also unable to respond appropriately to popular pressure for reform, largely because the monarchy itself felt threatened. In short, liberalisation is tolerated in Jordan when the regime's core support is not threatened, although, conversely, such a situation does not encourage the regime to expand the field of liberalisation. Furthermore, contrary to the experience elsewhere, the mobilisation of civil society does not necessarily support a democratisation process in Jordan, as the 'positive opposition' policy of the Islamic Action Front demonstrates. In any case, the professional syndicates – the major non-governmental arena in Jordan – reflect institutionalised elite interests that have no investment in substantive political change. It is only when there is real redistribution of power that genuine interest in reform emerges amongst the elite for then the state and monarchical patronage system cannot reproduce itself.

The ineffectiveness of civil society in the Jordanian context is an important theme taken up by Allen MacDuffee who argues that political liberalisation and democratisation are both part of the Hashemite survival strategy. Civil society in Jordan has not acted, as it would have been expected to, as a buffer between state and society but has been, instead, detrimental to the democratisation process. Although civil society in Jordan may have reflected associational life, its lack of effect on state policy and practice means that it has really acted as a cover for the unchanging socio-political reality of neo-patriarchy in the country. In addition, its activities have been blocked by legislation and the National Charter, since they require prior state approval, and the approval process, as well as subsequent operation, is controlled by the *mukhabarat*.

David Mednicoff addresses similar themes, drawing parallels from Morocco. The democratisation process inevitably forced the Hashemite monarchy to confront what he calls the 'king's dilemma'; in other words, how does a monarchy retain legitimacy and relevance during a political modernisation process? In the case of Jordan, it was the king's legitimacy that made domestic stability possible and thus provided a basis from which liberalisation could be initiated. Democratisation would depend on two factors – respect for the rule-of-law and for the role of civil society. However, it also depends on 'cultural framing' the process whereby such concepts are given a cultural relevance and may become the basis for a new institutionalised political hegemony. The problem is, at present, that Jordanian civil society is quiescent because of the effect of patronage-clientage and international non-governmental organisations have little effective role.

Renate Dieterich also refers to the role of patron-client relations in her discussion of the role of political opposition in Jordan. Since its establishment in the 1920s, the Hashemite monarchy has successfully pacified opposition forces through co-option or repression. She points out that opposition is an essential component of the democratic process but that, in Jordan, formal political opposition and its concomitant, non-governmental organisations, are weak and do not challenge the government, particularly since the democratic reforms undertaken at the end of the 1980s were reversed during the following decade. The reasons for this are, she argues, manifold and involve – in addition to the longstanding tradition of co-option of potential opposition by the regime – the fact that the breadth of democratic discourse is defined by the regime and that no alternatives to established patterns of power are available, for the opposition's main concerns are anti-Zionism and opposition to IMF-inspired reforms. In short, the failure of the opposition agenda reinforces an authoritarian regime.

Ali Kassay takes up a similar theme when he looks at external influences on the democratic process in Jordan by analysing the nature of the democratisation process there. He argues that initial moves towards liberalisation resulted from the need to redefine its regional role in a manner that would reinforce its links with the West in the wake of potential economic collapse, as did the peace treaty with Israel. However, once the treaty had been concluded, the regime was able to abandon its liberal pretensions and turn towards control of the press and the opposition. The outlook for political liberalisation and democratisation in Jordan is thus bleak if there is no external, as well as internal, pressure on the political system for real reform.

Quintan Wiktorowicz is interested in the role of non-governmental organisations in Jordan which should, according to conventional theory and practice, create collective empowerment through grassroots associationalism. The Jordanian situation, however, suggests that this assumption is not correct for, although the number of non-governmental organisations doubled between 1989 and 1999, they continued to be unpoliticised and political freedoms had not been enlarged. The reason for this failure appears to be that such organisations became instruments of state control in a regime survival strategy behind a façade of political liberalisation in order to confront an economic crisis. Since there was no pressure from civil society on the regime, the elites that controlled it ensured their control through the expanding non-governmental organisation sector.

The social background

Of course, such political control is rooted in social practice and Françoise de Bel-Air argues that the neo-patriarchal structure of the state mirrors the persistence of patriarchalism within the family. She points out, however, that demographic change in Jordan during the 1980s has adversely affected patriarchal family structures and that these adverse effects parallel the controlled liberalisation of political life under the hand of the king who played a sociological and psychological role in Jordan similar to that of the father in the family, whose authority is now threatened by the new roles adopted by his sons. The persistence of the Hashemite discourse in Jordan's collective life is underlined by Irene Maffi, in her analysis of the exploitation of national history to this end in Jordan's museums which has led to the marginalisation of genuine local history for the sake of the national Hashemite project.

Christine Jungen analyses the way in which this has led to the perpetuation of the role of tribalism inside political life. Hashemite authority has always depended on the relations between the Royal House and Jordan's tribes. However, tribal self-belief is also a constructed reality which has created an idealised vision of the past to justify present patterns of power and influence within the political system. She examines how this has been done in the Kerak region which is dominated by two tribal groups, the al-Majali and the Tarawneh. The al-Majali have based their tribal prestige on the leadership of a revolt against the Ottomans in 1910 as evidence of their rejection of central authority although, in reality, tribal leaders were always in the pay of the local Ottoman administration. The tradition, however, is now used to authenticate the status of modern tribal patrons in the region and to distinguish 'true' Jordanians from Palestinians settled in the country.

Ala al-Hamarneh addresses the issue of the Palestinians in Jordan by examining attitudes in the major refugee camps around Amman. Most refugees are Jordanian citizens and, until the late 1990s, expected to return to Palestine, although they now accept that this will not be the case. As a result, the refugee population and, indeed, the camps themselves are being integrated into the urban physical and social landscape of Amman – a process which was helped in the early 1990s by the integration of Palestinian refugees from the Gulf, whose accumulated savings created a temporary miniature property boom. In terms of political representation, for example, this is exemplified by the loss of influence of the Palestine Liberation Organisation over the refugees and its replacement by the Islamic Action Front which has, through its parent organisation, the Muslim Brotherhood, good access to the Royal Palace. Not even Hamas has been able to threaten the Front's hegemonic position on the Palestinian political scene in Jordan.

A tentative conclusion

As Jordan starts the new millennium, the record of the last decade of the twentieth century does not suggest that the promises of political, economic and social change that introduced it have been met. On the contrary, little real progress has been made. Political liberalisation has been halted, for the monarchy never lost its grip over the political system and exploited liberalisation for the sake of its own survival strategy. Once the peace treaty with Israel had been signed in 1994, it was abandoned, for a return to the old neo-patriarchal policies of the past, rooted as they were in the alliance between the monarchy and Jordan's powerful tribes. In any case, such a political system mirrored the social reality in which *wasta* – the systematised exploitation of influence for personal advantage – and patronage-clientage continued to be the dominant themes. Even economic liberalisation, from which so much had been expected, proved to offer little, both because of the failure of the peace dividend to materialise and because of the social context in which economic change had to be realised.

There has, however, been a change of regime, after the death of King Hussain in 1999. His successor has taken a far more activist approach to the question of economic change, although early enthusiasm may yet be blunted by the reality of the global and regional economies. In foreign affairs, too, links to Iraq have been quietly strengthened whilst the peace treaty with Israel has been marginalised in view of the on-going crisis in the Occupied Territories. Yet the old elitist structures remain, together with the habits of mind that populate them. The fundamental assumptions of Hashemite power appear to be unchanged, even if more modern concerns have also entered the political arena.

The most immediate question has, perhaps, been posed by events, late in 2001, in the United States. The destruction of the World Trade Centre in New York and the attack on the Pentagon in Washington on September 11 may well mark a turning-point in relations between the West and the Middle East, not least over the issue of international terrorism. There are, however, other fundamental regional concerns that have fed into this central issue and that will have decisive implications depending on how they are addressed, if indeed they are ultimately addressed at all. Jordan cannot stand apart from this process, for its own foreign policy and its domestic polity are directly connected to two of them – the Israeli–Palestinian crisis and the problem of Iraq – while its southern neighbour, Saudi Arabia, will have to reconsider its own links with the United States. Beyond this are the cultural and economic consequences of globalization, now no longer seen as an irresistible force but one that is amenable to human direction.

Jordan's pro-Western choice now stands in increasingly strong contrast to popular currents sweeping the Middle East in the wake of these events and the subsequent Western war against international terrorism. Yet there is no obvious alternative, only the choice for government as to whether Western initiatives receive only rhetorical support or wholehearted cooperation while coping with popular antagonism. King Abdullah's government will have to exercise caution if it is to appease its domestic and foreign constituencies successfully, for it cannot be seen to embrace the new American agenda wholeheartedly until American policy towards Israel and Iraq is transformed. Yet it has already accepted a strategic, pro-Western option and must now find a way of maintaining a cautious distance from the consequences of Western determination to deal with the phenomenon of terrorism. To square this circle will require imagination and initiative.

In short, change is now vital if Jordan's traditional survival strategy – walking the tightrope between Iraq and Israel and between economic success in a global context and failure in national isolation – is to succeed in confronting this new situation and creating the national consensus which will be required. Economic liberalisation will require genuine political liberalisation as well and that, in turn, can only be achieved if old social habits of *wasta* and patronage eventually cease to be the determinants of political life. For this to be achieved, the monarchy will have to learn how to place itself genuinely above the political scene and accept the implications of civil society whilst the organisations that make it up will have to learn the ability of acting outside the umbrella of royal power. It is not clear that either side can face the implications of such a choice and thus defuse the dangers of political extremism. Yet, if they do not, the outlook for Jordan in an increasingly globalised but polarised world, with a chronic political crisis along its western border, must be grim.

NOTES

1. L. A. Brand, *Jordan's inter-Arab relations*, New York: Columbia University Press, 1994.
2. Care should be taken in interpreting these figures for the Arab world's dominant position in imports and exports reflects the role of Iraq, as well as Saudi Arabia. In the case of Iraq, most Arab world imports are crude oil. The Arab world's

George Joffé

dominant position as a Jordanian export destination reflects the role of agriculture in Jordan's exports. Jordan's trade balance is heavily in deficit, hence the need for external rents to balance the external account:

JORDAN'S TRADE BALANCE, 1999–5

	1999	1998	1997	1996	1995
Imports (× 1,000 JD)	2,634,254	2,714,374	2,908,085	3,043,556	2,590,250
Exports (× 1,000 JD)	1,017,053	1,046,382	1,067,164	1,039,801	1,004,534
Trade deficit (× 1,000 JD)	1,617,201	1,667,992	1,840,921	2,003,755	1,585,716
Deficit / imports (%)	61.4	61.5	63.3	65.8	61.2
Deficit / exports (%)	159.0	159.5	172.5	192.7	157.8

Source: http://www.nic.gov.jo

Part I. FOREIGN POLICY

WALKING THE TIGHTROPE

JORDANIAN FOREIGN POLICY FROM THE GULF CRISIS TO
THE PEACE PROCESS AND BEYOND

Markus Bouillon

Since the late 1980s, Jordan has gradually become involved in a process of political openness and economic liberalisation. At the same time, various changes involving the domestic, regional and international agendas of the kingdom have taken place. Of particular significance among these processes were the changes in Jordan's regional environment as well as in the kingdom's international relations during the 1990s, as exemplified in Jordan's behaviour during and after the Gulf Crisis and in the conclusion of the peace treaty with Israel in 1994. How can Jordan's pro-Iraqi policy in the early 1990s and the apparent shift towards Israel and the anti-Iraq coalition in the mid-1990s be explained? Has Jordan's behaviour simply been erratic, or has there been a continuity in terms of the underlying objectives of foreign policy?

The following study of Jordan's foreign policy from the Gulf Crisis to the peace process and beyond argues that the foremost objective of all policies in the kingdom is regime survival and the subsistence of Hashemite rule. One major factor, of course, is the securing of an interrupted flow of capital transfers into the kingdom, on which Jordan remains dependent. While this has been a central characteristic of Jordanian foreign policy for decades and was a crucial factor in King Hussain's decision to opt for peace with Israel, there is an inherent tension between this objective and the second major goal, namely the maintenance of domestic political stability. It is this second feature that is the overriding concern of Jordanian policy-makers. In reconciling the two, Jordan's foreign policy is a process of continuously walking the tightrope between the necessities of international and economic survival and domestic stability.

This chapter focuses on the two major foreign policy issues the Hashemite kingdom was confronted with during the 1990s; first, the Gulf Crisis of 1990–1 and the shift towards the anti-Iraq coalition and, second, the conclusion of the 1994 peace treaty with Israel. Both events are analysed on three levels, regional and international power politics, the economic and political-economic context, and finally, the domestic political situation. Drawing these two events together, the continuity in Jordan's underlying objectives, until King Hussain's death in February 1999, will be demonstrated and the general objectives of Jordanian foreign policy be summarised on that basis. In theoretical terms, the Jordanian case demonstrates that a revised approach to foreign-policy analysis needs to take into account not only balance of power politics or the economic structure of a state, but also the specific configuration of state-society relations and the domestic political context.

Jordan in the Gulf crisis

A day after Iraq's invasion of Kuwait in the early hours of 2 August 1990, the foreign ministers of the Arab League condemned Iraq's attack and called for an immediate withdrawal. Jordan's representative abstained in the vote on the resolution and the government later argued:

The passage of this resolution effectively frustrated Jordanian efforts to arrange for a mini-summit, hardened the attitude of the Iraqi government [and] paved the way for the Arab League to abandon any attempts to keep the crisis within the boundaries of the Arab fold.[1]

Another resolution that strongly condemned the Iraqi attack was passed at an emergency Arab summit, held in Cairo on 10 August. This time, it was proposed that, if necessary, Arab forces would be dispatched to defend the Gulf States against Iraq. Again, Jordan's representative abstained, speaking in favour of a peaceful settlement within the region and seeking to avoid foreign intervention. The media, politicians and the public in the West were outraged. The firm alliance with the West, particularly the United States, had always been regarded as a guarantee for Jordan's survival in the turmoil of Middle Eastern politics.[2] How could the king now favour a peaceful settlement in the face of such an aggressive act; how could he defy his friends and allies in the West?

Officially Jordan obeyed the United Nations embargo now imposed against Iraq. However, King Hussain remained in touch with the Iraqi leadership throughout the crisis and did his best to keep Iraq open to imports – including strategic goods – despite the tightening blockade.[3] Pro-Iraqi demonstrations started on the first day of the invasion and continued until the end of the war. The rallies, at their peak involving some 70,000 protesters, were tolerated and occasionally even backed by the regime.

In late September, King Hussain and Crown Prince Hassan said that they would remain opposed to the military build-up in the Gulf. Whilst they demanded an immediate end to the presence of multinational troops in the Gulf, they also made it clear that Jordan did not condone the Iraqi take-over of Kuwait.[4] Jordan continued her diplomatic efforts to prevent a war. Together with Morocco and Algeria, the government drew up a peace plan towards the end of September, which was reportedly strongly biased in favour of Iraq. As a result, Jordan's relations to both the United States and Saudi Arabia deteriorated rapidly. When the United States took an increasingly uncompromising position, King Hussain's attempts to avert a war remained futile. Air strikes against Iraq were launched on 17 January.

Although Jordan officially declared herself neutral, the Jordanian cabinet immediately issued a statement in which it condemned 'what took place in the early hours of this morning as a brutal attack on an Arab Muslim country and people.'[5] Parliament accused the international coalition of blatant aggression against the 'Arab and Islamic nations.'[6] The king himself denounced the campaign of the international coalition against Iraq and stated in a speech on 6 February 1991, when the war had reached its peak: 'The real purpose behind this destructive war [...] is to destroy Iraq.'[7] To the United States, but also to the overwhelming majority of observers in the West, it seemed that King Hussain had just declared alliance with Iraq.

Regional politics and the balance of power

Jordan had been Iraq's closest ally in the Arab arena for almost a decade before the crisis and throughout the Iran-Iraq war.[8] This alignment was said to result from Jordan's desire to offset her own military weakness and to deter the two major regional powers, Syria and Israel.[9] But although some observers claimed that King Hussain's constant fear of military intervention from Syria formed the background to his view of Iraq, 'whatever the regime in Baghdad', and although Syria joined the anti-Iraq coalition, Damascus did not pose an immediate threat to Jordan before or during the Gulf Crisis.[10] Israel, on the other hand, was much more of a real threat, especially after the massive inflow of Soviet Jews at the start of the 1990s and with a Likud government in power that had repeatedly espoused the theory that 'Jordan was Palestine'. Iraq seemed to be the only potential deterrent to Israel. The desire to counter-balance Israel had led Jordanian policy-makers to play a central role in the establishment of the Arab Cooperation Council (ACC) in 1989, which brought together Jordan, Iraq, Egypt and North Yemen and enhanced Jordan's diplomatic and military position vis-à-vis Israel. Although the ACC faded away with Egypt's joining of the anti-Iraq camp during the crisis, Iraq still provided an important backup for Jordan towards Israel.[11]

The linkage between Jordan's position towards Israel and her support for Iraq was demonstrated when King Hussain stated in a speech on 9 December that 'the settlement of the Kuwait dispute should in some way be linked to a settlement of the Israeli-Palestinian dispute'.[12] He also criticised the United States for mobilising so rapidly when Iraq invaded Kuwait but failing to apply the same standards to the 23-year Israeli occupation of Jerusalem.[13] The king could speculate that the Americans would not let him fall despite deteriorating relations, and that on the contrary, they would need him in the long run. It was clear that the United States would launch a diplomatic offensive to resolve the Arab-Israeli conflict and that Jordan was one of the crucial players, which could not be left out if a peace settlement was to be achieved.

However, regional balance-of-power politics alone cannot provide a sufficient explanation for Jordan's stand. King Hussain's attempt to instrumentalise the Gulf crisis in order to press for a settlement of the Arab-Israeli conflict actually increased Jordan's vulnerability. Nobody knew what Israel's reaction to a war in the Gulf would be and Jordan ran the risk of being squeezed between Iraq and Israel, especially when Saddam Hussain began to threaten Israel, and Israel responded with promises of retaliation. It was because of this danger that Jordan officially sought to mediate and maintained neutrality during the crisis. Other factors, therefore, need to be considered to explain Jordan's position.

Rentierism and economic crisis

Given her modest economic resources, Jordan has traditionally relied on external assistance – after 1973 mainly from the oil-rich Arab states – and on remittances from workers in the Gulf. During the 1970s and early 1980s, Jordan experienced an economic boom, but with the decay of oil prices, the economy gradually descended into a deep crisis. In 1988, when Jordan's foreign debts amounted to more than $6 billion and the kingdom could not meet its obligations anymore, the Jordanian dinar was devalued by almost 50 per cent. In 1989, Jordan and the IMF agreed on a structural adjustment programme, inciting the violent riots of April 1989 when subsidies on basic commodities were removed almost overnight. It was under these circumstances that the ACC was founded in February 1989, in the hope that the alliance would not only be politically but also economically beneficial.[14]

However, bilateral relations with the oil-producing states, rather than the multilateral ties with Egypt, North Yemen and Iraq, were the vital ones for Jordan's economy: shocked by the riots, the Gulf monarchies rushed emergency transfers of aid and oil to Jordan to ensure the stability of the regime. Despite this, there was bitter feeling arising from both state and popular levels directed at the Gulf States, in view of the fact that such aid was only offered after these severe domestic upheavals had occurred. The government issued scathing attacks on them for failing to fulfil their promises of aid and only excluded one state from these reproaches – Iraq.

During the Iran-Iraq war, economic relations between Jordan and Iraq had intensified and the kingdom had benefited considerably from its support for Iraq, not only through generous loans and aid, but also in terms of exports and transit trade to Iraq. Although Iraq's economic power declined towards the end of the war, Jordan had become economically dependent on its neighbour by the late 1980s. This dependence emerged from three elements. Firstly, by mid-1990 some 70 per cent of all imports and some 25 per cent of all exports passing through the port of Aqaba were transit trade, most of which went to Iraq. Secondly, Iraq was Jordan's single largest trading partner. And thirdly, Iraq provided some 80–90 per cent of Jordan's oil requirements.[15]

A fourth factor, which must be taken into consideration, is that Iraq had been the only state to make a formal commitment in response to King Hussain's plea for aid at the May 1990 Arab summit in Baghdad, when the king openly admitted that the country was bankrupt.[16] Jordan's support for Iraq, therefore, was vital to its economic survival. Yet Jordan also relied heavily on both Kuwait and Saudi Arabia. Although their financial aid was not as generous as it had previously been, these two states were still the most likely potential Arab sources of aid and concessionary loans. In addition, both Kuwait and Saudi Arabia indicated their willingness to reward Jordan for joining the anti-Iraq coalition following the invasion. As Laurie Brand pointed out, 'Joining the coalition would have offered Jordan the possibility of increased Arab and Western aid to offset losses incurred during the crisis, whereas failure to join the coalition both ruled out any such assistance and offered no other options.'[17] Hence, Jordan's position vis-à-vis Iraq during the Gulf crisis, despite the close ties between the two countries, could as well be seen as economically counter-productive.

Domestic politics and the liberal experiment

Until the late 1980s, political freedom had been severely restricted.[18] With the deepening economic crisis and the riots of April 1989, however, the domestic political scene changed dramatically. The riots originated in the southern town of Ma'an, a community which the regime considered a 'bedrock constituency' for Hashemite rule, given the historical support there for the regime.[19] Now that he found himself threatened by his traditional social base, King Hussain adopted what has been called 'a policy of defensive democratisation.'[20] Within weeks, the unpopular prime minister was sacked and top government and administrative officials replaced. The first general elections in twenty-two years were held in November 1989.

It is only against this background of beginning political liberalisation that Jordan's stance in the Gulf crisis can be fully understood. With mass demonstrations and volunteers signing up to fight for Iraq in Amman, acting in accord with public sentiment was the safest course of action. Or as Peter Gubser has written: 'Many observers believe the king had little choice but to take the course that he did. Otherwise his throne would have certainly been threatened.'[21] Jordanians suffered from the blockade of the port of Aqaba and were shocked at the sight of the bombardments in Iraq and of attacks on Jordanian trucks on the Iraqi border. As high as the tide of emotions was, a policy of reversing the process of liberalisation and condemning Iraq could have swept the king out of power.

Moreover, there was the 'Palestinian factor' to be considered, which was perhaps the decisive one in the domestic arena. King Hussain, unexpectedly, did not link the issue of Iraq and Kuwait and the Arab-Israeli conflict since he had long sought to come to terms with Israel.[22] Many Jordanians, not only those of Palestinian origin but also East Bankers, compared the international responses to the Iraqi take-over of Kuwait and to the Israeli refusal to withdraw from the occupied territories and felt deeply betrayed by the apparent application of double-standards. This was where the overwhelming popular support for Iraq emerged from, and it only grew when Saddam Hussain attacked Israel and portrayed himself as a hero for the Arab cause.

The longer the crisis endured, the closer King Hussain moved towards the position dictated by his people. His popularity reached unprecedented levels. His fierce attack against the West in February 1991 illustrated the king's two-pronged approach. While officially, Jordan maintained political neutrality on the international stage, keeping open vital channels of aid and other support, Hussain

adopted a sufficiently pro-Iraqi and anti-Western tone at home to satisfy the demands of the population. The king was walking a tightrope between the requirements of economic survival and
international reputation on the one hand, and popular demands on
the other.

In this sense, the regional dimension of the Arab-Israeli conflict
stood behind the popular support for Iraq, but it was the latter that
forced the regime to adopt the position dictated by the people at a
time when opinions could be voiced relatively freely. It was not the Iraqi invasion and subsequent annexation of Kuwait as such, which inspired the Jordanian population. Rather, it was Saddam's clever
manoeuvre to turn the affair into a challenge to Western imperialism
and to Israel and Zionism that touched the people. And for the king,
identifying and to be seen as identifying with his people was simply
a matter of survival.[23]

Into the anti-Saddam camp

As soon as the war in the Gulf was over, Jordan began to steer herself
back on a middle course between Iraq on one side and the West and
its Arab allies on the other. Ties with the United States and particularly the European members of the anti-Iraq coalition quickly improved, especially after Jordan accepted the invitation to participate
in the Middle East peace conference at Madrid in October 1991.[24]
Relations with her Arab neighbours, however, remained strained.
The Egyptian press attacked King Hussain fervently when Jordan issued a White Paper in August 1991, in which it implicitly accused
Egypt of having contributed to the escalation of the Gulf Crisis.[25]
Saudi Arabia re-opened its borders to Jordanian trucks towards the
end of 1991, but relations deteriorated again in early 1992 and after
that, only slowly improved until they were fully restored in 1996.[26]

Relations with Iraq remained close at first. There were reports
about widespread smuggling of strategic goods to Iraq from Jordan
and the government campaigned vigorously against the UN embargo. The shift away from Iraq began in August 1992 when King Hussain met members of the Iraqi opposition in London and when an
Iraqi nuclear scientist was shot in Amman in December 1992.[27] From
then on, Iraq increasingly became a side issue whilst the peace process
began to dominate the foreign policy agenda.

The peace process, however, moved slowly. With the deportation
of 415 Palestinians accused of being *Hamas* activists to Lebanon towards the end of 1992, the hopes for a breakthrough were almost
dashed. When the United States and her allies renewed the air strikes

against Iraq in January 1993, King Hussain found himself walking the tightrope once again. This time, Jordan was caught between her attempts to restore relations with her former allies in the West and her commitment to the Madrid process on the one hand, and her attempts not to jeopardise relations with Iraq altogether. With events unfolding, however, the decision was made: only a day after the presentation of the Israeli-Palestinian Oslo Accords on 13 September 1993, the kingdom signed its own agenda agreement with Israel. When Saddam Hussain threatened Kuwait again just a week before the official signing of the Jordanian-Israeli peace treaty in October 1994, King Hussain reacted angrily, accused him of being responsible for the rising tension in the Gulf and warned that Jordan would react seriously to any threat to regional security.[28]

In 1995, the re-formulation of Jordan's position vis-à-vis Iraq manifested itself again. When Hussain Kamel Hassan, Saddam Hussain's son-in-law and trusted aide, and his brother defected to Amman, King Hussain welcomed and granted them asylum. The defectors called for the overthrow of Saddam Hussain and the king himself told an Israeli newspaper that it was 'time for a change' in the Iraqi leadership. Shortly thereafter, the king began to openly support opponents of the Iraqi regime, calling for an opposition conference and allowing some opposition parties to open offices in Amman. Jordan now appeared to have 'completed the circle' and 'become a permanent member of the anti-Saddam camp.' Jordan's shift towards the anti-Iraq coalition seemed complete in 1996, when relations with the United States and Saudi Arabia were fully restored, overtures were made in the direction of Kuwait and Jordan remained an enthusiastic and committed supporter of the peace process. Jordan exchanged one strong partner, Iraq, for a new one, Israel.[29]

Peace and a new balance of power

The Gulf Crisis had left Jordan regionally and internationally isolated. With the defeat of Iraq, it had lost its ally and Arab deterrent vis-à-vis Israel. Only the peace process enabled Jordan to assert a role for herself in the new regional order. Israel's refusal to negotiate with the Palestinian Liberation Organisation (PLO) until 1993 and her insistence that the Palestinians be part of a joint delegation with Jordan at the Madrid conference helped Jordan to assume a pivotal role in the peace process. In this sense, Israel played a key role in rehabilitating Jordan after the Gulf war.[30]

In a speech in October 1991, the king stated that there was no alternative to attending the conference and that missing this perhaps final opportunity would leave Jordan for ever weak and vulnerable. Jordan could not afford a repeat of her stance during the Gulf Crisis by opposing the United States in its drive to settle the Arab-Israeli conflict.[31] But while King Hussain assumed the role of broker and mediator between the Americans and Israelis on one side and Saudi Arabia and Iraq on the other, he kept a low profile and let the Palestinians make their peace deal first. It was in spring 1993 that it became clear that a full commitment to peace was the only viable option. Kuwait and Saudi Arabia announced their 'unified position' that normalisation with Jordan needed time in April, and with Jordan's inter-Arab relations remaining weak, peace was the king's obvious choice, especially when rumours about a pending Palestinian-Israeli deal started spreading.[32]

Although the remark made in June 1993 by the Israeli foreign minister, Shimon Peres, to journalists that a Jordanian-Israeli peace deal was in the making threatened to disrupt the balance, Jordan followed the Palestinians swiftly once the breakthrough was made public. Still, Hussain kept walking the tightrope well into 1994. After the Hebron Massacre early that year, which caught Jordan 'between hammer and anvil', he had to make a final decision. However once another attempt to restore relations with Saudi Arabia failed and the Palestinians signed their economic protocol with Israel in the spring, which overrode the economic agreements between Jordanians and Palestinians, the general lack of coordination among and the lack of support from the Arab states tipped the balance.[33]

In addition, it was American pressure, which led to peace. After the war, the United States said that it was prepared to 'let bygones be bygones but only step by step and with a royal commitment to helping the organisation of the peace conference.'[34] The pressure was so strong that one senior official judged: 'We should not be surprised if the Americans attempted to keep up the pressure on us until we've agreed to sign a peace treaty.'[35]

In this sense, what appeared to be a 180-degree turn from Jordan's alignment with Iraq towards signing a peace treaty with Israel was the result of the kingdom's weakness and isolation – which in turn were the consequences of its stance during the Gulf Crisis. Looking for new allies, King Hussain first signalled to the anti-Iraq camp that he wished reconciliation when he met Iraqi opposition figures in 1992. But only the peace process and the assumption of a role of mediator gave Hussain a chance to re-assert a role in regional and international politics and to make friends again, albeit not so much with his erstwhile allies among the Arab neighbours but with the Americans and the Israelis.

The re-formulation of Jordan's foreign policy towards Iraq and the strategic decision to make peace with Israel, which stood behind the former, were not abrupt shifts but rather carefully prepared steps. Jordan, attempting to restore relations with her former allies, at first pursued a cautious course of action and bargained hard. But it did not help. The Palestinians pursued an independent course of action, the Gulf States still resented the kingdom for its position during the crisis and the Americans would accept no less than a peace treaty before fully restoring friendly relations. Only peace fully rehabilitated Jordan in regional and international politics. The main reason for the re-alignment, however, was less Jordan's strategic isolation than its economic vulnerability.

Economic survival and the peace dividend

Due to the embargo against Iraq, Jordan's economy almost came to a standstill during the Gulf Crisis and her austerity programme had to be suspended. The Central Bank estimated that the economy suffered losses of more than $1.5 billion, or the equivalent of 35 per cent of Jordan's GDP in 1989, in 1990 alone. It concluded that only external assistance and foreign debt reduction could offset 'tremendous external financial gaps in Jordan's balance of payments in the forthcoming years.'[36]

Jordan was therefore left vulnerable to pressures from aid donors and had to present herself as a reliable ally to gain financial support. In a speech at the European Parliament in September 1991, King Hussain 'painted a grim picture' of the economic situation and pleaded for aid.[37] This factor explains Jordan's participation in the multilateral talks in Moscow in February 1992. Jordanian officials made it clear that despite the absence of both Syrians and Palestinians, Jordan could not afford to 'say no to the Americans, no to the Saudis and no to the rest of the world and still hope for Arab and international understanding and badly needed economic support.'[38]

Then, contrary to all expectations, the influx of 300,000 returning workers from the Gulf triggered an economic boom in 1992.[39] The so far uninterrupted flow of oil from Iraq actually increased during 1992 and Iraq remained Jordan's most important trade partner.[40] Hence, at this time, there was no economic need to rush the conclusion of a peace treaty when the apparent commitment to the peace process sufficed to secure a $380 million package of loans and grants for 1993 from the Paris Club of donors.[41]

However, Jordan depended on the United States to ease the sanctions against Iraq and to help her economic recovery in other areas.

When she continuously failed in her efforts to persuade it to relax the searches of ships bound for Aqaba, the port's transit trade shrank by more than 75 per cent, and shippers said the embargo cost Jordan's transport sector over $500 million in losses.[42] Saddam's decision in 1993 to withdraw Iraqi 25-Dinar notes from circulation and to close Iraq's borders, also cost Jordanians some $100 million in hoarded currency and interrupted the oil supply.[43] Moreover, it now became clear that the kingdom's economic boom of the previous year had only been short-lived. All these events, in addition to the reticent behaviour of Kuwait and Saudi Arabia proved that economically, there was no other option than peace, especially after a World Bank report optimistically claimed that peace could bring 'substantial benefits to Jordan's economy.'.[44] When the Palestinian-Israeli economic protocol was signed in April 1994 and threatened to exclude Jordan from reaping the peace dividend, the pace of Jordanian-Israeli negotiations became almost frantic.[45] Following the signing of the Washington declaration, which ended the state of war between Jordan and Israel, in July 1994, Jordan benefited from a windfall debt relief of almost $900 million. Once the peace treaty was signed, visitors started to flock into the kingdom, generating a boom in the tourism sector in 1995.[46] Amman also hosted the second Middle East economic summit and presented a long list of development projects to potential donors in October 1995. Yet economic ties with Iraq also remained close. The Jordanian energy minister visited Baghdad in September 1995, where he described relations with Iraq as '100 per cent normal' and said Amman would continue buying its oil from Baghdad.[47]

Jordan's hope for a peace dividend in terms of debt relief and aid explains the foreign policy shift after the Gulf Crisis. The fact that Jordan maintained economic relations with Iraq, which were as close as possible under the circumstances, illustrates that the rationale behind the re-alignment was less ideological than purely pragmatic. The sources of financial aid and support were less important than the fact that they should be available without disruption and in large quantities.

Changes on the domestic political scene

But the shift was only made possible through important changes on the domestic political scene. The ratification of the National Charter, a quasi-constitutional document officially aimed at strengthening the process of liberalisation, in June 1991, effectively underlined the legitimacy of the monarchy.[48] Thus strengthened, King Hussain appointed a new government, stripping the Islamists, five of whom had been included in the government during the crisis, of their influence in June 1991. The new prime minister, Taher al-Masri, was of Palestinian origin and well known for his good relations to the PLO, which was an important signal on the eve of the Madrid Conference.[49]

With his popularity at a peak after the Gulf Crisis, his first operation for cancer in September 1992 and the economic boom of that year, King Hussain began preparing the ground. The most prominent Islamist opponent of the regime, Laith Shubailat, was sentenced to death and, in a demonstration of the regime's power, pardoned a mere 48 hours later in November.[50] In December, two political parties were denied legalisation and the ratification of a new Press Law meant a severe restriction of press freedom.[51] These issues clearly dominated the agenda throughout 1992 and until the elections in November 1993, and dampened popular interest in the peace process for the time being.

In May 1993, the king appointed a new government, asking it to change the election law, which had enabled opponents of the regime to gain seats in parliament in 1989.[52] Due to some uncertainty about the reaction of the Palestinians in Jordan to the Oslo accords and the potential disruption of the delicate balance between Palestinians and East Bankers, the elections seemed in danger at first. But when the Islamists appeared to be losing ground, Hussain decided to get on with the elections. His tactics to change the election law succeeded in diminishing the Muslim Brotherhood's strength in parliament, and ensured that the latter would not sabotage the peace process and the IMF-prescribed programme for economic recovery.[53]

From now on, the regime made clear that expressions of discontent relating to peace would not be allowed.[54] The crackdown on the opposition continued, with serious measures in particular taken against the Islamists to prevent them from exploiting their potential to campaign against peace and normalisation.[55] At the same time, the regime started marketing peace by promising a huge peace dividend for everyone.[56] But selling peace created huge expectations, and when the anticipated peace dividend did not materialise immediately, especially for the average Jordanian, King Hussain must have concluded that peace and democracy would not go together.[57] In November 1995, he expressed his readiness for a showdown with the growing number of opponents to his policy vis-à-vis Israel.[58] By 1996, the 'episode of regime transition and re-consolidation' had clearly ended. After a period of free elections and significant widening of public freedoms, the pre-1989 boundaries and practices had gradually been reasserted.[59]

The regime's determination to resort to oppression manifested itself again in August 1996, when in striking similarity to 1989, the lifting of subsidies for bread led to riots. Speaking on television, the king threatened to use an 'iron fist' and any other means necessary to restore order, and blamed the Iraqi regime for inciting the unrest, once again a demonstration of how much Jordan had turned away from Iraq and realigned itself with the West and Israel.[60] In this sense, it was only in the context of the slide back into suppression that Jordan could pursue its policy of distancing herself from Iraq and making peace with Israel. The regime was stable and its foreign policy was not subjected to popular influence.[61]

Walking the tightrope again

The king's alignment with Israel was not to remain unstrained. The Israeli 'Grapes of Wrath' operation against Lebanon in spring 1996 first spoiled the relationship, and after Binyamin Netanyahu's assumption of power in Israel in June 1996, Israeli-Jordanian relations soon deteriorated further. Almost in response, it appeared, to King Hussain's personal visit to the parents of seven Israeli girls shot by a Jordanian soldier in March 1997, Netanyahu sent Mossad agents to Amman to assassinate the leading *Hamas* member, Muhammad Mish'al, in September. Israel also obstructed most projects of economic cooperation so that Jordan's foreign minister, Jawad al-'Anani, described relations between the kingdom and Israel as 'almost at a standstill and at a minimal level of coordination' in July 1998.[62] After the promise of the first MENA summits, the conferences were suspended in the aftermath of the last meeting in Doha in 1997, when, after Egypt and Saudi Arabia had already boycotted the proceedings, no participant volunteered to act as the next host.[63] Economically Jordan was as vulnerable as ever. Some 26 per cent of the Jordanian population suffered from absolute poverty by the end of 1997 and 45 per cent of all families lived on a monthly salary of at most 150 dinars.[64]

Relations with the Palestinian Authority were not particularly friendly either, since Israel's promise to grant Jordan 'high priority' in the negotiations over the future status of Jerusalem in the peace treaty. The separate peace agreements had not only resulted in economic competition but also in the 'bankruptcy of the confederal idea.'[65] Despite King Hussain's repeated attempts to help with Israeli-Palestinian negotiations, the Palestinians would not let him interfere with their affairs. In addition, Yassir Arafat was highly annoyed with the king's move to press for the release of *Hamas'* spiritual leader, Sheikh Yasin, following the failed Mossad assassination attempt in September 1997.[66]

The Palestinians were not the only potential partner with whom relations remained difficult. Syria had rejected Jordan's peace treaty with Israel, and King Hussain and President Asad did not even meet until 1996.[67] Rumours about plans for a joint Israeli-Jordanian dam to be built on the Israeli-occupied Golan Heights in August 1997 kept relations difficult and mutual accusations continued in what some commentators called a 'war of words' throughout 1998. Asad remained the only Arab leader not to call Hussain while he was undergoing treatment for his cancer in the United States during 1998.[68]

It was no wonder, therefore, that Jordan shifted closer to Iraq again. The implementation of the United Nations food-for-oil programme enabled both countries to maintain close economic ties.[69] Once again, in addition to Jordan's economic needs, domestic politics played a pivotal role. The 'National Front against Normalisation with Israel' had become a mass movement, which almost succeeded in cancelling the first Israeli trade fair in Jordan in January 1997. Jordanian businessmen called for a renewal of the Arab boycott against Israel and pressed at the same time for closer relations with Iraq, where most entrepreneurs had interests.[70] In what was almost a repetition of the events of August 1990, pro-Iraqi demonstrations took place when a renewal of the war in the Gulf seemed most likely in 1998. While King Hussain rejected a military attack against Iraq, he did not give in this time. Clashes between protesters and the police and the military occurred in Ma'an in February and resulted in eight casualties.[71]

In this sense, Jordan continued to walk the tightrope between her association with the West and Israel on one side, and her ties to Iraq and the Arab world on the other. The choice Jordan had made by making peace with Israel and re-aligning with the West was never put into question, but the kingdom maintained its economic links to Iraq, continued to balance between Iraq and Israel and to make the best of this bargaining position. King Hussain's strategy not to close doors on anyone and to keep open all options was proven successful once again towards the end of the 1990s.

Jordan's regional policy in the 1990s

Three factors stood behind Jordan's refusal to join the anti-Iraq coalition in 1990–1: regional politics, economic considerations and popular influence. Jordan had allied herself with Iraq in order to strengthen her position vis-à-vis Israel before the Gulf Crisis. With a decline in aid and remittances from the Gulf, Jordan had also become economically dependent on Iraq by 1990. Consequently, the kingdom stayed on Iraq's side and sought to take advantage of the crisis in order to press for a settlement of the Arab-Israeli conflict.

At the same time, it would have been easy to support the US-led coalition and then ask for a reward in terms of American pressure on Israel. Given the overwhelming military and economic power of the anti-Iraq coalition, it must have been obvious to the Jordanian regime that supporting the alliance against Iraq could have resulted in generous financial and strategic rewards after the war. For these reasons, strategic and economic, Jordan took a moderate position of neutrality and sought to mediate. Still, her tactical support for Iraq was clearly recognisable. It was the consequence of a popular domestic consensus in favour of Saddam Hussein, which threatened to destabilise the Jordanian regime.

While pursuing different lines at the same time – mediation on one side, support for Iraq on the other – the latter clearly had priority over the former, thus ensuring the survival of the regime. However, this short-term tactic threatened to undermine the conventional strategy of maintaining regime stability in Jordan, namely the securing of financial assistance, on which the kingdom has relied ever since its creation. Once the war was over, therefore, Jordan's foreign policy began to reflect the need for long-term economic security. Peace with Israel was the obvious choice, as it promised not only direct rewards from the West in terms of debt relief, but also benefits from economic cooperation with Israel and foreign direct investment. At the same time, the regime tightened its reign and made clear that it would not let the people interfere with Jordan's long-term interest. While there was an apparent shift in Jordan's foreign policy orientation, this shift did not mean a change in the underlying aims the kingdom pursued.

The alignment with Iraq was a domestic political necessity in the short run; participation in the peace process and the re-alignment with the West was a long-term economic necessity. What prompted the apparent shift in Jordan's foreign policy, therefore, was a change not in the regime's objectives, but in the weight of different factors impacting on policy-making in Jordan. During the Gulf Crisis, the precarious domestic political situation overrode any genuine foreign policy concerns. Jordan's foreign-policy behaviour in 1990–1 was directed inwards, it was domestic rather than foreign policy. After the Crisis, the regime had the time and the space to manoeuvre, and hence, it could pursue its foreign policy goals without interference from the domestic political scene.

It was only when the relations to Israel began to deteriorate in the context of a peace dividend which failed to materialise, that Jordan moved closer to Iraq again. Until the end of the decade, Jordan walked the tightrope again, between her commitment to peace and the hope for a peace dividend on one side, and her economic and strategic alignment with Iraq on the other. But again, domestic popular demands were a decisive factor, in addition to Jordan's economic needs. In this sense, Jordan's regional policy during the 1990s was characterised by continuity. The kingdom continued to balance between different lines of action simultaneously and while the impact of different factors changed the overall balance, Jordan's underlying objectives – ensuring the survival of the regime – did not change.

King Hussain, after forty-six years in power, died on February 7, 1999, not without leaving another surprise for observers in the West and elsewhere, when he dismissed his brother Hassan and made his son Abdullah crown prince, only a few days before his death. So far, King Abdullah II has walked in his father's footsteps by being friends with everyone. Reconciliation with Syria and with all the Gulf States has been achieved and Jordan's economic vulnerability figures much higher on the new king's agenda than domestic political liberalisation.[72] Walking the tightrope to ensure the survival of the Hashemite monarchy appears to be a continuous feature in Jordan's foreign policy even in the twenty-first century.

Objectives of Jordanian foreign policy

In 1994 Laurie A. Brand published her epochal study of 'Jordan's Inter-Arab Relations', arguing that it was the kingdom's economic structure as a rentier economy, which was at the heart of Jordan's foreign policy orientation.[73] Her work, however, focused on events prior to the 1990s and the Gulf Crisis was mentioned only in passing. As has been shown in this chapter, the crisis indicated that Brand's thesis was incomplete: it is insufficient to explain Jordanian foreign policy solely by reference to the kingdom's economic structure and situation, although the country's domestic political economy is certainly one major factor impacting on foreign policy decisions.

On the basis of the analysis of Jordan's stance during the Crisis and her strategic decision to make peace with Israel, one can conclude that generally, regime survival is the major concern influencing all areas of domestic and foreign policy. The conventional strategy of attaining this goal in terms of foreign policy is to secure financial aid for the kingdom. These rents are used to maintain social peace and thus, regime stability in Jordan. Officials themselves have often emphasised the importance of Jordan's foreign relations as the key to economic stability, and thus, to domestic social peace and regime security.[74]

Brand was therefore correct in asserting that the 'nature of the Jordanian economy, especially the structure or composition of state revenues' plays the key role in influencing the course of Jordan's foreign policy. As she wrote, the Jordanian regime 'made or had to make as a primary, conscious focus of its foreign policy, the collection of funds that enabled it to continue to play its allocative role, a role that underpinned the regime itself.'[75] This focus of Jordan's foreign policy on securing the uninterrupted flow of rents both restricts the manoeuvrability of the regime and accounts for alignment shifts. While Jordan is vulnerable in her dependency on other states and therefore subjected to the influence of regional and international donors, however, there is room for manoeuvre, and the need to continuously balance on the tightrope also involves some degree of flexibility and bargaining power.

In this sense, while Jordan has been subjected to pressures from international powers and has to respond to them, as she did when she opted for peace and the re-alignment with the West, she is able to bargain and balance between different commitments and sources of aid. This is illustrated by the continuity in Jordan's ties to Iraq on a functional level. More important than a whole-hearted re-alignment with the West was the fact that it sufficiently appeared as such to the international community. But this shift was necessitated by the state of Jordan's economy and her isolation in regional and international circles after the war.

Budget security is the overriding concern behind the kingdom's foreign policy. Behind this constant search for economic security stands a political-economic system, which is based on the allocation of incoming rents by the regime. Any change in Jordan's economic structure would instantaneously threaten the political system, which is underpinned by it. Jordan's alignments may change, but the kingdom's principal objective of maintaining the inflow of external assistance and the political-economic rentier system do not. Jordan's foreign policy, therefore, is an extension of domestic policy and serves to secure the foremost aim of all policies in the kingdom, regime survival.

The principal foreign policy goal of budget security is an important one, but it is merely one expression of the overriding concern with regime survival. Whenever the attainment of that foreign-policy objective conflicts with the primary goal of survival and stability, the latter will be more important than the former. This conflict arose during the Gulf Crisis, but it was firmly resolved again after the Crisis when peace was the choice of the day and King Hussain once again tightened his grip.

When Jordan took a position of official neutrality and implicit support for Iraq during the Gulf Crisis, most observers in the West were left dumbfounded. The Hashemite kingdom had been allied to the West ever since its creation. Few commentators ever dared to question Jordan's firm establishment in the Western camp. King Hussain was a favourite of the Western media. That the 'little king', as European and American tabloids called him, should refuse to condemn the West's number one enemy, Saddam Hussain, when he invaded Kuwait in August 1990, seemed completely unintelligible to most observers. Only few scholars in the West ever attempted to establish a more critical account of the king's policies, which would not only have contradicted the popular image of the king in the West but would also have meant to criticise an ally, whom Western governments considered a crucial partner in their quest to contain the influence of the Soviet Union and the radical Arab regimes during the Cold War.

It was the end of the Cold War that proved to be a watershed, in both the theory of international relations and the study of Jordanian politics. The study of Jordanian regional foreign policy during and after the Gulf Crisis reveals that the long-established picture of a conservative, ultimately pro-Western monarchy was a misleading fiction and disguised the actual themes underlying the kingdom's foreign policy. In retrospect, it was the scarcity of resources and Jordan's economic vulnerability, which had tied the kingdom first to Britain, then to the United States and thereafter, increasingly, to the conservative Gulf States. A more critical analysis of Jordan's policies reveals a domestic political system, in which the preservation of power depends on the successful obtaining and distributing of external assistance within the kingdom. King Hussain's first and foremost goal always was the survival of his regime and Jordan's foreign policy until today is subordinated to this overriding objective.

It is no coincidence, however, that the revision of orthodox views on Jordan occurs simultaneously with a renewed fervidity in the theoretical study of foreign policy and international politics. In the shadow of the Cold War confrontation between two superpowers, developing states were only seen as small powers, vulnerable to strategic pressure from the great powers. Jordan's regional policy during the 1990s, however, illustrates that rather than military security and external survival, economic security and domestic stability, or internal survival, are the overriding concerns of foreign policy. These concerns are common to most 'new' states, or developing states, as Mohammad Ayoob and other scholars have pointed out, since the end of the Cold War allowed moving beyond military concerns and balance of power politics.[76] Due to the incongruent nature of state and nation in the Developing World and the contested legitimacy of many regimes in the developing world, the principal concern of regimes is with domestically generated threats to the security of the government. Therefore, security cannot be considered apart from the internal structure of the state.[77] As a result, the realm of foreign policy is secondary to the sphere of domestic politics and the international repercussions of the actions that a state pursues are seen as of less importance than those consequences that most nearly touch the population.[78]

The most important explanatory variables for foreign policy, therefore, are to be found in the nature of a state, in its domestic political system and the economic structure underpinning it. The case of Jordan illustrates that the state, or in that case, the regime, pursues its own goals while walking a tightrope between international and domestic pressures. These goals result from the domestic nature of the state, and in the context of unconsolidated state structures in the Third World, often involve the preservation of the state, internal stability and regime survival. The strategies developing states pursue differ according to the specific challenges each state is confronted with and can only be explained with reference to the specific nature of state-society relations.

In the case of Jordan, the lack of resources and the resulting economic weakness necessitates that foreign policy ensures an uninterrupted flow of external assistance into the kingdom. These rents are distributed by the state in Jordan and thus serve to uphold social peace and to legitimise Hashemite rule. But as the ultimate rationale behind this foreign-policy objective is a domestic goal – namely, regime survival – domestic concerns can be expected to override this foreign-policy concern in the case that a conflict between the two arises. It is in this sense that Jordanian foreign policy until today is balancing, bargaining, and most importantly, surviving.

NOTES

1. White Paper: *Jordan and the Gulf Crisis August 1990-March 1991*, Government of the Hashemite Kingdom of Jordan, Amman, August 1991.
2. See, for example, S. Al-Khazendar (1997), *Jordan and the Palestine Question: The Role of Islamic and Left Forces in Foreign-Policy Making*, Reading, England:

Ithaca Press, and M. Haas, *Hussains Königreich. Jordaniens Stellung im Nahen Osten*, Munich: Tuduv, 1975.

3. U. Dann, *King Hussain's Strategy of Survival*, Washington Institute for Near East Policy Papers, 1992.

4. *Middle East International*, 28 September 1990.

5. Quoted in A. Baram, 'No New Fertile Crescent: Iraqi-Jordanian Relations, 1968–1992' in J. Nevo and I. Pappé (eds), *Jordan in the Middle East: The Making of a Pivotal State 1948–1988*, Ilford: Frank Cass, 1994.

6. *Middle East International*, 25 January 1991.

7. 'Address to the Nation by His Majesty King Hussain, Amman, 6 February 1991.' Reprinted in the White Paper. See also *Middle East International*, 22 February 1991.

8. On Jordanian-Iraqi relations prior to 1990, see L. Brand, *Jordan's Inter-Arab Relations. The Political Economy of Alliance Making*, New York: Columbia University Press 1994, and A. Baram, 'Baathi Iraq and Hashimite Jordan: From Hostility to Alignment', *Middle East Journal*, 45, 1 (1991).

9. A. Hillal Dessouki, and K. Aboul Kheir, 'The Politics of Vulnerability and Survival: The Foreign Policy of Jordan' in B. Korany, and A. Hillal Dessouki (eds), *The Foreign Policies of Arab States: The Challenge of Change*, Boulder, CO: Westview Press, 1991.

10. See, for example, Dann (1992), and R. Dallas, *King Hussain: A Life on the Edge*, London: Profile Books, 1998.

11. On the ACC, see C. Ryan, 'Jordan and the Rise and Fall of the Arab Co-operation Council', *Middle East Journal*, 52,3 (1998).

12. Quoted in Dallas (1998).

13. A. Lesch, 'Contrasting Reactions to the Persian Gulf Crisis: Egypt, Syria, Jordan, and the Palestinians', *Middle East Journal*, 45, 1(1991).

14. C. Ryan, 'Peace, Bread and Riots: Jordan and the IMF', *Middle East Policy*, 6,2 (1996).

15. Baram (1994).

16. *Middle East International*, 8 June 1990.

17. L. Brand, 'In Search of Budget Security: A Re-examination of Jordanian Foreign Policy', *Politics and the State in Jordan 1946 – 1996*, collection of papers given at an international symposium at the Institut du Monde Arabe, Paris, 24–25 June 1993.

18. On the domestic political situation before the 1990s, see K. Rath, 'The Process of Democratisation in Jordan', *Middle East Studies*, 30,3 (1998).

19. Ryan (1998).

20. G. Robinson, 'Defensive Democratisation in Jordan', *International Journal of Middle East Studiey*, 30,3 (1987). On democratisation and liberalisation in Jordan since 1989, see B. Milton-Edwards, 'Façade Democracy and Jordan', *British Journal of Middle Eastern Studiey*, 20, 2 (1993).

21. P. Gubser, 'Jordan and Hussain', *Middle East Policy*, 2,2.

22. On the long history of Jordanian-Israeli relations, see A. Shlaim, *Collusion Across the Jordan: King Abdullah, the Zionist movement, and the Partition of Palestine*, Oxford: Clarendon Press, 1998, and Y. Lukacs, *Israel, Jordan, and the Peace Process*, Syracuse University Press, 1997.

23. Dann (1992)

24. *Middle East International*, 5 April, 3 May, and 27 September 1991.

25. *Middle East International*, 13 September 1991.

26. *Middle East Economic Digest*, 35:48 (6 December 1991); *Middle East International*, 29 May 1992.

27. *Middle East International*, 11 September, 25 September, and 18 December 1992; *Middle East Economic Digest*, 36:39 (2 October 1992).
28. *Middle East International*, 26 August and 21 October 1994.
29. *Middle East International*, 25 August, 1 December and 29 March 1996; *Middle East Economic Digest*, 39:34 (25 August 1995).
30. Lukacs (1997).
31. *Middle East International*, 27 September and 25 October 1991.
32. *Middle East International*, 16 April 1993.
33. *Middle East International*, 18 April and 13 May 1994.
34. Dallas (1998)
35. *Middle East International*, 15 April 1994.
36. *Twenty Fifth Annual Report 1990*, Central Bank of Jordan, Department of Research and Studies, Amman, 1991.
37. *Middle East International*, 27 September 1991.
38. *Middle East International*, 21 February 1992.
39. T. Piro, *The Political Economy of Market Reform in Jordan*, Lanham MD: Rowman & Littlefield, 1998. On the role of the returning Jordanian and Palestinian workers and their impact on the Jordanian economy, see L. Deeb, 'The Economic Activities of the "Returnees" from the Gulf Countries and their Effect on Jordan's economy', in L. Blin and P. Fargues (eds), *L'Economie de la Paix au Proche Orient/The Economy of Peace in the Middle East*, Luisant: CEDEJ, vol. 1: Strategies, 1995.
40. *Middle East International*, 23 July and 9 July 1993.
41. *Middle East International*, 5 February 1993.
42. *Middle East International*, 23 July and 30 April 1993.
43. *Middle East International*, 14 May 1993.
44. *Peace and the Jordanian Economy*, Washington, DC: IBRD, World Bank, 1994.
45. *Middle East International*, 487 (4 November 1994) and *Middle East Economic Digest*, 38:14, (8 April 1994).
46. *Middle East Economic Digest* 38:47, 21 April 1995.
47. *Middle East International*, 22 September 1995.
48. *Middle East International*, 14 June 1991.
49. *Middle East International*, 28 June 1991.
50. *Middle East International*, 20 November 1992.
51. *Middle East International*, 18 December 1992.
52. *Middle East International*, 11 June 1993.
53. *Middle East International*, 8 October 1993 and 19 November 1993. On the elections and their consequences, see also Robinson (1997).
54. L. Brand, 'The Effects of the Peace Process on Political Liberalisation in Jordan', *Journal of Palestine Studies,* 28, 2 (1999).
55. *Middle East International*, 16 December 1994 and 23 September 1994.
56. On the marketing efforts of the regime, see A. Astorino-Courtois, 'Transforming International Agreements into National Realities: Marketing Arab-Israeli Peace in Jordan', *Journal of Politics*, 58, 4 (1996).
57. M. Bouillon and O. Köndgen, 'Jordaniens Friedensdividende 1994–1998. Eine Bestandsaufnahme', *KAS-Auslandsinformationen*, 9 (1998).
58. *Middle East International*, 15 December 1995.
59. L. Brand, *Women, the State, and Political Liberalisation: Middle Eastern and North African Experiences*, New York: Columbia University Press, 1998.
60. On the 1996 riots, see Ryan (1996).
61. See also M. Mufti, 'Elite Bargains and the Onset of Political Liberalisation in Jordan', *Comparative Political Studies,* 32, 1 (1999).

62. *Jordan Times*, 2–3 July 1998.
63. L. Plotkin, 'The Doha Conference: A Post-Mortem', *Peacewatch*, 149 (1997); Washington, DC: Institute for Near East Policy, Special Reports on the Arab-Israeli Peace Process, 21 November 1997.
64. Minister for Social Development, Khair Mamser, to *Jordan Times*, 16 March 1998. See also *Jordan Times*, 23 March 1998.
65. See M. Braizat, *The Jordanian-Palestinian Relationship: The Bankruptcy of the Confederal Idea*, London: British Academy Press, 1998.
66. *Middle East International*, 24 October 1997.
67. *Middle East International*, 21 June and 5 July 1996.
68. *Jordan Times*, 24 August 1997, and *The Star*, 28 August 1997.
69. *Middle East International*, 549, 2 May 1997.
70. *The Star*, 28 November 1996; *Jordan Times*, 5 January and 11 January 1997.
71. *Middle East International*, 13 March 1998 and 27 February 1998.
72. *Middle East International*, 12 March 1999, 23 April and 7 May 1999.
73. Brand (1994).
74. Ryan (1998).
75. Brand (1994), pp. 82–3.
76. M. Ayoob, *The Third World Security Predicament: State Making, Regional Conflict, and the International System*, Boulder, CO: Lynne Rienner, 1995 .
77. B. Buzan, *People, States and Fear: An Agenda for International Security Studies in the Post-Cold War Era*, New York: Harvester Wheatsheaf, 1991.
78. P. Calvert, *The Foreign Policy of New States*, Brighton: Wheatsheaf, 1986.

GOVERNANCE, ECONOMIC TRANSITION AND JORDAN'S NATIONAL SECURITY

Maen Nsour

Successful governments need coherent economic strategies to improve the well-being of citizens. Poorly conceived economic strategies can result in undue national hardships and popular reaction to ill-conceived policies is sometimes strong enough to bring governments down. Economic issues, therefore, are now receiving more attention as critical mechanisms through which the security of individual states and regimes can be realised over the long term. In other words, purely economic concepts such as increase in productivity, economic growth, economic reform, the integration of regional and international markets, and protection of income sources are also becoming part of the national security lexicon. Jordan is no exception here.

Three broad economic and social factors have been identified as potential sources of internal conflict and internal instability of a country: economic problems, discriminatory economic systems, and the trials and tribulations of economic development and modernisation.[1] First, when a country experiences economic problems, these problems can contribute to intrastate tensions. Unemployment, inflation, and resource competition, contribute to societal frustrations and tensions, and can provide the breeding ground for conflict. Economic reforms do not always help and can contribute to the problem in the short term, especially if economic shocks are severe and state subsidies for staples, services, and social welfare are cut. In short, economic slowdowns, stagnation, deterioration, and collapse can be deeply destabilising.

Second, discriminatory economic systems can generate feelings of resentment and levels of frustration prone to the generation of violence. Unequal economic opportunities, unequal access to resources and vast differences in standards of living are all signs of economic systems that disadvantaged members of society will see as unfair and perhaps illegitimate. Economic development is not necessarily the solution. Indeed, it can aggravate the situation: economic growth always benefits some individuals, groups, and regions more than others, and those who are on top to begin with are likely to be in a better position to take advantage of new economic opportunities than the downtrodden. Even if a country's overall economic picture is improving, growing inequities and gaps can aggravate intrastate tensions.

Third, economic development and modernisation can be taproots of instability and internal conflict. Better education and improved access to growing mass media raise awareness of differential social status. At the minimum, this places strains on existing social and political systems. It also raises economic and political expectations, and can lead to mounting frustrations when these expectations are not met. The result could be instability.[2]

Economic crisis in Jordan

The onset of the economic crisis in Jordan was signaled in 1989 by a serious deterioration in the balance-of-payments and pressure on reserves and the exchange rate. The balance-of-payments problem reflected both past domestic policy mistakes and external shocks. The consequence was a weakened control over macroeconomic policy. During the 1970s and 1980s the Jordanian government had relied heavily on external borrowing and Arab aid to finance fiscal as well as current account deficits; when capital inflows became meagre, it had few choices but to rely on more external borrowing and taxes. A weakening balance-of-payments position was thus accompanied by widening fiscal deficits and the distributional conflicts that accompany such macroeconomic instability. The Jordanian government responded with a structural adjustment programme agreed with the World Bank and the International Monetary Fund.

Fiscal, monetary and exchange rate policies are the three main instruments of the adjustment programme.[3] Fiscal deficits were attacked by measures for generating revenue, on the one hand, and for reducing expenditures, on the other. Measures for generating revenue included new sales and value-added taxes; increased license fees; increased charges for electricity and water; and sale of public enterprises. Measures for reducing expenditures were reductions in public capital expenditures; wage freezes; layoffs of public employees; discontinuation of some public services; privatisation of money-losing public enterprises; and campaigns for greater efficiency.

Adjustment also included such monetary measures as reduction of the volume of monetary emission to a level at or below rates of GDP growth; raising domestic interest rates; and eliminating subsidies to both producers and consumers. Furthermore, a key to the stabilisation process was an attempt in 1989 to maintain a more realistic exchange rate through the process of devaluation. Such devaluation was supposed to help in reducing trade imbalance through making exports cheaper and imports more expensive.

Economic structural adjustment was supposed to position the country to proceed with an economic strategy that would ensure future growth, employment, and improved levels of well being. Nevertheless, austerity programmes in Jordan have harmed not only the lower-income groups but also the middle class. Reductions in the civil service and parastatal organisations have directly and indirectly caused hardships. Demand contraction reduced demand for labour. The need to reduce the budget deficit led to eliminating food subsidies and other subsidies. Reduced public services did not always lead to an increase in the supply from private sources, and the poor in particular had to go without them. Where cost recovery was introduced, it reduced the access to health services and education. Tighter credit has made it difficult for small businesses to borrow. There were some offsetting benefits, but in general these measures have, no doubt, caused a degree of deprivation in the country.

Prime Minister Rawabdeh admitted in his policy statement before the House of Representatives in April 1999:

The Jordanian economy has moved from the phase of slow growth to that of regression. The recession is felt by every citizen. It is useless to deny or justify it by any theory ... our circumstances, living conditions, and limited sources of income make the negative effects of the recession more than the citizen can bear. Therefore, there must be urgent steps to stop the regression and return to quick growth. [4]

Indeed, malnutrition, ill health, inadequate shelter, and unemployment are evils; it does not matter whether they are caused by contractionist adjustment measures or by external shocks, by domestic misfortune or mismanagement, or by deep structural forces or misalignment of prices. Whatever their causes, top priority must have been given to their elimination.

If some evidence can be offered that the structural adjustment medicine is working in Jordan, the recovery so far is less than complete. While there has been some revitalisation of the indigenous economy, partly as a consequence of deregulation and liberalised trade and payment regime, perhaps the most challenging area for economic policy relates to continuing weakness in Jordan's ability to attract investments and in the country's export performance. The EU-Jordan Association Agreement, signed in November 1997, and the Free Trade Area Agreement with the United States, signed in October 2000, are good foundations. Nevertheless, even if market stimulus is a necessary ingredient for economic success, it is far from obvious that it will be sufficient to generate lively export growth. There is, at the moment, a need to create a vision of how Jordan can earn its way in international markets.

Economic debility and the dilemma of the welfare state

The welfare state inevitably contributes to the emergence of a healthy and educated population with higher social aspirations. When economic resources and opportunities become meagre, a significant portion of the population will feel excluded from socio-economic advancement and the country's development process. Welfare systems also create the problems of irreversibility and sustainability; it is easy to begin a programme of welfare provision when it is financially feasible, but difficult to terminate it when it is found financially unfeasible. Moreover, the state is expected by its citizens not only to continue the welfare programmes, but also expand them with the qualitative and quantitative expansion of the population. However, sustaining a certain welfare level requires an increase in the economic capacity of the state. Economic growth is, therefore, necessary either to sustain the welfare state or to reduce the dependence of the population on welfare measures.[5]

The quest for education, income, consumption, and higher career prospects in an economy characterised by a growing scarcity of economic resources and opportunities results in an increase in competition among individuals or social segments in the society. The visible growth of mass consumption among affluent groups clearly intensifies the sense of exclusion among other groups. Indeed, the sense of social exclusion escalates not only due to increasing competition for economic resources and opportunities but also due to their unfair distribution. Cuts in living standards, imposed by the need to correct a balance-of-payments deficit, are bound to hit lower-income groups in the society. The main concern should not only be the impact of adjustment on the lower-income groups, but also on relative income distribution – for conflicts over the division of benefits can be as serious as conflicts over absolute gains and losses. Individuals and social groups realise their social exclusion and experience frustration due to a high degree of awareness of and exposure to the visible growth in the rest of the society. The realisation of social exclusion and the right to social inclusion results in the formation of group identities of frustrated social groups. Social exclusion and frustration in the quest for socio-economic advancement constitutes a fertile basis for intrastate conflict and political opposition.[6]

A social segment that faced the harsh consequences of economic deterioration in Jordan comprised the country's new generations, the youth that was brought up within a welfare state. The younger generation in Jordan is proportionally large, and relatively healthy, educated, politically conscious, and ambitious. Yet, it was confronted by a competitive society characterised by an increasing scarcity of economic resources and opportunities. The economic capacity to provide resources and opportunities to meet rising social and political demands for socio-economic advancement fell short of its expectations.

In sum, an unsustainable paradox of the Jordanian welfare state was created by the growing scarcity of economic resources and opportunities relative to the escalating social and political demands. Economic mismanagement failed to produce the growth required in sustaining the competitive society. A *Jordan Times* editor once maintained that:

There is consensus that the top priority for the government . . . is to reform the economy, which suffers stagnation, and to alleviate poverty and unemployment. Most governments in recent years have had similar mandates but failed to attain much in terms of reversing the tide of poverty and rising unemployment.[7]

The youth population, with high aspirations for socio-economic advancement, was confronted with an increasing scarcity of economic resources and opportunities. The development of social aspirations for socio-economic advancement to achieve socially valued consumption patterns, income levels, employment and education in Jordan has exceeded the country's economic capacity.

Given the retreat in output and household incomes in Jordan, prospects for enhancing welfare and reducing poverty depend critically on the resurgence of robust, stable, and equitable growth. Growth is a necessary condition in order to provide income-earning opportunities for households, thereby enabling them to improve their incomes and living standards. Without the increase in the size of the national income and of the fiscal resources available, the government in Jordan will find it difficult to finance the required investments in social, human, and physical capital, or the redistributive policies needed to protect the poor in the Jordanian society. This, of course, has some serious security implications.

The conditions for forcible political opposition

Political conflicts are created when people feel that they have no access to institutionalised means of representing their grievances, and when state authorities are believed to be directly responsible for their exclusion. Social exclusion forms fertile ground for the emergence and sustenance of forcible political opposition.[8]

It is generally believed that liberal political systems are characterised by institutions in which decision-making is based on the will of the majority. Therefore, it is argued that the scope for non-violent means of achieving the goals is larger in such liberal systems than in exhaustively authoritarian political systems.[9] True, liberal systems permit the expression of grievances, but for a number of reasons the grievances of at least part of society are left unattended. The problem is acute in the face of widening gap between the rising social expectations and declining economic possibilities. Thus, those who were socially excluded begin to recognise that the system is ineffective in addressing their grievances. In theory, the voice of the excluded can be heard in a democratic system, but their social and political lobby may not be effective. This eventually erodes the possibilities for institutional means of achieving the goals, and leads to increased opposition.

With respect to the formation of human resources for forcible political opposition, the degree of awareness of the excluded and frustrated social groups is important. The degree of awareness becomes valuable input in political opposition, when social groups can judge their position against other groups in their own society, and understand their capacity and right to change the system according to their own specifications and standards.[10] In the advancement of the degree of awareness, education and the degree of exposure to information play a major role. When the majority of the employed are unable to advance socio-economically due to the declining economic capacity of the country, parties seeking political power could easily exploit this situation. Rami Khouri, a Jordanian political analyst, argues:

...King Abdullah ... recognised that the most serious threats to Jordan emanated from two related issues: economic stagnation and political discontent at home. The first threat was the young population's growing concerns about finding satisfying jobs and earning enough money to live a reasonably comfortable life; the second threat was many Jordanians' growing complaints about a pattern of discrimination, inequity, and favoritism in society, along ethnic, religious, geographical, tribal, cultural, or economic divides. This deadly combination of material and political discontent had to be addressed before it threatened the stability and well-being of the country.[11]

Economics and regime legitimacy

Common to both the preservation of the regimes and societies is an implicit expectation of the ruled that, in return for granting legitimacy to the rulers, the regime will provide some level of welfare or economic well-being for the society. A weak economy undermines a state's economic development and its ability to maintain social welfare programmes and employment for workers. This feeds back and increases the risks of threats to the legitimacy of the regime, as well as dissention especially where there is considerable economic disparity between groups.[12]

The state gains legitimacy in the eyes of the population through redistributing wealth, a welfare system, and various other subsidies. Stability is expected to last as long as redistribution is kept flowing from the state to its populace. Both stability and legitimacy are maintained as long as the state can channel to its citizenry. The state can be threatened as a result of a decrease in revenues which would undermine its ability to act as the main distributor.[13]

The Jordanian state draws its legitimacy from its populace using a combination of variables, the most dominant being Arab nationalism, Islam, and a welfare system. Developmental legitimacy is a core feature of the Jordanian state. Castells maintains:

A state is developmental when it establishes as its principle of legitimacy its ability to promote and sustain development, understanding by development the combination of steady high rates of economic growth and structural change in the productive system, both domestically and in its relationship with the international economy ... ultimately for the developmental state, economic development is not an end but a means.[14]

Economic development is not pursued as an end in itself, but as a means of securing internal stability. Developmental legitimacy leads to the consolidation of political legitimacy which, in turn, enables the regime to mobilise popular support to deter or withstand external and internal threats. Moreover, the greater the political legitimacy of its regime, the more the state has the capability to maintain the support of its populace in the face of economic crisis. If the populace does not accept the political legitimacy of the regime, and the state succumbs to internal strife, its capabilities are weakened or diverted. External enemies can take advantage of internal strife and use the internal enemies of the regime to destabilise the regime.

In Jordan the state has in effect attempted to satisfy the citizenry through provision of a host of services and economic activities paid through income received from rents.[15] As long as rents from the outside world – in the form of economic aid – were available, the state responded to those concerns of the population that it found necessary for maintaining its power and position. Since most of the state's revenues were not extracted from the population, the corollary sense of obligation and responsiveness to the society did not fully develop. In fact, all rentier states find themselves increasingly reluctant to liberalise their political systems.

After the 1989 economic crisis and when income was mainly based on taxation of domestic economic activity, calls for political liberalisation became more assertive. In fact, when the economic crisis broke out and austerity measures were introduced, widespread protest and public outcry against corruption and inequalities and calls for greater political freedom and participation transpired. Consequently, the political leadership in Jordan began the process of incremental political liberalisation in 1989. When the state faced fiscal crisis and resorted to increased taxation demands from within the society were generated for accountability and democratic institutions. Jordan's transition from rentierism, fostered by an ancient fiscal crisis, ushered in a form of political liberalisation which has allowed for a relatively free press, contested parliamentary elections and reduced restrictions on freedom of association.[16] The role of individuals at the helm of power was a key factor in the decision to liberalise. The decisive role of King Hussain in promoting political liberalisation and inclusionary politics was quite significant since many states facing a similar situation have resorted to repression instead. Indeed, taxation and the widening of the state's fiscal base were essential inducements for political liberalisation in Jordan. The state in Jordan sought through political reform to solve the pains of extensive economic belt-tightening and tax increases. Indeed, the link between fiscal crisis, reduction of rentier dependence and political liberalisation surely receives support in the case of Jordan.

The role of the state

After sifting through the accumulated historical evidence on one hundred years of growth in forty-two contemporary developing countries, Lloyd Reynolds concluded: 'My hypothesis is that the single most explanatory variable is political organisation and the administrative competence of government.'[17] Reynolds is right to give credit for growth to government, if only because it can destroy the impulse for growth by failing to create an environment in which it can succeed. It is customary, both in economic analysis and in public debate, to attribute the success or failure of a government's economic strategy to its competence and, occasionally, its integrity. The judgment may refer either to the government's choice of priorities or to its choice and/or implementation of particular policies. In the very short run, it is not inconceivable for a government, like anyone else, to make a mistake, even a serious mistake, especially when confronted with an unfamiliar problem. However, if a government continues to act 'incompetently' over a long period despite changes in its membership and advisers, or even more puzzling, if a succession of different governments continue to do so it is surely time to ask a rather obvious question: why do so many governments have one characteristic in common – incompetence?[18]

Policies require more than an appropriate institutional framework to produce the desired results: they need to be supported by a strong national consensus which is impossible without a high degree of social harmony. No matter how imaginative or theoretically sound a particular course of action may seem, it is bound to fail unless there is widespread national support for it.[19] In other words, whatever a country's economic potential, serious social division and the forcible political oppositions that normally accompanies it will ensure that its rate of economic progress lags markedly behind that of the countries with a more favourable socio-political environment. A Jordanian political observer has correctly argued:

Economic dialogue and modernisation of the Jordanian State must be the sole scientific dialogue. Efforts must be focused on bridging the gap between towns and rural areas and between the rich and the poor. When we overcome poverty and unemployment, we will automatically overcome regional rivalries. When people are occupied with work and production, their loyalty to the State and the land deepens. Horizons of cooperation open up to them and windows of subversive activity are shut.[20]

The economic and social characteristics of countries change over time and, as a result, priorities and policy mixes have to be altered to reflect these new conditions and needs. The success or failure of individual economies is largely determined by the ease with which their institutions and policies can be adapted to the new realities and problems. In other words, economic and institutional dynamics are closely related and will, therefore, progress and stagnate together.[21]

Moreover, the scope and ultimate success of an economic strategy will depend on the previously described conditions and on the ability, inventiveness, and political skills of those in power – with the former usually as the dominant factor. Factors conducive to successful state action include at least coherent bureaucratic traditions and a coherent corporatist network. Rational management of the economy requires a meritocratic bureaucracy that is competent and autonomous enough to obey its own logic which is one of utility maximisation, and prestigious enough not to be easily corrupted by outside interests.[22] In a political culture in which the public service is held in high esteem, it is easier to recruit amongst the best minds. On the other hand, corruption and mediocracy are self-enforcing phenomena as well: mediocre administrations can at best attract mediocre people, and corrupt governments attract corrupt people and encourage the corruption even of those who originally tried to enforce the common interest.

One of the main thrusts of economic structural adjustment in Jordan has been to trim the role of the state. The tasks left with government are, however, not only critical, but also in some ways complex – the manipulation of market-related policy instruments, the implementation of public investment programmes and the management of public infrastructure, and the delivery of social services. Nevertheless, economic reform in Jordan is, by and large, narrowing the range of government intervention and is supposed to leave the government with a more manageable set of tasks, but transfer of activities to the private sector has a significant degree of sensitivity, on grounds of economic efficiency, social desirability, and political feasibility.

The state has responsibility for the provision of services to the mass of the population. The deterioration in the delivery of social services has persisted, reflecting stringent resource constraints and a failure to implement new strategies of delivery and cost recovery. Macroeconomic structural adjustment did not do enough to improve the situation in the social sectors; while there is little evidence that structural adjustment had a regressive impact on the primary distribution of income, fiscal stringency has had a negative impact on the public provision of social services. Formulation of new sectoral strategies has been partial, support for the social sectors has not been informed by a coherent strategy to promote institutional reform, and progress in implementing new strategies has been limited.

Real salaries in the public service have collapsed, and the performances of many employees precisely match their vestigial incomes. Some senior civil servants survive on the perquisites of office. It could be argued that what is required is the rehabilitation of the state. Even when an essentially private economy is to be the model for the post-structural adjustment era, more effective state institutions are required in Jordan. King Abdullah puts it bluntly:

If we want to develop this country, we must enhance our methods and our management of the various problems it faces. Raising the level of administrative efficiency would certainly help our efforts to improve the economic situation ... We have a high unemployment rate as well as huge debts for a country like Jordan. Meanwhile, the governmental authorities continue to expand with very little potential. All these problems trap us in a vicious circle.[23]

Assuming structural adjustment has some further success and the private economy expands, the state will need to be reformed to be able to meet the needs of that development process, including the provision of essential infrastructure and social services and, as the private sector grows, the implementation of appropriate public actions to accommodate and orchestrate private economic activity. Even a minimalist state needs to fill gaps in the institutional arrangements for the private economy, including modifying the legal framework, sponsoring the development of new markets, and encouraging coordinating agencies.

The argument developed here is that effective government participation in development has both a bureaucratic and political dimension; transforming the state in Jordan will require movement on both fronts. In principle the definition of the agenda for bureaucratic reform is straightforward. The short-term need is for a careful definition of the responsibilities of government in the emerging economic situation and a systematic effort to put in place a reformed bureaucratic structure to tackle the identified tasks. The agenda for the rehabilitation of the state includes clarification of the required institutional structure, identification of appropriate human-power requirements, and the definition of an effective incentive system for the public service, involving fewer, but better paid public servants.

Emphasis has been placed increasingly on the importance of improved governance in Jordan. Reform of the public administration – of the budgetary system, of the civil service, of the government decision-making system, etc. – have been discussed widely. However, so far there has been little success in achieving comprehensive public sector reform. The most important steps in structural adjustment involved changes in key macroeconomic policies and decisions to dismantle various government controls. Reform of the institutions of government is a more complex task.

It is clear that the economic crisis set in train events that led to the dismantling of some ineffective instruments of state policy and a shift of resources from parasitic state institutions. However, it is far from clear that sustained growth will emerge from market forces, unaided by state intervention, while the capacity of state institutions has definitely not been restored in the structural adjustment process. As a result, the policy discussion in Jordan is shifting from structural adjustment to capacity building. In terms of this contention, that involves seeking means to increase the capacity of the state to make and implement policy and exploring whether the emerging political economy will be conducive to effective policy making. It is evident that the effective operation of a market economy in Jordan needs reasonably strong state institutions, a positive institutional environment, a stable macroeconomic setting, and the provision of economic and social services which are necessarily the responsibility of the state.

The first condition of successful economic transition is political stability. Without this the benefits of liberalisation (such as investor confidence) are unlikely to materialise, nor may there be the will to push reforms through. This would indicate that politically destabilising reforms – however sound in economic theory – would be counterproductive. Instability would also tend to reduce the extent to which the institutions of the state and the market can function.[24]

The existence of adequate institutions for the safeguarding of the rule of law, the protection of private property and the regulation of the market is another crucial prerequisite for successful liberalising reform. In apparently paradoxical terms, therefore, a strong state and regime in Jordan are much more likely to carry through economic reform than an undeveloped, truly minimal, or unstable political and state system.[25]

Another condition pertains to the available resources – natural, technical, and human. As Colclough puts it, 'Introducing a liberal regime in the context of impoverishment is very different from a setting (or early prospect) of dynamic growth.'[26] Indeed, the problems of vulnerable groups would then be likely to be much higher, and the difficulty of avoiding political problems and potential upheaval much greater. Similarly, a context in which great inequality prevails – which in itself is recognised as a rake on growth – will also make the adoption of liberalising reforms without compensatory programmes much more politically and socially unsettling. If reforms end up increasing such inequality they will be counterproductive in terms of long-term growth. For liberalising structural reforms to succeed in such circumstances, they must be designed in tandem with programmes to protect the most vulnerable (through social safety nets), and to reduce inequality (through basic services and education).

Economic reform and political change

Huntington along with many others asserts that a market economy fosters the development of democracy.[27] A number of reasons may be advanced to explain why economic liberalisation should produce this effect – even if often with a considerable time lag. The first is simply that an economic withdrawal of the state is likely to reduce its capacity for socio-political control, patronage, and co-option.

The second cluster of reasons concerns the effects such domestic and international trade liberalisation tends to have on civil society. The different components of economic liberalisation and their effects tend to help bring about some of the changes in social conditions and structures thus affecting the distribution of power resources (economic, intellectual, and otherwise). New forms of wealth and its distribution, technological change, and changing education are all part of these resources, and are almost inevitably affected by a process of economic liberalisation. It is plausible that political liberalisation would be boosted in the case of a wider distribution of such resources. One of the social effects of economic liberalisation will tend to be the expansion or strengthening of a middle class with some degree of independence from the state. That such a class is likely to develop its own political demands, however gradually, is conceivable.[28]

Because the political stock of the regime in Jordan was always high the country moved towards fundamental structural transformation of the economy and its management, and reforms included comprehensive opening up of trade and investment opportunities and have aimed more at economic efficiency than political survival. However, one has to admit that any further moves would probably require further political liberalisation in the country. At this point the dilemma consists of the futility of trying, through budget cuts, to convince people to take on more responsibility for their own well-being, while the government itself continues to maintain unquestioned authority. Equally futile, of course, is the bid of the private sector monopolies to inherit, under the guise of economic liberalism and privatisation, the productive assets of the public sector without assuming any of the social burdens.

Privatisation and liberalisation policies may indeed bring about fundamental changes, but for now, and for a while to come, they lead to the tipping of the balance towards the rich and, paradoxically, towards a large number of state-supported entrepreneurs who are making money in a thoroughly rigid market and are not necessarily compelled for economic or non-economic reasons to invest their money in productive activities. The least that can be said about these policies is that they are not very conducive to the creation of a free market.

Lack of political change will lead the country to a vexatious outcome. What can be done? The task involves thoughtful consideration of how to improve state-society relations in order to enhance the legitimacy of various existing polities, not merely leaders or even governmental institutions. A good polity can only be generated based on the rule of law, protection of legitimate economic activities and interests, a government's accountability to its citizens, effective measures to curb corruption, a participatory approach to development, easy access to information and services, and sound decision-making reflecting the actual needs of people.[29]

Economic reform is not a proper vehicle for increasing the political assets of the government. If anything, the reverse is the case. In order to become secure, polities need to rely on a supportive society in concrete and formulated ways.[30] But this support will not come about unless the state begins to seem less arbitrary in day-to-day life. Accordingly, any genuine discussion of economic improvements must begin here. In other words, attention must turn towards state structures. Put bluntly, an increase in the political assets of the state, required for enacting genuine economic reform, can only come about the reform of the state itself.

The state will have to address burgeoning demands for accountable, efficacious, honest and fair government. The demand for political reform will grow more urgent in the years ahead. Increasing demands for jobs in an economic system with already a saturated labour pool create the potential for unrest and oppositional mobilisation.

The sheer immensity of the prevailing socio-economic factors will not in itself cause political change. Only when the paucity of jobs, poor housing and the general inadequacy of public services is perceived as a failure of politics do these factors acquire political meaning. In this sense, economic inequity, unemployment, poor housing and public services will be politicised. Therefore, the government must continue to seek economic and political reforms that target material needs, but also it needs to divert political energies into regime support. When asked in an interview about the main political and economic challenges that face him at the domestic level, King Abdullah responded:

> The economic and democratic reform processes are the most prominent challenges in the coming stage . . . We have no illusion that these challenges will be easy or that they can be dealt with quickly. But we must confront them firmly, wisely, and patiently.[31]

National security through economic growth

The risk that threatens the stability of Jordan can stem from an ailing economy, poverty, high unemployment levels and deteriorating standards of living. Given the retreat in output and household incomes in Jordan, prospects for enhancing welfare and reducing poverty depend critically on the resurgence of robust, stable, and equitable growth. Growth is a necessary condition in order to provide income-earning opportunities for households, thereby enabling them to improve their incomes and living standards.

The government continues to play a critical role in fostering the development of policies and institutions that would do the most to spur growth. Bad government policies and inadequate institutional arrangements can also make things worse. Partial reforms that permit a greater capture of the state by oligarchs, loose fiscal policies, excessive licensing and regulations, poor incentives for new enterprise development and corruption all compromise growth and deny the poor the opportunities they need to improve their welfare.

In developing these policies, the government needs to bear in mind two sets of issues. First, transition remains a holistic process that requires movement along many fronts and that necessarily stretches the limited implementation capacity of most of countries. Mistakes may occur, but it is important to stay the course on the general direction of policy change. In this vein the costs of 'partial reform' are high and highlight the interdependencies between policy and institutional reforms, and between macroeconomic and microeconomic reforms.

Second, the growth of economic opportunities will have higher payoffs for the poor if that growth generates employment and real wages rise over time with increases in labour productivity. This requires that the poor gain more than proportionally from the emergent growth – an enormous challenge in view of the experience that job creation typically lags behind economic growth. But the government can adopt measures to enhance the job content of growth. For example, deregulating product markets, reducing barriers to entry for small businesses and upgrading vital infrastructure will foster the development of a more competitive private sector and maximise the potential for job creation.[32]

Whatever the specific package of growth policies adopted, these policies must take into account certain issues. First, the restructuring of existing state enterprises and the creation of new private business through new entry and privatisation are priorities and the future engine of growth.

Second, this restructuring has to be supported by a sound fiscal policy that can provide the basis for macroeconomic stability while allowing for adequate social protection for displaced workers and other vulnerable groups. This fiscal policy also has to permit critical investments in health, education and social infrastructure, so as to enable the population to take advantage of the benefits offered by the emerging market economy.

Third, the challenge of social protection in the face of enterprise restructuring and tightening budgets implies that social policy must be reconfigured in a way that makes the provision of social services more cost-effective. Government policies in the social sphere need to have a dual focus: providing social assistance to those adversely affected by enterprise restructuring and other macroeconomic and structural reforms and strengthening the education and skill development required for future growth.

To accommodate the social fallout from tightened budgetary constraints on enterprises, the government needs to strengthen the formal social protection system. The social role of the state in Jordan has to be reoriented away from paternalistic, poorly targeted benefits and toward policies that address poverty and vulnerability directly.

Growth will come primarily from an increase in labour productivity rather than from the expansion of the labour force. While workers' productivity is closely related to the level of capital investment, it can also be enhanced by human capital investments through education and training activities, and by improvement in health service delivery.

It has been argued:

The single most important change that has occurred under the leadership of King Abdullah has been a broad reorientation of Jordan's overall national role and horizons. Under King Hussain's long reign the Jordanian state survived and progressed by carving out for itself an effective geo-strategic role as an agent of political and developmental ideologies . . . Under King Abdullah, Jordan is a very different country today, focused almost totally on addressing its domestic economic challenges, and correspondingly defining a new global role for itself as a purveyor of human and technical capabilities.[33]

In Jordan, two processes shape the transition to a new economic model: integration and economic transition.[34] In both cases, economic policy has an important role to play. Jordanian policymakers are obliged to negotiate the integration of Jordan with other economies and to take measures to open, deregulate, privatise, and streamline the social role of the state in order to free up markets and release the vitality of entrepreneurship. The impact of these changes profoundly alters the nature of production and socioeconomic relationships – with the paradoxical result that new interventions by the state in the economy are required.

Whether liberal economic transition will be consistent, and thus successful, depends on how much power the state has over civil society and how autonomous its technocratic elites are vis-à-vis other elites, corporatist interests, and social movements. Massive economic, social and institutional changes have been tearing down some structures at the same time that new ones are being generated. This process will continue. Its dramatic consequences – the disempowerment of certain groups and the breakdown of certain relationships – have left some members of the society marginalised or even excluded. Meanwhile, new groups have emerged that can be considered new working classes. These social categories constitute spaces in which management enjoys much greater power than in the rest of the society.

The older welfare functions of the Jordanian state proved to be unsustainable politically and economically. They relied on deficit spending, promoted inefficiency, allowed resources to be siphoned off by high-income groups and were used for clientelistic purposes by the government. By the same token, however, liberalisation has not yet succeeded in offering an efficient, effective alternative. In fact, liberal reforms have allowed for more efficient and better quality services but only for higher income groups. Access to basic services has become much more restricted, and the effort to focus resources on the extreme poor is limited in scope. The old welfare state has not been replaced by markets that respond to demand and achieve Pareto optimality.[35] Markets in social services are indifferent to social inequalities, and they have numerous flaws and high transition costs.

A failure of the liberal model can have consequences that reverberate not only in the social and economic spheres; the very legitimacy of the state can be at stake, and a hard-earned space for crucial social compromise can be jeopardised. The reduction in state intervention in the social sphere reduces the total amount of resources available in the polity. The roll-back in social welfare programmes reduces the ability both of the state to alleviate the widespread failures of markets to provide an acceptable level of social justice in terms of access to health care, education, and social security. The state's renunciation of certain instruments of economic policy – various forms of price control, subsidies and transfer prices – not only weaken the state; they also weaken those organisations in civil society that represented their members' interests by constant lobbying within the policy-making arena.

In this way, both the state and civil society lose power capacities. Of course, the roll-back of the state is unlikely to be 'class neutral': Big business is likely to gain, and small business and labour are likely to lose. In a market-oriented society, those groups that can dominate markets will do well, while others will lose.

The politics of Jordan is in a state of flux and it is quite unclear how the economic groups strengthened under liberal economic policies will participate in the political process, how a lively small-scale sector and fledgling indigenous capitalists will impinge on enfeebled state institutions. A class of entrepreneurs is emerging and is expected to play an important role both in larger-scale economic sectors and in the political process.

State capacity is largely an organisational question. While the Jordanian state is under-resourced, the road to increased efficiency and capacity in the state runs through institutional reform. There are several areas where action is needed: increased fiscal capacity through tax reform; improved mechanisms for links between the state and key economic actors, improved internal functioning of state apparatus, including reduction of over-manning, clientelism, and corruption; and improved balance between the executive and legislative/judicial powers.

This is a massive agenda that will produce benefits for the state primarily in the long run. As a result, although the long-term benefits may be appealing, there is little incentive for any particular government, concerned with short-term political survival, to embark on these reforms. The immediate risks and costs are perceived to be high, and the benefits are seen to accrue only in the long-run.

There is one circumstance in which the Jordanian government might embark on these long-term reforms. If there exists a strong movement in civil society aimed at making the state responsive to its citizens, it is possible that this could be institutionalised in a number of civic movements in a way that might give state managers some incentive to embark on these reforms. It has been observed:

Domestic political change and further democratic advances move slowly, while economic growth reigns as the single, supreme issue for Jordan today ... The King seems to operate in the correct assumption that political reform will be easier to achieve in the future, once economic growth has been restored.[36]

There are many grounds for optimism about the future of Jordan as far as state-civil society relations are concerned. A shift toward sustained improvement, both in terms of sustained growth with equity and in terms of improved quality of democracy, will depend on internal pressures from the state in its drive to increase its power capacities. This drive could perhaps generate a mutually reinforcing spiral that will force social movements to respond.

MAIN ECONOMIC INDICATORS, 1997–2000*

	1997	1998	1999	2000*
Normal GDP ($ million)	6975.7	7385.9	7696.8	8112.4
Real GDP growth (%)	1.3	2.2	1.3*	2.0
Inflation (%)	3.0	3.1	0.6	2.0
Deficit/surplus (excluding grants) ($ million)	535.2-	786.8-	587.9-	577.5-
(as % of GDP)	-7.7	-10.7	-7.6	-7.1
Deficit/surplus (inducing grants) ($ million)	218.3-	500.8-	308.3-	197.2-
(as % of GDP)	-3.1	-6.8	-4.0	-2.4
External debt ($ million)	6451.6	7046.1	7304.2	7501.4
(as % of GDP)	92.6	95.5	95.0	92.6
Internal debt ($ million)	1287.6	1686.6	1757.5	1891.5
(as % of GDP)	18.5	22.9	22.9	23.3
Current account balance ($ million)	29.6	40.8	343.7	207.0
(as % of GDP)	0.4	0.6	4.5	2.6

*Estimates.
Sources: Central Bank of Jordan and Ministry of Finance.

GDP REAL GROWTH RATES 1990–9

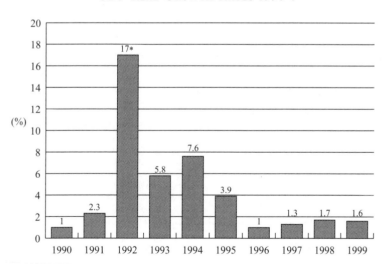

Following the Gulf War, the flood of returnees increased the GDP real growth rate.
Source: Bank of Jordan, Annual Report, various issues.

It is both desirable and likely that the Jordanian state seeks to expand its power capacities in the foreseeable future. It is both desirable and likely that social movements will become more institutionalised. The combination of these trends will be an increased organisational density in state-civil society relations. This could increase the possibilities for various forms of stable consensus politics at the expense of both 'populist' mobilisation and exclusionary elitist projects.

The Jordanian state will expand its power capacity, forcing civil society to respond. The outcome is likely to mean a more structured reform of politics, with greater regularity and a denser intermeshing of state and civil society. This could strengthen and improve the quality of democracy. This will happen to the extent that a whole series of rather specific issues become articulated as part of a large demand for enhanced citizenship.

NOTES

1. See Oskar Kurer (1997), *The political foundations of development policies*, Lanham, MD: University Press of America.
2. Although development widens the range of choices available, it also diminishes the range of socially expected choices. On the one hand, among the relatively deprived social groups, expectations of socio-economic advancement rise, in the context of the current local and global socio-economic environment. On the other hand, relatively deprived social groups experience a growing scarcity of economic resources and opportunities in relation to their expectations. Therefore, the strategic development problem faced by the state is the generation of economic resources and opportunities to meet the rising social expectations, rather than a set of pre-defined basic needs.
3. See Vinod Thomas, *et al.* (eds), *Restructuring economies in distress: policy reform and the World Bank*, Washington, DC: The World Bank, 1991. Also see Sebastian Edwards, *The sequencing of structural adjustment and stabilisation*, San Fransisco: International Center for Economic Growth, 1992.
4. Abd-al-Ra'uf al-Rawabdeh, *Government policy statement before the House of Representatives*, 3 April 1999.
5. See Irwin Collier *et al.* (eds), *Welfare states in transition*, New York: St. Martin's Press, 1999.
6. See Stephen Haggard and Robert Kaufman, *The political economy of democratic transitions*, Princeton University Press, 1995.
7. Jordan Times, 'Al-Rawabidah's "Tough Task",' *Jordan Times*, 7 March 1999.
8. See Klitgaard, Robert, *Adjusting to reality: beyond 'state versus market' in economic development*, San Fransisco: International Center for Economic Development, 1991.
9. See Kurt Weyland, *Democracy without equity*, University of Pittsburgh Press, 1996.
10. Ibid.
11. Rami Khouri, 'First year of King's Abdullah's reign', *Jordan Times*, 16 February 2000.
12. See Warren Samuels, *Fundamentals of the economic role of government* Westport,

CT: Greenwood Press, 1989.

13. Ibid.

14. Castells, 1992, pp. 56–7.

15. The rentier state argument holds that in states in which the main source of revenue is derived from outside the domestic economy (e.g. aid), the essence of the economy and the political system becomes one of getting access to the circulation of this rent (from viewpoint of the population), and allocating it for purposes of political stability (from the viewpoint of the rulers). In developing states in which the politics of rentierism has become part and parcel of the system's dynamics, these dynamics and the regime's calculation are also likely to inhibit far-reaching liberalisation. Not only will those parts of the population (including a state-dependent private sector) that benefit from the allocation of such rent resist drastic change, but the regime itself is unlikely to let go easily of the means of power and patronage that a politically stabilising allocation system affords it. The imperative of distribution and control over the rent circuit may therefore remain more important than that of efficiency and productivity. State apparatuses and public bureaucracies are often used as much as 'sponge employers' for sociopolitical reasons and for engendering the dependence of their employees, as for their official purposes. The option of slimming down the public sector therefore becomes politically loaded, implying socially and politically destabilising unemployment and a loss of regime control. In the end the outcome will depend on the available resources and their balance with increasing demands.

16. From the earliest days of its inception, the Jordanian state was dependent on foreign subsidy (external rent) for its income and revenue. The extent, form, and continuity of this subsidy made rentiersim the prime feature of the Jordanian state. Rentierism peaked in 1970s and 80s with important increases in the two primary features of Jordan's rentier economy – petro-dollar foreign aid and workers' remittances. Both of these sources of revenues declined after the Second Gulf War and after many of the expatriate workers from the Gulf returned unemployed, seeking jobs at home. The resultant budgetary deficits were rectified with increased taxation and through external and domestic borrowing.

17. See Lloyd Reynolds, 'The spread of economic growth to the Third World: 1850–1980', *Journal of Economic Literature*, 21, 941–80.

18. See Karl Polanyi, *The great transformation: the political and economic origins of our time*, Boston, MA: Beacon Press, 1944.

19. See Robert Holt, and John Turner, *The political basis of economic development: an exploration in comparative political analysis*, Princeton, NJ: Van Nostrand, 1966).

20. Muhammad al-Subayhi, 'Those who want to obstruct economic change', *Al-'Arab al-Yawm*, 25 April, 2000, p. 17.

21. See V. A. Muscatelli (ed.), *Economic and political institutions in economic policy*, Manchester University Press, 1996.

22. See Robert Klitgaard, *Adjusting to Reality: Beyond 'State Versus Market' in Economic Development*, San Fransisco: International Center for Economic Development 1991.

23. Ibrahim Nafi', 'Interview with Jordanian King Abdullah II,' *Al-Ahram*, 9 February 2000.

24. See Mohammed Ayoob, *The Third World security predicament: state making, regional conflict, and the international system*, Boulder, CO: Lynne Rienner, 1995.

25. See Haggard and Kaufman (1995).

26. C. Colclough, 'Structuralism versus neo-liberalism: an introduction' in C. Colclough and J. Manor (eds), *States or markets? neo-liberalism and the development*

     policy debate, Oxford: Clarendon Press, 1991, pp. 1–25.
27.   See Samuel Huntington, *The third wave: democratisation in the late twentieth century*, Norman: University of Oklahoma Press, 1991.
28.   See Haggard and Kaufman (1995).
29.   See Deutsch, Karl, *The nerves of government: models of political communication and control*, New York: Free Press, 1966.
30.   See Kurer, Oskar, *The political foundations of development policies* (Lanham, MD: University Press of America, 1997); and Kurt Weyland, *Democracy without equity*, University of Pittsburgh Press, 1996.
31.   George Sam'an and Salamah Ni'mat, 'Interview with Jordanian King Abdullah II bin-Husayn,' *Al-Hayat*, 12 May 1999, p. 7.
32.   See IMF Fiscal Affairs Department, *Should equity be a goal of economic policy?* Washington, DC: International Monetary Fund, 1998.
33.   Rami Khouri, 'First year of King's Abdullah's reign,' *Jordan Times*, 16 February 2000.
34.   Integration refers to the policies, negotiations, agreements and norms that in their early phases lower tariffs and eliminate nontariff barriers. Later on integration policies pursue more advanced objectives that include customs union, currency alignments and the coordination of finance policy.
35.   Pareto optimality is maximised allocative efficiency.
36.   Rami Khouri, 'First year of King's Abdullah's reign', *Jordan Times*, 16 February 2000.

Part II. THE DOMESTIC SCENE

THE EFFECTS OF EXTERNAL FORCES ON JORDAN'S PROCESS OF DEMOCRATISATION

Ali Kassay

Most of the literature on democracy in the Arab world tends to concentrate on the domestic dynamics that led to the start of this process in those countries where a degree of democratisation has already emerged.[1] The process of democratisation is presented as a top-down process through which patrimonial or neo-patrimonial regimes in rentier states,[2] which were faced with civil discontent fuelled by economic crises, sought to restore their shaken legitimacy by a variety of means, one of which was the incorporation of elements of democratic procedures into their systems of government. In doing so, these regimes sought to transform their societies from quiescent recipients of goods and services provided by the state (before the economic crisis), to partners in bearing the responsibility for the deteriorating economy. This explanation suffers from two shortcomings: the first is that it does not explain why the people were not also made partners in the decision-making process which sought a solution for the problem; and, moreover, it pays comparatively little attention to the international factors that encouraged Arab leaders to undertake the process of democratisation.

This study posits that the analysis of Arab democratisation would be incomplete without a closer look at the international dimension, an assertion that is supported by the high permeability of the Arab World to influences from abroad, mainly from Europe and North America. It is therefore considered important to include in the analysis the impact of international transformations that coincided with the start of Arab democratisation and that influenced them. These transformations include the global consensus on democracy after the collapse of communism, pressure for reform by international donor states and agencies, and increased activity in the Arab world by Western non-governmental organisations (NGOs). To do this, the discussion below will review briefly the available literature on democratisation and the means by which international factors influence it, then it will test the applicability of these theories to the case of Jordan. While this paper will concentrate only on Jordan, yet the hypothesis is not without relevance to other countries in the Arab Near East.

The Arab world, the rentier state and democratisation – the classic vision

While this study does not support any claim to Arab, Islamic, or Middle Eastern specificity, whether democratic or anti-democratic, it accepts the premise that the Arab world has lived for centuries under purely patrimonial states, in which the state was an extension of the sovereign who was its ultimate owner and who demanded total submission from all[3] and that this philosophy of government has persisted into modern Arab history. In other words, Arab societies have yet to experience a transition to democracy, which is taken here to involve two levels of transformation: at the state level, 'democratisation refers to a change in rules and procedures, which institute responsibility on the part of the rulers [towards the ruled], and at the societal level, it is a transformation of the individual from subject to citizen.'[4] Unlike the patrimonial or neo-patrimonial state, the democratic state has duties because its citizens have rights, not because the prince is benevolent and God-fearing.[5]

The demand for democracy has always ranked very low on the agendas of governments as well as mainstream opposition groups in Arab countries. To be sure, there have been thinkers and politicians who believed in and called for democracy, but they were marginal at best. Many reasons for this phenomenon are given (historic, cultural, religious), of which the most pertinent in modern times may have been the success of the rentier system during the 1970s and 1980s. During this period, the Arab world lived in relative stability that contrasted sharply with the preceding two decades. The principal economic feature of this period was the near total dependence of the state on exogenous sources of income that allowed it to assume the role of principal benefactor for the public. The oil crisis that followed the 1973 Arab-Israeli war and subsequent oil shocks, raised the price of crude oil, and hence the income of oil producing states to a mind-boggling level. The Gulf oil producing states poured money on a large scale on all services for their societies. They still had vast surpluses of money left, which, for reasons related to the Arab order that prevailed after the 1967 war, they shared with their Arab neighbours that were less endowed with natural resources. For their part, the latter group developed a style of government spending identical, though somewhat smaller in scale, to that of the oil producers.

The lavish distribution of state resources created a state-society relationship, the logic of which has been frequently expressed elsewhere as 'no taxation, no representation.' Of course, the distribution of state benefits to society was not necessarily equitable; but everyone was touched by these benefits to a greater or lesser degree, which reduced in a commensurate fashion society's desire to hold the state accountable. As a result, the social basis of power remained very narrow, and the channels of access to resources did not pass through the public sphere, but through personal relationships with an elite which determined how resources would be allocated.[6]

The outcome, Jean Leca argues, was to reject any call for democratisation because there is a link between the extraction of resources and democracy in a modern state. If governments have a low or non-tax base while investing in infrastructures, industries, education and health, they have the means to postpone accountability as long as there are enough other resources. But as soon as they are burdened with expenditures no longer covered by these resources, 'structural adjustments' loom large on the horizon: subsidies have to decrease, as well as the taxes on international trade and transactions. A sizeable part of the population will suffer more while being expected to contribute more to public resources through direct taxation.[7]

Demographic changes ran parallel to the drop in revenues and exacerbated the crisis of the rentier state.[8] In the case of Jordan, for instance, the improvement of health services during the seventies and early eighties reduced the child mortality rate and raised life expectancy, which raised the rate of natural population growth during that period to a staggering 3.8 per cent. It was becoming increasingly difficult for the state to meet the rising expectations of its rapidly growing population. In Jordan as well as elsewhere, the elite were faced with a choice: either they would expand their income and thus safeguard the clientelist system, or they would open up the political systems and let other social groups share in the privileges.

So far this review of literature supports the premise that democratisation came as a response to the economic crisis of the rentier state. This study posits that the accepted explanations do not pay enough attention to the importance of the West as an ally of many Arab states whether rich or poor, and hence the importance of Western calls for administrative reforms and political liberalisation that came in the end of the 1980s and during the 1990s, which were inspired by the liberal belief that democratic governments create regional stability and are more efficient in utilising the resources available to them.

International factors and democratisation

During the 1980s the programmes that were prescribed to help developing countries achieve economic recovery were purely economic, based on free-market neo-liberal economic theory. As the experience of purely economic reforms progressed, it became clear that no economic project was likely to succeed unless minimum conditions of responsible government behaviour were met, such as political legitimacy and institutional efficiency. However, the problem with demanding reforms of the institutions of state, and linking such reforms to economic assistance, was that this linkage would attract protests of interference in the affairs of sovereign states. Moreover, it would have been beyond the mandate of multilateral banks and agencies, such as the World Bank and the IMF to demand such reforms. To overcome this problem, donors devised terms such as 'good governance' and 'promoting civil society', which allowed sensitive questions to be discussed in apparently technical and politically innocuous terms.[9]

One of the objectives of donors became to promote democracy by promoting the development of centres of economic power through economic liberalisation programmes, and political power through the development of civil society institutions that are independent of the state. Economic liberalisation, coupled with the increased dependence of the state on locally generated revenue is believed to make the call for government accountability inevitable. The enhancement of civil society is believed to have a direct impact on democratisation, through two primary functions: these may be labelled the pluralist and educational functions. The pluralist function is based on the principle that, by organised collective action, groups can hold their own and protect their interests vis-à-vis other groups in society and vis-à-vis the organs of the state. The educational function is a process 'of socialisation into democratic norms, through a process of learning by doing.'[10]

In a study on the international context of democratisation in the Arab world,[11] Moore identifies five factors:

1. Cultural diffusion and demonstration effects – which entail the transfer of the constituent ideas of an ideal democratic polity through the media, while demonstration effects refer to the rippling effects from a nation or a group of nations undergoing significant liberalisation and democratisation.

2. Foreign governmental policies and aid – while it may be incorrect to assume that foreign pressure and aid alone would be sufficient to produce democratic transformation, yet successful pressure helps

raise the costs of internal repression and holds out rewards for greater liberalisation.

3. Non-governmental activities – this refers to the recent increased presence in Arab world of and its concern with – non-governmental organisations. There has developed a symbiotic relationship between international organisations and regionally based groups, wherein international groups depend on local groups for the bulk of their information, while local groups depend on the international organisations to publicise their plight and, most importantly, to pressure the local government.

4. Regional security environment and regional actors – excessive spending on defence can result in a crowding out of the private sector limiting the formation of independent political spheres of power able to influence a regime opening.[12]

5. International fiscal environment and policy – this factor encompasses two distinct pressures which are argued to be the most powerful external factors shaping democratisation in the Arab world. The first consists of changes in the international economic environment, specifically the constriction of external rents. The second, which results from the first, comprises conditionality imposed by the International Monetary Fund (IMF) and the World Bank, in that the introduction of policies of which they approve is a precondition of the loans which they dispense.

The case of Jordan – the classic vision

Jordan's dependence on foreign assistance goes back to the creation of the state in 1921.[13] Realising the inadequacy of their country's natural resources, the rulers of Jordan benefited from the country's central location, regional disputes and, later, the Cold War to weave a clever web of regional and international relations that made Jordan's well-being a concern for Western and conservative Arab states.

These relations were based mainly on mutual security interests, namely the fight against communism and against the revolutionary tide that swept the Arab world in the 1950s and 1960s. In due course this network of relations developed into an almost universal consensus that Jordan was a vital element in maintaining regional security and stability.[14] The Iraq-Iran war, during which the Gulf monarchies felt threatened by the prospects of an Iranian victory that would bring the Islamic revolution to the borders of Saudi Arabia and Kuwait, added a further dimension to Jordan's importance, since Jordan was the principal route through which Iraq imported supplies for its war effort. The point here is that Jordan has always been dependent on its

TOTAL LOANS AND GRANTS FROM THE U.S.A, TO JORDAN,
1952–95

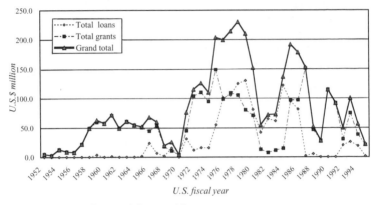

Source: U.S. Overseas Loans and Grants, vol. I.

international relations for its survival and economic solvency. During
the 1970s and 1980s the three main sources of external assistance for
the Jordanian treasury were the oil-rich Arab states, the United
States and, to a lesser extent, Western Europe, both on a bilateral basis and through European Union programmes.

The drop in oil prices dealt a double blow to the Jordanian economy. It reduced the transfers from oil producers on which Jordan was
dependent, as well as the remittances of Jordanian citizens working in
Gulf, which had become another important source of hard currency.
To make things worse, this coincided with a drop of economic assistance from the West, especially the United States, to a very low level.
The government, which had come to base its legitimacy on its ability
to provide for society, found itself increasingly unable to maintain
the spending levels of previous years. But successive governments
were reluctant to reduce their spending, thereby undermining the base
of the clientelist system in Jordan. When cuts were made, they affected government investments rather than running expenses.

The summer of 1988 saw a run on the Jordanian dinar which
brought down its exchange rate from $1=JD 0.33 to $1=JD 0.71. This
was catastrophic for a country that imported most of its consumption. The government was forced to turn to the IMF in the spring of
1989 to seek $275 million in standby credits and assistance in resche-
duling its foreign debts. As part of the deal, the government agreed
to a five-year economic stabilisation programme that involved more
prudent borrowing policies, strengthening foreign reserves, reducing

inflation through tight credit policies, improving the current account balance, reforming the tax system, and reducing the budget deficit.[15]

The last item – reducing the budget deficit – meant the very risky step of reducing government subsidies on basic goods. With the memory of bread riots in Egypt, Tunisia and Algeria fresh in its mind, the Jordanian government refused to lift the subsidy on basic food-stuffs such as bread, rice, and staples. But on April 16, 1989, it hiked the price of cooking gas, gasoline, diesel fuel and kerosene by 10–30 per cent. This came at a particularly unpropitious moment, since it coincided with the start of Ramadan, the Muslim month of fasting and asceticism, when Jordanian household expenditure on consumer goods reaches its peak.

Riots broke out almost immediately after the announcement. They started in Ma'an, a trucker's town that was already suffering from the drop in road transportation between the port of Aqaba and Amman and between Aqaba and Iraq, which had come to a virtual stand-still after the end of the Iraq-Iran war. The riots soon spread to other towns and villages, whose populations were predominantly if not entirely from the East Bank, communities that are considered the backbone of support for the regime.

It is important to note two things about the riots: the first is that the rioters did not criticise the king, but they expressed themselves freely against the government, which they accused of flagrant corruption and whose resignation they demanded. The second point is that the rioters did not make any calls for democracy, civil liberties, or greater respect for human rights. Such considerations do not appear to have been in the minds of the rioters. Instead, they made dichotomous demands: the elimination of government corruption on the one hand, and on the other, the incorporation of their communities more closely into the circles in which favours were distributed. Demands for democracy and civil liberties appeared on the list of grievances much later, mainly through the pronouncements of the professional associations which, being based in Amman, took no part in the riots.

The response of the king was to appoint a new cabinet on April 27, which he ordered in the letter of appointment to end corruption, favouritism, clientelism, and nepotism, and to restore full parliamentary life to Jordan. The instructions to end corruption, favouritism and nepotism were to reappear in every letter of appointment thereafter.[16] As for the restoration of parliamentary life, the cabinet acted swiftly to fulfil its mandate, organising elections in November of the same year, that were recognised by all observers and commentators as free and fair.

   The link between civil discontent with the economic situation and
the restoration of parliamentary life[17] seems, therefore, undeniable.
For one thing, Prince Hassan, then crown prince of Jordan, acknowledged that 'Jordan could not sustain the painful medicine of economic stabilisation without political liberalisation.'[18] Brynen also refers
to several interviews with a former prime minister and several close
advisors of the king in Amman between July and August 1989, in
which they said that 'there seemed little choice other than to forge a
new social contract, an implicit – and sometimes explicit – quid pro
quo whereby a real democratic opening would be offered for acceptance of continued economic austerity.'[19] To the economic imperative, Salamé adds two other political objectives: to Jordanise the
Jordanian citizens of Palestinian origin by incorporating them in the
political process, and to restore or forge new ties between the Palace
and society, after the dislocation of classic tribal structures that were
highlighted by the riots of 1989.[20]
   Whilst this discussion does not deny the importance of these factors,
it argues that they do not describe the full picture. For one thing, democracy was not a demand of the rioters, so there was no quid pro
quo as such. Moreover, the government remained unwilling to reduce
its control over all activity in the country even after democracy was
restored. The resumption of parliamentary activity, however, satisfied the second demand of rioters in that 120 representatives of their
communities (80 deputies and 40 senators) were incorporated in the
favour-distribution system. Yet, to explain fully the evolution of Jordan's process of democratisation, one needs to look beyond the country itself, to the international arena.

External influences on Jordan's democracy

This study posits that, in 1998, Jordan was faced with a challenge
more serious than the economic situation alone. It faced the danger
of the disintegration of its network of regional and international relations that was vital for its survival. This network of relationships consisted of a four-tier alliance system:
1. There was, first, a strategic alliance with the West against the
spread of communism and Arab revolutionary nationalism. This alliance focused on a central great-power patron, which was Britain until
the 1950s, and then became the United States, but it did not exclude
other Western friends, whose value was to increase Jordan's margin
of manoeuvre vis-à-vis the central patron. One element that enhanced
this alliance was the existence of 'an uneasy political consensus in Israel' that supported Jordan.[21]

2. Second, there was a strategic alliance with the oil-rich conservative Arab monarchies against revolutionary Arab regimes. During the 1960s and 1970s this alliance served both parties well. During the stage of institution-building, the oil-rich states were able to draw on the expertise of Jordanian military trainers, civil servants, and school and university teachers, who could be trusted not to disseminate revolutionary propaganda in their respective institutions. In return, Jordan received considerable financial and political assistance from these states and its economy benefited from the remittances that were sent by its expatriate workers to their families back in Jordan. During the 1980s, a new element entered into this alliance, the Iran-Iraq war, during which Iraq was seen as the only regional power capable of checking the expansionist ambitions of the Iranian revolution. Jordan gained importance during this period as Iraq's principal ally and outlet to the sea.

3. Third came a series of shifting tactical alliances with Syria, Iraq, and Egypt, the objective of which was to prevent the rise of an alliance between these three states against Jordan. By the end of the Iran-Iraq war, this alliance combined Jordan with Egypt and Iraq, which were drawn together by the need to support Iraq in its war against Iran.

4. Finally, there was an alliance with the non-Arab states beyond Jordan's immediate Arab neighbours, namely Iran, and later Turkey. The alliance with Iran, which was strong under the Shah, collapsed when he was ousted by the Islamic revolution. Attempts to replace it by an alliance with Turkey during the mid-eighties proved unsuccessful.

This alliance system was beginning to unravel by the end of the 1980s. The strategic alliance with the West had lost much of its logic with the disappearance of both the communist threat and the Arab revolutionary tide. Even the Israeli consensus in favour of Jordan suffered under the Likud governments. Less sensitive than their Labour rivals to the regional and domestic constraints that prevented Jordan from signing a separate peace with Israel, elements in the Likud started to discuss the 'alternative homeland' solution, which meant transforming Jordan into a Palestinian state. There was also talk of coupling this formula with the 'transfer,' a euphemism for the forcible eviction of the Palestinian inhabitants of the West Bank to Jordan. This prospect was a source of serious worry for Jordanian rulers, which was compounded by the Soviet Union's decision to permit its Jewish citizens to emigrate to Israel. This decision threatened to reverse the demographic trend whereby the population growth rate of Arabs outstripped that of Jews in Israel as well as the Occupied Territories, which threatened Israel with a demographic time bomb. Moreover, such a reversal strengthened the case of Israelis that called for the transfer and the alternative homeland solution.

The alliance with the Gulf States also lost much of its value to the Gulf States for three reasons: their diminished income, the disappearance of the Arab revolutionary threat, and the end of the Iran-Iraq war in 1988, following which Iraq alienated its former Gulf allies by seeking to become a regional hegemon. The perception that Jordan was the principal ally of Iraq had become a liability, but Jordan could see little by way of alternatives. Even the tactical alliance with Egypt and Iraq was weakened by divergent regional and international ambitions of each country. Unable to secure assistance from traditional sources, Jordan became increasingly dependent on the assistance that it received from the World Bank and the IMF. This assistance, however, was linked to reforms, as documents published by these institutions, during that period and subsequently, state clearly.[22] But economic assistance alone was not sufficient. Jordan was desperate to restore its standing among its Western allies who, for their part, had turned their attention to Eastern Europe where the retreat of the Soviet Union had allowed former East Bloc countries to shed their communist ideology and to embark on a process of political and economic liberalisation. Wherever Jordan turned in the West, it found its interlocutors preoccupied with the new democracies in Eastern Europe.

The cultural diffusion and demonstration effects appear to have operated here in a modified manner. The example of East Europe showed Jordanian decision-makers not that democracy was desirable, but that democratising countries received Western assistance. By trying to become a regional leader in democratisation, Jordan knew that it would anger some of its more conservative neighbours, but it hoped that its new regional role would be compatible with Western priorities. In this sense, the objective of democratisation was not to reform the clientelist system, but to acquire the means to preserve it.

Whether democratisation would have been sufficient in restoring Western assistance to Jordan is an impossible question to answer because the Gulf crisis and war superseded and overshadowed all other developments in the Middle East. Jordan's position over the Gulf crisis was seen by the West, correctly or otherwise, as pro-Iraqi, which widened the gap between Jordan and its traditional protectors and benefactors. Short of alternatives, and realising the need to consolidate the domestic front, Jordan could only forge ahead with democratic reform. It revoked the state of martial law, repealed the ban on political parties, and introduced a new Press and Publications law, which was criticised by journalists at the time for not being liberal enough, but which is now lauded as the most liberal that Jordan has ever known.

The turning point came in 1994 when Jordan signed the peace treaty with Israel. This act immediately raised its status to one of the West's top priorities in the region. The United States declared Jordan a non-NATO strategic ally, wrote off its debt, and raised aid levels progressively from a minimal amount to the point where Jordan became in less than a decade the fourth largest recipient of U.S. economic and military assistance in the world – $1 billion over three years.[23] Jordan was also selected to host the MENA conference, which was a great opportunity for the country to attract foreign direct investments. In addition, Jordan became one of the first countries in the region to sign a partnership agreement with the European Union. Jordan's membership of the World Trade Organisation was rushed through in record time in the year 2000. And to top it all up, the United States signed a free trade zone with Jordan in the year 2000 which, at the time of writing, awaits ratification by the legislatures of both countries.[24]

In short, peace with Israel succeeded where democracy had failed to restore the flow of Western funds to Jordan. But the improvement of the regional security environment did not have the effect of reducing spending on defence and clearing the path for the evolution of the private sector and the formation of independent political spheres of power able to influence a regime opening. The Jordanian-Israeli peace treaty was not preceded by a national dialogue in Jordan that prepared public opinion for this major political step. Instead, the Jordanian public had been assured repeatedly that their government would not break Arab ranks by signing a separate peace treaty. However, the Oslo accord between the Palestinian Liberation Organisation (PLO) and Israel, which took everyone by surprise, accentuated Jordan's fear for the status of its eroding regional role if it waited any longer, and so it hastened to conclude its own peace treaty within a year of the accord. There was not the time to prepare public opinion for this step, nor the possibility of doing so, since announcing such a plan in advance would have been certain to attract strong opposition from Syria as well as Egypt and the PLO, all of whom later criticised Jordan for what they considered to be precipitous action.[25]

A strong movement developed in Jordan that opposed the peace treaty, which centred on the Muslim Brotherhood Movement and its political arm, the Islamic Action Front, as well as the professional associations. The associations threatened any of their members who accepted normalisation with Israel with dismissal, a move that would prevent the member from practising his profession. The opposition knew that the peace treaty was irreversible, but they sought to empty it of its content by preventing 'normalisation', or the evolution of normal relations and exchanges with what they continued to consider as the 'Zionist enemy'. The government feared that anti-normalisation sentiment might have been strong enough to persuade the population to give the Muslim Brotherhood a majority in the 1993 parliamentary elections. But, at the same time it needed to have the peace treaty ratified by parliament. It was imperative, therefore, that the parliament elected in 1993 should be of a composition that would approve the peace treaty.[26] The United States' Human Rights Report of 1994 did not comment on the elections, but the 1997 report acknowledged that parliamentary elections in 1993: were largely free and fair although there were opposition accusations of government misconduct.[27]

Domestically, some people started to exercise their newly restored rights and to push for more. The Muslim Brotherhood-supported government, which was appointed in 1989, introduced a draft law requiring officials to declare their assets, which the senate succeeded in freezing, though not in killing it off completely. Islamic Action Front deputies made calls for a new election law in which the more densely-populated areas, where their strength lay, would receive a level of representation proportionate to their demographic weight. The press started to contradict government statements frequently, and to prove them wrong too often for comfort.[28] Criticism of the government's performance became all too common in the press. The weeklies, in particular, revelled in allegations of misconduct among government officials, and published composite photographs ridiculing them. It is important to stress here that these criticisms were not always fair or well founded. Reports of misconduct were, quite often, either poorly researched or completely groundless; which gave rise to calls for stiffer punishments for cases of libel, and for reforms of the legal system to enable it to process these cases more swiftly. Instead, the government chose to fall back on the old and tested practices that it had learnt under martial law.

The government and the press. While such behaviour by the opposition and the press is not uncommon in a democratic society, it is usually considered outrageous and shocking in a fledgling democracy, whose officials developed their careers in the context of clientelism and under martial law. This combination develops a political culture that does not tolerate any questioning of authority (such as the call for accountability), and that is deeply mistrustful of any initiative that is independent of close and direct state control (such as the institutions of civil society).[29] Such behaviour is seen as a slide towards anarchy. In Jordan, therefore, all criticism of the government's performance was labelled as an attempt to discredit the country internationally, hence as a threat to national security. Critics of this mindset argued that this was merely the pretext that officials used in order avoid accountability.

The government reacted in May 1997 by introducing emergency amendments to the 1993 Press and Publications Law, which had the effect of closing down thirteen of the more sensationalist weekly tabloids, and muzzling all other publications in the run-up to the parliamentary elections in November of that year. These elections were described in the U.S. State Department Human Rights Report 1998 as follows:

The Electoral Law (enacted just before the 1993 Parliamentary elections) and the distribution of parliamentary seats deliberately favour regions with populations known for their traditional views, . . . i.e. rural and Southern Jordan. Over 500 candidates competed in the November 1997 parliamentary elections, despite a boycott by Islamist and other parties. There were many reports of registration irregularities and fraud on the part of candidates. Restrictions on the press and on campaign materials also had a negative effect on the campaign, which elicited much debate over the fairness of the electoral law and its implementation. Voter turnout was significantly lower in most urban areas than in rural areas. Centrist candidates with ties to major tribes dominate the new Parliament.[30]

The amendments to the Press Law were annulled on January 26, 1998 by the High Court of Justice which found them unconstitutional, but they were replaced during the same year by a new law, which was found to be even more restrictive by journalists. It banned the media from publishing any material that touched any of fourteen subjects including the King, the Royal Family, the Armed Forces, security agencies, the economy, the judiciary, heads of Arab, Islamic, or friendly states or their diplomatic missions in Jordan, or any crime at any stage of execution, investigation, or trial.[31] If a lawsuit was pressed against a publication, the court was authorised to order the suspension of that publication pending trial, which could take years.[32] The law was not enforced down to its most minute details; but these bans were like a sword of Damocles, ready to come down on any journalist or publication that exceeded acceptable bounds, which persuaded most journalists and their chief editors to exercise strict self-censorship.

In explaining the objective of the law, the acting prime minister and minister of information highlighted the government's concern to show the country in a good light abroad by stating, during a press conference on June 15: 'I do not care if people accept or reject peace with Israel. But many journalists are publishing stories that make the country look bad . . . I shall stop them from writing because the purpose of a journalist is to give a good image of the country.'[33]

Journalists launched an intensive lobbying campaign to have the draft law repealed or amended, but to no avail. This led some of them to seek international pressure to support their cause. In a personal crusade, activist Sa'eda Kailani, of the Arab Archives and Studies Centre, lobbied the European Parliament to take a stand against the Jordanian Press Law. Other journalists sought the support of international human rights organisations, which heaped scorn on the law. On August 14, three days after passage of the draft law through the Lower House, letters were sent by Article 19, Human Rights Watch, and Reporters Sans Frontières to Senate President Zayed Rifai calling on the Upper House to amend the draft in a manner compatible with press freedom and freedom of expression.

International criticism of the 1998 Press and Publication Law continued after its enactment. In September 1998 the Euro-Mediterranean Human Rights Network published a report authored by Sa'eda Kailani entitled: 'Black Year for Democracy in Jordan: The 1998 Press and Publication Law'.[34] After an exchange between the Secretariat of the Network and the Director of Press and Publication, the Secretariat expressed its continued concern over many of the provisions of the law, and its opinion that the 1998 Press and Publications Law was in violation of the internationally guaranteed right to freedom of expression. Nor did the fact that the law was passed by Parliament diminish their concerns.[35]

In response to domestic and international criticism, the government produced a new draft law, which was promulgated on 22 September 1999. Some elements of it were more liberal: it halved the capitalisation requirement for weekly publications, transferred the power to revoke a publication's license from the minister of information to the court system, reduced fines, withdrew the court's authority to suspend a publication and cancelled the list of taboos. Critics of the law argue that each one of the taboos is already covered in other laws, which carry even stiffer sentences than the press and publications laws do.

Attacks on non-governmental organisations. The international pressure on the government, which was solicited by NGOs, may not have been the only reason for changing the law. Another factor may have been the government's desire to attract to Jordan wealthy Arab satellite television stations, which went to Bahrain and the United Arab Emirates in preference. However, pressure from international NGOs appears to have been an important contributing factor, judging by the government's reaction to local NGOs, some of which are registered as non-profit -making private companies. This reaction highlights further the sensitivity felt against any criticism reaching foreign ears.

In June 2000, in an unprecedented move, the Office of the Controller of Companies in the Ministry of Industry and Trade requested non-profit companies to produce new financial and administrative regulations and to submit them to the office, along with full disclosure of all their income and expenditure and activities to date, within a month of receiving the request. The Controller of Companies explained that this was being done in order to impose clear and strict control over non-profit companies, so that they would be compatible with acceptable principles of disclosure and transparency.[36]

On June 8, the president of the Bar Association addressed a letter to the prime minister, calling on the government to 'close down all centres and institutions that work in the field of human rights and women's rights and that receive financing from foreign embassies and agencies ... and that conduct activities and seminars devoted to downgrade the respect for Jordan.' The letter went on to say that these research and study centres were involved in intelligence gathering that posed a threat to national security, which 'falls under the heading of high treason.'[37] The principal target of this attack was lawyer Asma Khader, the director of Al-Mizan Group, who is a principal activist against crimes of honour.[38] Ironically, the campaign against crimes of honour has the open support of many members of the Royal Family.

At the same time, the Jordan Press Association opened an investigation into Nidal Mansour, its secretary-general and director of the Centre for the Protection and Defence of Journalists. He was charged with receiving funds from foreign sources, which is illegal by Jordanian law, unless the activity for which the funds were solicited was approved by the Minister of Information, and the funds channelled through the Ministry of Planning.[39] On June 11, the head of the Parliamentary Freedoms Committee announced that the Committee would soon request full information about all human rights organisations, their objectives, and their motives. He was quoted as saying that he had

... almost certain information that some organisations receive funding from foreign sources, and some external centres of power to work in Jordan with the objective of marring its image ... External parties try to exploit issues, no matter how small, to mar Jordan's image and cast doubt about the truth of its democracy, as part of a plan and a conspiracy that aims to denigrate Jordan.[40]

This controversy has yet to be resolved but the prevalence of this political culture that rejects accountability and suspects any initiative that is independent of close government control, in the executive as well as the legislative branch, especially after the elections of 1997, has created a tug of war that is normal in any process of democratisation. In Jordan the line is drawn between the combination of the government and parliament seeking to maintain absolute state control on all forms of public activity, and on the other hand, elements in society that seek to exercise and expand their margin of civil liberties. The importance of external factors and of international public opinion to democracy in Jordan can be seen in the fact that each side justifies itself by claiming that the action which it advocates would improve Jordan's international standing, while the opposite would harm it. In this contest the king is the ultimate arbiter who defines the rules and limits of the game. For instance, both King Hussain and King Abdullah have asserted that democracy is an irreversible process; at the same time, it would have been difficult even for the most democratic-minded decision-makers to ignore the excesses and lack of professionalism of some publications, which frequently published reports against officials that were pure fabrication.

Beneath the authority of the ultimate arbiter in the form of the monarchy, these two contesting groups are constantly mindful of Western reactions to their acts. Conservatives realise that Western assistance is more closely linked to Jordan's regional policies than its domestic policies, hence a modicum of restrictions and falsification of elections would pass unnoticed. However, they also realise that overt restrictions of civil liberties would not fail to attract a negative reaction. To quote Moore, successful pressure helps raise the costs of internal repression and holds out rewards for greater liberalisation.

Liberals, for their part, realise that Western sympathy is an important asset to their cause. But the importance of this asset is tempered by the fact that supporting democracy and civil society are only two of a whole range of Western interests, and that other interests may be of a higher order of priority. This is not the case with Western NGOs, whose range of interests is much narrower than governments; but whose influence is much more limited. In addition, the legacy of the culture of national liberation that prevailed in the 1950s and 1960s renders close association with Western institutions, whether governmental or non-governmental, susceptible to accusations of collaboration and treason. Another danger facing Jordanian NGOs is their dependence on external sponsoring partners (mainly donor agencies) for their funding, which may reduce their need to garner local support (and donations). This, in turn, would limit their interaction with local society, and hence their capacity to influence it.[41]

The purpose of this analysis has been to demonstrate that democratisation in Jordan has been a far more complex phenomenon than is usually realised, in which the external environment plays a crucial role. Its general conclusions can be summed up as set out below:

1. The classic outlook on democratisation in the Arab world explains the phenomenon in terms of the economic crisis of the rentier state, which has become unable to maintain the level of government expenditure needed to support the clientelist system on which it operates, so it offers its citizens democracy in return for economic austerity. This outlook, however, does not pay adequate attention to the external factors that have influenced democratisation in the Arab world. These factors include the cultural diffusion and demonstration effect, foreign government policies and aid, non-governmental activities, changes in the regional security environment and international fiscal environment and policy.

2. Taking Jordan as a case study, the crisis that the country faced was far more serious than one linked simply to the economy. Jordan's regional role, which is at the core of its network of regional and international relations and hence vital for its survival and economic well-being, was eroding. Jordan needed desperately to redefine its regional role to ensure the resumption of lavish foreign assistance.

3. Jordan's attempts to regain Western assistance during the late 1980s were unsuccessful, largely because the West was preoccupied with another international development, the collapse of the Soviet Bloc, and the emergence of democracies in Eastern Europe. This was quickly picked up by Jordan, which concluded that, since emergent democracies were strong candidates for Western assistance, it might therefore succeed in gaining such assistance by becoming a regional leader in democratisation. In this sense, democratisation may not have been an attempt to reform the rentier economy, as the classic outlook suggests, but an attempt to gain the means to preserve it.

4. The disappearance of government-to-government transfers, that had enabled Jordan to create a rentier or semi-rentier economy, increased the country's dependence on international donor agencies, the World Bank and the IMF, whose aid packages required, in addition

to fiscal policies, institutional reforms aiming at better governance. The declared policies of these institutions consider that democratic reforms are essential for the efficacious management of resources.

5. In addition to international donor agencies, Jordan's traditional Western allies started to encourage recipient countries to embark on a process of liberalisation and democratisation.

6. A fourth element that pushed towards democratisation was the greater involvement of international human rights NGOs, which formed a symbiotic relationship with local NGOs campaigning for similar objectives.

7. Peace with Israel in 1994 succeeded in restoring Jordan to a position of high priority in the Western strategic calculus, and restored aid to a very high level. However, the enhancement to Jordan's security that the peace treaty brought did not result in greater liberalisation. A strong anti-normalisation movement developed in the country, to which the government responded by tightening the margins of liberty.

8. As in any society going through a process of democratisation, there developed an anti democracy backlash by officials and legislators whose careers had developed under martial law. Their political culture considers calls for accountability to be a challenge to the authority of the state, and it is mistrustful of any initiative that is independent of direct and close state control. Their case was strengthened by the excesses of some publications, which frequently published unfounded allegations of misconduct and which carried composite photographs ridiculing government officials. The margin of manoeuvre of this group, however, is limited by the King's commitment to democracy. On the other hand, some elements in society abuse the civil liberties by indulging in unfounded criticisms and attempts at character assassination, which weakens the case of those who seek to expand the margin of liberties.

9. In this give and take, the importance of external forces is evident in the fact that both groups seek to justify their positions by claiming that the policies which they advocate would improve Jordan's international standing, while the opposite would harm it.

NOTES

1.   See for instance R Brynen, 'Economic Crisis and Post-Rentier Democratisation in the Arab World: The Case of Jordan', *Canadian Journal of Political Science*, XXV (March 1992), pp. 69–98; G Salamé, 'Sur la causalité d'un manque: pourquoi le monde arabe n'est-il donc pas démocratique?', *Revue Française de Science Politique*, 41 (June 1991), pp. 307–41; J. Leca, 'Democratisation in the Arab World: Uncertainty, Vulnerability, and Legitimacy. A Tentative Conceptualisation and

some Hypotheses', paper presented to the conference organised by the Mattei Foundation, Varenna, 4–6 June 1992; and E. Murphy, 'Legitimacy and Economic Reform in the Arab World' in S. Behrendt and C.-P. Hanelt (eds), *The Future Role of the State in the Middle East and North Africa*, Gütersloh: Bertelsmann Foundation, 1998.

2. For a discussion on the rentier state see H. Mahdavi, 'The Pattern and Problems of Economic Development in Rentier States: The Case of Iran' in M. Cook (ed.), *Studies in the Economic History of the Middle East*, Oxford University Press, 1979. See also H. Beblawi, and G. Luciani (eds.), *The Rentier State*, London: Croom Helm, 1979. Brynen, (op. cit.) draws a distinction between rentier states (in the case of the Arab world, the oil rich states) and semi-rentier states, which lacked natural resources and depended on transfers from rentier states to create a rentier type economy. His paper describes Jordan as a typical example of semi-rentier states.

3. For an analysis of the modern Arab concept of leadership see B. al-Khadra, *The Prophetic Caliphan model: A Theory on the Concept of Leadership among Arabs*, Amman: Jordan University, 1982.

4. P. Moore, 'The International Context of Liberalisation and Democratisation in the Arab World', *Arab Studies Quarterly*, summer 1994, p. 44.

5. Leca (1992), p. 14.

6. Ibid., p. 39.

7. Ibid., pp. 40/41.

8. W. Weidenfeld, J. Janning and S. Behrendt, *Transformation in the Middle East and North Africa*, Gütersloh: Bertelsmann Foundation, pp. 38–40.

9. C. Hewitt de Alcantara, 'Uses and Abuses of the Concept of Governance', International Social Sciences Journal, 155 (March 1998), pp. 105–13.

10. A. Hadenius, and F. Uggla, 'Making Civil Society Work, Promoting Democratic Development: What can States and Donors Do?', *World Development*, 24, 10, (1996), pp. 1621–39.

11. Moore, op. cit., p. 44

12. Moore, op. cit. quoting R. Looney, 'The Economic Impact of Defence Expenditure in the Middle East', Naval Postgraduate School (1990), pp. 16–17.

13. M. Wilson, in her book *King Abdullah, Britain, and the making of Jordan*, Cambridge University Press, 1987, draws a vivid picture of the state's dependence on assistance from Britain in its early days.

14. For a discussion of Jordan's network of international relations see A. Mouftard, and J.-C. Augé, 'La politique étrangère et régionale héritages, contraintes et inflexions', *Maghreb-Machrek*, 164 (April-June 1999), pp. 123–40.

15. R., Brynen, op. cit., p. 95.

16. For a discussion of Jordan's fight against corruption see S. Bino, 'Public Responsibility and accountability', paper delivered at the Fifth Jordanian Scientific Week held on the theme of developing Jordan's competitiveness, September 1997. See also A. Kassay, 'Administration and efficiency, bureaucratic reform – the case of Jordan', *Mediterranean Politics*, 3, 3 (summer 1998), pp. 52–62.

17. Strictly speaking, parliamentary life was restored to Jordan in 1984, not in 1989. Parliament had been suspended in 1974 due to the impossibility of holding elections in the West Bank (which was under Israeli occupation), from which half of the deputies for the Jordanian parliament were to be elected, and because deaths had depleted the parliament, elected in 1967. In 1984 a constitutional amendment was introduced, whereby dead members from the East Bank were replaced by means of local elections, and those from the West Bank were replaced by new ones elected by the remaining West Bank deputies. This move, which permitted the

old parliament to reconvene, was precipitated by political events, mainly the failure of the Jordanian-Palestinian coordination which had started after the expulsion of the PLO from Lebanon in 1982. However, this formula also became unworkable after the disengagement of legal and administrative ties between Jordan and the West Bank in August 1988. A second constitutional amendment was introduced, whereby the Chamber of Deputies came to comprise 80 members, all of them elected in the East Bank. There is unanimity among analysts that the general parliamentary elections of November 1989 marked the real restoration of parliamentary life to Jordan.

18. Interview with Jordan Television, 22 April 1989, quoted by Brynen, op. cit.
19. Brynen, op. cit., p. 95.
20. Salamé, op. cit., p. 331.
21. U. Dann, *King Hussain and the challenge of Arab radicalism: Jordan, 1955–1967*, Oxford University Press, 1984, 4.
22. For a description of the World Bank's outlook on the role of the state, see *World Bank Report 1997*, esp. Part 3 on reinvigorating institutional capability, pp. 76–142.
23. Comments by Deputy Secretary of the Treasury Stuart Eizenstat during his visit to the Qualified Industrial Zone in Irbid on 26 June 2000, *Jordan Times*, 27 June 2000.
24. Ibid.
25. This topic gave rise to an abnormally sharp exchange between Egypt's Foreign Minister Amr Mousa and King Hussain during the Amman MENA summit. Mousa criticised what he termed 'sprinting into normal relations with Israel'. At this the King, who had already spoken, took the floor a second time, something he had never done before, to reply that Jordan was only following the precedent that Egypt had set ten years previously.
26. For a discussion of the 1993 elections and the emergency legislative changes introduced immediately before them, see A. Mouftard, and F. Charillon, 'Jordanie: les élections du 1993 et le processus de paix', *Maghreb Machrek*, 144 (April–June 1994).
27. U.S. Human Rights Report on Jordan, 1996, U.S. Government website, www.state.gov/www/global/hu. . .rights/1996hrp.report/Jordan/html
28. The case best known internationally related to Israel's attempt to assassinate Hamas leader Khaled Mash'al in Amman. The initial government statement said that there had been a scuffle between Mash'al's guards and two Canadian tourists, while independent *Al-Arab Al-Yawm* (whose chief editor at the time later became minister of information) reported that this was an attempt by Mossad to assassinate Mash'al. *Al-Arab Al-Yawm*'s version proved to be the correct one.
29. One of the remarks most representative of this mindset was made by a deputy explaining democracy in Jordan. He said: 'His Majesty ordered for elections for the new parliament and he ordered to impose democracy as a rule in the state.' Quoted in S. Fathi, *Jordan, an invented nation?* Hamburg: Deutsches Orient-Institut, 1994, 271.
30. United States Department of State Human Rights Report, 1998, U.S. Government web site www.state.gov/www/global/hu...rights/1998hrp.report/Jordan/html
31. Articles 37 and 39, *The Press and Publications Law* no. 8, 1998, author's translation.
32. Article 50, ibid.
33. Notes taken by the author who was present at the minister's meeting with the press.

34. The Secretariat of the Euro-Mediterranean Human Rights Network, Copenhagen.
35. Letter addressed by the Euro-Mediterranean Human Rights Network to the Director of Press and Publication on 4 December 1998, ref. 330/Euromed.
36. *Al-Ra'i*, 4 June 2000, author's translation.
37. All Jordanian dailies, 8 June 2000. In particular *Al-Dustour*.
38. 'Crime of honour' is the term used to describe the murder of women by their male relatives on suspicion that they may have indulged in immoral practices. Normally the murdering male relatives receive very light sentences, up to three years' imprisonment. The campaign to eliminate these crimes was first launched by journalist Rana Hussaini, and now enjoys the support of members of the Royal Family.
39. *Shihan*, 10 June 2000.
40. Al-Arab Al-Yawm, 11 June 2000
41. A. Hadenius and F. Uggla, op. cit., p. 1635.

LIBERALISATION OR DEMOCRATISATION?

THE LIMITS OF POLITICAL REFORM AND CIVIL SOCIETY IN JORDAN[1]

Ranjit Singh

Have the top-down political reforms initiated in 1989 put Jordan on the path to a democratic transition?[2] This study presents an historical analysis of the constraints on regime change in Jordan. Focusing on the nature of opposition demands, the present liberalisation period is compared with the monarchy's formative experience with liberal politics, the brief government of Sulayman al-Nabulsi (1956–7). The analysis suggests a logic of political reform in Jordan relevant today. The study contends that the secular decline of the monarchy's historical antagonist, the Jordanian left, since the prior liberal period provided the regime and its conservative allies with the incentives to tolerate liberalised politics in the 1980s and 1990s. Propertied elites linked to the regime have historically played a pivotal role in determining the fate of political reform.[3] The prospect of demands for the redistribution of wealth early in the liberalisation process induced these elites to support an authoritarian backlash in 1957. Furthermore, the lack of such demands since the 1980s facilitates the 'façade democracy' equilibrium of today – electoralism without an accompanying diffusion of power.

Historically, the regime's limits on liberalisation have been defined by the popular mobilisation of two demands: one to reduce the power of the monarchy (represented by republican and Pan-Arabist ideologies) and the other reflecting Marxist-inspired demands to fundamentally alter the existing distribution of wealth. These demands have traditionally co-existed in the reform agendas of Ba'athist, Communist and numerous other leftist groups that dominated opposition politics before the 1980s. They are not, however, a part of the reform agenda of the mainstream Islamic movement, the Jordanian Muslim Brotherhood and its offshoot political party the Islamic Action Front (IAF), that replaced the left as the regime's primary opposition before 1989.

It is axiomatic that the King will not risk liberalisation if he believes the process will cede meaningful power to a movement that challenges the authority of the monarchy. Therefore, in both liberalisation periods, it is highly improbable that King Hussain would have allowed a fair election if he foresaw leftist control of government as the likely outcome. According to the following analysis, the King's decision to risk a fair election in 1956 and again in 1989 rested largely on the belief that the process would produce a legitimated parliament dominated by loyal moderate centrists and traditional conservatives. By marginalising the Jordanian left, Hussain viewed such moderate-right parliaments as instrumental to consolidating (1956) or affirming (1989) his institutional power during periods of crisis.

Rising demands for a republic or union with Syria and Egypt in 1957 threatened the authority and even the existence of the monarchy. Had the King faced these demands alone, he would eventually have been forced to accept a diminished role or risk costly and uncertain repression. While many among Jordan's nascent bourgeoisie espoused liberal values, most of the groups that supported Hussain in the April 1957 crisis (tribal leaders, landed and status elites, and the army) resisted neither state authoritarianism in the pre-1956 period nor the subsequent decision to liberalise. The increasing disproportionate influence of leftist Jordanian 'radicals' – after the 1956 election – proved to be the turning point. The rising prospect of socialist reforms jeopardised the material interests of propertied groups and classes. Radicalism thus enabled Hussain to rally these conservative elites to preserve his throne and oust the elected government. As a result, the political interests of the monarchy and the economic interests of key elites fused in April 1957 to ensure radical demands were not implemented. With additions, this authoritarian regime persists today.

Based on this interpretation, the study suggests some limitations on prospects for democracy in contemporary Jordan. In this volume, a common defining element of any transition from political liberalisation to democratisation is a diffusion in the distribution of authority within the political system. That is, democratisation requires that the authority of the Hashemite monarchy at some point become subject to question.

The 'moderate centre' presently dominating the Jordanian regime, parliament, and civil society is ill-suited to this task, however. The fusion of economic and political interests, the exhaustion of the left after decades of repression, and the rise of loyalist Islamists have resulted in the political primacy of what is more appropriately termed a 'moderate right'. This development, it is argued, has important repercussions for democratisation. First, the present liberalisation process persists largely because Jordan's propertied elites have not faced demands for a redistribution of wealth. This is a result of the incapacity of the Jordanian left to mobilise subaltern classes that may benefit from and support such demands. Second, any attempt to do so increases the probability of another authoritarian backlash by those elites who profit materially from the present system. As a result, the left's inability to mobilise its traditional social base both encourages elite toleration for limited liberalisation while leaving the probability that the reform process will expand to encompass the interests of subaltern groups low.

In sum, the well-consolidated authoritarian regime in Jordan places limits on civil society that supercede the much-cited legal restrictions. The theme of Jordanian politics continues to be a monarchy 'above politics' yet exercising power in a manner little changed by more than a decade of liberalisation. Elected representatives and civil society remain essentially toothless before the authority of the King, occupying political 'space' while leaving the power of reform largely in the hands of the monarch and other traditional, status quo-oriented ruling elites.

It is important to acknowledge from the outset that foreign intervention and regional affairs have influenced Jordanian politics more than most countries. However, the approach used here views external factors as important to liberalisation to the extent that they play out amongst and influence domestic balances of power and interests. This approach thus favours the analysis of how the political and material interests of domestic actors (the monarchy, its supporters, and opponents) interact to produce outcomes.

A final word about terminology. In this chapter, 'regime' refers to the Hashemite king and his shifting but identifiable base of supporters during the relevant periods. The regime therefore comprises the more rigid, authoritarian core of the Hashemite state that evolves only slowly. The person of the monarch, King Hussain (1953–99), remains unchanged for virtually the entire period under consideration. Since the periods under study are ones of relatively liberal politics, 'government' denotes the more variable elected *majlis al-nuwwab* (lower house of parliament) as well as the cabinet of ministers. With the onset of liberalisation, the composition of the parliament is subject to elections. The cabinet, however, is liable to influence by election results but ultimately serves at the approval of the King in accordance with the Jordanian constitution of 1952. After the authoritarian reaction of 1957, the cabinet therefore became part of the regime. Furthermore, the constitution also grants the King power to dissolve parliament when he deems it necessary. In sum, while there is frequent overlap of members between the two, 'regime' refers to the authoritarian heart of the state, and 'government' denotes those parts of the state subject to contestation once liberalisation begins.

The rise and fall of liberal politics: the al-Nabulsi government

Despite its brief tenure, the period between the election of October 1956 and the fall of the government of Sulayman al-Nabulsi in April 1957 is considered to be the high-water mark for liberal politics in pre-1989 Jordan.[4] Liberalisation occurred at a time in Jordan's history, beginning with the 1951 assassination of King Hussain's grandfather Abdullah I, in which powerful external and internal tensions nearly undermined the precarious state. The Cold War rivalry polarised Jordanian politics. Regionally, the Egyptian Free Officers' revolution of 1952 and the struggle for power in Syria spurred both countries to play heavy-handed roles in Jordan's affairs. This trend was exacerbated by ideologies 'imported' from the 'free' Arab republics that framed domestic conflict over the future of Jordan. Local actors (particularly Palestinians) introduced new ideas and strategies into Jordanian politics: Nasser's Pan-Arab nationalism, Syrian Ba'athist socialism, communism, and the Egyptian Muslim Brotherhood's conservative Islamism.

On the societal level, Abdullah's decision in 1950 to incorporate the West Bank dramatically altered the state's socio-economic and political composition. In addition to the influx of dispossessed refugees, the hundreds of thousands of Palestinians brought a new, more urbanised, educated and politicised element to Jordanian politics with suspect allegiance to the Hashemite king.[5] The new Palestinian citizens also exacerbated Jordan's historical scarcity of resources as they competed with the more rural and tribal East Bank 'Transjordanians' for access to state largesse and upward mobility.[6]

In sum, by 1956 the state was in danger of being pulled apart by the Cold War rivalry, which spurred violent street confrontations, or disappearing altogether within a Pan-Arab union with an anti-royalist Arab republic. From May 1955 until October 1956, six loyalist prime ministers failed to ensure stability. Hussain's decision to hold a free election at this restive moment therefore seems contradictory or forced, especially in light of the severe repression resorted to in other moments of regime danger (such as the 'Black September' crisis of 1970–1). The King's decision, however, was consistent with his own institutional interests.

Hussain, still in his early twenties, had yet to establish his hold on power within the state and society. The Hashemite monarchy was critically weakened by Abdullah's assassination, the brief and ineffective reign of Hussain's father Talal, and the subsequent period of regency. Consequently, executive power had effectively become the domain of a series of prime ministers led by the repressive Tawfiq Abu al-Huda. Reclaiming Hashemite authority was therefore Hussain's primary goal.

Yet Hussain's initial attempts to consolidate the power of the monarchy proved unsuccessful. For example, his popular decision in March 1956 to dismiss Glubb Pasha, the head of Jordan's military and the despised symbol of British influence for Arab nationalists, was superseded by Nasser's dramatic stand against imperialism in Suez (indeed, many Jordanians falsely attributed Glubb's ouster to Nasser, not Hussain).[7] An earlier decision to dissolve the unpopular 1954 parliament engineered by Abu al-Huda had won the King some tentative approval among liberals. More to the point, it also left vacant a tempting and potentially dangerous (and unconstitutional) political space. This space provided the King with an alternative means to confirm his authority. Dann's analysis of the view from the throne at this time neatly surmises Hussain's attitude towards a possible freely elected parliament:

The king, who was the origination of all policy, might be persuaded to compromise to some extent for the time being but would certainly retain his position as the arbiter in difficult or controversial questions.[8]

However, a fair election, by definition, may produce an uncertain outcome and therefore entails risk. Hussain sought to consolidate his power; he was therefore unlikely to permit a fair election unless he and his advisers were confident that it would serve this end by returning a relatively subservient and loyalist parliament. Analysis of the domestic balance of interests and power provides insight into how the King viewed the election's expected outcome as favourable.

First, despite its decline the monarchy still had significant resources and potential bases of support. The violent clashes over the Baghdad Pact in late 1955 and early 1956 made apparent the army's importance to the regime.[9] Moreover, Hussain cultivated the support of East Bank tribal leaders, many of whom had benefited from close ties with Hussain's grandfather Abdullah.[10] Also with a potential vested interest in the monarchy were traditional, usually landed, notables whose influence and privileges were threatened by instability and radicalism. Many of these individuals, such as village *mukhtars* and other status elites, formed the leadership of or were associated with Jordan's Muslim Brotherhood, which upheld the Islamic legitimacy of the monarchy and respect for private property.[11] In contrast to their close relations with the Hashemites, the Brotherhood's leaders blamed Nasser for their counterparts' persecution in Egypt, and vigorously opposed leftist ideologies.

Second, from the perspective of the palace the primary opposition in Jordan during this period may be divided ideologically into two categories. The National Socialist Party (NSP), Jordan's only indigenous political party in 1956, represented the political 'moderate centre'. The foreign-backed Ba'athists and Communists comprised the 'radical' opposition. Both radical movements traced their origins outside Jordan.

Since Abdullah I's death in 1951, the NSP had emerged as the strongest electoral force in Jordanian politics.[12] NSP support straddled the increasingly divergent East and West Banks. Led by Sulayman al-Nabulsi, the political and economic platform of the party was typically ambiguous, but considered to be moderate and loyalist.[13] NSP leadership comprised mostly wealthy liberals determined not to leave the political field open to Ba'athists and Communists.[14] The party's 'socialist' label was therefore seen at the time, especially by the left but also by NSP members themselves, as an opportunistic 'socialism of the last minute' rather than a true ideological commitment.[15] Indeed, NSP socialism, as it existed, was rooted in nationalism rather than class struggle, emphasising the international distribution of wealth, not domestic.[16] Furthermore, al-Nabulsi was considered to be a modest, patriotic figure with liberal instincts that pushed him to tolerate radicals but not to share their demands for sweeping social change. His earlier support for the Baghdad Pact was seen by both the King and his British advisers as evidence of a tempered, pragmatic view of Arab nationalism.[17]

In stark contrast to al-Nabulsi and the NSP, the other major ideological parties in Jordanian politics, the leftist Ba'ath Party and the banned Communists (electorally active under the label 'National Front') were viewed by the King and his supporters as radicals.[18] Both groups, aided by Hussain's rivals in republican Egypt and Syria, overtly opposed monarchism in direct conflict with the principles of Hashemite rule. In addition, both parties sought to implement a political union with their foreign benefactors, a policy that threatened to weaken or eliminate the monarchy.

Radical candidates, like those of other parties, focused on the more dramatic international and regional issues during their 1956 election campaigns. Ideologically, however, both Ba'athism and Communism embraced programmes for fundamental socio-economic domestic change, centered on a socialist redistribution of wealth via pro-peasant

Ranjit Singh

and labour policies, anti-feudalism, and progressive land reform. In principle, therefore, their agendas jeopardised the privileges of Jordan's landed and status-based elites, with the possible exception of the army.[19] Among the disaffected Palestinians of the West Bank, however, particularly refugees in camps, the radical combination of anti-imperialism with redistributive reforms found a natural constituency.

Even so, radical leftists had yet to prove their ability to win more than two or three seats in any competitive parliamentary election.[20] The proven electoral strength of the NSP in prior competitive elections made it likely that another would return the moderate centre party to its former parliamentary influence. Hussain himself calculated that the radical parties would repeat their earlier poor performances, producing a 'reasonable parliament' with not more than 'two or three extremists.'[21] Prior elections, fair or not, had also demonstrated the persistent ability of the 'old-order' Arab Constitutional Party (ACP) and other non-ideological, pro-Hashemite 'independents' to gain strong pluralities in parliament.[22] In sum, a fair election would most likely provide Hussain with a predominantly moderate loyalist parliament as well as bolster his legitimacy as a liberal. The election seemed to pose little risk of empowering radicals who threatened the power of the monarchy.

Accordingly, elections for the 40-member parliament were held in October 1956 in an atmosphere regarded as substantially free from regime interference. In terms of the distribution of seats, we may say that the King's calculations were correct. The Ba'ath gained two seats and the Communists three, all from the West Bank. Conversely, the NSP won 12 seats, 5 from the East Bank and 7 from the West Bank, making it the best represented party in parliament. The remainder of the seats were filled by the loyalist ACP (5 seats), Muslim Brotherhood (4 seats), and independent candidates (13 seats).[23] Some independents held known sympathies for one party or another, but many if not most were non-ideological conservative notables linked to the regime.[24] Politically, the election therefore delivered a strong majority of traditional loyalists and moderate nationalists. Socio-economically, the election also favoured candidates with an interest in the existing system of distribution of wealth.[25]

More ominously, however, the results also demonstrated sharp differences in support for leftist movements among Palestinians and Transjordanians. Discounting loyal nationalists (which included many members of the NSP), the monarchy's hard core of traditional supporters, conservatives and Islamists, won 13 of 20 seats in the East Bank, but only 4 of 20 in the West Bank.[26] Urbanised West Bank

Palestinians had voted for anti-status quo, mostly leftist candidates in droves: because of this new constituency, Communist and Ba'ath-ist candidates combined (i.e. radicals) mobilised more voters than the NSP, despite the latter's much greater allotment of seats in parliament.[27]

As leader of the most successful political party, al-Nabulsi accepted the King's eventual offer to lead the government. Hussain was pleased to set the precedent of the monarch appointing the prime minister, not the winning party.[28] What Hussain probably could not have foreseen, however, was his liberal new prime minister's determination to form a coalition cabinet on the basis of shared nationalism. Al-Nabulsi's cabinet comprised six members of the NSP, three independents, one Communist and one Ba'athist. In terms of the distribution of parliamentary seats, this government gave the radicals roughly proportionate influence. However, while moderate centrists dominated the parliament, radicals held sway in the volatile streets, especially in the more densely populated West Bank towns.[29] This influence was multiplied by the appointment of Pan-Arabist Ba'athist leader Abdullah Rimawi as Minister of State for Foreign Affairs, a critical portfolio at a time when international issues drove Jordanian politics.[30] Communist leader Abd al-Qader Saleh became Minister of Agriculture, responsible for land relations.

From the perspective of the King, the policies of the al-Nabulsi government quickly proved intolerable. The radical ministers and members of parliament used their intimidating ability to mobilise the street to push their agendas. In subsequent weeks, radical ministers and MPs demonstrated their disregard for the monarchy through demonstrations, dismissals of Hashemite officials, and diplomatic and security decisions taken without consulting the King. In February 1957, Ba'athist Rimawi implied during a press conference that the parliament, not the King, was the chief policy maker in Jordan.[31]

Acting on Hussain's order to control radicalism, al-Nabulsi's appeal to tone down radical rhetoric and activities – 'Don't embarrass the government' – was rebuffed.[32] By the spring of 1957, the Eisenhower Doctrine, which proposed replacing British aid to Jordan with American in exchange for Jordanian support against Communism, had clarified the divisions both within the al-Nabulsi government and between it and the regime. Many members of the NSP favoured exchanging declining British assistance for American.[33] In April, radical-influenced Army units clashed with loyalists, and the King reacted forcefully. Hussain dismissed the cabinet, dissolved parliament, and banned all political parties.[34] Following an embittered radical congress held in the West Bank town of Nablus, the first

experiment with political pluralism under Hussain ended swiftly with
the imposition of martial law.

The liberal al-Nabulsi government, by incorporating actors hostile
to the monarchy, strayed far beyond the limits envisioned by the
King in his struggle to assert his own role 'as the origination of all
policy.' The ensuing crisis stemmed from the fact that the al-Nabulsi
government did not represent the moderate and conservative nationalist majority that was elected to parliament.[35] The radicals' ability
to mobilise the Jordanian street, particularly Palestinians with uncertain allegiance to the monarchy, produced their disproportionate
influence.

Had the King faced rising demands for a republic or union with
Egypt or Syria alone, he would eventually have been compelled to accept a diminished role or risk costly repression. Hussain's hesitancy
to take forceful action against the radicals before the April 1957 crisis
stems from two concerns. Instability within the officer corps, preceding the liberalisation period, made repression an uncertain option.[36]
Hussain therefore needed to ensure a broader domestic base of support, without which such forceful action may have proven counter-
productive.[37]

However, most of the groups that supported Hussain in April
1957 had actively resisted neither state authoritarianism pre-1956 nor
the subsequent decision to liberalise.[38] It cannot be assumed that in
the absence of threats to their material privileges these elites would
have rallied against liberalism and republicanism.[39] Theoretically,
both authoritarian and democratic political systems are capable of
safeguarding the interests of propertied elites.[40] For Jordan's privileged groups and classes, therefore, threats to the authority of the
King were one thing, as witnessed by the fact that most had stood by
as the monarchy weakened following Abdullah's assassination. By
1957, however, given the radicals' socialist inclinations and ability to
mobilise subaltern groups, their potential victory over Hashemite
authority also foreshadowed future demands for widespread socio-
economic reform.

As radical influence over policy increased at the expense of the
monarchy, so did the anxiety of propertied elites. The acquisition of
power to implement redistributive reform by Ba'athists, Communists
or their supporters threatened to sweep aside traditional socio-economic elites, as indeed happened to analogous groups in neighbouring
Egypt, and eventually Syria and Iraq.[41] Therefore, as a group Jordan's
privileged elites could not have seen a potential radical government as
anything less than disastrous to their interests. In the last weeks before
the crisis, the King's persistent references to any opposing his power

as 'Communists,' accurate or not, reinforced the perception of a unity of interests with those elites who feared socialist reforms.[42]

Once they perceived their own material interests were in danger, status quo elites and their clients had few incentives to commit to liberal politics and support an elected government against the King. Not only did the bedouin core of the army prove loyal,[43] on the same day that West Bank students demonstrated for the return of the leader of an alleged coup attempt, Hussain received oaths of allegiance from two hundred tribal chiefs.[44] Members of the Muslim Brotherhood, led by village *mukhtars* and other propertied and status elites, clashed violently with radical supporters in the street. Following the crisis, the King drew from these constituencies to appoint a new loyalist government that cemented his status as the primary actor in Jordanian politics.

Traditionalists and the moderate liberals, including members of Jordan's growing bourgeoisie, thereby confirmed their preference for privilege over pluralism. A case in point, the new illiberal government came to be headed in 1959 by Haza'a al-Majali, an experienced politician from an elite landholding family who had founded the NSP in opposition to the despotism of former prime minister Tawfiq Abul Huda.

The collapse of liberalism has been described as 'a coup from above'[45] and 'the Hashemite Restoration',[46] emphasising the agency of the King. More accurately, the 1957 crisis represents an anti-liberal backlash against urbanised ideologues undertaken by propertied, largely East Bank rural notables and their clients who quickly saw their material interests coincide with those of the monarchy. The result was a more resilient authoritarian regime that fused political and economic interests. With additions, this regime persists today.

Continuity and change in regime-opposition relations: political liberalisation since 1989

Three levels of explanation for the renewal of electoral politics in 1989 are commonly cited. The first points to immediate causes, specifically the increased level of civil disturbances sparked by IMF-related subsidy cuts, culminating in the violent April 1989 riots.[47] The second emphasises deeper structural causes rooted in Jordan's political economy. Citing Jordan's status as a 'semi-rentier' state, this explanation is founded in the 'rentier state' thesis which holds that as decreasing external sources of incomes compel regimes to seek increased domestic revenues (taxation), more demands for representational politics will appear.[48] The third type of argument stresses the political wisdom and agency of King Hussain and actors within the regime. This approach views the liberalisation process as one of tactical 'defensive democratisation' or a regime 'survival strategy.'[49]

These accounts insufficiently explain Hussain's decision to renew liberalisation in 1989. Simply put, there would not have been a free parliamentary election in 1989 had the King faced the level of radical mobilisation and influence he confronted in 1957. Hussain's decision to resume electoral politics in 1989 coincided with an absence of significant challenges to his authority. Whatever other factors may have inspired Hussain, liberalisation would not have been a meaningful option if this necessary condition had not first been met. The nature of the opposition matters.

Given the longitudinal design of this study, it is necessary to underscore the importance of the al-Nabulsi period to Hussain's decision to first renew electoral politics and later permit political parties.[50] For the King and his advisers, the experience of 1956–7 informed their basic understanding of the perils of liberalisation. 'Adnan Abu 'Odeh, chief political adviser to Hussain, explains: 'The basic issue (in 1989) for me, and us in the government, was to avoid the 1956 experiment.'[51] Hussain's decision to renew liberalisation thus included one irreducible consideration: that all involved in the election be aware of 'the line that cannot be crossed' – that the authority of the monarchy was beyond question. To hard-line supporters within the regime, threats to the monarchy are still equated with an unacceptable risk of profound socio-economic change engendered by liberal politics. Accordingly, to understand how the King calculated the costs and benefits of liberalisation we must assess the condition of the ideological left in Jordan in 1989.

Numerous external and domestic events resulted in important shifts in the Jordanian political landscape during the 1970s and 1980s. For the purposes of this study, the steady erosion of the left's organisational capacity corresponding with the rise of conservative Islam, specifically the Muslim Brotherhood, represents the key transition. It is highly unlikely that the King would have risked a fair election in 1989 without this shift in the domestic balance of power.[52]

By the 1980s, leftist factions and underground parties had gained an institutional platform in the professional syndicates. Although vocal and important, the elitist syndicates were poor substitutes for mass mobilisation political parties.[53] The regime, via repression and cooptation, had successfully crippled the Jordanian left's ability to effectively mobilise its traditional constituencies. While the left remained into the 1990s ideologically redistributive,[54] its reduced capacity to mobilise support transformed its political status. Once a broad-based if quarrelsome political movement, by the mid-1980s the left was fragmented and suffering from a dearth of leadership. Election results at both the national and syndicate levels in the 1980s and 1990s support this conclusion.

With regard to the monarchy, the formerly radical Palestinians, Ba'athists, Communists, and others had moderated beyond recognition in comparison with earlier periods. Several months before the 1989 election, for example, leftist politicians united with representatives of the other major political trends to approve a 'National Program' that explicitly recognised Jordan as a constitutional monarchy.[55] The radical, anti-royalist leftist programme was out. Even Hussain's hard-line chief of public security felt he could dismiss the Jordanian left as a significant threat to the monarchy by 1989.[56]

As a former leftist activist remarked, the left didn't even consider the increasingly influential Muslim Brotherhood a part of the opposition.[57] Indeed, the Brotherhood historically represents a nucleus of support for the Hashemites, as its members demonstrated in the 1957 crisis. The movement explicitly recognises a mutuality of interests with the monarchy.[58] In addition, its conservative social agenda is guided by what one leader describes as a conscientiously 'evolutionary, not revolutionary' approach to Islamic reform.[59] Such tempered expressions of moderation by Brotherhood leaders, many themselves members of a privileged class, may not accurately reflect the aspirations of some of their followers, especially Palestinians in refugee camps.[60] However, throughout the 1980s the Brotherhood focused its domestic activities on relatively innocuous education and social development issues in a manner consistent with this 'evolutionary' approach.

In addition to this critical shift in domestic politics from left to right, the rapid growth of the Jordanian economy in the late 1970s allowed the Hashemite regime to incorporate new elements of support, particularly wealthy Palestinian businessmen, merchants, and state employees.[61] Correspondingly, more economic elites saw their material interests as linked to the stability of the throne. Hussain's decision to sever Jordan's administrative ties to the West Bank in 1988 may have accentuated this trend, albeit in ways that are still far from clear. Apart from transforming the political orientation of the country, the historic break seems to have exacerbated tensions between Jordanians of East Bank and West Bank descent. By providing a new basis for 'Transjordanian nationalism',[62] which disparages leftist ideologies as 'foreign' or 'Palestinian', Jordanians of Palestinian origin (often with leftist backgrounds) may have felt it more necessary to prove their loyalty to the monarchy after the 1988 break than before.[63]

As in 1956, accurate prediction of the likely political distribution of seats resulting from a fair parliamentary election was possible. The 1984 by-election provided early evidence of growing support for Islamists.[64] However, Hussain and his advisers had more sophisticated tools at their disposal in 1989. These included, according to a cabinet minister at the time, two opinion surveys quietly conducted by the regime in urban areas in the weeks before the election. The surveys predicted that Islamist candidates would enjoy large levels of support in the election, while the popularity of leftist candidates was limited and declining as the election approached.[65]

Consequently, in 1989 the King could confidently predict that a fair election would return a parliament dominated by candidates affiliated with the Muslim Brotherhood as well as the usual non-ideological, pro-regime 'independents',[66] While complicating relations with Israel, this likely composition would not present a challenge to his institutional authority. The unusual degree of unity within the regime over Hussain's weighty decision supports the conclusion that others foresaw a similar outcome.[67]

The November 1989 parliamentary election resulted in Muslim Brotherhood candidates taking 22 of the 80 parliamentary seats, with another 10 to 14 seats going to independent Islamists. As predicted, the conservative Islamic bloc became the largest in the elected lower house of parliament. Leftists, Pan-Arabists, reformists and liberals (running as individuals) gained between 10 and 15 seats. This was the first time leftists held seats in parliament since 1957. Conservative and loyalist traditionalists, rural community leaders, former officials and bedouin leaders held the remaining 31 seats.[68] In sum, the election created an overwhelmingly loyalist and moderate parliament. As one observer remarked: 'If Hussain was disappointed with the election outcome, he does not show it.'[69]

This time, however, the King was not inclined to place his faith once more in a moderate parliament alone. Although none of the candidates in 1989 espoused reforms that threatened the monarchy or even a change in the system,[70] Hussain's next move sought to ensure continued loyalty and that political power would not diffuse. The result was the National Charter of 1991,[71] a document 'larger than the parliament' signed by representatives from all major political groupings in Jordan 'which set the parameters the King wanted'. The conservative impetus behind Hussain's initiative was 'to overcome the psychological barriers that arise [regarding] political pluralism because of the 1956 experience.'[72] Accordingly, the Charter ensures certain liberties to political parties and other actors in exchange for assurances that the authority of the monarchy remains beyond question. An important effect of the Charter was to quell the fears of hard-line regime supporters concerning renewed liberalisation. Abd al-Hadi al-Majali, speaker of the lower house of parliament and a fervent Transjordanian loyalist, tellingly describes the Charter's utility as two-fold: nationalistic, ensuring that political parties remain 'absolutely Jordanian'; and regulatory, 'we are democratic, but we will approve who is going to run for the election.'[73] Only after the creation of the National Charter did Hussain allow political parties to become legal and lift martial law in 1992. The new political party law permitted the Brotherhood to form the Islamic Action Front, but refused to legalise the Ba'ath and Communist parties.

Given the tone of Jordanian politics since liberalisation, it is doubtful that hard-line concerns in 1989 were justified. The most influential movement under liberalisation, Islamists led by the IAF, has shown no desire to contest the authority of the monarchy. Instead, the party's parliamentary aims are deliberately limited by a measured view of reform consistent with what IAF leader Abd al-Latif 'Arabiyat terms 'positive opposition', in which the party seeks neither ultimate authority nor material gain.[74]

In critical issues (such as the 1993 electoral and press laws, the 1994 peace treaty with Israel, and the continuing struggle over normalisation with Israel which has united the secular and Islamic oppositions) the monarchy, through the King-appointed cabinet, has clearly retained the capacity to deflect the will of elected representatives and civic associations.[75] Opposition representation in parliament has declined steadily since 1989. After more than a decade of liberalisation, the persistent ability of the monarchy's 'old guard' allies to deny meaningful political reform has come 'as a shock' even to 'the self-styled liberal reformists within the establishment'.[76]

From liberalisation to democratisation? Observations on the limits of political reform

Despite the continuing optimism and interest in Jordan as an example of relatively successful liberalisation,[77] this concluding section redirects attention to a more enduring concern: the persistence of the authoritarian regime. Ultimately, this question must be addressed through a study that locates Jordan within a set of methodologically comparable cases. With this caveat in mind, however, the preceding analysis allows for some informed observations of the obstacles confronting would-be democratic reformers. Can Jordan move beyond liberalisation towards democratisation?

Since 1989, a top-down liberalisation process has occurred: regime interference in parliamentary elections is bounded, elections are convened regularly, political parties are legal, and voter participation is essentially unrestricted. In contrast to the period 1956–7, however, Jordanians have yet to meaningfully debate the role and powers of the Hashemite monarchy. Political inclusiveness (the right to participate) has thus preceded competition (permissible opposition) in Jordan.[78] In this sense, the sustained liberalisation process since 1989 has been less competitive than the brief experiment of 1956; representatives of political and civic groups in the 1990s debated regional and domestic issues without questioning the distribution of authority within the state.[79] Jordan has therefore yet to begin a process of democratisation.

To draw a finer distinction, opposition groups in Jordan, in attempting to ensure sustained liberalisation, have accepted limits on political reform itself. This is in itself may not seem an unfavourable act. Democratisation theorists emphasise the instrumental value of 'pacts', formal or informal agreements that provide mutual guarantees to actors that ensure each side's vital interests.[80] These guarantees, it is argued, propel the democratisation process by marginalising actors at the political extremes. The Jordanian National Charter represents a formal political pact between opposition groups and the monarchy. However, by keeping the status of the monarchy off the bargaining table, the Charter demonstrates its utility as an impediment, not impetus, to the diffusion of power within the state. While tying the hands of opposition groups, the Charter has effectively permitted the regime to slowly constrict democratic rights through a variety of quasi-legalistic mechanisms, such as manipulation of electoral laws, a trend that culminated in the 1997 electoral boycott. Political parties and civic associations have been compelled to defensively focus their energies on the political *process* in Jordan, not the political *system*. The National Charter is therefore a conserving, not democratising, pact.[81]

The interpretation of Jordan's political history presented in this essay places the problem of democratisation squarely within an historical structural framework. The concentration of political and material interests within the regime combined with the subsequent socio-political shift from left to right weighs heavily upon prospects for democratisation.[82] A clear impetus for democratic reform of the political system is lacking in Jordan today. The regime's core supporters have not yet faced the societal pressures necessary for them to view substantive democratisation and its attendant freedoms favourably.

The rightwards shift in political society has ensured that demands for the redistribution of wealth and challenges to the authority of the King have not been a concern to the regime. Today's propertied elites, who underpin the monarchy, have therefore continued to tolerate limited liberalisation. However, any political mobilisation of Jordan's subaltern groups and classes (via increased liberalisation or a revival of the left) is likely to give rise to the same redistributive demands that increase the risks of regime repression, not tolerance. The reformer's dilemma works in cycles: present suppressed levels of mobilisation also keep down the costs of repressing any challenge to the monarchy's authority, even an indirect one.[83] Jordan has not yet entered a scenario where the threat posed to democratisation by redistributive demands is offset by, for example, a deconcentration of resources or economic growth leading to a serious reduction in poverty.[84]

The dilemma of democratic reform is rooted in Jordan's present civil society and balance of class power. A 'moderate centre' is often considered to be a prerequisite for democratisation.[85] With the left moribund and political and economic power concentrated, however, the bulk of today's party leaders, parliamentarians, and civic group activists actually constitutes a 'moderate right'. Jordan's political and economic elites, including most leaders of political parties and many NGOs, have few incentives to part from the authoritarian system that maintains their material benefits. The general deficiency of market reform and privatisation in Jordan is indicative of this conservatism. The fusion of elite material interests with the political interests of the monarchy appears to be preventing the emergence of an autonomous private sector that might view its interests as distinct from the authoritarian regime. A recent study finds the salient aspects of Jordanian economic liberalisation to be 'a domestic coalition more interested in maintaining its standing within the economy ... and the use of state-owned enterprises for political purposes.' Those responsible for guiding privatisation are more interested in 'trying to maintain their privileged positions', while 'the private sector is not enthusiastic about a state withdrawal from the economy because that would remove the stabilising hand of the state.'[86]

Furthermore, Jordan's 'moderate right' makes it unlikely that political reform will encompass the material interests of subaltern groups and classes, a basic component of social and political equity. Rising Transjordanian nationalism may be constraining influential Palestinians, the liberal elite perhaps most willing to promote substantive political reform. The secular decline of the left weakened the political parties that have historically demonstrated the greatest capacity to effectively mobilise the economically unprivileged. Current economic reforms continue to place the greatest burdens upon the left's traditional popular bases, via subsidy cuts in basic commodities as well as other measures. With high unemployment (15–20 per cent), the impoverished condition of Palestinians in refugee camps (historically the kingdom's most volatile element), and more than one-third of Jordanians living below the poverty line, a latent constituency for redistributive reform exists that Islamists have not tapped into.[87] It is noteworthy that civil disturbances in recent years, including the 1989 and 1996 rioting, were not accompanied by significant political organisation. Jordanian political parties of all stripes are very wary of association with these protests linked to economic grievances.[88] Given the material demands behind the riots, the reluctance or inability of leftist parties to formally coordinate with demonstrators is striking, particularly in historical perspective.

The analysis presented here sheds a discouraging light on the potential of Jordanian civil society to move today's process of liberalisation towards democratisation.[89] The current emphasis on civil society as a mobiliser for democracy in Jordan is empirically hard to justify. As in many Middle Eastern countries, Jordanian civil society has generated far more scholarly interest and international support than actual political reform. In contrast, this study suggests that both civil society and political reform are operating under powerful historical structural constraints that preclude the incorporation of demands from below and systemic change. This pessimistic conclusion, it is argued, explains the comment frequently heard in Amman that no 'real' opposition or political parties exist in Jordan today.

NOTES

1. Field research for this study was made possible by a pre-doctoral fellowship from the Near and Middle East Research and Training Act and the American Center of Oriental Research.
2. In this volume, political liberalisation is fundamentally a process whereby members of a specific population within a state gain the ability to influence the political process and the behaviour of political elites through mutually recognised mechanisms which are generally accepted to be formal elements within the political system itself. In Jordan in 1956 and 1989, this process began with parliamentary elections largely free from regime interference, in which candidates with diverse political agendas were allowed to participate. A core aspect of democratisation, by contrast, is the replacement of neo-patrimonial political systems with pluralistic ones in which authority is diffused. With regard to political parties, in 1956 all major opposition parties were legal with the exception of the Communists. Communist candidates therefore, with the knowledge of the regime and public, ran successfully under the label 'National Front'. In 1989, all political parties were

formally illegal. However, the King suspended the most restrictive impediments on candidates with opposition party backgrounds found in the 1986 electoral law. Parties were subsequently legalised in 1992. It is also important to note that even in cases where parties were illegal, the political affiliations of individual candidates in 1956 and 1989 were generally common knowledge.

3. The term 'propertied elites' in this study broadly indicates those groups and individuals who have a vested material interest in the existing distributional system. Apart from large landholding elites and wealthy merchant families, the term also encompasses 'status' elites, such as village *mukhtars*, tribal leaders, and other notables, whose status in Jordan traditionally stems from material wealth. Bedouin tribesmen have historically comprised the core of the Jordanian army. These tribesmen are materially linked, through patron-client networks, to tribal leaders. It is worth noting that the dissatisfied Jordanian 'Free Officers' were disproportionately of peasant, not tribal, social origin. M. Al-Masri, 'Al-Urdun 1953–1957: dirasa siyasiya', master's thesis, University of Jordan College of Higher Studies, 1995, pp. 173–4.

4. Numerous interviews with Jordanian officials and academics, fall and winter 1999.

5. An opinion survey of Palestinian refugees in Arab countries conducted in 1952–53 found 'a growing minority' with pro-Egyptian or Syrian political sentiments, while 'those who are nominally citizens of Jordan strongly resent their own Jordan government as a "tool of Downing Street."' F. Bruhns, 'Study of Arab refugee attitudes', *Middle East Journal* 9, 2 (spring 1955), pp. 130–8. A detailed and contemporary sense of the dramatic political impact of the incorporation of Palestinians is found in D. Lerner, *The Passing of traditional society: modernising the Middle East*, New York: The Free Press, 1958, pp. 303–49.

6. The merger of the West and East Banks brought the population of Jordan to 400,000 Transjordanians, 400,000 refugees, and 500,000 West Bank Palestinians. T. Piro, *The political economy of market reform in Jordan,* Lanham, MD: Rowman and Littlefield, 1998, p. 29. The rise of Palestinian influence roughly coincided with the rise of 'real' opposition in Jordan. No significant demands were made to expand politics beyond the realm of tribal leaders, government bureaucrats, and the like, and no movement appeared to question the authority of the King, until after the Second World War. See A. Sa'adeh, *Al-mu' arada al-siyasiyya fi sab'aiin ' aman, 1921–1991*, Amman: Mutab'a al-Destur al-Tijariyya, 1998, pp. 1–34.

7. U. Dann, King Hussain and the challenge of Arab radicalism: Jordan, 1955–67, Oxford University Press, 1989, p. 32. The Egyptian radio programme, *Sawt Al-Arab*, was widely listened to in Jordanian towns and villages, and portrayed Hussain as a 'stool pigeon' of British interests.

8. Dann, op. cit., p. 42.

9. R. Satloff, *From Abdullah to Hussain: Jordan in transition*, Oxford University Press, 1994, p. 137.

10. Hussain carefully encouraged this support through state largesse. For example, in February 1955 Hussain distributed 8,000 dunums of fertile land in the Jordan Valley to tribesmen who had participated in the Arab Revolt led by his great-grandfather Sharif Hussain. Chronology in *Middle East Journal* 9, 2 (spring 1955), p. 170.

11. From its inception in the mid-1940s, the Muslim Brotherhood in both the West and East Banks was led by local notables whose leadership status depended on wealth and honorific titles. Encouraged by the monarchy, the generally apolitical Brotherhood maintained strong links to the army, the National Guard, local

business communities, and many prominent national politicians. The organisation paid little attention to workers and, initially, students, who were strongly influenced by leftist political parties. For the social origins of the Brotherhood's
leadership and members, see I. Ghurayba, *Jama' at al-ikhwan al-muslimiin fi al-
urdun 1946–1996*, Amman: Dar Sindibad li Al-Nashr, 1997, pp. 45–73, and A. al-
Kakhan, 1995, 'Al-ikhwan al-muslimun', in M. al-Kaylani, *Al-harakaat al-Islamiyya fi al-Urdun wa Filastin*, Amman: Dar al-Bashir, pp. 37–91.

12. The NSP was formally organised in 1954. The following numbers therefore reflect
    parliamentary seats won by individuals who later formed the party. Three parlia-
    mentary elections were held in the period 1950–4. In each election deemed rela-
    tively competitive (1950 and 1951), NSP members won 10 or 11 seats in the 40-
    member body, and only one seat in the 'rigged' election of 1954. This made it the
    best-represented political 'party' in each competitively elected parliament. See
    N. 'Aruri, *Jordan: a study of political development (1921–1965)*, The Hague:
    Martinus Nijhoff, 1972, p. 35.

13. 'A, Naqrash, 'Al-siyasaat al-dakhiliya fi 'ahd hukumat al-Nabulsi' in H. Hourani,
    (ed.), *Hukumat Sulayman al-Nabulsi (1956–1957)*, Amman: Dar Sindibad li al-
    Nashr, 1999, pp. 169–75.

14. Z. Salama in ibid., p. 162.

15. M. Al-Kayad in ibid., p. 93.

16. Ibid., 86. Satloff notes that the 1956 Suez Crisis produced a 'lowest common de-
    nominator' politics in Jordan, as even conservatives were compelled to adopt 'the
    most extreme nationalist positions or drop out.' Satloff, 152.

17. 'Among British observers, it was hoped the NSP would wind up "rather as the
    Congress Party did in India."' Satloff, 153. Hussain himself described al-Nabulsi
    years later as a moderate: 'I really believe he was "middle of the road" not an ex-
    tremist.' Interview with Hussain cited in Satloff, p. 153. Jamal al-Sha'ir, al-Nabul-
    si's aide in the 1970s, relates that Hussain accepted Nasser's suggestion in later
    years that he allow al-Nabulsi to play a role in government once more. Al-Nabulsi
    rejected the offer, al-Sha'ir explains, because of his opposition to the current US
    Rogers Plan. Interview, 28 November 1999.

18. Despite the parties' ideological differences, Devlin's analysis of Iraqi prime minis-
    ter Nuri al-Sa'id's take on the Ba'ath and Communists is illustrative of how Ha-
    shemite monarchists viewed these parties: 'there was, for all practical purposes,
    no distinction . . . Both [parties] were socialist and opposed to the established and
    traditional order.' J. Devlin, *The Ba' ath party: a history from its origins to 1966*,
    Stanford, CA: Hoover Institution Press, 1976, p. 73.

19. As in Syria, the Jordanian Ba'ath party in particular exerted efforts to penetrate
    the officer corps, with some success. M. Al-Mu'ayta, in Hourani (ed.), p. 56.

20. The Communist Party in Jordan was formed in 1951, and banned by the regime.
    The Ba'ath Party was legalised in 1955. Despite these unfavourable circum-
    stances, members of each party participated in the previous elections with their
    political affiliations common knowledge. See H. Hourani, 'Intikhabat tishriin al-
    awal 1956 wa al-majlis al-niyabi al-khamis' in Hourani (ed.), pp. 21–39. In the
    two competitive parliamentary elections cited above (1950, 1951), Communist
    and Ba'athist candidates won no more than three seats. 'Aruri, p. 35.

21. Satloff, pp. 150–1 and Dann, p. 38.

22. The Arab Constitutional Party was a 'bloc' party without a popular base whose
    membership was restricted to influential persons. Like other 'old order' parties in
    neighboring countries, it 'spoke for the regime and adhere(d) to the status quo.
    The party goals are always secondary to the personal goals which is (*sic*) to perpe-
    tuate their self-installed leadership.' 'Aruri, p. 101.

23. The rejectionist Islamic *Tahrir* party, calling for the establishment of a caliphate, gained one seat. Its MP was the only one to vote against the formation of the al-Nabulsi government. Significantly, all Muslim Brotherhood MPs voted for al-Nabulsi.

24. This conclusion is supported by the fact that only 15 of the original 40 MPs lost their seats in the 'packed' pro-Hashemite Samir al-Rif'ai parliament that coalesced in the year following the crisis. 'Aruri, pp. 149–50.

25. According to Hourani 40 per cent of MPs were landed and 32.5 per cent are defined as 'bourgeois', (20 per cent could be classified as workers). Hourani, 34. According to Hourani's analysis of the social background of the 1956 parliament, the Jordanian bourgeoisie at that time consisted of merchants or businessmen with contacts with foreign companies, with many MPs essentially *'ibna' al-'a'ilaat,'* or scions of the notable families. Interview, 27 October 1999.

26. H. Hourani, in Hourani (ed.), p. 33.

27. The NSP received 72,000 votes, the Communists 51,000, and the Ba'ath 34,000. I. Hijazin, in ibid., p. 127.

28. Dann, 40.

29. Since their incorporation, Palestinians had come to lead the local opposition press. 'The Palestinians relentlessly pushed Jordan towards extremism *vis a vis* the West and Israel, and toward mob rule at home.' Lerner, p. 312.

30. Rimawi had been appointed to the Ba'ath National Command in Syria in 1954. Devlin, p. 67.

31. Dann, pp. 50–1.

32. I. Hijazin, in Hourani (ed.), p. 131.

33. I. Madanat, in ibid., p. 143.

34. Significantly, al-Nabulsi was permitted to stay on as foreign minister, but he soon resigned.

35. J. al-Sha'ir in Hourani (ed.), p. 72.

36. From the palace's perspective, the costs of choosing repression solely through reliance on the army (then known as the 'Arab Legion') could not have been certain. First, dissatisfaction within the officer corps, originating in the 1948 war and exacerbated by rising radical influence within the officer corps, inspired some Jordanian officers to seek a greater political role for the Army and themselves. Accordingly, the Jordanian 'Free Officers' looked to their revolutionary Egyptian counterparts as role models. Second, Army officers began conspiring to oust Glubb Pasha *before* informing Hussain of their plans. M. Mu'ayta, in ibid., pp. 51–60. While their goals aligned with Hussain's regarding Glubb, learning that the officers were willing to conspire independently without first seeking his approval, could not have comforted Hussain. 'Once the Free Officers became known, the loyalty of the army was not assured.' 'A. Muhafezeh in ibid., p. 201.

37. It is commonly asserted, especially by leftist Jordanians, that the United States and Britain were key allies in helping the King oust the al-Nabulsi government. This argument appears insufficient. The monarchy's relationship with the US and Britain was also Hussain's chief political *liability* in that period of intense nationalism and anti-imperialism. Consistent with the approach used here, historian 'Ali Muhafaza has pointedly observed that any foreign power seeking to repress the nationalist al-Nabulsi government was 'in need of organised, internal Jordanian figures with their own programme and circumstances that permit its implementation'. Muhafaza, 'A. in ibid., p. 209.

38. Historically, resistance to Hashemite authority by Transjordanian elites stemmed from taxation issues. Sa'ada, pp. 5–30. In the early 1950s, political opposition originated in the heavy-handed actions of prime minister Tawfiq Abul Huda. Dissent

was at that time primarily oriented towards the person of the prime minister, not the state, as indicated by the fact that Abul Huda's repression sparked opposition from *all* ideological parties and movements, including the Muslim Brotherhood which supported the monarchy. M. al-Masri, pp. 93–7.

39. There is increasing empirical evidence that a diversity of elites, social groups, and classes, including those commonly considered to be 'children of the state,' demonstrate remarkable flexibility with regard to their political preferences for authoritarianism or democracy once their material privileges are assured. This flexibility of regime preferences is captured by Leigh Payne's 'adaptive actor' approach and Eva Bellin's theory of 'contingent democrats'. Payne, L. (1994), *Brazilian industrialists and democratic change*, Baltimore: Johns Hopkins University Press, 1994; E. Bellin, 'Contingent democrats: industrialists, labor, and democratisation in late-developing countries', *World Politics*, 52, 2 (January 2000), pp. 175–205.

40. L. Payne, xv.

41. See 'Aruri on the persistence of old-order 'bloc' parties in Jordan. 'Aruri, 101.

42. 'Aruri, pp. 138–9.

43. Following the crisis, the army was immediately purged, the officer corps bedouinised, and rewarded: the post-crisis regime allotted more than half of Jordan's 1957–8 national budget to the Army. Chronology in *Middle East Journal*, 11, 4 (autumn 1957), p. 422.

44. Chronology in *Middle East Journal*, 11, 3 (summer 1957), p. 297.

45. H. Al-Shayaab, in Hourani (ed.), p. 204.

46. Satloff, p. 172.

47. This 'conventional wisdom' explanation is commonly cited in media reports, interviews with Jordanian officials and analysts, as well as academic studies.

48. The most influential work in this vein is H. Beblawi and G. Luciani (eds), *The rentier state*, London: Croom Helm, 1987.

49. For example, see G. Robinson, (1998), 'Defensive democratisation in Jordan', *International Journal of Middle East Studies*, 30,3 (August 1998), pp. 387–410; or Brumberg's application of 'survival strategies' to Arab cases in D. Brumberg, (1995), 'Authoritarian legacies and reform strategies in the Arab world', in R. Brynen, B. Korany and P. Noble (eds), *Political liberalisation and democratisation in the Arab world: volume 1, theoretical perspectives*, Boulder, CO: Lynne Reinner, 1995, pp. 229–59.

50. Due to space limitations, the 1984 supplementary parliamentary elections to fill seven vacancies in the West Bank are not addressed. Both the decision to revive the 9th parliament and the results of the limited election are consistent with the broader shift in domestic balances of power and palace calculations described here.

51. 'Odeh 'Adnan Abu clearly describes the significance of the al-Nabulsi period in palace thinking in 1989 and the early 1990s: 'The basic issue for me, and for us in the government, was to avoid the 1956 experiment . . . In other words, I wanted to make sure that all of (the participants) would support the constitution as it is and the monarchy, the Hashemite monarchy, as the pivot of the political system and the state . . . It is the line that cannot be crossed . . . because if it happens again democratisation would be aborted again, and two abortions would make it impossible for democracy ever to conceive.' Interview, 29 December, 1999. Abu 'Odeh remained in the Royal Palace as political adviser to Hussain's son, now King Abdullah II, until the year 2000. In a recent book, he contends that to Hussain, 'the monarchy and Jordanian national interests are one and the same.' Thus, the lesson of 1957 for the King 'was that political pluralism posed a threat to the

constitution – or rather to the monarchy itself if it was not practiced within the confines of the Jordanian national interests.' 'A. Abu 'Odeh, *Jordanians, Palestinians and the Hashemite kingdom in the Middle East peace process*, Washington, DC: United States Institute of Peace Press, 1999, p. 82. Abd al-Hadi al-Majali, Director General of Public Security from 1985–9, presents a more hard-line formulation: 'When the regime thinks that anybody wants to step on its responsibilities ... the regime will interfere. And all powers will be with the regime – nobody can threaten it.' Interview, 21 December 1999.

52. This analysis departs from the 'conventional wisdom' that Islamic movements present a threat to liberal politics. While the ultimate effects of Islamism on democratisation cannot yet be assessed, it appears that the rise of the Jordanian Muslim Brotherhood, given its moderate agenda, was necessary for liberalisation to begin.

53. Concerning the loss of mobilising capacity among workers' syndicates, for example, in the late 1970s and 1980s, see 'I. Ahmad, 'Awda' al-haraka al-naqabiyya al-'ummaliyya al-urduniyya wa muhimmatuha al-rahina', *Al-Urdun Al-Jadid*, 11 (October 1988), pp. 55–72.

54. See the review of party agendas in N. Al-Khateeb, *Al-ahzab al-siyasiyya wa duruha fi anzhimat al-hukum al-mu'asareh*, Karak, Jordan: Mu'teh University, pp. 387–400.

55. L. Adoni, 'Lifting the lid', *Middle East International*, 3 November 1989, p. 10. The 'National Program' collapsed, however, because the Muslim Brotherhood objected to its support for the PLO's peace programme with Israel.

56. Interview with Abd al-Hadi al-Majali, 29 December 1999.

57. Interview with Hani Hourani, former member of the Popular Front for the Liberation of Palestine and later the break-away Democratic Front for the Liberation of Palestine, 12 October 1999.

58. Abd al-Latif 'Arabiyat, presently head of the Islamic Action Front (the Muslim Brotherhood's political party), contends: 'The monarchy is Islamically legitimate, and has the same Arab and Islamic goals as the Muslim Brotherhood. It would never take measures against Islam.' Interview, 18 November 1999.

59. Interview with Abd al-Latif 'Arabiyat, 29 November 1999.

60. According to Hani Hourani, the prior experiences of subaltern groups with radical and leftist ideologies, especially Palestinian refugees, has created expectations among some of the Brotherhood's supporters that its present leaders cannot represent. This may help to explain why some observers of Jordanian politics interviewed in late 1999 contend that support for the Brotherhood has eroded since the onset of liberalisation in 1989.

61. Although it is difficult to determine its level of support amongst the various classes and cleavages in Jordanian society, analysts concur that the Hashemite regime has succeeded in broadening its base of popular support in recent decades, particularly since the 'Black September' crisis of 1970–1. For example, see 'I. Ahmad, (above) for a description of how the regime consistently sided in the 1970s and 1980s with owners of capital against labour interests. More broadly, Anderson notes that 'the regime has spent the last forty years successfully establishing firm bases of support from among all the different classes of the population.' B. Anderson, 'Liberalisation in Jordan in the 1950s and 1990s: similarities or differences?', *Jordanies*, 4, December 1997, p. 211.

62. Abu 'Odeh told the author that his book was originally intended for the late King Hussain as a warning of the possible negative consequences of increasing tension between citizens of Transjordanians and Palestinian descent. Interview, 29 December 1999.

63. In interviews with several present and former officials of both West Bank and East Bank origins, mention was made that Palestinians are often viewed by East Bank Jordanians as transmitters of 'un-Jordanian' ideas. That is, ideas that threaten the monarchy or the regime. Taher Al-Masri, of Palestinian origin and prime minister from June until November 1991, explains his ouster thus: 'Those Jordanians, either conservatives or those that believe that a Palestinian should not reach such a position, they were many . . . in their minds I represent Palestine more than I represent Jordan.' Interview, 16 December 1999.

64. In the 1984 by-election, Islamist candidates won one-half of the seats (3 of 6) available to Muslim candidates. The remainder of the seats went to individuals considered to be moderate liberals or traditionalists. See analysis in 'Nata'ij al-intikhabat (taqayyam ijmali)', *Al-Urdun Al-Jadid*, 1 (July 1984), pp. 81–96.

65. Interview with Ibrahim 'Izz al-Din, Minister of Information. 12 December 1999. According to 'Izz al-Din, 'These surveys were conducted by a professional body, one month before the elections and a few days before. [The surveys] were extremely clear that the Islamic movement was winning, and specifically at the end (as the election neared) they were winning more than before.' Asked specifically about how accurately the surveys predicted support for leftist candidates in the 1989 election, 'Izz al-Din responded: 'We had a very clear indication of what to expect.' The surveys were not available for study. Hussain's adviser Abu 'Odeh concurs: based on the regime's intelligence reports, 'it was obvious to us that the rising political force was the Islamic force.' Interview, 29 December 1999.

66. Days before the election, one journalist predicted that candidates who support political reform (leftists, Pan-Arab nationalists, and independent liberals) would win six to ten seats in the 80-member parliament. 'The majority is expected to come from influential traditional candidates.' L. Adoni, 'Lifting the lid', *Middle East International*, 3 November 1989, p. 10.

67. Robinson notes that in contrast to the expectations of the comparative literature on democratisation, the political opening in Jordan in 1989 was not attended by significant cleavages within the ruling elite. G. Robinson (1998).

68. L. Adoni, 'King Hussain leads Jordan into a new era', *Middle East International*, 17 November 1989, p. 3.

69. Ibid. Hussain's political adviser Abu 'Odeh recalls Hussain's remarks at a post-election press conference: 'Those who don't like the outcome should understand that we like it as it is'. Interview, 29 December 1999.

70. L. Adoni, 'Lifting the lid', *Middle East International*, 3 November 1989, p. 9.

71. An English translation of the Charter is available on the internet at http://www.kinghussein.gov.jo/chart.intro.html.

72. The above quotes are from 'Adnan Abu 'Odeh. Interview, 29 December 1999.

73. Abd al-Hadi al-Majali. Interview, 21 December 1999.

74. Abd al-Latif 'Arabiyat. Interviews, 18 and 29 November 1999. 'Arabiyat's summary of the IAF's approach to governance and political activism is found in 'A. 'Arabiyat, 'Ma'aalim al-tajdid fi al-haraka al-islamiyya fi al-Urdun' in 'A. Muhafaza (ed.), *Al-ahzab wa al-t'addudiyya al-siyasiyya fi al-Urdun*, Amman: Mu'assasat Abd al-Hamid Shoman, 1997, pp. 123–35.

75. For a survey of the means utilised by the regime to stall or override opposition from civic organisations and political parties, see B. Anderson 'The status of "democracy" in Jordan', *Critique*, 10 (spring 1997), pp. 55–76.

76. S. Kamal, 'Old guard on top', *Middle East International*, 28 January 2000, p. 12.

77. For a recent example of Jordan's exemplary status in the literature on democratisation in the Middle East, see Sa'ad al-Din Ibrahim's contribution to a recent survey of civil society and democratisation in the region, entitled 'A call for Arab

constitutional monarchies'. In this essay, Ibrahim finds the democratisation process in Jordan (and other Arab monarchies) so promising that he suggests, in line with another Arab intellectual, that Arab republics initiate a new social contract with their leaders allowing presidents to hand-pick their successors in exchange for citizens' 'true democracy'; i.e., that Arab republics be transformed into constitutional monarchies. S. Ibrahim (ed.), *Al-mujtima' al-madani wa al-tahawwal al-dimuqrati fi al-watan al-'arabi: al-taqrir al-sanawi 2000*, Cairo: Markaz Ibn al-Khaldoun, 2000, pp. 19–22.

78. R. Dahl, *Polyarchy: participation and opposition*, Yale University Press, 1971. According to Dahl's classic comparative study, this sequence (inclusiveness before competition) has not favoured progress towards democracy (polyarchy).

79. The two exceptions that I am aware of where individuals challenged the monarchy's authority since 1989 are former independent Islamist MP Layth Shbaylat and former MP Toujan Faysal. Both are no longer members of parliament. Chief Political Adviser to the King 'Adnan Abu 'Odeh tellingly explained Shbaylat's mistake as failing to have an organisation behind him. Interview, 29 December 1999.

80. For example, see G. O'Donnell and P. Schmitter, *Transitions from authoritarian rule: tentative conclusions about uncertain democracies*, Baltimore: Johns Hopkins University Press, 1986; T. Karl, 'Dilemmas of democratisation in Latin America,' *Comparative Politics*, 23, 1 (October 1990), pp. 1–23; and G. di Palma, (1990), *To craft democracies: an essay on democratic transitions*, Berkeley: University of California Press, 1990.

81. For a critical view of how such pacts effectively assure the survival of authoritarianism, see R. Fatton, 'The impairments of democratisation,' *Comparative Politics*, 31, 2 (January 1999), pp. 209–29.

82. Due to space limitation, the effects of the Black September 1970–1 civil war in Jordan are not addressed. The regime's victory over the *fidayeen* served to further enforce a mutuality of interests between economic elites and the monarchy. T. Piro, *The political economy of market reform in Jordan*, Lanham, MD: Rowman and Littlefield, 1998, pp. 60–3.

83. Evidence indicates that despite its turbulent history Jordan has historically been characterised by low levels of political mobilisation and participation. Even in this day of legalised parties and competitive elections, name recognition of the IAF, the party best represented in parliament during the liberalisation period, was about 34 per cent in 1997, while only about 1 per cent of Jordanians admit to having ever belonged to a political party. See Markaz al-Dirasaat al-Istratijiyya, 'Istila' li al-ra'i hawl al-dimuqratiyya fi al-Urdun: al-nata'ij al-awwaliyya'. Amman: University of Jordan, 1998, pp. 19–21.

84. The danger of redistributive issues to processes of democratisation is a common theme in the literature of comparative regime change. See the discussion in D. Yashar, *Demanding democracy: reform and reaction in Costa Rica and Guatemala, 1870s-1950s*, Stanford University Press, 1997, pp. 20–1, and E. Bellin (above).

85. See the synopsis of current democratisation theory in Fatton, p. 211.

86. Piro, pp. 94–5.

87. As Robinson points out, the election and party programmes of the Muslim Brotherhood and IAF are noteworthy for their economic as well as social conservatism. G. Robinson, 'Can Islamists be democrats? The case of Jordan', *Middle East Journal*, 51, 3 (summer 1997), pp. 373–87.

88. In interviews conducted in The fall and winter of 1999 with secular and Islamist party members, interviewees distinctly emphasised that while their parties sympathised with the demonstrators, they played no direct role in facilitating their

activities. In some cases, including the Muslim Brotherhood and some leftist groups, party leaders gave direct orders to subordinates not to become associated with the demonstrators.

89. Some may argue that the professed commitment to reform of Hussain's successor, Abdullah II, presents another possible means towards democratisation. To date, Abdullah has focused his public energies on modernising Jordan's bureaucracy (often through well-publicised incognito visits to state facilities), stressing national unity, and promoting economic ties and development. Abdullah's views concerning political reform are presently difficult to assess. It is important to recall, however, that the young Hussain considered himself to be a liberal moderniser in line with the ideals of his era. K. Salibi, *The modern history of Jordan*, London: I. B. Tauris, 1998, pp. 179–80. Jordanian pundit Rami Khouri notes: 'Until the King gets out of the business of politics, there will be no real democracy.' From meetings with Abdullah, Khouri does not believe the King has yet realised this conflict. Interview, 30 November 1999.

MONARCHICAL STABILITY AND POLITICAL LIBERALISATION
CONNECTIONS BETWEEN JORDAN AND MOROCCO

David Mednicoff

Despite the hopes of many both outside of and within the Middle East, most governments in the region continue to have less open and representative institutions than in other parts of the world. A burgeoning literature among observers of this phenomenon notes the pressures that economic problems and civil society seem to create for political liberalisation while also underscoring the slow pace with which such liberalisation emerges.[1] In the meantime, the trajectory of Arab politics in the next decade remains elusive because of this apparent resistance to change.

Jordan, however, has been part of two trends that may shed light on Arab politics more generally. First, the Jordanian monarchy, like other Arab royal regimes, has been remarkably stable in the past three decades. Second, as in Morocco, but in contrast to non-monarchies like Syria, a smooth, well-prepared transition process[2] from the long-standing king to his designated filial successor seems to have taken place. These two trends beg the following question. Are there connections between Arab monarchy, generational transitions and the prospects for political liberalisation?

This analysis answers this question in the affirmative. Building on a comparison between the political processes and recent legacies of the comparable cases of Morocco and Jordan, it concludes that both the prospects and pressures for long-term political liberalisation are high. Before focusing on the factors that lead to this conclusion, the logic of comparing these two cases will be discussed, followed by a summary of the political situations inherited by their new kings.

Morocco and Jordan: comparable political cases

The year of 1999 focused dramatic attention on a clear connection between Jordan and Morocco. In each country, only a few months apart, the ruling kings, each of whom had been in power for some four decades, died entrusting their countries to their eldest sons. King Abdullah II of Jordan and King Muhammad VI of Morocco are each in their thirties, and, unlike their fathers, completed significant portions of their educations outside of their countries in the West – although King Hassan of Morocco did undertake higher education in France. Thus, the peaceful transition between fathers and sons in each country highlighted both the longevity of these two post-colonial monarchies and the sense that a generation with new priorities might be assuming the mantle of leadership in two Arab societies.

Yet these similarities between Morocco and Jordan are not merely coincidental. Rather, they reflect broader shared facts of political history and economics. The primary similarity between the contemporary histories of the two countries is the way in which their kings built on similar claims of personal status and skilful manipulation to attempt to associate their monarchy with the basic identity of their nation. In the case of both Jordan and Morocco, Western colonial powers assumed that ruling through a king from a local elite family, both claiming descent from the Prophet Muhammad's bloodline, would provide a credible, yet weak, puppet regime in their own interests.[3] Yet, in somewhat different ways, kings Abdullah of Jordan and Muhammad V of Morocco managed to transform their office into a leitmotif of national character, which in turn became central to the political legitimation of their successors, Hussain and Hassan.

King Abdullah, according to one historical account, used his secret contacts with Israel and more open connections with Britain to undermine indirectly the concept of Palestine as a political entity, thereby consolidating the idea of Jordan's heretofore un-established and unrecognised territorial integrity at the centre of Arab regional politics.[4] Muhammad V, for his part, became the symbol of Moroccan aspirations for independence from French colonial rule, which allowed him to assume the mantle of actual national leadership when independence came in 1956.

But in both cases it took successors with unusual mixtures of political skills, survival instincts and plain luck to create the idea of the monarchy as Jordan's and Morocco's pre-eminent national institution. Thus, the period from 1953 in Jordan and from 1961 in Morocco until 1999, when Hussain and Hassan became the two longest-ruling world leaders after World War II, is most apt for comparison. The two countries differed in population size, demographic divisions, proximity to the Arab-Israeli conflict and other salient features. Nevertheless, there were fundamental similarities in their domestic politics, foreign ties and economic options under Hussain and Hassan.

In domestic politics, both kings weathered direct threats to their rule in the 1960s and early 1970s to establish a clear system of monarchical domination of political institutions and culture. Neither king was afraid to make use of political repression, whether in Hussain's case of crushing the Palestinian revolt in 1970 or in Hassan's case of destroying his enemies in the military in the early 1970s. But an even more pervasive aspect of the two kings' efforts to control their countries' politics was the constant struggle to depict the monarchy as the lynchpin of their society.

The unceasing use of the media to glorify the political system was a characteristic of Arab and non-Arab states throughout this period. However, in Morocco and Jordan this general strategy took the specific form of inflating the dynastic importance and historical grounding of the two monarchies. However modern and fragile the foundations of the two post-colonial monarchies might have been, the image that the kings themselves tried to embody and the media apparatus they controlled constantly fostered was of a seamless blend of traditional legitimacy and modernism.

As has been argued in more detail with regard to Morocco,[5] much of the energy of the two kings was given to solidifying their image in political culture as the essential embodiment of their nations' achievements and aspirations. Although the constant assertion of this cultural image did not in fact make it so,[6] the coupling of this rhetoric, actual political repression and the mixture of luck and skill involved in the monarchs' endurance did work to limit the options for would-be political opposition.[7] Both Morocco and Jordan exhibited through the latter parts of Hassan's and Hussain's reigns the appearance of political pluralism and the reality of monarchical domination of actual politics.

The image and eventual stability of these two monarchies led to a similarity in their international relations. Given their self-inflated ability to combine tradition and modernity and given their endurance, they became known as 'Arab moderates' in prominent Western countries like France, the United Kingdom and the United States. Part of this sense also stemmed from a genuine inclination on the part of both regimes to maintain good connections and trade with Western countries. Given their respective frictions with socialist Algeria and Palestinian nationalism, it also suited Moroccan and Jordanian geopolitical needs to look towards Europe and North America.

Because Kings Hassan and Hussain acquired the 'moderate' label, both played roles on the stage of Middle Eastern diplomacy that outweighed their countries' cultural, military or economic importance. This in turn provided further ammunition for the barrage of rhetoric which their governments' media directed to the task of demonstrating the inseparability of the two kings and their countries' global prestige. Even with the lack of popularity among Western officials of Morocco's war to annex the former Spanish Western Saharan territories and, especially, of Jordan's refusal to combat Iraq's take-over of Kuwait in 1990, Hassan and Hussain continued to enjoy prominence and privilege on the world stage.

The strong connection of Morocco and Jordan to international and, especially, powerful Western countries' politics may have been necessary for economic reasons, but has not been costless. The necessity comes out of the critical shared economic fact between the two monarchies – neither is an oil-exporting nation. Because Jordan, much more than Morocco, has received significant aid from and exported labour to wealthy oil monarchies of the Persian Gulf, it might be termed an indirect rentier state. But the drop in oil prices in the early 1980s ended this source of prosperity and made Jordan, like Morocco, reliant to a significant extent on Western sources of trade and aid.

One cost of this economic situation for both countries has been their vulnerability to the policies and priorities of Western-dominated multilateral finance organisations, and, in particular, the International Monetary Fund. IMF austerity measures lowering price supports on bread led to massive riots in Morocco in 1984 and 1990 and in Jordan in 1989. It is quite possible that concerns brought on by this rioting propelled the two kings to attempt to revive the countries' elected parliaments.[8] In any case, the experience of Jordan and Morocco with the IMF is but one of the more obvious manifestations of the two countries' shared hopes and challenges to benefit more from the Western-run global economy.

The causes and constraints of managed monarchical liberalisation

Why did two kings who were autocratic survivors, like Hassan of Morocco and Hussain of Jordan, undertake at least the appearance of significant political liberalisation beginning in the late 1980s? To the extent that generalisation is possible,[9] three, perhaps four, factors common to both cases seem likely to have driven the process. These are the growing pressures for economic reform, if not complete privatisation; the increasing limitations on the two regimes' abilities to dominate the mass media; the overthrow of authoritarian regimes and the wave of democratisation in Eastern Europe and the very stability enjoyed by the two kings for so long.

The first factor stems from the political and economic linkages between each Arab monarchy and the West described above, as well as from the more general failure of developing countries to build competitive economies through predominantly state-owned economic institutions. Two knowledgeable experts discredited in the early 1990s the general predilection for Arab economies to rely on large, bureaucratic state sectors as a strategy for rapid industrialisation and diversification.[10] The neo-liberal economic vision informing this argument may obscure the dearth of catch-up options available to postcolonial developing countries. Nonetheless, both Morocco and Jordan have accepted for about a decade at least the principle that privatisation of state-owned firms is necessary to realise whatever hopes the countries have for global economic competitiveness.

With this acceptance came the necessity to expand the participatory basis of the Jordanian and Moroccan states. Analysts of the linkage between Arab economic privatisation and political liberalisation have stressed that impulses toward the former do not necessarily lead to dramatic shifts in the latter.[11] Yet the basic need that reducing or reinventing the state sector creates for regimes to find support in non-state economic actors means that 'privatisation and democracy . . . reinforce one another.'[12] Indeed, at least one knowledgeable analyst argues that economic reform did connect to Jordan's political liberalisation of the early 1990s.[13]

A second impetus for political reform came from the two monarchies' decreasing abilities to dominate political images and discourse within their countries. Two related developments presaged this change. First, improvements in communication and information technology meant that Jordanians and Moroccans had increasing access to television stations and newspapers that were not under state control. For instance, while the Moroccan government attempted to control and tax access to television satellite dishes in the early 1990s, this proved in the end impossible, exposing a wealthy elite to a significantly wider array of TV stations than had been the case before. As cross-sections of the population read and saw alternatives to the constant images of the advanced and democratic nature of the monarchy, a wide range of private and semi-private media began to sprout, in turn accelerating an impression of liberalised politics and civil society.

As communication technology increasingly allowed a wider range of Moroccans and Jordanians to see outside of their countries, so too did it allow outsiders to see in. In particular, the very openness and connections of the two countries to Western countries and visitors heightened the scrutiny they faced from a particular sort of outsider, the human rights monitor. In Morocco, Western-based international human rights organisations were particularly successful at finding ways to embarrass King Hassan. Because groups like Amnesty International disseminated their findings to a wide audience, especially within Western countries, they could affect foreign images of Morocco, sometimes at an official level.[14]

The clear consternation that the king manifested in response to a scathing journalistic book about his regime's human rights violations that became a bestseller in France[15] led to a major deterioration in relations between the two countries. In response to the attack on his image represented by this book, Hassan authorised a counter-text also published in France in the form of a collection of interviews with a different French journalist.[16] But the lesson for Hassan's regime was clear – outsiders had the ability to publicise effectively aspects of the regime very much against the modernist and pluralist images which state-controlled media had laboured to instill for decades. Logically, it made sense for the king to undertake political measures that could address the gap between what the Moroccan and non-Moroccan media said about the monarchy.

A third factor relevant to political liberalisation by Kings Hussain and Hassan emerged at the end of the 1980s was the collapse of the authoritarian regimes of Eastern and Central Europe, mostly by peaceful means. One clear effect of this geopolitical earthquake was to decrease the influence of key non-monarchical authoritarian Arab regimes such as Syria and Libya. But more important for members of the Jordanian and Moroccan political elites was the 'demonstration effect' of non-violent democratic change in countries in a similar peripheral position to Western Europe as the Middle East.[17]

With the decline in influence of regimes identifying themselves with Soviet-style socialism, more representative political alternatives received increasing attention among Arab political activists, including both secular and Islamist ideas. In Morocco, one sign of this trend was a spate of high-level academic conferences on the political and economic lessons of Eastern Europe. The long-standing rulers of Jordan and Morocco made use of their tactical political skills to insert themselves into the dialogue by embracing limited actual liberalisation and unlimited rhetoric of liberalisation.

In fact, it is possible that the political liberalisation undertaken by the two late kings was as much the result of intention as pressure. At least within the limits of dominance of national politics by the monarchy, both Hussain and Hassan had attempted diversification of their governments and parliamentary elections before the late 1980s and 1990s. Perhaps the three factors described above dovetailed with a sense on the part of both monarchs that their stability had withstood a sufficient test of time to allow for a period of political institutional change and expansion. The need to provide the back-drop for a stable transition for their successors and the ultimate pre-servation of their monarchies also cut in the direction of regime opening. Both kings certainly embraced their new democratic politics with gusto and rhetorical flourish.

Whatever the precise weights of the causes of the political liberali-sation that characterised the last part of Hassan's and Hussain's lives, the process and effects in both cases were similar in their scope and limitations. Both liberalisation processes led to three major develop-ments – a revitalisation of parliament and parliamentary elections, an expansion of civil society and political discourse and an effort by the two kings to use these developments to concentrate, rather than de-centralise, their political control.

All of these developments were, of course, interrelated. The logic that co-opting the Muslim Brotherhood and other potential challen-gers to the regime by holding elections, giving very limited powers to Parliament and allowing the growth of a politically quiescent civil so-ciety could bolster King Hussain's control is discussed at length else-where in this volume.[18] It is instructive, however, also to consider briefly the pattern of Moroccan political expansion from the late 1980s to King Hassan's death, for it is quite similar to what occurred in Jordan.

One difference between Jordanian and Moroccan politics was the multiplicity of political parties functioning in the latter country for most of the period since national independence in 1956.[19] These par-ties, which did represent a diversity of social and political viewpoints, were allowed to operate as long as they voiced their acceptance of the monarchy as the organising principle of Moroccan politics. Even with these restrictions, the palace did not allow the country's politi-cally impotent parliament to be dominated by parties that were autonomous from the state. Thus, the parliaments elected in 1977 and 1984 consisted mainly of members of 'independent' political par-ties that were essentially sponsored by the government.

Yet the Istiqlal and Union of Socialist Popular Forces (USFP), the two parties with a history of ideological perspectives and mem-bership distinct from the palace elite, used the late 1980s and early 1990s as a time to press for more representative elections and a genu-ine function for parliament. In a move that the regime trumpeted as an example of 'Hassanien democracy', these parties in 1990 actually introduced a no-confidence motion against the government after riot-ing in Fes in 1990.[20] Even though the motion predictably failed, it high-lighted the ability of some of the political elite to publicise the need for political reform as an implicit alternative to the socioeconomic tensions associated with Fes and the incidents that had occurred there.

King Hassan promulgated a new Moroccan Constitution in 1992, giving parliament the right to endorse or reject the government and to demand answers to particular questions from ministers. Elections for parliament followed the next year and, as verified by an international team of observers,[21] were characterised by a higher degree of transparency and fairness than had existed in prior contests. With the USFP and Istiqlal holding 106 of the 333 seats in the parliament, the new deliberative body engaged in much more vigorous political and socioeconomic debate than in the past.[22]

As Morocco's parliament became more lively, indigenous human rights, journalists' and women's movements emerged, suggesting a more diverse and influential civil society. Despite the conclusion of a prominent Moroccan social scientist that the country's political culture was unlikely to be fertile ground for civil society,[23] the movements mentioned above were able to contribute to a climate in the country where there was much more talk and even some action on political liberalisation. In particular, Morocco's human rights climate improved markedly, to the point that the regime closed and eventually even acknowledged the existence of a particularly infamous political prison on the southern slopes of the Atlas mountains.

The extent of political liberalisation in Morocco outstripped that in Jordan and possibly any other Arab society.[24] Yet the results remained explicable in terms of the 'survival' hypothesis discussed throughout this book. As one observer puts it, 'the quantitative increase in associative activity is thus less an indicator of civil society's strength than the state's way out of the inertia of the formal political game between the palace and political parties.'[25]

In other words, in Morocco, as in Jordan, the late king attempted to bolster and reinvent his political relevance by facilitating the activity of civil and political organisations bound by his manipulations but used as evidence of the country's democratisation. Before Hassan died, the process of contestation within the confines of the monarchy again yielded a new constitution and elections for parliament that in 1998 produced a government dominated by the USFP and its leader, Abderrahman Youssifi. Once again, the actual significance of this 'opposition government' was much less than its importance in the late king's constant efforts to ensure the completion and perfection of Moroccan democratisation.

Therefore, the pattern of Morocco's politics in the 1990s only heighten the conclusion of other chapters in this book on Jordan; that liberalisation is less significant as a signal of genuine democratisation than as a variation on the long-standing pattern of royal monopolisation of the political arena. Yet, it is nonetheless possible that the liberalisation which has taken place has created new political dynamics, particularly in the context of a succession of kings in both countries.

A new generation of rulers: prospects and pressures for liberalisation

The decades of struggles for political survival successfully mastered by Kings Hassan and Hussain ended abruptly in 1999 with their deaths. Yet in each case, a smooth and non-violent transition took place, in which both were succeeded by their oldest sons. Another way of looking at the last stage of the reigns of the old kings is as an effort to provide a sufficient balance of centralised stability and political opening to allow their sons breathing room to lead their countries in different directions. The question is whether these new directions are less authoritarian.

In part because of the clear power-control mechanisms developed by both Kings Hassan and Hussain, their sons Muhammad and Abdullah may be able to preside over a greater degree of genuine political liberalisation. The dual facts of the contemporary longevity of the two monarchies and the preparations that were undertaken to secure the successions have given the two new kings a legacy of political stability and a modicum of political legitimacy. This point should not be over-stated; it would be both foolhardy and reductionist to assert that there is something inevitable about monarchies in Morocco and Jordan. Rather, the assertion is that the carefully-fostered succession process and the image of stability in each country are political assets which Muhammad and Abdullah can either use or squander.

Legacies of the fathers. The two kings bequeathed three more specific political legacies to their eldest sons. First, the free use that both regimes made of cultural domination, political control and co-optation and repression when expedient has crippled most anti-regime opposition. This has been particularly true with respect to Islamist opposition, although Morocco and Jordan have handled this issue differently.

Thus, it is possible that the pessimistic assessments to be found elsewhere in this volume concerning liberalisation under King Hussain, which could be easily applied to his Moroccan counterpart, are beside the point. The point is that the late kings' strong-arm tactics to ensure their regimes' survival and perhaps consolidate their nations' identities may allow their successors breathing room to pursue more genuine political openings. Neither Kings Abdullah nor Muhammad face powerful legal or clandestine opposition to their regimes.

Of course, virtually every Middle Eastern and many other authoritarian systems have been characterised by a variety of efforts to eliminate genuine political threats to their rule. What makes the contemporary situation of Morocco and Jordan different from Syria, another example of patrilineal succession, is the nature of the monarchical regimes' legitimacy claims. This legitimacy claim is the second of the three specific political legacies passed to Muhammad VI and Abdullah II.

Throughout their long period of rule, kings Hassan and Hussain each worked hard to foster the idea that their regime and dynasty were inseparable from the political well-being of their country. What distinguishes these rulers' efforts from that of many of their peers was their relative ability to embed themselves in the historical continuity of their respective societies. While these efforts to be sure in no way established the 'Alawi and Hashemite dynasties as the inevitable heads of state of Morocco and Jordan, they did facilitate a limited popular connection of the monarchy and political legitimacy.

The two kings were able to appeal to popular political legitimacy in three significant ways. First, the historical grounding of the kings' dynasties, however inflated this was by the state media which they controlled, allowed them to identify themselves with both local traditional roots and modernist cosmopolitanism. In Morocco, Hassan used his mastery of both Arabic and French and his combination of national dynastic inheritance and French education to great advantage. His media apparatus tirelessly associated him as appropriate with Moroccan tradition and international respectability. This association was plausible because he was in fact part of a dynasty that had ruled over Morocco since 1672. Similarly, Hussain played up his dynasty's role in the World War I Great Arab revolt to accentuate his local roots.

For countries like Morocco and Jordan which have struggled to chart a post-colonial course between clear local identity and global respect, the fact that their kings could straddle both of these poles was important. Yet, in addition to this, their ability to claim local political legitimacy was augmented by two further factors. First was Hassan's and Hussain's Islamic pedigree. The kings took great pains to combine constant popular awareness of their dynasty's status as descendants of the tribe of the Prophet Muhammad with symbolic roles in religious rituals. In Morocco, the claim that Hassan's frequent use of the caliphal metaphor of *amir al-mu'minin* (Commander of the Faithful) has led Moroccans to associate him with Islam[26] has been debated and subjected to understandable scepticism.[27] Yet the greater plausibility of the Sherifian traditional Moroccan monarch's claim to lead his nation's religious community relative to his counterparts in Algeria or Tunisia helps explain the comparative weakness of Islamist opposition in Morocco.[28]

A third factor that allowed the Jordanian and Moroccan kings to enjoy political legitimacy was their use of their status as monarchs to propagate the idea that they stood above, from or outside of the political fray. Each of the five versions of the Moroccan constitution promulgated under Hassan II has included clear provisions that explicitly stated the king's position above politics. Although not true, the idea that the king's position was outside the actual political arena provided four likely boosts to his legitimacy.

First, it encouraged people – with some success – to dissociate particular policies and partisan politics more generally from the palace.[29] For example, even though longtime minister of the interior and strongman, Driss Basri, acted in consort with the late Moroccan king, Moroccans are much more likely to blame the former than the latter for Moroccan political oppression.

Second, it allowed for more popular expression of political dissent than in a system such as Syria's where the leader and government are more difficult to view as separate. In Morocco, the political parties with an autonomous popular base, until the government formed in 1997, played the role of opposition within the system. These parties' newspapers could openly criticise policies and behaviour of the 'government' without risking reprisals from the king. Thus Moroccans, and particularly potential opponents of the regime within the elite, had a mechanism for blowing off political steam that was separate from a critique of the monarchy.

Third, the idea that the king in Morocco and Jordan was outside the political fray allowed for frequent rotations and dismissals of government officials without real change in the power of the monarchy. Taken with the possibility for critique of the government mentioned above, this meant that there was a limited sort of political accountability in the two Arab monarchies that was different from that which would be available in other forms of non-elected systems. Thus, individual ministers and entire cabinets in both Morocco and Jordan have been dismissed by the king without implicating the basic political structure of either country.

Fourth and finally, the myth of the king's apolitical status tended to support the idea that politics was an unattractive, even dirty business that ordinary people would best avoid.[30] Diffusion of the idea that politics does not merit the involvement of citizens in general has the effect of reducing potential demands and interest in participation on the regime, thereby decreasing the problem of legitimacy for an unelected ruler. Regardless of its truth value, the proposition that the king's apolitical status made him more akin to the people than the government he controlled was a justification for popular apathy and quiescence.

In short, Kings Hassan and Hussain fostered the legitimacy of their political systems by their efforts to incarnate both tradition and modernity, their personal Islamic status, and their ability to depict themselves as above their countries' political squabbles. The combination of these specific trends is the second of the three broader political legacies of the former kings that may be relevant to their sons' prospects for more genuine liberalisation. The third of these legacies is the two countries' general image in Western countries, which has given them significant access to financial and other aid.

Due in part to the political legitimising strategies followed above, the quasi-traditional kings of Jordan and Morocco never defined their regimes by articulating an anti-Western nationalist ideology or turning away from close relations with Western countries. Indeed, following the overthrow of many of these systems in the 1950s and 1960s, the remaining Arab monarchies at times needed outside help to endure the pressures of the Nasserist and pan-Arabist political influences in Arab politics during the height of the Cold War. This, along with the very longevity of the two kings' regimes and their relative pragmatism with respect to Israel, led to decades of close ties between the major Western powers and the two Arab monarchies.

Hassan and Hussain clearly cultivated these ties for their own purposes of enhancing their roles on the world diplomatic stage and improving their fiscal resources and prestige at home. Nonetheless, as discussed above, they developed their image as Arab 'moderates' in the West. With the end of the Cold War and the contemporary military and economic global dominance of the West, and particularly the United States, this is an important potential asset for the young kings Abdullah and Muhammad. In the first half of 2000, the favourable reception and aid packages that both kings were given by US President Bill Clinton reinforced the impression that longstanding warm relations with Western nations had tangible benefits for Jordan and Morocco.

To summarise, the new rulers of Morocco and Jordan came to power in 1999 with at least three political assets that were connected to their status as the inheritors of long-ruling, occasionally repressive monarchs. First, they have faced no immediate, salient overt threats to their regime. Second, they have been able to make fairly credible legitimacy claims for a non-elected government, and these claims lessen potential demands for broader political participation. Third, they have enjoyed better access to Western markets, material and monetary aid than many other authoritarian countries with similarly small economies.

Prospects for the sons. The question relevant to this volume is what, if anything, these political assets suggest in terms of the prospects for political liberalisation in Jordan. The answer to this question seems to be that these assets tend to raise the probability for success for whatever broad political posture the Jordanian king adopts. Having no obvious opposition, enjoying some legitimacy and benefiting from respect in the international community, King Abdullah has significant maneuvering room to chart his own and his regime's future political course.

Yet there are internal and external pressures pushing Jordan in the direction of liberalisation. On the internal side, perhaps the most important, if most banal, of these pressures is the need for the new king to stand out from his father. This is the flip side of the coin of the continuity represented by Jordan's political transition. On the one hand, as discussed, Abdullah has considerable political assets that stem from the fact that he succeeded to his position peacefully and without a disruption to Jordan's basic political structures. On the other hand, this means that the new king has a special challenge to carve out his own political identity unique from that of his late father. In particular, it is crucial that the new king builds his support through a different underlying coalition of the political elite from his father's.

King Abdullah's early socialisation suggests that the political identity he would build for himself involves more genuine political liberalisation. He attended school in the United States, married a wife of Palestinian origin, speaks fluent English, and has shown other signs of cosmopolitanism and a high level of comfort in Western societies. While it is important not to make too much of these points, it is probably significant for his politics that an important part of Abdullah's socialisation took place in pluralistic contexts.

External pressures on Jordan even more clearly suggest the need for further political liberalisation. These pressures can be lumped under the rubric of globalisation, although it is clearly not necessarily the case that globalisation is a single set of processes or one that tends to political opening.[31] The three major external pressures that tend to favour political liberalisation are the challenge of the global market, the proliferation of communication media and the increasing transparency of Jordanian society and the local sensitivity to a variety of transnational actors implied by the first two pressures.

As other chapters of this book discuss in greater detail, Jordan faces considerable difficulties in reforming and expanding its economy. The contemporary 'historically unique confluence or clustering of patterns of globalisation . . . in all dimensions of economic activity'[32] means in part that countries like Jordan have little possibility of opting out of the global marketplace or of the international regimes and organisations that regulate this marketplace. The limited economic impact of Jordan's expected 'peace dividend' with Israel is the strongest reason that the country's elite expresses disappointment with the 1994 treaty.

The fact that Jordan faces a strong challenge to create and anchor its niche in the global economy is not in itself an argument about political liberalisation. Indeed, economic growth is used by governments to justify limited political openness at least as much as it encourages democratisation. However, in a small economy such as Jordan's with limited financial clout to defy international expectations, there is more reason to believe in a link between the country's dependence on the world economy and steps towards liberalisation. This is because, however selectively or even hypocritically, wealthy advanced economies and multilateral economic actors frequently link business or aid to privatisation, human rights or political accountability. As capable as governments may be to resist or give the false appearance of satisfying such conditions, the sensitivity of an economy such as Jordan's makes these conditions a genuine source of political pressure. At least one veteran analyst argues that, 'Whatever limited democratisation might have occurred in the Middle East was the indirect outcome of . . . the financial crisis of the state and globalisation.'[33]

A second change of a technical nature is also a source of pressure on Jordan to liberalise its politics. This is the spread of information technology which tends towards greater social transparency. Since Kings Hassan and Hussain built some of their stability on propagating specific cultural articulations of their legitimacy through the national media, the growth of satellite television and the Internet have undermined this strategy. The administrative apparatus of the Moroccan and Jordanian states, formidable though it may be, cannot control or censor all of the potential sources of information available to economic and political elites within their societies.

The result of this is an increasing elite fluency with, and ability to make use of, media techniques and sources that were much less available even a decade ago. Through transnational and more varied national televised and on-line media, Jordanians and Moroccans of means are able to absorb and disseminate easily a wide variety of social and political messages. The proliferation of such media itself need not encourage political liberalisation. But, in the specifically authoritarian monarchical context of Jordan, it may tend in this direction for two reasons.

First, as Manuel Castells has argued, the growing media dominance of politics tends to amplify popular political cynicism and decrease the perceived capacity of national governments.[34] On the other hand, issue-oriented, humanitarian, non-partisan issues such as human rights may in fact revitalise people's connection to politics.[35] If valid, these two points imply for societies like Jordan that a decline in loyalty to the regime is likely to occur along with a tendency to appreciate the type of issues like human rights and global equity that are connected with political liberalisation.

Second, the ready availability of a much wider variety of political discourse accompanying the globalisation of communications provides elites with a greater range of ready rhetoric and ideology relating to democracy. Since democracy was a term used by both the Moroccan and Jordanian monarchies to characterise their regimes, the increased public currency and contestable content of the term possible through contemporary media technology lessens the regimes' abilities to insist on their own self-referential definitions.

The discussion earlier in this chapter of Morocco's improvements in its human rights climate in the 1990's is an example of how activists' appeals to the language or meaning of democracy can constrain a regime that trumpets its own version of democratic rhetoric. In a context such as Jordan's, the monarchy has staked itself on connections to political liberalism within a traditional context, rather than on radical nationalism. Therefore, the proliferation of diverse indigenous and external discourses on democracy facilitated by contemporary communications technology create pressures for the regime to more fully realise its rhetoric.

Connected to the previous points but worth mentioning in its own right is the greater exposure to transnational interactions and influences involved in the growing globalisation of money and media. The French and German organisations sponsoring this volume and the conference that brought together its authors are an illustration of this trend. One of the signal characteristics of globalisation has been the growing number and importance of such transnational governmental and non-governmental organisations.[36] If such organisations do not mean the effective end of national sovereignty, they do suggest the fragmentation and internationalisation of internal domestic policy-making. In such a climate, the stakes and interests that some governmental organisations and many non-governmental ones have in aspects of political liberalisation could be a considerable pressure on

a government like Jordan's that is highly dependent on foreign aid
and the global market but lacking the clout of states like China or
even Egypt.

In short, together with his Moroccan peer, the young king of Jordan faces a domestic political situation in which he has a number of
political assets that could help him to forge his own approach to the
evolution of Jordanian politics. These assets may be of particular value should he choose to adopt and further a more genuine policy of
political liberalisation than that which his late father pursued. Considering this alongside the fact that the pressures of Jordan's place in
the global environment tend towards liberalisation, there is some reason to believe that the country may in fact be opening up its politics.

Conditions, caveats and comparative contrasts

In 1968 Samuel Huntington made an influential argument that monarchies were unlikely regimes to survive political development, in
large part because the dynastic basis of their authority precluded effective power sharing or political liberalisation. Other essays in this
volume affirm the logic of this argument in noting the fundamental
lack of real decentralisation that characterised the late king of Jordan's attempted liberalisation.

Yet, Jordan, and the comparable case of Morocco along with it,
has been one of the rare countries in which traditional monarchies
have indeed survived decades of political development. Just as the
survival of Kings Hussain and Hassan may have defied expectations,
the political landscape inherited by their sons Abdullah II and Muhammed VI may leave more grounds for liberalisation than their
fathers' own centralising tendencies would suggest. Indeed, if they
are able to circumnavigate the formidable challenges to their continued political relevance, the very traditionalism and even inflexibility
of monarchies may paradoxically turn into assets of local legitimacy
and stability. These assets are potentially very useful to a gradual process of political liberalisation, which the current Moroccan and Jordanian monarchs appear to support.

Whether the new king of Jordan is able to in fact preside over a
transition to a more genuinely democratic Jordan polity is nonetheless a very open question, the answer to which will depend on a variety of factors, of which four are particularly crucial. First, a more
autonomous, diverse civil society than that observed by others in this
volume will have to develop. Second, a more robust local Jordanian
social construction of the meaning of content of democracy and the
role of the monarchy in a genuinely democratic regime will need to

emerge. Such a social construction will have to include the institutio-
nalisation of more consistent respect for, and application of, the
rule-of-law. Third, Jordan must succeed in diversifying and privatising its economy and, thereby, stabilising economic expansion.
Fourth, a favourable international and regional climate is critical for
Jordanian economic development and political liberalisation.

In short, King Abdullah's potential to initiate a process of true democratisation in Jordan will not only be contingent upon his own political legacy and orientation, but on a great deal of skill and luck as
well. Furthermore, there are a number of ways in which Jordan faces
challenges different from those of Morocco. For one thing, Jordan's
political parties and state institutions are less developed than those in
Morocco. One particularly troubling indicator of this has been the
Jordanian government's low level of income taxes as a percentage of
total state revenue.[37] Secondly, Jordan's small size and lack of natural resources may give it less potential economic capacity than a country with Morocco's general diversity and particular phosphate and
newly-discovered oil reserves. Thirdly, even considering its Berber situation, Morocco has nothing approaching the deep source of social
cleavage for Jordan represented by the continued Palestinian refugee
problem.

The biggest challenge of all for King Abdullah is the re-emergence
of the king's dilemma. Is there any doubt that a genuine process of democratisation will eventually mean the end of a large amount of the
Hashemite monarchy's political power? Indeed, as the king enmeshes
himself with political and economic reformers, the sense of apolitical
credibility that has been so important a rhetorical support for the
two contemporary Arab monarchies is unlikely to endure. Whatever
the new king's temperament and tendencies with respect to liberalisation, there is always reason to doubt that a leader given autocratic
power will relinquish this power willingly.

With all of these concerns, there are three salient points worth re-
peating that nonetheless point towards the possibility that Abdullah
II's commitment to political liberalisation will go farther than his
father's. First, together with Hassan II of Morocco, the strategy that
Hussain used to bolster the monarchy by asserting a constant connection between it and Jordan is less available in today's globally-net-
worked cultural landscape. Second, Abdullah's inheritance from his
father of relative legitimacy and stability gives the new king substantial assets on which to chart his own political course. Third, the Jordanian monarch's apparent predilection and transnational pressures
both point towards the likelihood of political liberalisation.

In June 2000 Abdullah replaced conservative Prime Minister

Abdur-Ra'uf S. Rawabdeh with a more liberal figure. Echoing the even more symbolic and substantive sacking of Morocco's former strongman Driss Basri by Muhammed VI months earlier, this move led to renewed Jordanian calls and hopes for 'economic reform that goes hand-in-hand with political liberalisation.'[38] In a famous article that remains very influential among political scientists, Dankwart Rustow argued that a conscious move towards democracy required a prior sense of community to succeed.[39] This sense of political community is part of the legacy bequeathed to Abdullah by Hussain. The king of Jordan, like his fellow young monarch on the Western edge of the Arab world, enjoys an image as a popular reformer that might have been much slower to form, were it not for this political legacy of his father. The question for Jordan, and Morocco as well, is to what extent the new king will be able to build the political and social capital to transform this image into reality.

NOTES

1. The most extended examples of this are the pair of two-volume studies: A. R. Norton (ed.), *Civil Society in the Middle East*, Leiden: E. J. Brill, 1995–6, and R. Brynen, B. Korany, and P. Noble, 1995, 1998, *Political Liberalisation and Democratisation in the Arab World*, Boulder, CO: Lynne Rienner.
2. See, for example, Jon B. Alterman, 'Fathers and Sons', *Washington Post*, 18 June 2000, p. B2.
3. For more on the Jordanian case, see M. C. Wilson, *King Abdullah, Britain and the Making of Jordan*, Cambridge University Press: 1987. Among the better works on Morocco's colonial history is A. Laroui, *Histoire du Maghreb*, Paris: Maspéro, 1970, published in English and by Princeton University Press 1977.
4. Wilson, 214.
5. See D. M. Mednicoff, 'Civic apathy in the service of stability? Cultural politics in monarchist Morocco', *Journal of North African Studies*, 3, 4 (winter 1998), 1970, 1–27.
6. For a sceptical analysis of the Moroccan case, see Chapter 5 of H. Munson. *Religion and Power in Morocco*, Yale University Press, 1993.
7. See, for example, Q.Wiktorowicz's contribution to this volume and I. W. Zartman's, 'Opposition as Support for the State' in G. Luciano (ed.), *The Arab State*, University of California Press, 1990, 220–46.
8. Brynen, 'The Politics of Monarchical Liberalisation: Jordan', in Brynen, Korany and Noble (eds), 1990; vol. 2, 1998; 75 and M. Mufti, 'Elite Bargains and the Onset of Political Liberalisation in Jordan', *Comparative Political Studies* 32, 1 (Feb. 1999), pp. 100–29.
9. Mufti's article concludes that in the Jordanian case, many of the specific steps of political liberalisation were undertaken on fairly narrow grounds of political strategising between the regime and the Islamist opposition. The end dynamic, according to Mufti, created a logic for political liberalisation stronger than either party may have intended.
10. A. Richards and J. Waterbury, *A Political Economy of the Middle East*, Boulder, CO: Westview Press, 1990. Jordan and Morocco are treated most specifically on

pp. 208–11. See also I. Harik and D. J. Sullivan, *Privatisation and Liberalisation in the Middle East*, Bloomington: Indiana University Press, 1992.

11. See, for example, D. Brumberg, 'Authoritarian Legacies and Reform Strategies in the Arab World', in Brynen, Korany and Noble, vol. 1 (1995), pp. 229–59.
12. I. Harik, 'Privatisation: The Issue, The Prospects and the Fears' in Harik and Sullivan (1992), p. 21.
13. L. Brand, 'Economic and Political Liberalisation in a Rentier Economy: The Case of the Hashemite Kingdom of Jordan' in Harik and Sullivan (1992), pp. 184–5.
14. For more on the issue of human rights movements and politics in North Africa, see S. E. Waltz, *Human Rights and Reform – Changing the Face of North African Politics*, Berkeley: University of California Press, 1995, especially pp. 203–13.
15. G. Perrault, *Notre Ami le Roi*, Paris: Gallimard, 1990.
16. Hassan II (interviewed by E. Laurent), *La Mémoire d'un Roi*, Paris: Plon, 1993.
17. G. Ben-Dor, 'Prospects of Democratisation in the Arab World: Global Diffusion, regional demonstration, and Domestic Imperatives' in Brynen, Korany and Noble, vol. 1 (1995), pp. 311–16. The relevance of Eastern Europe for Morocco is noted in vol. 2 (1998), p. 177.
18. See especially Wiktorowicz's chapter.
19. See my chapter 'Morocco' in F. Tachau (ed.), *Political Parties of the Middle East and North Africa*, Westport, CT: Greenwood, 1994, pp. 380–421.
20. Mednicoff (1998), pp. 17–21.
21. See International Foundation for Electoral Systems, *Report of the IFES Monitoring and Observation Delegations*, 25 June 1993, pp. 104–6.
22. A. Baaklini, G. Denoeux and R. Springborg, *Legislative Politics in the Arab World*, Boulder, CO: Lynne Rienner, 1999, p. 118.
23. A. Saaf, 'L'hypothèse de la Société Civile au Maroc,' in el-Aoufi (ed.), *La Société Civile au Maroc*, Rabat: SMER, 1992, p. 14.
24. Baaklini, Denoeux and Springborg (1999); pp. 130–1. Yemen and Algeria both experienced more dramatic periods of liberalisation but the liberalisation was reversed in Algeria and is tricky to assess in Yemen, coming as it did along with an incomplete unification of the former separate South and North Yemeni states.
25. B. Korany, 'Monarchical Islam with a Democratic Veneer: Morocco' in Brynen, Korany and Noble, vol. 2 (1998), p. 174.
26. See Clifford Geertz's well-known discussion of this issue in Geertz, *Islam Observed*, University of Chicago Press, 1968, pp. 76–82, and the more recent, broader discussion of this idea by M. E. Combs-Schilling, *sacred performances: Islam, Sexuality and Sacrifice*, New York: Columbia University Press, 1989.
27. See, for example, Munson (1993).
28. Recent Tozy article in *Le Monde Diplomatique* (XX).
29. Baaklini, Denoeux and Springborg (1999), pp. 252–3.
30. An interesting discussion of the way the Arabic word for politics, *siyyasa,* is so tarnished in the Moroccan context can be found in M. Bennani-Charaibi, *Soumis et Rebelles, Les Jeunes au Maroc*, Paris: Fennec, 1994, p. 202.
31. Perhaps the best of the general volumes in the burgeoning literature on globalisation is the collective volume of D. Held, A. McGrew, D. Goldblatt and J. Perration, *Global Transformations*, Stanford University Press, 1999. Some remarks on globalisation and global political change of relevance to our collective book can be found on pp. 444–52.
32. Held (1999), p. 425. See also pp. 227–35.
33. N. N. Ayubi, *Overstating the Arab State*, London: I. B. Tauris, 1995, p. 401.
34. *The Power of Identity*, Oxford: Blackwell, 1997, pp. 310–12 and 342–5.

35. Ibid., pp. 352–3.
36. Held (1999), pp. 53–7.
37. Ayubi (1995), pp. 411–58. The difference in Jordanian and Moroccan measures of income taxes as a proportion of total state revenue can be found in Table 12.1 on p. 456.
38. 'Relief and Hope', Editorial, *Jordan Times*, 19 June 2000.
39. Rustow D. A. 'Transitions to Democracy: Toward a Dynamic Model', (1970) reprinted in L. Anderson, *Transitions to Democracy*, New York: Columbia University Press, 1999. The volume is a set of contemporary reflections and applications of Rustow's argument.

EMBEDDED AUTHORITARIANISM

BUREAUCRATIC POWER AND THE LIMITS TO
NON-GOVERNMENTAL ORGANISATIONS IN JORDAN

Quintan Wiktorowicz[1]

The 1989 transition to democracy in Jordan unleashed new expectations about political participation, freedom, and justice. Emboldened by a liberalised electoral arena, previously marginalised and excluded political voices held quiet optimism that political liberalisation measures would ineluctably reduce repression. This hope was predicated upon a belief that freedom in the political arena would eliminate state violence, intimidation, and authoritarian practices to uphold the dignity of civil liberties and freedoms. Yet more than ten years later, citizens of Jordan's 'new democracy' still experience substantial limitations to political freedom. Despite a series of relatively free and fair elections, the legalisation of political parties, and the boisterousness of parliament, the regime continues to limit opposition and dissent. Demonstrations, civic organising, the press and other modes of political participation are circumscribed by lingering authoritarian practices that are temporally juxtaposed with institutions of procedural democracy.[2]

This repression, however, is not typified by the overt, brutal forms of physical coercion that characterised the martial law period; rather it is what may be termed 'embedded authoritarianism'–social control projected through a complex array of administrative procedures, legal codes, and informal regulative practices designed to constrain opposition without resorting to violence. In embedded authoritarianism, the primary agent of control is the bureaucracy, not the *mukhabarat*, the military or totalitarian instruments, such as those utilised in China, Iraq, Burma and other dictatorial systems. Wrapped in the rhetoric and sanctity of democracy, the Jordanian regime can no longer afford blatant repression. Instead, power and control are embedded in bureaucratic processes, masked beneath the veneer of visible democratic institutions and practices. In such a political system, legal codes and administrative procedures become the new instruments of repression, manipulated to limit challenges to regime power.[3]

Embedded authoritarianism allows the Jordanian regime to claim the mantle of democracy while expanding control and repression through the bureaucracy. Because elections are held and political participation has expanded, the regime can point to concrete indicators of procedural democracy. At the same time, alternative political views and oppositional collective action are limited by regulative practices, which prevent real opposition from mobilising in civil society. Lucia Port and Samih Farsoun describe such a system as 'an electoral regime embedded in an authoritarian state'.[4] It is a 'façade democracy', concerned more with regime maintenance and control than democratic values.[5] In its pursuit of social control and stability, the Jordanian regime supports formal political participation while simultaneously utilising embedded authoritarianism.[6]

This paper explains how embedded authoritarianism is used to perpetuate regime control over non-governmental organisations (NGOs), frequently touted as the institutional manifestation of civil society and necessary for the consolidation of democracy. NGOs are seen as viable alternative centres of power capable of articulating societal interests and checking state power;[7] and the expansion of the NGO community is often interpreted as a sign of a robust democratic culture.[8] Yet, as this paper argues, the aggregate expansion of NGOs should not be confused with its qualitative significance. Although the number of NGOs in the kingdom has nearly doubled since 1989, they remain depoliticised and circumscribed by the realities of embedded authoritarianism; and the proliferation of grassroots organisations has not engendered greater freedom in civil society.

The logic of the transition and NGO expansion

To a large extent, embedded authoritarianism reflects the logic of the 1989 political transition. The transition to democracy was not a benevolent gift; it was part of a 'survival strategy' by a semi-rentier regime designed to reassert control in the midst of an economic crisis.[9] As a semi-rentier state, Jordan derives substantial revenues from the outside world rather than from domestic production. Sources of 'rent' have included subsidies (provided by the British, Americans, and Arab countries) and workers' remittances from Jordanians employed in the Gulf. Reliance on this rent weakened accountability to society because the state was able to provide basic goods and services without imposing economic burdens on its citizens[10]–in other words, 'no taxation, no representation'.[11] In such a system, the social contract is one in which 'the state is expected to provide a certain level of economic security, in exchange for which society grants leaders considerable political autonomy'.[12] Legitimacy rests upon the ability to enhance quality of life, rather than democratic principles, and there is an implied political right to economic security.[13] The state thus reduces 'formal politics to the issue of distribution and participation to the realm of consumption'.[14]

While the rentier social contract perpetuates non-democratic political structures, it is also vulnerable to external factors that undermine sources of rent. The decline in oil-related revenues in the 1980s, including foreign aid from Gulf countries and workers' remittances, undermined the logic of the social contract; and the subsequent financial crisis served as an important catalyst for democratisation. High levels of debt, inflation, and the return of expatriate Jordanian workers strained the financial capabilities of the state. Initially, the Jordanian regime believed it could postpone economic reforms by borrowing money, but in January 1989 the government was stunned when it was forced to withdraw a loan request ($150 million over seven years) because there were few subscribers. This repudiation of Jordan's creditworthiness shocked policy-makers who had previously ignored the issue and prompted action.[15] Because of its weak credit potential, Jordan was forced to capitulate to an International Monetary Fund (IMF) structural adjustment package that included harsh austerity measures. The subsequent economic reforms eliminated subsidies on basic goods and threatened public sector employment, which constituted about 50 per cent of all employment in the kingdom.

Without avenues of political participation, those affected by the changes were unable to voice their concerns through formal political structures and instead carried their grievances into the streets. After fuel prices increased, a series of riots erupted and shattered the control of martial law. People filled the streets in several southern towns, replicating images from the *intifada* (uprising) in the West Bank by wearing red and white kaffiyas, hurling stones at security forces and blocking streets with burning tires and barrels.[16] For the regime, what was most disconcerting was not the protests themselves, but rather who protested. The southern towns are populated by Jordanian tribes loyal to the Hashemites and serve as the backbone of support for the regime. The fact that traditional regime supporters, and not marginalised opposition figures, were responsible for the riots signaled that change was necessary. Following the riots, King Hussain announced his decision to hold elections and implement democracy. Democratisation thus served as a means for reinforcing ties to the king's traditional constituency of support by providing political space for the frustrations of groups adversely affected by the economic austerity measures.[17]

Following the king's decision, NGOs in Jordan grew substantially.

This included not only the expansion of traditional development NGOs, registered at the Ministry of Social Development (MOSD), but also newer cultural organisations, many of which sought to address sensitive political issues such as human rights, civil liberties, and political freedoms. While the number of local NGOs registered at the MOSD and the Ministry of Culture in the five years prior to the 1989 transition to democracy grew by only 24 per cent (from 391 to 477), the five subsequent years (1989–1994) witnessed a 67 per cent growth rate (from 477 to 796).[18] Although charitable NGOs still dominate the NGO community (see Figure 1), the most substantial growth following political liberalisation in 1989 came from cultural NGOs. From 1989–1994, charitable NGOs grew by a robust 47 per cent, but this pales in comparison to cultural NGOs, which expanded a remarkable 271 per cent (from 42 to 156 organisations) (see Figure 2).

Figure 1. COMPARATIVE GROWTH OF NGOs, 1985–94

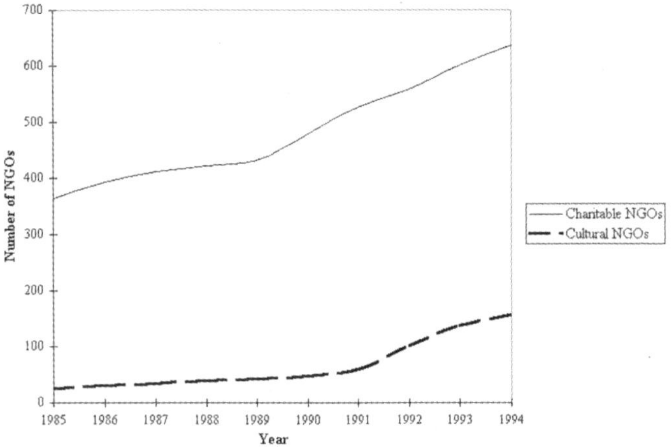

Source: Calculated using information from the Ministry of Culture, 1996, and the General Union of Voluntary Societies, 1996.

Although this reflects a quantitative expansion, any understanding of NGO growth must be informed by the logic of the transition. It was a 'defensive democratisation',[19] driven by the need to maintain stability and social control, not by a benevolent desire for enhanced political participation. Economic reforms were necessary, but carried consequences for stability; and political reforms were seen as a way of placating disaffected groups. Daniel Brumberg refers to this as the 'democratic bargain'–'an arrangement by which democratic reforms are used as a device to obtain economic reform'.[20] The regime in-

Figure 2. GROWTH RATE OF LOCAL NGOs, 1985–94

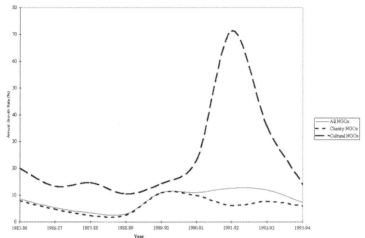

Source: Calculated using information from the Ministry of Culture, 1994; the Ministry of Social Development; and the General Union of Voluntary Societies, 1996.

itiated the transition in the belief that by opening the political system it could prevent widespread opposition to needed economic changes, thereby maintaining stability. As a result, the regime has fostered the aggregate expansion of the NGO community through greater organisational opportunities, but, as the next section explains, it utilises embedded authoritarianism to maintain a relatively quiescent civil society that enhances socioeconomic development without challenging regime power or control.

Limitations to NGOs

While collectivities ostensibly enjoy the freedom to form NGOs since democratisation, the state manipulates the application of the law and administrative practices to guarantee that formal grassroots organisations are not utilised to challenge the state or government policies. In order to organise in civil society, an interested group must meet three primary conditions. First, NGOs must limit their work to a particular set of activities registered by the state and abide by administrative and oversight requirements. This limitation is designed to enhance the state's regulative capacity. Second, voluntary organisations cannot engage in any 'political' activities, as defined by the state. Political activities are channeled into political parties, which to this point have had very little impact on politics and hold little importance

in society. The NGO community, which represents the strongest organisational matrix in society, is thus depoliticised. And third, assertive and critical opposition leadership through NGOs is prohibited.
The state directly interferes with NGO leadership structures to prevent and remove members it deems threatening to state interests. All
of these conditions are enforced through selective regulative practices
and the manipulation of the law, thus creating a less visible system
of repression through embedded authoritarianism.

Conditions for participation. The legal basis for NGOs was established in 1936 with Law 33. Subsequent revisions were made in 1956,
1965 and finally in 1966. The Law of Societies and Social Organisations, Law 33 of 1966, is the current law applied to voluntary organisations in the kingdom.[21] It covers all voluntary societies and
organisations comprised of at least seven individuals who have organised 'to provide social services without any intention of financial
gains or any other personal gains, including political gains.' This includes organisations devoted to charity, culture, science and training,
and sports activities (Article 2).

To form an organisation, a minimum of seven individuals, at least
21 years old, must first draft an internal law that clearly stipulates
the goals, objectives, and activities of the prospective organisation.
The application must include the names, ages, occupations, and addresses of all founding members. It must also describe the conditions
for membership and contributions, the selection process for the administrative committee, how finances are administered and the structure of the general assembly meetings.[22] The minister of social
development, with input from both the governor of the district where
the NGO would be registered and the General Union of Voluntary
Societies (GUVS) approves applications for charitable activities.
There is no cultural union, so the ministry of culture approves cultural societies without any kind of coordination. The respective ministry
has full discretion to reject or accept applications. Most oppositional
groups are rejected at this point and prevented from forming an
NGO. If approved, the internal law of the society serves as a rigid
guideline for permissible activities at the society; and the government
must approve any changes.

NGOs apply to a specific ministry for permission to operate and
their activities are therefore confined to that ministry's purview of
regulation. Thus if an organisation is applying to the ministry of culture, it must demonstrate that its activities will only be in the field of
culture. If applying to the ministry of social development, the organisation must show that it will only engage in charity or socioeconomic

development activities. NGOs are thus channeled into separate bureaucratic units where the respective administrative agency is charged with overseeing a particular category of activities. Organisations registered at one ministry are not permitted to engage in activities that cross into the administrative responsibilities of another state agency. For example, cultural societies cannot cross into other areas of organisational work such as politics or charity. This separation makes it easier for the state to effectively monitor and regulate all NGO work in the kingdom because there is functional differentiation in administrative responsibilities. In practice, these categories are not absolutely discrete and some overlap occurs, especially at charitable organisations, which may provide some cultural activities as well. But this is more an exception to organisational patterns than the rule.

The internal law further narrows the range of activities to a specific subset within the broader field of interest. Within the field of charity, for example, a society might receive permission to open a centre for the disabled, but not to form an orphanage. Or an organisation might receive permission to provide job training for women, but not to offer programmes for the deaf. The state can strike specific activities from the proposed list. For example, the Othman Bin Affan Society, one of the most successful charitable societies in Zarqa, is permitted to provide a variety of services, but is not allowed to engage in marriage-related activities, such as matching prospective marriage partners or providing financial assistance to young couples to lessen the financial burden of a wedding. The ministry official who reviewed the application simply drew a line through that portion of the proposal and then issued a permit.[23] Such discretionary power allows the state to shape the specifics of NGO activity in the kingdom.

Law 33 provides the state with legal standing to regulate the minutia of NGO activities and institutes mechanisms for surveillance that help sustain the administrative divisions and prevent the use of NGOs for oppositional purposes. The most important requirement is that the organisation must maintain a detailed record of all its activities, which is submitted in an annual report to the state. This record includes information on finances, correspondence, board meetings, fixed assets, revenues and disbursements, and working members (Article 15). In addition, the law provides the state with sweeping opportunities to interfere in the affairs of any organisation through inspections: 'the general manager or any employee in the department is entitled to visit any society, committee or union to examine its financial records to ensure that its money is spent in the manner for which it was established according to the law' (Article 14). The law emphasises the surveillance of financial activities to ensure that money is not used for unregistered activities, which are not monitored by the state. Ministry officials also attend elections to the administrative boards and must approve the results (Article 17).[24]

All of these requirements arm the state with the legal basis for dissolution should an organisation wander beyond the confines of the internal law or fail to provide the state with the information that renders oversight possible. Most dissolutions occur because the organisation does not fulfill its specified goals, engages in activities for which it is not registered, fails to meet regularly, or does not provide the administrative agency with relevant records, especially financial records.[25] The most frequent cause of dissolution is prompted by an NGO's failure to provide relevant information and detailed reports—in other words, failure to provide the information necessary for administrative oversight. In 1995, eleven charitable societies were dissolved.[26] In 1996, eighteen were closed. In January 1997 alone, five organisations were canceled by the ministry of social development.[27] The ministry of culture has also suspended numerous cultural organisations. Despite democratisation, the state retains its right to control NGOs and is willing to cancel any organisation that does not comply with the instruments of oversight and regulation.

In many instances, the state stops short of canceling a society and instead reorganises the leadership and organisational structure.[28] If there is a violation of the legal and bureaucratic requirements, the regulating Ministry has the right to dissolve the administrative committee of any society and replace it with a temporary one until new elections are held (Law 33, Article 18). Usually, the dissolution of the administrative committee occurs if there is insufficient attendance at board meetings or if there has been a violation of the internal law. In one case, the ministry of social development removed the administrative board members of the Jericho Society in Amman because there were continual disagreements and disputes among the board members. The ministry reasoned that the society was unable to achieve its goals because of this disarray and dissolved the administrative board. A temporary committee was appointed for six months during which time it went through all of the society's records and assets and reorganised the entire NGO. After the reorganisation, new elections were held and the society continued its work.[29] This demonstrates the discretionary power and leeway the state has to interfere in the internal affairs of NGOs.

Limits to political activities. In its quest to control NGOs and prevent the emergence of an organised opposition through civil society, the state strictly prohibits any transgression into the political sphere. Political activities of any kind are only permitted through political parties, which were formally legalised by The Political Party Law, Law 32 of 1992. This law stipulates that 'The use of the premises, instrumentalities, and assets of associations, charitable organisations and clubs for the benefit of any partisan organisation, shall be prohibited' (Article 14). This separation between NGO activities and politics is also reflected in Law 33 of 1966, which prohibits the use of NGOs for political gain (Article 2). Events, lectures, and activities are regulated so that they maintain an unambiguously apolitical content and work that wanders into the political realm can lead to legal proceedings, closure and imprisonment.

Government officials argue that new political freedoms provide opportunities to organise in politics through political parties and that any political activities should be confined to this space.[30] The productivity and utility of political parties, however, is questionable. In the November 1997 parliamentary elections, for example, not only did the opposition parties boycott, but those who ran for seats did so mostly outside the party system, relying instead on tribal affiliation to mobilise votes and support.[31] In reality, political parties hold little relevance for people, even in politics. In a survey in 1995 by the Center for Strategic Study (CSS) at the University of Jordan, only 50 per cent of those surveyed had even heard of the Islamic Action Front Party, at the time the single largest political party bloc in Parliament. Less than 25 per cent were aware of any other party, and awareness quickly diminished with smaller political parties (see Table 3). This level of awareness is certainly related to the novelty of political parties and their rapid proliferation since the political party law was enacted, but it is also due to the fact that political parties, even the largest ones, have little impact in society.[32] In the most recent survey by CSS in 2000, 98.6 per cent of respondents indicated that they had never joined a political party and 92.6 per cent stated that they had no intention of doing so in the future.[33] Despite the relative insignificance of parties in society, the state only permits political activities through political parties, which are regulated at the Ministry of the Interior. Political content in other venues of organisational work, such as NGOs, is suppressed.

The state utilises embedded authoritarianism to ensure that the integrity of the separation between politics and all other forms of organised work is upheld, and there are numerous examples of state intervention designed to reinforce this division. Since democratisation began, cultural NGOs, in particular, have increasingly felt the weight of state control. Many grassroots organisers in the cultural arena claim that issues such as democracy, human rights and political

freedom are cultural issues. These NGOs therefore attempt to incorporate political themes into organisational activities, only to face
reprisals from the state as it seeks to protect administrative distinctions. In one incident in January 1997, for example, the Kerak Cultural Forum was canceled because of alleged 'political activities' after
a lecture by Layth Shubaylat in which he criticised the government.[34]
Members of the society intended to form another organisation but
the Ministry demanded that they first form a new administrative
committee. The members refused and a new organisation was never
formed.[35]

LEVEL OF AWARENESS OF POLITICAL PARTIES

	% of respondents aware of party
Islamic Action Front Party	42.6
Pledge Party	20.7
Arab Socialist Ba'ath Party	16.8
Communist Party	15.1
People's Democratic Party	9.6
Reawakening Party	8.3
Progressive Democratic Party	7.6
Popular Unity Party	5.6
Arab Ba'ath Progressive Party	5.0
Democratic Socialist Party	5.0

Note: Parties below 5 % awareness level – 13 parties – are not included.
Source: Center for Strategic Studies (1995: 32).

Following the closure of the Karak Cultural Forum, Ahmad al-
Qudah, then minister of culture, issued a directive that banned any
cultural meetings from taking place anywhere in the kingdom without prior approval from the cultural manager in the respective governate. This was generally viewed as a direct reaction to the speech by
Shubaylat and engendered virulent opposition from cultural societies
throughout Jordan. Members of the Jordanian Writers Association
believed the directive was aimed at their society after it hosted a cultural week entitled 'debate of choices,' which focused on the political,
economic, cultural, and creative issues facing the country.[36] Though
the directive was eventually rescinded, other lectures about issues
such as the temporary Press Law, the economy and the peace treaty
were canceled and there is continuous interference in the freedom of
assembly to prevent NGOs from discussing political issues.[37]

In the following September, the subsequent minister of culture, Qa-
sem Abu Ein, sent a directive to cultural societies warning them to refrain from political activities, citing Law 33, which prohibits any
kind of political activity and confines the work of cultural societies to

the realm of 'culture'.[38] There was an ensuing confrontation between the Minister of Culture and the Jordanian Writers Association over the 'political nature' of some of the association's work. The Minister claimed that the association was illegally involved in political activities and that it was hosting illegal organisations (i.e. unregistered political parties). The association president, Fakhri Kawar, responded that 'any cultural activity will one way or another include politics in it' and asserted the association's right to 'conduct political activities because they are part of culture.' The minister even went so far as to charge that the association's meeting to discuss the issue of whether the organisation should be involved in political activities was illegal. He sent a letter of complaint to the minister of the interior stating that the organisation was involved in political work. He sent another letter to the Jordanian Writers Association warning that the ministry would close the organisation if it persisted in any 'political, tribal or sectarian activity'.[39] Regardless of societal opposition to such government actions, the regime utilises legal codes to limit the politicisation of NGOs.

Control of leadership. In addition to these direct tactics, discretionary state power is continuously used to prevent the emergence of leaders in NGOs who could constitute viable threats to the regime's power. In particular, all elections, leaders and members must be cleared by the security apparatus and other state agencies. Although it is not explicitly stated in Law 33, all volunteers as well as administrative board members must first be approved by the 'security department',[40] a euphemism for the *mukhabarat* and public security at the ministry of the interior.[41] These agencies are charged with the responsibility of preventing group work that threatens the security of the state, national unity, or the Hashemite regime. This input in registration decisions represents the veto power and informal involvement of the security apparatus in embedded authoritarianism. Through this power, the state enjoys absolute control over the composition of volunteers in NGO activities and is able to shape and mould the make-up of participants in the voluntary sector. The state uses this power to exclude particular individuals, deemed threatening to the regime, from participating in NGOs.

One Islamic cultural society, for example, was forced to exclude certain individuals from membership because these individuals were considered overly critical of the state and the regime. The *mukhabarat* approached the leaders of the organisation and dictated which individuals to exclude from membership. Without this exclusion, the state would have rejected the application for registration and the society would have been prevented from engaging in activities. At this same society, a member of the administrative committee, who is critical of the Jordanian regime, was brought in by the *mukhabarat* for questioning. His release was conditioned upon his resignation from the administrative board. The *mukhabarat* forced him to remove himself from a position of leadership within the society and only permits him to act as a working member.[42]

The state utilises its prerogatives and embedded authoritarianism to prevent the emergence of leaders within civil society who might use formal organisations to challenge the regime. By controlling administrative board elections, the composition of membership, and the leadership in NGOs, the state prevents real opposition from forming in NGOs. Most importantly, the state does not permit any transgressions into the political realm. It categorises and segregates different aspects of organisational activity to facilitate regulation and augment state power. NGOs have absorbed associational aspirations since 1989, but they are limited by the imperative of state social control.

A transition to democracy does not necessarily mean that a regime has relinquished its right to social control and power. On the contrary, if democratisation is motivated by a 'survival strategy' intended to ensure the political survival of the regime, it is likely that other policies and practices in politics will follow a similar logic. As Mahmood Monshipouri argues, abrupt transitions from authoritarianism to political freedom through 'shock democracy' do not always entail concomitant changes outside the formal political sphere because there is insufficient time to foster the cultural, material and political resources necessary for such changes.[43] Regimes that open political participation to enhance prospects for survival may resort to repressive practices outside the electoral arena to ensure this survival and control. Embedded authoritarianism encapsulates some of these practices.

Embedded authoritarianism points to a subtle process of control that is projected through bureaucratic processes, regulations, and practices. It hides within the complexities and requirements of the law, maintaining an outward appearance of rational legalism while subtly manipulating rules to suit regime interests. In instances where a regime has democratised, yet continues to repress, the form of coercion is more often characterised by embedded authoritarianism than physical repression. This latter form of repression does not end, but it appears most frequently in instances where embedded authoritarianism has failed to provide the necessary social control to uphold regime power. It is used as a supplement when embedded authoritarianism does not work or is an inadequate mechanism of restraint.

The bureaucratic power that circumscribes NGOs in Jordan has not dissipated since King Abdullah's coronation. Despite much optimism about the democratic inclinations of the new king, there has been little movement toward emancipating NGOs and other informal political actors from the constraints of embedded authoritarianism. If anything, NGOs find themselves increasingly under attack in the new millenium. The government's current draft on an amendment to the law governing charitable organisations, for example, proposes strengthening administrative oversight of NGO finances and the ability of the ministry of social development to change organisational leaderships.[44] Other attacks are currently percolating in parliament, where Ghazi Obeidat, chairman of the Lower House Public Freedoms and Citizens' Rights Committee, has called for an investigation into NGOs that receive foreign funding, claiming that 'it is against the law for Jordanian organisations to have links to foreign parties and receive funds from them because nobody gives you anything without wanting something in return'.[45] Others have gone even further, charging NGOs that receive foreign funding with treason. The Jordanian Bar Association, for example, recently stated: 'We've noticed a spread in centres that work under different names and goals of human rights, women and information centres . . . It is proved that those centres receive funding from foreign embassies . . . which is considered an interference in the country's affairs and a threat to its political and social security.'[46] Since a substantial number of NGOs in Jordan receive funding from international donors such as the United State Agency for International Development (USAID), the Friedrich Naumann Foundation, the European Union and the International Management and Training Institute, this may render NGOs vulnerable to an even stronger application of embedded authoritarian practices.

In the end, embedded authoritarianism and its continued application to NGOs in Jordan are about power and how to maintain that power. At times such control may mesh with traditional physical repression while at others it may become an accepted limit for associational life, a structure of limitations embedded into the collective subconscious of society without question. It is the latter condition that is most dangerous since it leads to an unquestioning acceptance of the conditions of power and control that structure politics. The hope created by the 1989 transition has been disappointed, sacrificed by the regime to perpetuate its own power and stability. The face of repression has changed, but limitations persist. To realise real political freedom and democracy in Jordan embedded authoritarianism must be recognised and dismantled.

NOTES

1. Funding for this project was provided by the American Center for Oriental Research and the Jordanian-American Binational Fulbright Commission. Some material in this paper first appeared in Quintan Wiktorowicz, 'The limits of democracy in the Middle East: the case of Jordan', *Middle East Journal*, 53, 4 (autumn 1999), pp. 606–20; and idem, 'Civil society as social control: state power in Jordan', *Comparative Politics*, October 2000.

2. Q. Wiktorowicz, 'The limits of democracy in the Middle East: the case of Jordan', *Middle East Journal*, 53, 4 (autumn 1999), 606–20.

3. It should be noted that such systems are qualitatively different from the bureaucratic-authoritarian regimes of Latin America that emerged in the 1970s and 1980s. I share Dominguez's narrow definition of bureaucratic-authoritarianism, which 'emphasises their use of state violence against regime enemies, the coalition of the military and certain upper class and middle-class groups, the important role of corporate military rule, and the excluding and demobilising features of the regime' (J. I. Dominguez, 'Political change: Central America, South America, and the Caribbean' in Myron Weiner and Samuel P. Huntington (eds), *Understanding political development*, 1987, p. 73. In contrast, embedded authoritarianism is a technique used to project authoritarian practices within the context of democratic elections and enhanced political freedom. In addition, embedded authoritarianism places more emphasis on the use of the bureaucracy than the military or instruments of violence (though these are still used to some degree). For more on bureaucratic-authoritarianism, see G. O'Donnell, *Modernisation and bureaucratic authoritarianism: studies in South American politics*, Politics of Modernisation series, no. 9. Berkeley: Institute of International Studies, University of California, 1973, and D. Collier (ed.), *The new authoritarianism in Latin America*, Princeton University Press, 1979.

4. S. K. Farsoun, and L. P. Fort, 'The problematics of civil society: intellectual discourse and Arab intellectuals', unpublished paper, 1992, p. 42.

5. S. E. Finer (1970, *Comparative Government*. London: Pelican; M. Bennoune, 'Algeria's façade democracy', *Middle East Report* (March–April 1990); B. Milton-Edwards, 'Façade democracy and Jordan', *British Journal of Middle East Studies* 20, 2 (1993), 191–203.

6. This is not to argue that physical coercion, torture, and the techniques of the *mukhabarat* do not exist in Jordan, only that the balance of social control mechanisms has shifted away from these forms of repression to more subtle bureaucratic instruments, many of which existed during the martial law period. Physical coercion, such as the repression of demonstrators or torture, most often emerges in instances where embedded authoritarianism fails, as the regime fumbles to regain social control.

7. For the relationship between NGOs and political change, see J. Clark, (1991), *Democratising development: the role of voluntary organisations*, London: Earthscan, 1991; B. Loveman, 'NGOs and the transition to democracy in Chile.' *Grassroots Development* 15, 2 (1991): 8–19; N. Chazan, 'Africa's democratic challenge: strengthening civil society and the state.' *World Policy Journal 9*, 2 (spring 1992), 279–307; G. White, 'Civil society, democratisation and development: (I) clearing the analytical ground' (1991), *Democratisation*, 1, 3 (autumn 1994); and M. Edwards and D. Hulme (eds), *Too close for comfort? NGOs, states and donors*, London: Macmillan, 1996.

8. R. D. Putnam, *Making democracy work: civic traditions in modern Italy*, Princeton University Press, 1993.

9. L. A. Brand, 'Economic and political liberalisation in a rentier economy: the case of the Hashemite Kingdom of Jordan' in I. Harik and D. J. Sullivan (eds), *Privatisation and liberalisation in the Middle East*, Bloomington: Indiana University Press, 1992; R. Brynen, 'Economic crisis and post-rentier democratisation in the Arab World: the case of Jordan', *Canadian Journal of Political Science*, 25, 1 (March 1992), pp. 69–97, and 'The politics of monarchical liberalism: Jordan' in B. Korany, R. Brynen and P. Noble (eds), *Political liberalisation and democratisation in the Arab World*, vol. 2: comparative experiences, Boulder, CO: Lynne Rienner, 1998, and K. Rath, 'The process of democratisation in Jordan', *Middle Eastern Studies*, 30, 3 (July 1994): pp. 530–57.

10. G. Luciani, 'Allocation v. production states: a theoretical framework' in H. Bablawi and G. Luciani (eds), *The rentier state*, London: Croom Helm, 1987; G. Luciani, 'Economic foundations of democracy and authoritarianism: the Arab world in comparative perspective', *Arab Studies Quarterly* 10, 4 (autumn 1988); G. Luciani, 'The oil rent, the fiscal crisis of the state and democratisation' in G. Salamé (ed.), *Democracy without Democrats? The Renewal of Politics in the Muslim World*, London: I. B. Tauris, 1994.

11. Luciani (1988), op. cit., p. 463

12. Brynen (1992), op. cit., p. 75

13. S. K. Farsoun, 'Class Structure and Social Change in the Arab World: 1995' in H. Sharabi (ed.), *The next Arab decade: alternative futures*, Boulder, CO: Westview Press, 1988, p. 231

14. D. Singerman, *Avenues of participation: family, politics and networks in urban quarters of Cairo*, Princeton University Press, 1995, p. 245.

15. R. B. Satloff, 'Jordan's great gamble: economic crisis and political reform' in H. Barkey (ed.), *The politics of economic reform in the Middle East*, New York: St. Martin's Press, 1992, pp. 134–7.

16. L. Andoni, 'Jordan' in R. Brynen (ed.), *Echoes of Intifada: regional repercussions of the Palestinian-Israeli conflict*, Boulder, CO: Westview Press, 1991, p. 178.

17. Satloff, op. cit. and M. Mufti, 'Elite bargains and the onset of political liberalisation in Jordan', *Comparative Political Studies* 32, 1 (February 1999), pp. 100–29.

18. Ministry of Culture, *Annual report*, Amman: Hashemite Kingdom of Jordan; Ministry of Social Development, 1995.

19. G. Robinson, 'Defensive democratisation in Jordan', *International Journal of Middle East Studies*, 30 (1998), 387–410.

20. D. Brumberg, 'Authoritarian legacies and reform strategies in the Arab world.' in Brynen, Korany and Noble (eds), *Political liberalisation and democratisation in the Arab world*, vol. 1: *Theoretical perspectives*, Boulder, CO: Lynne Rienner, 1995, 230.

21. Law 33 is similar to laws governing voluntary work in other Arab countries as well. For a discussion of the parallel Egyptian law, see S. E. Ibrahim, 'Egyptian Law 32 of 1964 on Egypt's PVOs and Pfs: a critical assessment', unpublished study, 1993; D. J. Sullivan, *Private voluntary organisations in Egypt: Islamic development, private initiative, and state control*, Gainesville: University of Florida Press, 1994, 17–18; M. Zaki, *Civil society and democratisation in Egypt, 1981–1994*. Cairo: Konrad Adenauer Foundation, 56–7, 61–2; and A. Kandil, *Civil society in the Arab world: private voluntary organisations*, Washington, DC: Civicus, 1995.

22. The state requires that all members of the administrative board are elected democratically. This is an important point for scholars who argue that democratic indicators may be found in grassroots organisations. It is an imposed democracy,

not a selection process that is freely chosen. This is not to say that organisational activists would not otherwise invoke democratic principles in the selection process, but that it is impossible to argue that it is an indication of the potential for democratic consolidation in Jordan.

23. President of the Othman Bin Affan Society, interview with author, 18 March 1997.
24. A GUVS official confirmed that this is enforced in practice.
25. GUVS official, interview by author, 28 October 1996; Administrative Committee for the Union of Voluntary Societies, Amman Governate, 1996.
26. General Union of Voluntary Societies (GUVS), *Executive Council Report*, Amman, 1996, 39.
27. Mahmoud Kafawee, Director of Charitable Organisations at the Ministry of Social Development, interview by author, 28 March 1997.
28. The state also routinely issues warnings to organisations.
29. Hashem Azzan, interview by author, 17 February 1997. Azzan was a member of the appointed temporary committee.
30. Director of Cultural Exchange, ministry of culture, interview by author, 8 October 1996; Director of Charitable Organisations, Ministry of Social Development, interview by author, 28 March 1997.
31. For more on the role of tribes in Jordanian politics and elections, see L. L. Layne, *Home and homeland: the dialogics of tribal and national identities in Jordan*, Princeton University Press, 1994, chapter 5. Details about the role of tribes in the 1997 parliamentary elections can be found in numerous articles in the *Jordan Times*, *al-Ra'y*, and *al-Destour* around the time of the elections.
32. There are currently twenty registered political parties.
33. *The Star*, 8 June 2000
34. Shubaylat is considered one of the most radical opposition figures in the country. He considers himself an opposition figure first and an Islamist second (Layth Shubaylat, interview by author, 13 March 1997). He was also the president of the Engineers' Association. He has directly criticised the King and the royal family in various speeches, for which he has served time in jail at numerous points. Members of the Islamic movement have mixed views of Shubaylat. Some view him as an inspiration, while others describe him as an egomaniac.
35. Women's movement activist who presented a lecture at the society just prior to its cancellation, interview by author, 20 March 1997.
36. *The Star*, 23 January 1997.
37. Human Rights Watch, 1997.
38. Ibid., pp. 31–3.
39. *Jordan Times*, 20 September 1997.
40. A. El Khatib, 'The experience of NGOs in Jordan (a brief description)', paper presented at the Experts Meeting on Strategies for Strengthening NGO Networking and Research in the Middle East, Arab Thought Forum, Amman, 26 March 1994, pp. 20–1)
41. In all registration decisions, the governor of the district where the organisation would operate is consulted. Islamists and other social movement actors claim that the governor acts on behalf of the *mukhabarat*.
42. During my research I interviewed ten members of this society. These sources will remain anonymous for their safety.
43. M. Monshipouri, *Democratisation, liberalisation and human rights in the Third World*. Boulder, CO: Lynne Rienner, 1995.
44. *Jordan Times*, 2 June 2000.
45. Ibid., 12 June 2000.
46. Ibid., 9 June 2000.

THE WEAKNESS OF THE RULED IS THE STRENGTH OF THE RULER

THE ROLE OF THE OPPOSITION IN CONTEMPORARY JORDAN

Renate Dieterich

'Democracy does not mean you can read or say anything.' (Mahmoud Sharif, Jordanian Minister of Information, 1993)

The functioning of a democratic system is clearly bound to the existence of an opposition. By definition, the opposition questions the policies of the government in a bid to alter its political course or even to seize power. The interaction between the ruling majority and such an opposition is vital for a healthy democracy and the way the opposition is treated by the ruling majority may serve as a 'litmus test' for democracies. Systems which oppress important opposition groups, as did, for example, the 'popular democracies' in the former East Bloc, can only be considered 'façade democracies'.[1]

The analysis of opposition movements in democratising states is therefore helpful for an overall assessment of the whole process of transition from authoritarian to more democratic forms of rule. These transitions need the firm support of the people both in an organised way and as spontaneous mass participation. Many democratising states have witnessed strong popular support during times of upheaval, with huge mass demonstrations involving different sectors of civil society. This participation of the ruled in the process of change leads to a situation where the regime has no choice but to break resistance with brute force or to concede – at least partially. But once an authoritarian regime has yielded, the commitment of civil society towards real change and the inclusion of the opposition in the transitional process becomes more crucial than ever. A powerful opposition, committed to reform and non-violent change and able to gather important political groups outside the former regime is central for a successful transition.

In 1989 Jordan started a domestic political process that has become known as 'democratisation' or 'political liberalisation'. It is evident that important changes on the domestic scene have taken place since then. However, more than ten years later, an evaluation of the democratic transition also reveals severe shortcomings in democratic development. While far-reaching reforms characterised the early years, setbacks have diminished or even reversed some of the consequent democratic freedoms since the mid-1990s. It will be argued here that these setbacks were not only created by the regime – the monarchy and its security apparatus, the economic elites and tribal forces who together have ruled Jordan for decades – but may also be attributed to the weak status of Jordan's political opposition. In order to illustrate this point, a brief discussion to the Jordanian manner of dealing with political opposition in the early days of the emirate is necessary.

Political opposition in Jordan in historical perspective

Though the roots of the modern nation-state in what was later to become the Emirate of Transjordan date back into the nineteenth century,[2] opinion groups and political opposition against the new central power did not emerge before the 1920s when the Emir 'Abdullah started to build up the Emirate with the help of the British. During this early period in the Emirate, opposition came mainly from Arab Nationalists and from the Bedouin tribes.

Amman, as the new capital of the state, became the centre of political action in the 1920s. Syrian Nationalists, many of them adherents of the *Hizb al-Istiqlal* (Independence Party) who had fled Syria after the fall of the Faisal government, gathered in Amman where both the British mandate force and the Royal Court were located. They were to be of special importance for the effective operation of the embryonic state apparatus. In the beginning, the *Istiqlalis* sided with Abdullah because they hoped that he would support their ideas of a Greater Syria but when they realised that Abdullah was used by the British as a tool to fulfil the mandatory power's aspirations in the region, they became his opponents and were subsequently expelled.[3] Subsequent governments were then mainly composed of migrants from neighbouring Palestine. They owed their economic and political influence as much to the mandatory power as to the Emir and were therefore loyal to the rulers of the country.

The Bedouins, who were the other important social group in the country, feared a loss of power which would inevitably be the consequence of the establishment of a central power in Transjordan and British military aid was necessary to put down several tribal rebellions during the early years of the Emirate. Abdullah soon realised that his reign would be much more secure if he included elements of the tribal opposition in his administration and in the armed forces, while the Bedouin *sheikhs* on their part became aware of the benefits of participation in the new state apparatus.[4]

Eventually, by the end of the 1920s, Abdullah had succeeded – though only with strong British support – in neutralising opponents and in consolidating Hashemite rule in Transjordan. The nucleus of a 'Transjordan for the Transjordanians' movement loyal to the Hashemites emerged during these years and was significant throughout the 1920s and 1930s.[5] There was no social group, however, which would have had the power to challenge the new system of rule and a new political and economic elite in the country was still to emerge. The political game of co-opting the more moderate elements among his political opponents instead of radicalising them through suppression – which Abdullah played so well – was to become one of the central features of Jordanian politics until the present day. Except for some historical writings which are mainly descriptive in content, not much research has been undertaken on Jordanian politics in the 1930s and 1940s[6] but the available evidence suggests that the Hashemite reign was stabilised without major challenges and that political activists who would have been able to question the Transjordanian regime's policies and actions were preoccupied with the events in neighbouring Palestine.

In contrast, the 1950s and the first years of King Hussain's reign were characterised by domestic unrest. Cautious experiments with gradual democratic freedoms were hastily stopped when mass demonstrations, Egyptian propaganda and the activities of the leftist and nationalist movements seemed to endanger the Hashemite throne. King Hussain did not hesitate to curb the basic constitutional rights of his subjects by imposing martial law and dissolving all political parties in 1957. Many political activists were imprisoned or exiled, but the pattern of co-option established by his grandfather was carried on by the young king so that prominent figures from the ranks of the opposition were included in the cabinet or the administration of the country in subsequent years. Until the end of the 1960s, the domestic situation in Jordan was relatively calm and the former organised opposition was silenced. The only major exception was the Jordanian-Palestinian military confrontation in 1970 and 1971, the 'Black September' episode.

The 1970s were characterised by the economic boom, which enabled the state apparatus to expand its services and to supply its citizens with numerous benefits. The growing number of working migrants in rich oil states, mainly in the Gulf, reduced the potential for domestic political opposition. With political parties still outlawed, the only outlet for discontent were the professional associations

which maintained their democratic structures during this period and
thus became the main forum for the opposition. This highly politicised role of the associations has been maintained up to the present
day.

The economic boom years ended in the 1980s and with Jordan's deteriorating economic situation, the articulation of political dissatisfaction became louder again. Important segments of Jordan's
growing middle class now called for democratic reforms and an end
to the authoritarian style of government. The numerous statements
made by the professional syndicates or by women organisations and
cultural associations demonstrate the depth of these demands.[7] The
intransigent position of Prime Minister Zayed Rifai and his cabinet at
the end of the 1980s[8] exacerbated the domestic tensions that already
existed, which finally culminated in the spring of 1989.[9] However,
what broke the ground for the democratic opening was a spontaneous
popular upheaval and not the success of the opposition.

The April 1989 riots and after

The impoverished part of the population which was hit hard by the
IMF inspired economic 'reform programme' protested against a rise
in prices of several basic commodities but also demanded more democratic rights.[10] The riots persuaded the regime to engage in a significant liberalisation of the authoritarian political system and these new
developments allowed Jordan's opposition forces to participate in
the political process in a way unknown for most of the period since
the independence of the state. They also offered the Jordanian people
an option for political participation, which could have resulted in a
substantial change in domestic politics.

By the 1990s, the opposition could be categorised in four groups,
namely the Islamists (independents and organised), leftists, nationalists and a handful of well-known and reputable individuals without
any group affiliation. These forces, which can be generally identified
by their ideological orientations except for the individuals involved in
opposition, are supported by elements of Jordan's civil society, especially the professional associations and to a lesser extent, women's
and cultural organisations and student councils. The Palestinian factor, which is so dominant in Jordanian society, is not reflected in the
structure of the opposition. This is partly due to the legal framework
which prohibits political groupings with organisational or financial
links across international borders with any non-Jordanian group. It
is also partly due to the legacy of the military confrontation between
East-Bankers and the Palestinian *fedayin* in the 1970s. Palestinians

who do not explicitly refer to their national background, however, can be found in all political movements in Jordan.

Though the importance of pressure from below for the democratic development that took place in 1989 must be taken into consideration, the process was mainly a top-down liberalisation in which the governing elites tried to defend their position without a substantial loss of power. Behind the scenes, a battle between hard-liners and reformers took place.[11] The old forces within the powerful security apparatus still had a strong grip on the political scene, a phenomenon which is counter-productive to any democratic transition. All the attempts to liberalise the political system were done with care in order to avoid an erosion of the bases of the Hashemite rule in Jordan. To keep the fragile balance of granting more freedom but refusing real power sharing now became the most difficult task for the old ruling elites.

The legal framework and the National Charter. Jordan is a constitutional monarchy with an elected parliament but the king and the cabinet, which is appointed by royal decree, dispose of a significant influence on the decision-making process which is guaranteed by the constitution. The potential for popular participation was, therefore, limited from the beginning of the 'new democratic era'. To allow a greater amount of freedom without endangering the core interests of the ruling group, a new legal framework for the liberalisation process was shaped through three important documents, the National charter, the Political Parties Law, and the Press and Publications Law.

National pacts have proven to be a successful tool for democratic transitions in various countries.[12] In some cases, the bargain between the ruling group and opposition forces has led to a fruitful outcome of the confrontation between ruling authoritarian circles and the opposition, in terms of more democratic freedom and the introduction of different political forces into the decision-making process. In fact, in some cases fierce opponents of the ruling group were invited to participate in developing such pacts in order to co-opt and pacify them. From this point of view, the Jordanian National Charter[13] is probably the most important document of the democratic initiative and reflects a liberal approach to the issue. However, its effects on Jordanian society have, at the least, been ambiguous.

A commission, including many members of the opposition, was appointed by the Royal Court to work out the Charter. Proposals to draft it as an annex to the constitution were made and demands to submit the draft to a national referendum were heard. But eventually, the population was excluded from the whole process of drafting and approving the Charter. Instead, it was ratified in June 1991 by a 2,000-member National Congress appointed by the Royal Court. Both the formulation and the acceptance of the document were transferred to non-representative bodies created by the old regime while the representatives of the people, elected through free and democratic voting procedures, only played a very marginal role as members of the National Congress. Even more disappointing from the standpoint of democratic freedoms was the fact that the Charter did not acquire any official status but was designed merely as a declaration of goodwill without any legally binding function. The chairman of the commission, Ahmad Obeidat, later remarked:

If it (the Charter) were being put in the form of legislation, used by the legislative and the executive authority, it would have the validity of the constitution. Without this, the Charter would only remain ink on paper.[14]

The statements about pluralism and democracy in chapter 1 and 2 of the Charter, beginning with a reaffirmation of the legitimacy of the Hashemite monarchy, were to be most important for future political life in Jordan.[15] The Charter paved the way for the opposition to organise itself in political parties and defined the limits on freedom of expression and of the media. But at the same time, it was an instrument designed to co-opt the opposition and to bind it to the ruling elites. Despite the noble ideas embodied in the Charter, its inherent promise of more democracy cannot be realised because the document is not legally binding and the constitutional court, long demanded by parts of the opposition, still does not exist. Furthermore, because of the opposition's participation in drafting the Charter, it was now bound to adhere to it. Thus the Charter will be an important point of reference for the regime whenever it wishes to curtail the opposition in the coming years, instead of accelerating the democratic transition. King Hussain's warning to his critics in 1995 may serve as only one amongst many:

My eagerness to maintain the democratisation process, political pluralism and respect for human rights is unlimited. However, each individual should know what those rights mean. Everyone should know he has responsibilities that he must bear [. . .]. All these responsibilities are based on the National Charter.[16]

The Political Parties Law, promulgated in 1992, enabled the organised opposition to legalise its structures, but also contained specific conditions which allowed the regime to control them. Today, nearly all trends are represented on the Jordanian party scene in a spectrum from the Communists to several Ba'athist groupings and even to parties with doctrines linked to Islam. Though there were eventually more than twenty political parties, nearly all of them failed to secure broad support from the Jordanian public.[17] In general, the influence of political parties – whether from the opposition or from loyalist groups – has been marginal, with the notable exception of the Islamic Action Front (see below).

The new Press and Publications Law, promulgated in 1993, lead to the emergence of a broad press scene with dozens of weeklies and tabloids of different trends. Though the law totally excluded certain sensitive issues from public discussion, such as the role of the armed forces and the security apparatus or the monarchy itself, the new democratic spirit was reflected in the spread of issues which had been taboo before and were now tackled by the press. After 1994, the weeklies became a central tool for the opposition in its fight against the politics of normalisation with Israel. The press in consequence became more and more a target of criticism and threats from the regime. In 1995, the prime minister, Zaid Ben Shaker, sharply warned the press, during a visit to the Jordan Press Foundation which publishes the semi-official Arabic and English dailies *al-Ra'y* and *Jordan Times*:

The government does not mind criticism or hearing the views of the opposition, but it can by no means tolerate any harm to the country and its achievements. [...] The government will always ... accept constructive criticism aimed at safeguarding national interest and achievements realised over the past four decades. [...] Any denial of these achievements is tantamount to treason. We would hold account [*sic*] those people who do harm to the country and its achievements.[18]

Ongoing tensions between the government and the press since 1995 reached a climax in 1997, when the government under the leadership of Abd al-Salam al-Majali imposed a new Press Law during a period when parliament was in recess. Under the new law, the freedom of the media was drastically curtailed.[19]

Electoral participation. Though the parliament as the legislative power is the weakest of the three powers within the state, the prime minister still needs its vote of confidence for his appointment. All draft laws have to pass the lower and the upper houses before they come into force and the old elites, therefore, have good reason to fear a parliament dominated by the opposition. During the 1989 parliamentary elections, which were generally considered to have been free and democratic, opposition candidates (Islamists, Leftists and Nationalists) were able to secure nearly half of the seats in parliament, while conservative loyalists and tribal figures had a difficult time gaining seats. The subsequent parliament, which sat from 1989 to 1993, dared to discuss topics as sensitive as corruption in the highest offices of state and was the most outspoken and critical parliament Jordan has known. In order to reduce the opposition's – mainly Islamist – influence, the election law was changed in 1993, a decision which set in motion a rollback of the whole democratic process.[20] This change in the electoral law which was initiated by the king and enforced by royal decree without the approval of the parliament which had been dissolved shortly before, was rejected by all opposition forces but could not be challenged by legal means because it did not contradict the constitution. Though the Islamists initially called for a boycott of the November 1993 elections, they later changed their minds and participated in them despite their disapproval of the new law.

The elections in 1993 and particularly in 1997 were much less democratic than the 1989 campaign had been and the presence of the opposition in parliament was substantially reduced. Only 26 of the deputies in the 1993–7 parliament could have been considered as members of the opposition. This setback in the representation of opposition culminated in the 1997 parliamentary elections.[21] While Communists, Ba'athists and the Leftist Jordanian Unionist Democratic Party fielded candidates, the Islamists and seven smaller parties boycotted the elections and thus deprived themselves of a possible participation in the decision-making process. The boycott was first of all meant to protest against the 1993 Election Law which was seen as favouring independent and tribal candidates over ideologically committed and party affiliated activists. But it was also directed against the general decline in public freedoms since 1994, as well as the Jordanian-Israeli peace treaty and the subsequent policy of normalisation. These have been, in fact, the main topics of opposition interest since the mid-1990s to which it has devoted itself uncompromisingly.

A heterogeneous 'boycott front' consisting of the eight parties, the professional associations and several independent personalities published a National Salvation Programme in which they offered a solution for Jordan's ongoing political and economic crisis.[22] Yet, even on this occasion, when unity was vital, the opposition did not appear united but was split into several factions. It was an experience which demonstrated very well the fragmentation and disorganisation of the Jordanian opposition. Their political fight – resembling more and more a battle by Don Quixote – has led neither to an abrogation of the much-discussed Election Law nor to withdrawal from the peace treaty with Israel nor, indeed, to a noticeable extension of democratic freedoms. In that respect, the Jordanian opposition has completely failed.

The Islamist decision to boycott the elections did not lead to a decisive loss of influence for them because they derive their position in Jordanian society not only from their purely political activities but also from their widespread social services. The smaller parties, which were already of minor importance, emerged from the boycott more marginalised than before, however. For them, the decision to restrain from participating in the elections was definitely counterproductive.

National democratic discourse and national dialogue

Limits on public freedom and democratic rights are defined by the regime and the relevant documents and institutions such as the constitution, the National Charter or relevant laws. The intransigent position of the regime towards opposition claims is mirrored in what will be called here the national democratic discourse and which creates the framework for all political action. The central features of this 'national democratic discourse' can be discovered by analysing important documents of the 'democratic transition', such as the National Charter or various speeches by prime ministers or from the king himself.

Only a minor part of the formal political discussion is actually carried out in parliament, while the Jordanian regime uses different channels to communicate with the opposition. This is euphemistically called the 'national dialogue'. The king and his prime ministers, as well as other leading members of the cabinet, meet regularly with representatives of influential organisations, especially from the professional associations, the ranks of the Islamists and tribal circles. Even an occasional glance at Jordan's newspapers reveals the frequency with which such informal meetings are held. The court and the government use these meetings as an important access to the public mood and a means by which to judge the levels of public discontent. During these meetings the various factions make their demands and formulate their criticisms. They are as well an important opportunity for the regime to co-opt those who are willing to restrict or even abandon their criticism in exchange for influential and lucrative posts in government and administration.

An analysis of the numerous speeches made by the late King Hussain, his heads of government and various ministers reveals certain features that are central to any understanding of the regime's perception of democracy. Central terms which reoccur regularly are 'national unity', 'the united [Jordanian] family', 'higher national interest', 'responsible freedom', 'responsible discussion' and 'national guidance'. None of these terms is clearly defined but all of them are used whenever the regime tries to silence the opposition. The Jordanian citizen is accorded numerous rights guaranteed by the constitution and the various laws, but before he can exploit these rights, he has to fulfil his duties towards the state. Democratic freedoms are granted only for those who use them in a 'responsible way', because 'democratic society is a society of free, but responsible discussion'.[23]

The media has a special role in this 'responsible discussion'. Again and again the representatives of the press have been warned not to cross certain 'red lines' introduced by the regime: 'Under democracy, the national responsibility of the media [. . .] increases. [. . .] The media should be guided by the supreme national interest', King Hussain commented as early as 1991.[24] And in 1995, he turned on the opponents of the peace treaty whilst addressing high ranking army officers: 'Democracy does not mean crossing red lines in order to undermine national unity here and destroy everything of value in this country,' he said.[25] Using threatening tones, he warned the opposition to refrain from its criticism:

Democracy does not mean anarchy or transgressing the country's law and order . . . nor does it mean harming national unity, denigrating every accomplishment, and assassinating the good reputation of our country and its people . . . We will continue to observe these phenomena which fight democracy in the name of democracy and we shall confront them in an appropriate manner, according to the constitution and the law.[26]

Freedom of expression – either in the press or anywhere else – discovers its limits when central decisions of the regime are threatened. These limits even legitimise censorship:

Censorship exists in all democratic states . . . censorship existed in Jordan and will continue to exist under democracy because it is the government's responsibility to protect the people's morals. (. . .) Publications that are confiscated are those which violate the press and publications law. (. . .) democracy does not mean you can read or say anything.[27]

This concept of 'responsible freedom' and the inviolable 'higher national interest' did not vanish with the death of King Hussain but has been passed on to the new King Abdullah II who tells his subjects:

It is not anybody's right or that of any side whoever it may be, to monopolise the claim for truth or that of the higher national interest, or to exploit the climate of freedom, democracy or tolerance or to abuse the laws in this country, or its traditions and noble values, or to harm its image and bright reputation.[28]

The regime views itself in the role of an authority for national gui-dance, responsible for the observance of the self-defined rules of the democratic game. Those who try to cross these invisible 'red-lines' will be ostracised immediately. Freedom of expression and freedom in the media are thus restricted in many respects. The blurred con-cepts of national unity, *al-wahda al-wataniya*, and the 'higher na-tional interest', *al-maslaha al-wataniya al-'uliya,* define the boundaries of democratic freedom. While freedom of expression, pluralism, mutual respect between political actors, peaceful political competition and respect for human rights are central elements of the 'national democratic discourse', the boundaries of freedom of expres-sion are quickly reached when the 'higher national interest' is touched. While the regime allows a plurality of opinions, no construc-tive pluralism where the opinion of the other would be taken into con-sideration before vital decisions are made is permitted. The 'higher national interest' is always endangered when the monarchy, the struc-ture of the regime or important decisions such as the peace process are questioned. Criticism in these fields is deemed as damaging the nation and is therefore unacceptable.

Important laws, which have been promulgated since 1989, such as the Political Parties Law and the Press and Publications Law, have also been subordinated to the regime's definition of democracy. Am-biguous and vague formulations in both laws open ways for the re-gime to intervene in political life at its will. As representatives of the people in parliament, most of the opposition forces have taken part in the process of drafting and discussing these laws, but because of their minority position in the Lower House, they have not been able to sub-stantially change their content. Thus, the rules of the 'democratic game', as defined by the regime, are the only valid ones and they squeeze the Jordanian opposition into a rigid system of restrictions.

The Islamist opposition

By far the most important and influential political group outside the ruling elite is the moderate Islamist opposition; namely, the Muslim Brotherhood (*jama' a al-ikhwan al-muslimin*) and its political wing, the IAF – Islamic Action Front (*hizb jabha al-'amal al-islami*). In general, Jordanian politicians who refer to Islam can rely on a broad constituency and in this the Jordanian example does not differ from other Islamic states in the region. The Jordanian Muslim Brother-hood, the main Islamist force in the country, has always proven to be loyal to the Hashemite dynasty. Nevertheless, the results of the No-vember 1989 parliamentary elections where more than one third of

the newly elected deputies were either members of the Muslim Brotherhood or claimed to be independent Islamists[29] came as a surprise
for political analysts as much as for King Hussain himself.[30] Though
this strong Islamist representation was reduced by the 1993 elections
and even more so in 1997 when the Islamists boycotted the elections,
the importance of the Brotherhood's ideology for the Jordanian public cannot be underestimated. In 1999, the IAF decided to return to
the official political arena and participated with success in the municipal elections.

Both the election programmes of the Muslim Brothers in 1989
and of the IAF in 1993 called for public freedoms, press freedom and
human rights, but they clearly drew a red line when it came to issues
which might contradict 'Islamic values'. They asked for special committees which were to enforce the observance of the 'pureness' of the
media or school and university textbooks; a proposal that cannot be
seen as anything else but Islamic censorship. Indeed, the term 'freedom' as perceived by the Brotherhood is always a 'responsible freedom' which does not cross certain 'red lines'. In that the Islamists and
the regime clearly agree. These 'red lines' are defined by the Islamists
themselves for they alone want to hold the monopoly of 'true Islam'.
Thus, their interpretation of democracy and civil rights is thrown
open to question. Their way of dealing with critics was clearly revealed during the 1989 election campaign, when their position on women's rights was sharply criticised by the female candidate for a
parliamentary seat, Toujan Faisal. For this she was attacked by some
Islamist forces outside the *Ikhwan* who wanted her to be designated
an apostate. The Brotherhood officially pretended to be neutral in the
affair, but commented:

We declare that freedom of expression should be dealt with honestly and
within the framework of decency and high morality. It is unacceptable in
terms of either logic or reason for writers – male or female – to exploit the
right to freedom of expression to pour their outrage over religious people and
the Islamists.[31]

The Jordanian Muslim Brotherhood and the IAF have both been
sharp critics of various Jordanian governments but they have never
challenged the legitimacy of Hashemite rule. On the contrary, they
know quite well that their very existence is closely connected to the
monarchy's goodwill and would be threatened once they started to attack the king. They are even willing to participate in the government,
as they proved in 1991 in the cabinet of Mudar Badran.

Splits in the ranks of the Islamists began in the early 1990s but were
sharpened after the Jordanian-Israeli peace treaty when the question

of a possible participation in future governments became one of the major concerns of the IAF. While the hard-liners rejected any form of cooperation with a government that dealt with the 'Zionist enemy', in the wake of the 1994 peace treaty, other Islamists opted for a more pragmatic stand and welcomed the idea of participation. While the problem has not been finally solved, the pragmatism of the *ikhwan* has played an ever-increasing role in their actual political behaviour.

This can, for example, be seen in their participation in the municipal elections in 1999. Despite the fact that they were hampered by the government in the 1995 municipal elections, through vote rigging and interference which prompted the IAF to withdraw some of their candidates on the election day, they decided to participate in the 1999 municipal elections. These elections turned out to be a major success for the IAF which was able to gain seats in the cities of Irbid, Ruseifa, Zarqa, Madaba and Amman, in addition to winning the post of the mayor in Irbid.[32] This successful participation may even be a signal for a possible Islamist participation in the 2001 parliamentary elections. The Brotherhood now seems more determined than ever to keep its good relations with the regime and to stabilise the ruling order, even at the expense of abandoning its core political positions.

The professional associations and their political fight

The professional associations in Jordan provide a forum for the technocratic elite of the country and had been substitutes for political parties in the martial law era. The most influential ones are the associations for engineers, medical professionals and the bar. Whilst the associations have always seen their main responsibilities being directed their to respective professions, they also take clear standpoints on domestic and international issues. Throughout the 1980s they called for democratic reforms and public freedoms and the internal elections of the associations are considered to have been run on democratic principles. The political activities of the associations were tolerated by the regime because it sent out important signals about the political climate in the country at times when national suffrage was suspended. Whilst Leftists and Nationalists had dominated the associations in the 1970s and in the first half of the 1980s, a strong Islamist presence that emerged in the internal elections thereafter indicates the ideological shift that has occurred among Jordan's technocratic elite and also shows how deeply the Islamist trend is rooted in the country.

When parliamentary life was eventually resumed and political parties re-emerged after 1989, the regime called on the associations to give up their political interests. The associations, however, refused to do so and insisted on their right to political action. The growing margin of democratic freedom now allows them to make themselves heard and to publish their opinions in the numerous new newspapers that have appeared. Ever since the signing of the Jordanian-Israeli peace treaty, they have been spearheading the anti-normalisation struggle which strongly opposes all official and private dealings with Israel. Precisely because of this engagement the Royal Court and various cabinet members have warned the associations on several occasions to refrain from political action and to return to their 'professional duties'. Thus, for example, King Hussain criticised the associations for their resistance to the peace treaty:

... the minority will not monopolise the leading posts in these ... unions and professions. This minority discusses things which it does not have the right to discuss at the expense of duty and the basic role it should play.[33]

Until now, the associations have insisted on their political work, though their influence is limited. Threats to dissolve them because of their struggle which emerges into the public arena at times of open confrontation between themselves and the regime have not materialised. The very presence of the associations is, on the one hand, a clear proof of the existence of a civil society in Jordan which is willing and able to participate in the country's development. On the other hand, the associations do not have a formal, institutionalised venue in which to pursue their national politics. Representatives of the associations have regularly been involved in consultations and discussions with members of the regime, but this is merely part of the 'national dialogue' which is pursued by the Royal Court and the government to secure the inclusion of all important segments of society in the decision-making process. For example, members of the associations were met by then prime minister, Abd al-Karim Kabariti, in 1996 when bread prices were raised. But while Kabariti campaigned for their support for the government's action, he did not accept their criticism of the decision.[34] Thus the inclusion of the associations is neither institutionalised nor does it have any binding or permanent function for the ruling circles inside the regime. The associations may oppose certain decisions of the government, they may discuss their standpoint with government representatives and with the king, but they may never actively alter the course of policy.

Dissidents and shifting alliances

Jordan's opposition has never been united, although its members do agree on certain topics such as the anti-normalisation struggle or the rejection of the Electoral Law. Sharp disagreements exist among the opposition about the influence the various groups try to exert on the 'national movement': the secular opposition accuses the Islamists of exploiting their position to the disadvantage of the secularists while the Islamists are powerful enough to pursue their goals without the help of the secularists. The latter fear the intolerance of the Islamists, were they ever to gain a major share of power. As a result, despite frequent calls for the creation of a united national front, the opposition has never managed to field their candidates on a joint ticket.[35]

But this disunity within the opposition which is grounded on ideological differences is exacerbated by factors which are deeply rooted in Jordanian society. The social fabric of modern Jordan which still relies heavily on family bonds and informal *wasta* networks (clientelist relationships) makes political opposition a difficult task. Opposition politics have long been strongly identified with certain figures who cannot bring themselves to unite in one coherent movement. Instead, everyone fights on his own thus squandering opportunities for real change, a fact which is clearly demonstrated by the examples of Laith Shubeilat and Ahmad Obeidat.

Ahmad Obeidat, a former director of the Jordanian Intelligence Service and former prime minister, is viewed as a reliable and honest politician by the public. A senator in the Upper House since 1984, he was urged to resign in 1994 when he refused to vote in favour of the peace treaty.[36] Since then he has become one of the most outstanding critics of the treaty and was marginalised by the regime because of this stance. In 1997, he was among the defenders of the Jordanian soldier Dakhamseh who had shot dead seven Israeli schoolgirls in the Jordan Valley. Obeidat was expected to become a leading figure in Jordan's national movement and several attempts were made by the opposition to build up a national platform under his leadership, but all of them failed. Whilst being respected by the public and being very familiar with the inner circles of power, Obeidat has so far failed to use his influence to tie together the various components of the opposition or to negotiate between the regime and its opponents. Finally, he was reintegrated into the inner circle of power when he was appointed as a senator to the Upper House in 1997.

Laith Shubeilat, a member of a prominent family from Southern Jordan, is certainly the most ambiguous figure among Jordan's opposition politicians. Whilst being an advocate of democratic freedom in the 1980s and a firm supporter of the anti-corruption campaign of the early 1990s, he has become a fanatic anti-normalisation fighter since 1994. Shubeilat, a long-time president of the influential engineers association, alienated even his Islamist colleagues because of his inflexible standpoint towards the regime. He was imprisoned twice; for high treason in 1992 and for *lèse majesté* in 1996.[37] He likes to present himself as a lone fighter against Western and especially 'Zionist' domination and he has always refused to become part of any organised political group. His good contacts with the Iraqi leadership enabled him to free several Jordanian prisoners in Baghdad in December 1997, applauded by the public and thus embarrassing the king and his cabinet who were still negotiating with Saddam Hussain on the issue.

It is not an accident that both Obeidat and Shubeilat are from important East Jordanian families. On the contrary, it would hardly be feasible for a Palestinian Jordanian to criticise the regime as openly as they do. For both men, the peace treaty with Israel has worked as a catalyst for their political struggle, and in their stand towards the normalisation of relations they even risk being completely marginalised.

Other prominent figures among Jordan's deputies from the ranks of the opposition, such as Nazih Amarin from Kerak or Toujan Faisal who was the only female deputy between 1993 and 1997, have done much valuable work in promoting the democratic freedoms of their electorate. But they have always acted on an individual basis and, to date, no attempt to unite the ranks of the opposition has succeeded. Whilst tribal figures are usually found among the loyalists, the events of the spring of 2000 demonstrated the possibility of shifting alliances whenever the old consensus between regime and society is endangered. In April 2000, 44 deputies, most of them with a tribal background, signed a petition to the king in which they complained over the performance of the Abd al-Raouf al-Rawabdeh government and asked for his resignation.[38]

The motives behind this severe criticism of the prime minister can be detected in the radical programme of economic reform that is being pursued under the new King Abdullah II. The old elites, long used to benefiting from a wide range of material and immaterial concessions granted by the regime, now feel the pains of a loss of these benefits in the course of the privatisation process. The fact that the prime minister finally resigned in June 2000 shows that the traditional ways of satisfying the old elites in order to restore the balance of power between regime and society still applies, but the dangers of an initially loyal Lower House radicalised by a sudden cancellation of old contracts have become visible.

Jordan under Abdullah II

The death of King Hussain in February 1999 and the succession of his eldest son Abdullah did not lead to a fundamental change in the way in which the country is ruled. During the first year of the new King's reign, it has become clear that hopes for more democracy will not be fulfilled in the near future. King Abdullah II is much more committed to an uncompromising course of economic liberalisation and the integration of Jordan into the global economic system than to a more participatory style of governance.[39] Whilst this policy may alienate important segments of the old oligarchy in the country from the Hashemite system and lead to a further impoverishment of broad sectors of society, it is also the case that working conditions for the opposition will become more difficult than ever.

By eagerly pushing a pro-Western political and economic agenda, combined with a social modernisation campaign, Abdullah is risking a collision with broad sectors of Jordanian society, both inside and outside the establishment. At the same time, however, it will be difficult for the diversified opposition to form a broad, effective coalition with a unified agenda.[40]

Abdullah II has inherited the tradition of the 'national dialogue' and has quickly become accustomed to it. For example, his first meeting with representatives from the Muslim Brotherhood was held as early as March 1999.[41] The new king has not fundamentally altered the way of handling the opposition. Indeed, in his crackdown on the radical Palestinian movement, *Hamas* and parts of the Jordanian Islamist movement, in 1999,[42] he demonstrated that he does not tolerate any force that might endanger his pro-Western policy of 'modernising Jordan'.

Jordan's opposition is weak and has remained so in spite of the 'democratic opening' in 1989. This weakness is grounded on both the nature of Jordan's political system and on the close symbiotic relationship between the regime and its opponents. In addition, structural impediments, such as the marginal role of parliament in the decision-making process; specific features of Jordan's society, such as the special importance of tribal relations or smouldering Jordanian-Palestinian tensions; and the legacy of three decades of martial law have prevented the opposition from building up a powerful base from which to fight for its goals. The highly fragmented structure of the Jordanian opposition is complemented by the emergence of prominent individuals acting as leading opposition figures. It is the interplay of all these factors which has led to the fatal weakness of the opposition in the post-1989 era. In addition, while popular unrest and mass demonstrations marked the beginning of the process in 1989, the masses have rarely been allowed to express their protest on the streets and remained remarkably silent during most of the years in the last decade.[43]

Together with the other important political opposition force in the country, the professional associations, opponents to the regime since the mid 1990s, have become preoccupied with combating the official politics of normalisation, the United Nations embargo against Iraq and the structural adjustment initiated by the IMF. The 'democratic spring' which started after the April 1989 riots was only short-lived: while democratic freedoms were increased in the years 1989 to mid-1993, subsequent years revealed a heavy-handed return of the old authoritarian style of rule. Nonetheless, the years between 1989 and 1993 were characterised by a constantly widening margin of democratic freedoms, a fact which was reflected in the various activities of opposition groups. But the regime soon reacted to the danger it perceived the opposition, inside and outside parliament, to represent for regime security. The election law was changed in order to reduce the influence of the opposition and there is clear evidence to support the allegations of massive vote rigging in the 1995 municipal elections and the 1997 parliamentary elections.

Public support for organised political groups is likewise weak, except for the Islamists. It was only during the Gulf War in 1991 that public demonstrations of discontent were permitted. Otherwise, whenever people went into the streets despite government bans, they suffered fierce reactions from the security apparatus. After 1993 the arena for public discontent slowly became narrower with each passing year and press freedom was more and more curtailed. Whilst diverging opinions on certain government decisions may be tolerated, criticism of the king or rejection of the regime as such will immediately be sanctioned. Advocates of a regime change are usually subjected to legal sanction and are therefore rare among the ranks of the opponents. Attempts by the Islamist, Nationalist and Leftist forces to resist key decisions of the regime, such as the 1993 Electoral Law or the peace treaty in 1994, were timid and never went as far as provoking open conflict.

The change in the leadership of the country has not yet led to a widening of the democratic process and hopes for more democratic freedoms have not materialised. The new king, like the late King Hussain needs strong financial support from the West to keep the country going.[44] Therefore, the scope for political action both on the domestic and the international scene is narrow. The faltering economic system of the country is also one of the reasons for the reluctance of the opposition to take a clear position against the regime. To survive economically, Jordan has no choice but to obey to the IMF economic reform programme and to secure the goodwill of the international donor community. The granting of such foreign aid, which is mainly Western, is bound to the existence of a 'moderate' and pro-Western regime in Jordan committed to 'democratic reform'. Therefore, any revolutionary change in the country would lead to an immediate cut off of this aid, a fact which cannot be ignored by even the most radical critic.

To date opposition groups have not been able to build a united platform. Though secular groups and the Islamists joined ranks at the national level to combat the politics of normalisation with Israel after the signing of the 1994 peace treaty, the alliance is full of ambiguities and contradictions and has not led to a unified stand on the issue.[46] Despite official declarations of a common goal, the Islamist and the secular groups competed with each other in every election since 1989.

Since the mid-1990s the positions of the opposition and the regime have solidified to such a point that movement in any direction seems hardly imaginable. The hopeless battles against the politics of normalisation and the economic reform programme have led to a virtual stagnant situation for the opposition and confrontations with the regime have simply become unproductive political spectacles. Political life in Jordan in the beginning of the twenty-first century seems to be frozen and the only chance that this situation may change lies in the possibility of a sharpening conflict between the traditional elites, new economic reformers and an opposition which will be trapped between the two other protagonists. As the contemporary situation evolves, in short, it seems that the actors on Jordan's political scene may soon be playing with a new deck of cards.

NOTES

1.　I am indebted to Schirin Fathi for her valuable comments on an earlier draft of this article. The expression is borrowed from B. Milton-Edwards, 'Façade democracy in Jordan', *British Journal of Middle Eastern Studies* 2 (1993), pp. 191–203.

2.　In contrast to the frequently heard thesis about Jordan being the 'most artificial state' among the Middle Eastern nations, newly published findings point to the legacy of an authentic Transjordanian experience from Ottoman times. See E. Rogan, *Frontiers of the state in the late Ottoman empire*, Cambridge University Press, 1999.

3.　See U. Dann, 'The political confrontation of summer 1924' in U. Dann (ed.), *Studies in the history of Transjordan, 1920–1949: The making of a state*, Boulder, CO: Westview Press, 1984, pp. 81–92.

4.　M. Hamarneh, 'Social and economic transformation of Transjordan, 1921–1946', unpublished dissertation, Georgetown University, 1985, p. 211.

5.　See Hamarneh 142.

6.　With the notable exception of A. Amawi, 'State and class in Transjordan: A study of state autonomy', unpublished dissertation, Washington, DC. A shorter account of the political positions of the opposition during these years can be found in M. Sa'ada, *Al-mu'arada al-siyasiya fi-l-urdunn fi sab'in 'aman 1921–1991*, Amman: Matabi' al-dusturiya al-tijariya, 1998, 23ff.

7.　See the various statements and pamphlets published in *al-urdunn al-jadid*, vols 1/1984, 2/1984, 3–4/1985, 5–6/1985 and 10/1988.

8.　The crackdown on the already docile press or the incidents at Yarmouk University in 1986 are only two examples of the authoritarianism of the Rifa'i government.

9.　It seems noteworthy that nearly all public unrest and rioting in Transjordan and Jordan in the twentieth century has occurred in rural areas, in the South of the country. This was for example the case in the 1926 uprising in Karak and Shobak, the 1989 riots, the 1996 'bread riots' in Karak or the 1998 riots in Ma'an. The major cities have hardly been touched by unrest.

10.　For a chronology of the riots see H. Abu Rumman, 'Waqa'i' intifada al-rabi' al-urdunniya', *al-urdunn al-jadid*, 14 (1989), pp. 32–55; for a deeper analysis see N. Timmermans, *Le soulèvement jordanien d'Avril 1989. Elément annonciateur de changements socio-politique au sein de la population de la Jordanie du Sud?*, Paris: Institut d'Etudes Politiques, Mémoire de DEA, 1991.

11.　M. Mufti, 'Elite bargains and the onset of political liberalisation in Jordan', 106, *Comparative Political Studies* 1 (1999), pp. 100–29.

12.　See e.g. L. Anderson, 'Political pacts, Liberalism and democracy: The Tunisian National Pact of 1988', *Government and Opposition*, 2 (1991), pp. 244–60.

13.　The term 'National Charter' has a clear connotation in Jordanian history and refers back to the 1920s and 1930s when Arab Nationalists held several 'National Congresses' in their efforts to oppose the British mandatory policy in Transjordan. The Charter of the 1990s was thus intended to stand in line with the anticolonial movements of Arab nationalism in the 1920s and tried to construct a continuity of political life from the early days of the emirate up to the present.

14.　H. Dobers, W. Goussous, Y. Sara (eds), *Democracy and the Rule of Law – in Germany – in Jordan,* Amman: Konrad-Adenauer-Foundation, 1993, p. 49.

15.　This important aspect of tying all political forces to the monarchy has been mentioned earlier – see L. Brand, '"In The beginning was the state . . .": The quest for civil society in Jordan', in A. Norton, (ed.), *Civil society in the Middle East*, vol. 1, Leiden: Brill, pp. 148–85.

16.　FBIS-NES-95-087.

17. For an overview of the emergence of political parties after 1989 and an assessment of the Political Parties Law see R. Dieterich, 'Where authoritarianism and tribalism meet: legal constraints and societal conditions of party activism, 1989 – 1997' in R. Bocco (ed.), *The Hashemite Kingdom of Jordan, 1946–1996: Social identities, development policies and state-building*, Paris: Karthala, 2001.

18. *Jordan Times*, 19 Nov. 1995.

19. For details of the developments in Jordan's press law see J. Campagna, 'Press freedom in Jordan', *MERIP* 206 (spring 1998), pp. 44–8, and A. Jones, *Press, regime and society in Jordan since 1989*, Montreal: Consortium Universitaire pour les Etudes Arabes, 1997. The 1997 Press Law was declared as in contradiction with the constitution by the High Court of Justice, but the new 1998 draft law which was accepted by the parliament in July 1998 is similar in its repressive nature. See *Jordan Times*, 17 and 18 June 1998, for the draft.

20. The introduction of the one-person-one-vote-law and its consequences have been discussed and analyzed in depth elsewhere; see e. g. A. Amawi, 'The 1993 elections in Jordan', 15ff, *Arab Studies Quarterly* 3 (1994) 15–27, and G. Robinson, 'Defensive democratisation in Jordan', 397ff., *International Journal of Middle East Studies*, 3, (1998), pp. 387–410.

21. See Amawi, *The 1993 elections*, for the 1993 parliamentary elections and the special edition of *Jordanies* for the voting of 1997, *Jordanies* 5–6 (1998).

22. See *as-sabil*, 28 Oct.-3. Nov. 1997.

23. Final speech of King Hussain before the National Congress which voted on the National Charter, in *Al-mithaq al-watani*, Amman: Press and Publications Department, 1991, pp. 57–61.

24. King Hussain in his letter of designation to Zaid Ben Shaker, in FBIS-NES-91–226.

25. Speech by King Hussain to army officers, FBIS-NES-95–218.

26. King Hussain in his speech to the parliament about the opponents of the Jordanian-Israeli peace treaty, in *Jerusalem Post*, 3 Dec. 1995.

27. Minister of Information Mahmoud Sharif in FBIS-NES-93–044.

28. King Abdullah II, speech from the throne, 1 November 1999.

29. In numbers: 32 out of the 80 seats of Jordan's lower house went to the Islamists

30. See his statements during a press conference on the occasion of the elections, in FBIS-NES 89–218, and Mufti, *Elite bargaining*, p. 108.

31. Press statement of the Islamist block, 3 Nov. 1989, in FBIS-NES-89–212.

32. See *Al-Ra'y*, 17 July 1999.

33. FBIS-NES 95–113.

34. See *Jordan Times*, 29 July 1996.

35. Only recently the secular and the Islamist opposition failed to unite on the occasion of the municipal elections, see *Jordan Times*, 3 May 1999.

36. See J.-C. Augé, 'The non-Islamist opposition, as reflected by the elections; is the sum of the parties and of those who do not belong to any "party" equal to a whole?' Jordanies 5–6 (1998), pp. 297–335.

37. For the details see R. Dieterich. 'To raise one's tongue against His Majesty – Islamist critique and its response in Jordan: the case of Laith Shubeilat' in L. Edzard and C. Szyska (eds), *Encounters of Words and Texts*, Hildesheim: Olms, 1997, pp. 159–76.

38. See *The Star*, 20 April 2000.

39. See L. Andoni, 'King Abdullah: In his father's footsteps?' pp. 80ff., *Journal of Palestine Studies*, 3 (2000), pp. 77–89.

40. Andoni, *King Abdullah*, p. 88.

41. The opposition for its part may hope for concessions on certain points; thus for

example when the new king,during the meeting with the Islamists, promised to release more than a dozen of its supporters who had been arrested earlier. See *The
Star*, 25 March 1999.
42. The *Hamas* office in Amman was closed and major representatives of the movement were expelled in the autumn of 1999.
43. Exceptions were the pro-Iraqi demonstrations which mirrored the sentiments of
the Jordanian populace during the Gulf War of 1991, the bread riots in Karak in
1996 and the pro-Iraqi demonstrations in Amman and Ma'an in 1998. Demonstrations against the conclusion of the peace treaty with Israel in 1994 did not take
place because they were prohibited.
44. See B. Milton-Edwards and P. Hinchcliffe, 'Abdullah's Jordan: New King, old
problems', *MERIP* 213/1999 (winter 1999), pp. 28–31.
46. See *The Star*, 8 April 1999, for the attempts to build a united committee against
the politics of normalisation.

Part III. SOCIAL CHANGE

HOUSEHOLD POLITICS TO DOMESTIC POLICIES

THE EFFECT OF DEMOGRAPHIC TRANSITION ON SOCIO-POLITICAL PATTERNS OF DOMINATION[1]

Françoise de Bel-Air

The aim of this study is, first, to explore the consequences of a long-term process (the demographic transition in Jordan) on household-level patterns of domination – the 'hierarchies of gender and generation'.[2] Second, it will suggest a relationship between these major changes in population and family structure, on the one hand, and alterations in the domestic power structure in Jordan, specifically, the trend towards democratisation there. Third, we shall question the role of new social policies implemented during the last decade of the twentieth century. We will show that these policies actually follow the changes they were supposed to induce and are used to monitor further political evolution, in an attempt to smooth the transition from patriarchal order, crystallised in King Hussain's 'neo-patriarchal' state,[3] to a new socio-political structural model.

The effect of the demographic transition on the patriarchal family

The demographic transition[4] in Jordan can be described as 'high' and 'short', as Crude Rates of Natural Increase (CRNI) peaked in 1980 at a very high level (36 per cent) and began to decrease five years later to reach a level of 25 per cent by 1990.[5] In effect, until 1980, the first phase of fertility transition was in operation. Mortality rates were controlled during the 1950s. As a result, the Infant Mortality Rate (IMR) fell from 22 per cent in 1930 to an average of 16 per cent in the years between 1955 and 1960,[6] thereafter declining further to reach 9 per cent in 1970, as a consequence of progress in the sanitary conditions and medical care in Jordan from the 1950s onwards. This decrease, however, did not have the effect of reducing fertility rates. From an estimated level of seven children on average per women in the 1960s, Total Fertility Rates (TFR)[7] had risen to levels which were

Figure 1. EVOLUTION OF THE TOTAL FERTILITY RATES (TFR), FROM 1970 TO 1997

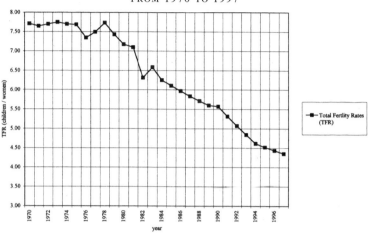

Source: adjusted civil status data, 1979 and 1994 census, Fertility Surveys

among the highest in the world – almost eight children per woman on average, throughout the 1970s (Figure 1).

After 1980, the second phase of fertility transition began, to be followed immediately by the third phase. From 1980 until the present, fertility rates have shown a constant and regular decrease, from a high average level of 7–8 children per woman in the 1970s, to 4.3 children per woman on average in 1997. An analysis of generational histories[8] demonstrates that the generations born in the 1950s, who started their reproductive life in the 1970s, are the last to show behaviour trends towards high fertility. From the 1961–5 generation onwards, fertility rates are lower for all ages, showing a clear gap between the histories of these two generational groups (Figure 2). Given the inertia inherent in demographic evolution, this situation demonstrates a very striking development in behaviour patterns and fertility models since the 1970s. This is closely related to changes in the institution of patriarchy, which has conditioned the specific mode of demographic transition witnessed in the region.[9]

Patriarchal families in transition. One of the most frequently used definitions of the Arab family – as characterised by the following six traits: extended, patrilineal, patrilocal, patriarchal, endogamous and occasionally polygynous[10] – refers more to an ideal, to representations than to a tangible reality of family structures.[11] Nevertheless,

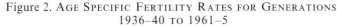

Figure 2. AGE SPECIFIC FERTILITY RATES FOR GENERATIONS
1936–40 TO 1961–5

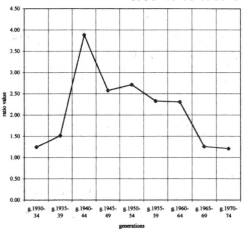

Source: WFS 1976, JFFHS 1983, JPFHS 1992 and 1997

certain characteristics of the Jordanian environment bear witness to the existence of a patriarchal order within the family, in terms of 'hierarchies of gender and generation'. As Moghadam points out, 'In classic patriarchy, the senior man has authority over everyone else in the family, including younger men, and women are subject to distinct forms of control and subordination'.[12] As will be shown on the microsocial level, the emergence of this form of male/elderly domination comes both from endogenous – demographic – factors, and from exogenous factors, such as modes of wealth accumulation, education and imported models of family structures.

The period until 1980 could be described as the 'golden age of patriarchy', as all the indicators of social and economic development needed to develop such a system came together. Regarding the established relationship between female education and patterns of fertility, evidence from worldwide surveys demonstrates that fertility levels decrease as the levels of female education improve. At the same time, differential levels of education between men and women will also have a great impact on the domination of the former over the latter within the household, thus helping the construction of a patriarchal family structure.

Since no real education system had been set up in Jordan before the 1950s, the generations born before 1940 could not benefit, in their vast majority, from serious involvement in education. Figure 3 shows the balance between men and women in terms of widespread lack of

Figure 3. INEQUALITIES IN EDUCATION BETWEEN MEN AND WOMEN
FOR GENERATIONS 1930 TO 1974

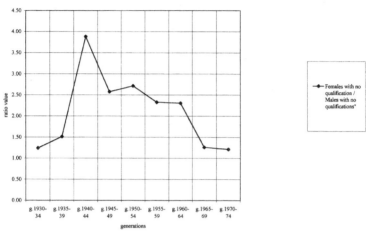

Source: Housing and Population Census 1979; Manpower, Unemployment and Income Survey 1993.

qualifications. Within the generations born after 1940, up to the beginning of the 1960s, the gap between men and women deepens, suggesting that boys were far more intensively enrolled in school than girls, thus implying acute domination of men over women. The generations between 1940 and 1944 show the biggest gender gap, with almost four times more women being without qualifications than men. Yet these generations, and their successor generations, which show more than twice as many women lacking qualifications compared with men, are the fertile generations up to 1980.

This relatively low level of female education reflects on marriage patterns: older generations, born in the period up to the early 1960s, did not see their marriage plans postponed or even cancelled for reasons of study. Indeed, marriage was almost universal,[13] unions happened at a relatively young age (25.5 years for men and between 20.5 and 21 years for women[14]), the average age gap of five years between spouses reflecting male domination within the couple. These figures showed little change until the late 1970s, as was the case with the proportion of early marriages celebrated with women aged less than 20 years old, which stood at 28 per cent of the total in 1961 and was still 22 per cent in 1979.[15] Apart from increasing the risk of pregnancy, thus influencing fertility rates, early and universal marriage has also contributed to confirming the patriarchal family model in society, both in theory and practice, for individual fate is linked to marriage and family and thus encourages male union with a younger, less educated woman.

Furthermore, a set of economic factors – the 1973 oil boom with the concomitant emigration of workers to the Gulf and the consequent flow of remittances – have contributed to reinforcing patriarchal values. The specific mode of wealth accumulation experienced after 1973 led Jordan to be described as a 'rentier state',[16] induced an 'inhibition of the fertility transition', and 'acted to provide a reprieve to the patriarchal order'.[17] Yet this scenario reveals a pattern of evolution that contradicts the general pattern observed for fertility transition, which otherwise emphasises the decisive role of the economic welfare of households in the process of fertility decline.

In the Jordanian case, the mass migration of workers to the Gulf between 1973 and the early 1980s boosted the national economy, as well as the household economy because of remittances sent by expatriate workers to their families. On the household level, the improvement in living standards during the period 1975–84[18] lifted material constraints on early marriages as well as on fertility, so that parents, who were still willing to have large families may have been encouraged to do so a few years earlier than would otherwise have been the case. These remittances, furthermore,[19] allowed the state to provide for social infrastructure in the education and health sectors – the 1970s, for example, was the decade which witnessed the most rapid growth in the number of schools; a factor which helped to uncouple fertility from the disincentive of associated costs.

More important was the fact that oil wealth had the social effect of discouraging women from entering the labour market, for the entry of women into the workplace is a factor which is normally considered decisive in producing a decrease of fertility. At the household level, remittances provided by expatriate kinship members effectively replaced a salary, making women's access to professional life unnecessary. At the macroeconomic level, immigration was co-opted to develop modern services and expand sectors of the economy now boosted by remittance income, thus avoiding once again the use of local female labour. Until 1979, the proportion of women involved in economic activity was no more than 7 per cent.[20]

Lastly, emigration may have had another consequence which contributed to the persistence of high levels of fertility – the import of cultural models from the Gulf countries. The governments of those countries, rich in resources but with small populations, were at the time anxious to encourage high birth-rates, promoting large families and encouraging women's exclusion from the public sphere. Furthermore, since a woman whose husband worked in the Gulf was usually

placed under the control of her husband's family, migration to the
Gulf could be seen as likely to promote 'conservative' family models.[21] Even women's increasing levels of education during the 1970s
seemed to be unconnected from the evolution of their social status
which would usually have been associated with it because of the
strength of patriarchal model. If fertility trends between countries at
the end of the 1970s are compared, the comparison reveals that educated women in Jordan, even if they had lower fertility than their less
educated peers, still bore more children than uneducated women in
other countries. For example: 'An illiterate Tunisian woman gives
birth to less children than a Jordanian woman who went to school for
four to six years'.[22]

After 1980, however – at the start of the second phase of the demographic transition – a crisis within the patriarchal family could have
been anticipated. Yet, at the end of the 1980s – as Jordan had just entered the last phase of its demographic transition process – all those factors which had contributed to the reinforcement of patriarchal models
and high fertility levels had been profoundly modified, thus launching
the process of redefinition of role redistribution within the family. First,
the average age of marriage increases after 1980. The 1961–5 generations, who were entering the marriage market at the beginning of the
1980s, experienced an increase in the age of marriage that had remained stable until the decade had opened. The average age of women
at marriage rose by almost three years over the next decade – from
21 years old in 1979 to 25 years old at the end of the 1980s. Men experienced a similar evolution; their age at first marriage increased from
25.5 years in 1979 on average to 28 years at the end of the decade.[23]
Women's rates of education also increased significantly. Along with
the boost in education levels of the overall population from the 1970s
onwards,[24] female enrolment rate in secondary education rose from
38.4 per cent in 1976 to 47 per cent in 1983, most of the increase having
concerned the rural areas. In 1984, in higher education, women accounted for 44.2 per cent of students[25] and for 33 per cent in 1976. This
situation had a great impact on early marriage and fertility, as witnessed by the drop in age-specific fertility rates from 133 in 1976 to 49
in 1983 for the 15–19 age group.[26] If the rise in education levels played
its expected role, economic factors such as the economic crisis at the
end of the1980s, and women's access to the labour market, were not
linked with fertility and social change in a straightforward manner.

After the secular decline in oil prices in the 1980s, from 1984 onwards the share of remittances in Jordan's GNP and the amount of
aid given by foreign powers, specifically from the gulf states, which
together covered more than 50 per cent of GNP, started to decline.[27]

Emigration flows also stagnated.[28] At the same time, foreign debt in the second half of the 1980s began to reach uncontrollable levels.[29] It seems that the effect of the slow-down of economic expansion in Jordan during the first half of the 1980s, the moment when fertility rates started decreasing, was not particularly appreciated by the population at the time, as government was still spending on infrastructure development and private consumption levels were still raising steadily. We can thus assume that remittances and foreign aid – following a 'rentier' pattern – may have boosted social conservatism (patriarchal power) and levels of natural increase, but, contrary to other countries,[30] their stabilisation happened before the effects of the economic crisis could be felt. Throughout the 1980s, as fertility rates decreased, the pattern of social evolution was closer to one marked by the 'modernisation' of social structures. As expected, in line with steep increase of women's education rates, their access to the labour market started increasing, from a total of 7 per cent of women aged 15 and more in 1979 to 14 per cent at the end of the 1980s,[31] a twofold increase in ten years. Nevertheless, after the onset of the economic crisis at the turn of the 1990s, rates of female activity stopped expanding,[32] perhaps because of an increase in unemployment in the 1990s.[33] Moreover, rural areas were the most affected by the fall of fertility levels during the 1990s, which significantly reduced the gap between urban and rural fertility behaviour. It can thus be assumed that the model of fertility decrease witnessed during the 1990s includes a dimension of 'Malthusianism of poverty',[34] affecting the poorest populations in urban and rural areas, which will be shown below to be the most vulnerable.

In fact, rural regions because their decline in fertility occurred later were not affected by the same combination of fertility determinants which, in urban areas, acted together to change, or reflect changes of social models, as well as to influence the power structure within the family between men and women and between generations. A purely demographic factor – the population pressure within the household – seems, however, to have played an essential role in the process of threatening patriarchal family structures in poor rural regions, by changing the dynamics within the household. The increase in family size mechanically led to a shift of paternal authority towards one of his sons. Solidarity and authority came to be exerted along an horizontal axis, among collaterals, whereas the vertical axis – where traditionally the father as the oldest male dominated – lost its coherence. In short, starting from the 1980s, a period of maximal population pressure and household size, the power of age was being replaced by power of numbers.

The argument here is that, given age at first marriage until the end of the 1970s (25.5 for men and 20.5–21 years for women on average), the high reproduction rates of up to eight children on average per woman and the context of low mortality, the eldest child will progressively replace its ageing parents, specifically for their youngest brothers and sisters. Thus, as the domination of boys can still be observed, even if reduced by girls' increasing rates of education and professional activity, eldest sons progressively challenge their ageing fathers for power within the household.

Since comprehensive data on age differences among members of a household were unavailable, use has been made here of indicative fieldwork data. Evidence from fieldwork conducted in a village near Kerak[35] in the early 1990s supports this hypothesis. Among households surveyed the age difference between first-born and last-born was 11.5 years. If we consider only the heads of households aged 45 and above, having terminated their fertile life in conditions of relatively low mortality without having experienced the subsequent decrease in fertility, the gap between first and last birth is 17.5 years. Since the age difference between spouses is almost six years in these older couples, a women aged 45 will terminate her fertile life when her husband is already more than 50 years old. The last baby will have brothers and sisters 15 to 20 years older and when it reaches the age of 10 to 15 years, its father will be no younger than 60. It is most doubtful that these children will be under the control of these ageing parents. It is more likely that they will fall under the responsibility of older brothers and sisters, aged at that time between 25 and 30 years and not yet married – for, as was established the age at marriage increased from the 1980s onwards. Since these age groups acquire a comparative increase in demographic weight as the vertical ties of domination fade, horizontal ties of solidarity can only be strengthened among brothers, cousins and other members of the same, now numerous, age group. Nevertheless, the transition was not complete and was also potentially destabilising, for the emerging power of sons was not officially acknowledged. Although the father no longer effectively directed the household, he still proclaimed himself the head of household, an attitude which implies potential tension between generations.

This fieldwork data is also supported by survey data collected at the end of the 1980s in Amman,[36] which displays a strong correlation between the spatial distribution of large-size households and households where the head is fifty years old or more. This data demonstrates the spread of inter-generational tension at the end of the 1980s as an emerging challenge to the dominance of age and a transitional stage between two micropolitical situations – the classical patriarchal family and a transitional family structure. Even if the transition is progressing in urban areas of the country, in line with women's access to education and professional life, in the rural areas, where women's activity is more constrained, transitional experiences of this kind have been more violent. In fact, they developed into macropolitical demands because of the heavy dependency of population on the state in these regions and because of the greater effect of the 'neo-patriarchal' nature of the regime there. In essence, the challenge to the father's absolute power within the family developed into a challenge to the absolute power of the father of the nation – the King.

From patriarchal family to 'neo-patriarchal' system

In fact, the state has participated in the construction of the patriarchal family within a neo-patriarchal system of political domination. We saw that the patterns of fertility in Jordan were conditioned by patterns of family formation and power relations within the household – in terms of generating a strong patriarchal family, itself reinforced until the 1980s by the specific economic and political conditions discussed above. However, this structure of power, witnessed at the microsocial level, has not only been reinforced, but has also been created by political conditions. Patriarchy has been constructed and fashioned to implement the neo-patriarchal political system in Jordan, the role given by law and practice to the father reflecting the natural allegiance considered due to the head-of-state. Inevitably, the evolution of factors which had led to a strengthening of the patriarchal family has also had an effect on the macropolitical level, within the neo-patriarchal system.

Indeed, references to a 'tradition' of patriarchal family structure does not reflect the reality on the ground, but is really a dominant model of reference. As shown by many authors, tradition is 'invented'[37] and, among other factors, mortality levels prevailing in the past never allowed for large, exclusively father-headed households to embody an effective norm in family structures,[38] suggesting the same pattern for the Arab world.

Other factors would include oil wealth, remittances, and foreign aid, all of which helped to block social change on the macrosociopolitical level, in the same way that they did at the microsocial level of the household. The eviction of women from public life, the call upon foreign immigration to manage emerging sectors of the developing economy, as well as the development in Jordan of a welfare state system of social support, have blocked the emergence of alternative social claims and contributed to an increased dependency of citizens towards the state itself. Just as a father has control over the members of his family because he is the eldest, most educated and in charge of economic power, the state redistributes to citizens the product of remittances in the shape of social infrastructures, but keeps them away from the engineering process of the economic development through its ability to call on immigrants, thus preventing the emergence of a local, politically-conscious and potentially destabilising working force.

The parallel drawn here between the state's and the father's mode of political domination reflects the theory of 'neo-patriarchy', a system within which 'traditional models of sexual relations and typical forms of exercise of power and authority within the family have produced patriarchal models of political authority in the Arab world, [as] traditional patriarchy made an alliance with the strong state system imported from Europe'.[39] 'A central psycho-social feature of this type of society, whether it is conservative or progressive, is the dominance of the father (patriarch), the centre around which the national as well as the natural family are organised. Thus between ruler and ruled; between father and child, there exist only vertical relations'.[40] In such a system, the necessary interdependence between the patriarchal family and the macropolitical system requires the state to protect and strengthen the patriarchal family. On the economic level, the family is assimilated into a production unit, through the allocation of economic wealth managed by the father, for intergenerational wealth flows are characteristic of patriarchal family structures.[41] On the social level, the provision of social infrastructures and of imported manpower – as described above – prevents the access of women into the public sphere, thereby sustaining male domination and contributing to the stability of social institutions, reinforced, for instance, by legal measures enforcing the father's power over his wife and children.[42] In return, on the political level, the patriarchal model of domination, based on allegiance rooted in kinship relations, provides a model of political domination of state over citizens implicitly presented as rooted in blood relations, thus unquestionable, but also eternal, relating to the 'innate' aspect of Muslim society. Neo-patriarchy is a political system based on a 'naturalisation of social arbitrariness',[43] as witnessed clearly, for instance, in the vocabulary used in King Hussain's speeches, when he refers to himself as 'the father', to the Jordanians as 'his children' and to Jordan as 'their house'.[44]

This raises an associated question; namely, whether dependency towards the state implies allegiance to patriarchal families. In fact, in an examination of the geographical distribution of demographic factors related to a predominantly patriarchal family structure,[45] one region seems particularly relevant: the governorate of Ma'an, where the indicators show extreme values, and to a lesser extent, Tafieleh, as well as Mafraq, a steppe region in the east of the country. Furthermore, their spatial distribution is very close to that of the geographical distribution of the state's dominant role in the provision of employment.[46] At the same time, these distributions display a structure similar to that reflecting instability of family structures: the spatial distribution of highest divorce rates.[47] This demonstrates the vulnerability of large-size patriarchal families.

Changes in neo-patriarchal domination. As might have been expected, the vulnerability of the patriarchal family and powerful demographic pressures in rural areas of the country were reflected in the fact that the 1989 riots erupted in these regions after the 1988 economic crisis. The failure of the neo-patriarchal system of domination, mainly as a result of demographic pressures, was an important element in the implementation of the process of political liberalisation which followed the disturbances.

The mainly rural regions in the south and, to a lesser extent, the east of Jordan, have been tied to the Hashemite regime by a social contract, in which allegiance has been offered in return for protection since the 1930s, a well-known process in the Middle East and particularly described in Jordan itself.[48] However, Jordanian rule over the West Bank, backed by Britain and the United States, meant that financial aid from western countries (mainly from the United States) started flowing into the country. As negotiations with foreign states and the management of aid depended on an emerging class of bureaucrats who were generally educated urbanites, funds and development aid were progressively directed towards urban areas.[49] Consequently, the first surveys on poverty conducted in the 1980s[50] disclosed that the rural regions of the south were the most strongly hit by poverty in the kingdom, for the state continued to be the biggest provider of infrastructure, employment and services, but did not properly fulfil the terms of the original implicit contract of 'allegiance for protection'.

The failure of welfare state policies after 1988 and the implementation of an IMF-style structural adjustment plan, requiring, amongst other measures, a decrease in the public expenditures have, as a result, hit the those regions most dependent on state assistance most severely, at a moment when the patriarchal family structure was at its most vulnerable because the peak in demographic pressure within households had led to a growing frustration over the distribution of power within the family. The violent anti-regime demands in the south, directed against the power of the neo-patriarchal system, which had failed to protect and provide for its 'children' while imposing its absolute authority, led to the implementation of a process of political liberalisation in 1989. Indeed, this emancipation of the nation's 'children' ran in parallel to claims of youth against the power exerted over them by their elders – demands, in effect, for the end of patriarchy. The economic transition, then, seems to have acted as a catalyst for a social and political crisis that could have been anticipated.

Fertility regulation and social change – demographic policies in context

Until now, we have described a process of demographic transition, leading to social transition. It is a process that has followed a trend essentially determined in part by progress in female education and in part to attempts to change the power structure on the micropolitical (household) level and on the macropolitical level. We now turn to the issue of whether or not and to what extent this rapid evolution is also due to the numerous population and social policies implemented in Jordan since the 1990s, in the wake of pressure by foreign states and international agencies. It will be demonstrated that the policies, in fact, shadow the socio-political evolution they were supposed to dynamise. This, in turn, poses the question as to why such policies are conducted – as part of a process of intervention or to monitor the side-effects of the so-called spontaneous socio-political transitions experienced by Jordan at the turn of the 1990s?

Population policies: history, aims, means, assessment. Even if fertility in Jordan has reached levels among the highest in the world, population policies did exist in the country. Jordan's first population policy was designed as early as 1972, after concern about population issues started being expressed at the international level. In the 1960s, Western governments, particularly the United States, together with international and United Nation's agencies as well as private foundations, started exerting pressure on the Third World countries they were supporting, for the design and implementation of government-initiated population policies and for permission for voluntary organisations concerned with population growth to operate on their soil. Jordan, being heavily dependant on foreign, particularly American, aid, had to comply with these demands. In December 1964, a *fatwa* was issued by the Mufti of Jordan, Sheikh Abdullah al-Qalqili, which allowed 'the use of medicine for contraception, or even for abortion before the embryo or the foetus is ensouled'.[51] In the same year, in 1964, Family Planning and Protection Association (FPPA) established a branch in Jerusalem.[52]

In 1972, at an experts meeting convened in Amman by the Department of Statistics, the following elements of a proper policy were proposed: 'In order to help families determine the number of their offspring, family planning services should be made available in Ministry of Health clinics, other branches of government should assist by providing information, and voluntary bodies in the field should be given support'.[53] In 1973, the government established the National Population Committee under the chairmanship of the Ministry of Labour, with a mandate to formulate and implement a national population policy and to address all population-related activities. Opposition to the initiative emerged at all levels of the government apparatus and the new institution took no action, apart from arranging for the supply – import and marketing – of birth control devices, as well as supporting the opening of clinics by voluntary organisations (such as the Jordanian Family Planning Association) subsidised by the government and by the Ministry of Health, through its network of Mother and Child Health Centres, while international agencies, such as the United Nations Fund for Population Activities (UNFPA) opened offices in Amman.[54] In short, throughout the 1970s and the 1980s, family planning policy in Jordan was not mandatory or activist in nature although the necessary infrastructure did exist and birth control devices were available in the country.

At the very end of the 1980s, voluntary activist measures began, starting with the revival of the National Population Committee by Princess Basma, King Hussain's sister, in 1988. The Commission's brief was widened and a general secretariat was set up as its executive arm.[55] Progress since then has been measured. After the launching of policies mainly geared towards health improvement and birth spacing,[56] the 1993–7 five-year plan was the first planning document to explicitly mention the necessity 'to balance population growth and resources', in hardening the official position towards natural increase dynamics. In 1996, a new National Population Strategy (NPS – sometimes referred to as 'Revised Work Plan for Birth Spacing 1997–2000' that was more clearly directed towards birth control) was endorsed by the government.

The latest strategy is very comprehensive, covering the domains of reproductive health, information, education and communication, women in development, labour, natural resources and the environment and housing. Population growth, however, is considered as the key issue in the programme. The improvement of the situation in all the domains covered in the strategy depend on it, even if representations of the cultural background of society leads to a degree of self-censorship. Indeed, the NPC states that the strategy should be implemented in order for Jordanians to 'decide freely and responsibly the number, spacing and timing of their children, have the information and means to make these decisions, and attain the highest standards of sexual and reproductive health, in line with the religious and cultural values of Jordanian society'.[57]

The plan objectives are to raise the Contraceptive Prevalence Rate (CPR) from 39 per cent of users of modern methods, to 47 per cent by the year 2000, increase the availability of family planning services, raise the level of knowledge of proper usage of modern contraceptive methods, improve the systematic dissemination of health information, especially on family planning for both men and women and increase the participation of voluntary and international organisations and Non-Governmental Organisations (NGOs) in the provision of family planning. The programme itself is based on the *Shari'a* (Islamic religious law), the constitution and the National Charter, in order to ensure that it fits within the cultural and political context of the country and to avoid as much controversy as possible. The focus of the information it provides is the proposal that 'family-planning is an essential contribution to the well-being of the family'. Muslim leaders were particularly targeted by the information campaign, because they were seen as potential opponents to birth control. Booklets were targeted at them, explaining the legacy of family planning within Islam through Quranic quotations endorsed by Sheikh Tamimi, the Chief Justice of the Islamic Court in Jordan.[58]

In 1995, USAID, UNFPA, IPPF and the European Community provided funding for the programme. The World Bank and the Japanese International Cooperation Agency were also supposed to play a major role in health services funding, particularly reproductive health and family planning.[59] Service delivery is provided by the public sector – the Ministry of Health, mainly through its network of Maternal and Child Health Centres, the Royal Medical Services, UNRWA and the Jordan University Hospital, as well as by NGOs.[60] In 1999, the number of NGOs involved in the provision of family planning services totalled 400 throughout the kingdom.[61] Training, research and evaluation, and information services are, in short, provided by a set of institutions marked by their diversity.[62]

In view of the widespread range of agencies involved in the reduction of birth control rates over the 1990s, the assessment of the effect of policies on fertility changes is complex. Though contraception is considered a major proximate determinant of fertility and, by

Figure 4. DESIRED FERTILITY AND REAL FERTILITY PER REGION

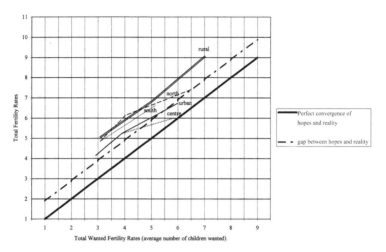

Source: WFS 1976, JPFHS 1990 and 1997.

extension its correlate, the family structure, its share in the process of birth rate decline has not been discussed. In order to determine if high fertility can be linked to lack of availability of services, or more generally to unmet needs in terms of contraceptive services, Figure 4 compares total fertility rates (TFR) of women from 1976 to 1997, with desired fertility rates.[63] Unmet needs would be characterised by a noticeable difference between the TFR and the desired rate. Variations would also occur, with the gap between the TFR and the desired rate increasing in times of high fertility, thus demonstrating the impossibility of women to control by themselves the number of their children.

However, for urban and rural areas, as well as for the three main regions in Jordan (north, centre and south), data from the surveys are remarkably closely aligned. The slope of the regression line is 0.9, a figure close to 1, suggesting a good correlation between wanted fertility and actual fertility, whatever the fluctuations. The gap between this line and the regression line representing perfect convergence of behaviour with expectation is nevertheless of the order of 0.9 points. This means that, whatever the circumstances, women gave birth to almost one child more than they wished to, whether or not fertility rates were high and family planning services were available. In other words, the provision of family planning services did not change deci-

sions with respect to family size. Fertility, in short, is a definite preferred objective in Jordan and changes in fertility can be controlled
by women themselves, as was demonstrated by the sharp decrease in
fertility in the 1980s, long before an effective population control policy was designed and implemented. Indeed, in 1983, only 26 per cent
of married women used a birth control method, close to the level of
23 per cent use reported in 1976, during a period of high fertility,
whereas, in 1990, the figure had risen slightly to 35 per cent. A further
point of interest which reinforces this conclusion, is the increase of
use of traditional birth control methods, in parallel to the increase in
use of other 'modern' methods – from 5 per cent in the 1970s and
1980s to 12 per cent in 1997, methods which were always available
but not always used. In short, birth control practice follows the desire
to limit the family size, but fails to promote new models of fertility.
The increased practice of birth control is not the cause of the drop in
fertility, but the result of a reduction of the number of children
women wish to have. Policies, in short, have followed the trend,
rather than induced it.

Family planning as a tool of globalisation and political stability. In
view of the fact that birth control policies may not have a direct impact in changing models of fertility, at least in the initial periods of
policy implementation, it is legitimate to question the utility of developing massive infrastructures to provide education, training and information have, in view of the significant funding that is involved.
Since the 1960s, international emphasis has been placed on the link
between population growth and environment deterioration. This, in
turn, has led to a globalisation of the issue of demography, of the idea
that population control is a duty, both to a specific country itself
and also to the international community. This idea of a common duty
leads, in turn, to the idea of common mechanisms to achieve birth
regulation, through the 'reduplication of a standard policy' which has
proven to be effective in a specific context to other countries and circumstances. 'The nation-states become the framework of a relatively
uniformed implementation of a world policy',[64] whilst international
agencies and western states are the most active in promoting and
funding population policies in the developing world.

   This uniformity of policy is evident, not only in the methods recommended, but also in the identification of the issues to be tackled and
the definition of target groups to be specifically approached, for they
are created by the simple fact that they are designated as targets –
the poor, refugees or 'unmet needs', for example. This is certainly true
in Jordan for, even if the description given here of the aims and means

made use of in Jordanian policy seem to reflect great care to avoid controversy and adapt policy to a national context, the actors and the pressure groups involved are targeted in accordance with a vision of society imported from abroad.[65] It follows that the use of the same methods of field analysis throughout the world would lead to the creation of identical social categories or pressure groups, because they would be defined by the policies. A good example of this process of standardising field analysis and policy-making is given by the development of international programmes of observation of demographic dynamics through the World Fertility Surveys in the 1970s, the Fertility and Family Health Surveys in the 1980s and the Population and Family Health Surveys in the 1990s. These studies have been conducted in several countries in the world through the same organisational system, the same questions have been asked and same socio-economic patterns of sample distribution has been observed. This provides for comparison of demographic situation over time and space – a fantastic scientific asset but politically questionable since the results serve as policy tools.

Population policy can be seen also as a tool for ensuring stability because it allows for the monitoring of domestic issues in order to satisfy international requirements. Population policies are designed for a long-term periods of implementation because of the long time span over which demographic changes occur. As such, a policy is implicitly designed within the context of the situation current in the country when the policy is introduced and of the fears then current. In the case of Jordan, the reality and perceptions of the demographic aspect of the internal and regional balance-of-power is well known and may be behind the stagnation in population control implementation by the state in the 1970s and 1980s.[66] The design of a policy can then be seen as an attempt to achieve stability and to solve current problems in the future by a careful monitoring of decisions that would inevitably have an impact on the issue of identity and the related political power game. The state is in fact present in the process of policy-making and implementation, for even if the share of the public sector in the provision of family planning services was only 23 per cent in 1997,[67] the Ministry of Health remains the biggest spender, with 36 per cent of total funding in 1995.[68]

Furthermore, for a country heavily reliant on external funding, aid given to Jordan in this connection can be seen as a new source of income that has a trickle-down effect on improvements in other sectors, such as medical services, and thus a remote effect on social and political stability. Nor are the amounts of aid involved insignificant. The figures for the beginning of the 1990s demonstrate this: UNFPA had granted Jordan $10 million since 1976; and the World Bank had given a $13.5 million loan for the implementation of a Primary Health Care Project, out of a total of $30.5 million over a seven-year period. Another $35 million loan had been made to other health projects, together with $73 million to finance a ten-year Human Resource Development Project – and all these projects were related to family planning issues. In addition, USAID had provided a $15 million for a health, population and nutrition package; IPPF gave to its Jordanian branch $0.5 million for two years, while approximately $70,000 were given by small agencies. For 1995 alone, $7.4 million was provided by all donors for family planning purposes.[69]

The totality of the aims targeted also raises hope for the side-effects of family planning policies in terms of investments in related fields, such as development and women's issues. At the same time, the implementation of birth control policies along with other activities such as female empowerment, is internationally a sign of openness, of desire to follow a pattern considered universal and of empowerment of the individual, that goes implicitly hand in hand with acceptance of democracy and the westernisation of socio-political structures – a factor that leads to positive appreciation of the country on the international level and thus helps it sustain its stability.

Conclusion: the purpose of demographic and political transition

In Jordan, the very high but short demographic transition during the 1980s did not smooth political transition at the end of the decade because of the previous explosion of growth rates. The claims for power addressed by young adults to the holders of patriarchal power within the household were reflected at the macropolitical level, as the neo-patriarchal power of King Hussain was challenged. On the social level, increasing education rates played an essential role in progressively dissociating women from early marriage and childbearing. Population policies were proven not to have induced any of these changes but display, instead, socio-political models of individual and female empowerment – the antithesis of patriarchal power.[70] Nevertheless, this trend towards the standardisation of social dynamics and power distribution relies heavily on the apparatus of the state in the provision of services and infrastructures. This, in turn, could create an increased dependency between citizens and the state, as policies become more comprehensive and voluntary. This increased dependency of citizen on the state, moreover, also mirrors the increased dependency of developing world states on international institutions and western governments, achieved through the transfer of increasing amounts of development aid. In short, political transitions leading towards the standardisation of political behaviour rely on the monitoring of social and demographic behaviour at the micro-level.

NOTES

1. This article is a more in-depth study of issues discussed in an earlier more general and comprehensive article: F. de Bel-Air, '"La lutte démographique pour le pouvoir" – Population et politique en Jordanie (1948–98)' in R. Bocco (ed.), *Le royaume hachémite de Jordanie. Identités sociales, politiques de développement et construction étatique en Jordanie, 1946–96*, Amman: CERMOC/Paris, Karthala, 2000.
2. P. Fargues, 'Changing Hierarchies of Gender and Generation in the Arab World' in C. Obermeyer (ed.), *Family, Gender and Population in the Middle-East Policies in Context*, American University of Cairo Press, pp. 179–98.
3. H. Sharabi, *Neopatriarchy: A Theory of Distorted Change in Arab Society*, Oxford University Press, 1998.
4. This term refers to a general scheme of evolution of human populations, characterised by an evolution from a 'pre-transitional balance' (high mortality, high fertility), to a 'post-transitional balance' (low mortality, low fertility). The evolution of annual Crude Rates of Natural Increase (CRNI) (ratio of natural growth, or excess of births over deaths in a given year, to average population in the same year) marks the three phases of this process:
    – high fertility rates continue but a progressive reduction in mortality rates leads to high or accelerating population growth rates.
    – growth rates stagnate, due to slower rates of increase of life expectancy at birth, coupled with a decrease in fertility.
    – growth rates decline because of a drop in fertility rates
    (G. Tapinos, *Eléments de démographie*, Paris: Armand Colin, 1985, pp. 221–2).
5. Central Bureau of Statistics, *Preliminary Report on the Result of the Housing and Population Census 1994 and Sample Survey 1994*, Amman: Central Bureau of Statistics, 1996, p. 4.
6. U.N. Data, quoted by O. Winckler, *Population Growth and Migration in Jordan, 1950–1994*, Brighton: Sussex Academic Press, 1997, p. 18.
7. The sum of age specific fertility rates in a given year (children born in a given year, according to age group of their mother, divided by the total number of women in the age group).
8. The figures provided in chart 1 (Total Fertility Rates (TFR), expressed in children per women) are periodic measures, calculated on the basis of 'hypothetical' (or synthetic) cohorts, the women in each age group in a given year being aggregated to build-up a fictive generation. This procedure reflects periodic events and behaviour patterns, so as to allow for comparison of the fertility situation on a year-by-year basis.
9. P. Fargues, op.cit., p. 179.
10. R. Patai, *Society, culture and change in the Middle East*, Philadelphia, University of Pennsylvania Press, 1971, p. 84.
11. For instance, multinuclear families account for less than 10 per cent of all families in Jordan.
12. V. Moghadam, *Development and Patriarchy: the Middle-East and North Africa in*

Economic and Demographic Transition, World Institute for Development Economics Research of the United Nations University, Working Paper no. 99, 1992.

13. Only 1.6 per cent of men and 2.4 per cent of women in age group 45–49 years were classified as 'unmarried' in the 1979' and census: Hashemite Kingdom of Jordan, Results of Housing and Population Census 1979, vol 2: East Bank, Amman Department of Statistics, 1983.

14. Figures calculated by use of the Hajnal method, using the proportion of unmarried persons in each age group as presented in the 1961 census: Hashemite Kingdom of Jordan, *First Census of Population and Housing- 18 November, 1961, vol. 1: Final Tables: General Characteristics of the Population*, Amman: Department of Statistics, 1961.

15. There was no difference between rural and urban areas, Hashemite Kingdom of Jordan, op. cit.

16. L. Brand, *Jordan's Inter Arab Relations: The Political Economy of Alliance Making*, New York: Columbia University Press, 1994.

17. P. Fargues, op. cit.; pp. 181–2.

18. GNP per capita rose by 65.8 per cent, household consumption expanded and indicators of social development improved, as salaries increased . . . (F. Czichowski (1991) 'Migrations internationales et répartition du revenu en Jordanie', in G. Beaugé and F. Buttner (eds), *Les migrations dans le monde arabe,* Paris: CNRS, 1991, pp. 303–27.

19. The remittances amounted to 3 per cent of GDP in 1970, 14.2 per cent in 1975, 23.4 per cent in 1977, 20 per cent in 1980 and 25.6 per cent in 1984, when it peaked, to be followed by a precipitate decline thereafter. F. Cichowski, *Jordanien. Internationale Migration, Wirtschaftliche Entwicklung und Soziale Stabilität,* Hamburg: Deutsches Orient-Institut, 1990.

20. Hashemite Kingdom of Jordan, op. cit.

21. Y. Courbage 'Fertility Transition in the Mashriq and in the Maghrib: Education, Emigration and the Diffusion of Ideas' in C. Obermeyer (ed.), *Family, Gender and Population in the Middle-East: Policies in Context,* American University of Cairo Press, 1995, pp.81–104. Comparing migration patterns in Morocco and Egypt, the author describes variations in the models encountered by the two sets of migrants and the effect on their fertility behaviour.

22. P. Fargues, 'La baisse de la fécondité arabe', *Population*, 6 (1988), p. 992.

23. Hashemite Kingdom of Jordan (1983), op. cit.; Hashemite Kingdom of Jordan, *Manpower, Unemployment, Immigrants and Poverty in Jordan*, Amman: Department of Statistics, 1991.

24. From 1973 to 1991/2, the number of students increased by 4.8 per cent annually, a rate higher than the demographic increase of the population as a whole.

25. Enrolled in universities and community colleges

26. A. Hammouda, 'Policy implications and future programme issues of family planning and fertility reduction in Jordan' in *The Egyptian Population and Family Planning Review*, Cairo University, 1988; Hashemite Kingdom of Jordan, *Jordan Fertility Survey (JFS) 1976*, 'Summary of principal findings, World Fertility Survey', Amman Department of Statistics, 1976, p. 8; Hashemite Kingdom of Jordan (1984), *Jordan Fertility and Family Health Survey (JFFHS) 1983*, 'Report on principal findings', Amman: Department of Statistics, Division of Reproductive Health, 1984, p. 43.

27. From 25.6 per cent of GNP in 1984 to 17 per cent in 1987 for remittances, from 28 per cent of GNP in 1984 to 10.9 per cent in 1987 for Gulf aid (F. Czichowski, op. cit., pp. 252, 270).

28. G. Anderer, *Die Politische Ökonomie eines Allokationssystems – Jordanien und*

die Internationale Arbeitsmigration seit 1973, Frankfurt am Main: Lang.

29. It rose to 200 per cent of GDP in 1988. P. Dougherty, 'The pain of adjustment – Kerak's bread riots as a response to Jordan's continuing economic restructuring programme: a general overview', *Jordanies* 2, (December 1996), pp. 95–9.

30. Like Jordan, where the evolution of fertility rates mimics the evolution of remittances (– see P. Fargues, 'Contrôler les naissances ou contrôler la famille ? Interprétation de la politique démographique en Egypte, du socialisme au libéralisme', paper presented at the Sixth Franco-Egyptian Meeting on Political Sciences, Institut du monde arabe (Paris), 19–21 May 1995, pp. 1–27, and P. Fargues, 'State Policies and the Birth Rate in Egypt: From Socialism to Liberalism' in *Population and Development Review*, 3, 1, (March 1997), pp. 115–38.

31. Hashemite Kingdom of Jordan (1983), op. cit.; Hashemite Kingdom of Jordan (1991), op. cit.

32. According to a 1997 survey, the female activity rate was stagnant around 15 per cent of women aged 15 and more: Hashemite Kingdom of Jordan, *Manpower and Unemployment Survey 1997*, Amman: Department of Statistics, 1998, pp. 1–447. Analysis of female activity patterns in Amman is provided by M. Kawar 'Young Working Women in Amman: Workplace and Household Perspectives', *Jordanies*, 2 (December 1996), pp. 107–13.

33. At the beginning of the 1980s, unemployment was almost non-existent in Jordan (– see F. Czichowski (1990), p. 317), but reached very high levels after the second Gulf War (between 20 and 30 per cent of active population, according to various sources).

34. M. Cosio, 'Malthusianisme de la pauvreté au Mexique' in Institut National d'Etudes démographiques (INED), *Populations, l'état des connaissances. La France, l'Europe, le monde*, Paris: Editions La Découverte, 1996, pp. 255–6.

35. F. de Bel-Air (1997), 'Les structures familiales à Mhyy' in A. Mahmoud, A. Omoush, M. Biewers and F. de Bel-Air (eds), *The Village of Mhyy – A Socio-Anthropological Study*, Documents of Mu'ta, no. 48 (1997), pp. 255–81 (in Arabic).

36. F. de Bel-Air (1996), 'Amman, lieu de passage ou cité multiple- Eléments sur la structure des ménages' in J. Hannoyer and S. Shami (eds), *Amman, ville et société*, Amman: CERMOC, 1996. Data were collected by the municipality of Amman in 1987.

37. E. Hobsbawm and T. Ranger (eds), *The Invention of Tradition*, Cambridge University Press, 1992.

38. W. Goode, *World Revolution and Family Patterns*, New York: Free Press, 1963; P. Laslett, *Household and Family in Past Time*, Cambridge University Press, 1972.

39. G. Salame, 'Une démocratie sans démocrates?' in *Démocraties sans démocrates, politiques d'ouverture dans le monde arabe et islamique*, Paris: Fayard, 1994, p. 106 (author's translation).

40. H. Sharabi, *Neopatriarchy- A Theory of Distorted Change in Arab Society*, Oxford University Press, 1988, p. 7.

41. V. Moghadam (1992), op. cit.; A. Findlay and M. Ma'ani, Migration, Inter- Generational Wealth Flow and Fertility Decline: A Jordanian Case Study, unpublished, 1990, inspired by the wealth-flow theory of John Caldwell.

42. This domination was effective until the beginning of the 1990s, for example regarding the necessity of the husband's or father's agreement for a women to be delivered a passport, or regarding the mother's responsibility in case of illegitimate birth.

43. 'Naturalisation de l'arbitraire social' – P. Bourdieu, 'A propos de la famille

comme catégorie réalisée' in *Actes de la recherche en sciences sociales*, no. 100 (December 1993), pp. 32–6.

44. See, for instance, King Hussain's speech when returning from hospitalisation in the United States, 1992.

45. Highest fertility rates, earliest female age at marriage, biggest age difference between husband and wife, education gap between men and women, highest average age of the head of household.

46. Due to lack of data available at the region's level, the indicator used is the proportion of employers and own account workers (i.e. non-state employees) within the employed population aged 15 and more in 1979 (HKJ, 1983). The governorate of Ma'an shows the smallest proportion of 'non-state employees' (20 per cent, versus 25 per cent for the country as a whole).

47. From 1985 to 1993, more than 25–30 per cent of marriages were dissolved by divorce in Ma'an, showing an increasing trend, whereas the national average was 20–17 per cent (civil status data).

48. T. Tell, 'Paysans, nomades et Etat en Jordanie orientale : les politiques de développement rural, 1920–1989' in R. Bocco, R. Jaubert and F. Métral (eds), *Steppes d'Arabie*, Paris: PUF, 1993, pp. 87–102; T. Tell, 'Les origines sociales de la glasnost jordanienne' in R. Bocco and M.-R. Djalili (eds), *Moyen-Orient. Migrations, démocratisation, médiations*, Paris: PUF, 1994, pp. 201–19.

49. T. Tell (1994), op. cit..

50. Ministry of Social Development, *The Pockets of Poverty in the Hashemite Kingdom of Jordan*, Amman: Ministry of Social Development, 1989; Ministry of Social Development, *Report on Poverty: Facts and Characteristics*, Amman: Ministry of Social Development, 1993.

51. A. Omran, *Family Planning in the Legacy of Islam*, London: Routledge, 1992, p. 255.

52. With the restriction that it would focus its activities on family planning, but not birth control; see R. Al-Qutob, Towards Family Planning Policy in Jordan, Amman: UNFPA, CST Working Papers, no. 9, 1994, p. 5.

53. G. Gilbar, *Population Dilemmas in the Middle East*, London: Frank Cass, 1997, p. 74.

54. USAID had been in Jordan since the 1950s, providing health services.

55. The Queen Alia Fund for Social Development hosted the Committee. The staff required was recruited with the help of USAID and UNFPA, and sixteen members representing the Ministries of Labour, Education, Information, Health, Higher Education, Religious Affairs, The Armed Forces, the Department of Statistics, the Queen Alia Fund for Social Development, the four public universities of the Kingdom, Mu'ta University, JUST and Yarmouk University were included in the team. The NPC is now an Non-Governmental Oorganisation, specifically in charge of co-ordinating the policy, with governmental, non governmental and commercial sector and implementing the population activities in Jordan – R. Al-Qutob, op. cit., p. 6.

56. The National Birth Spacing Programme, adopted by the government in 1993.

57. National Population Committee (NPC), Jordan: Family Planning Communication Strategy 1997–2002, Amman: NPC General Secretariat, 1997, p. 5.

58. National Population Committee (NPC), op. cit., p. 5.

59. W. Winfrey and I. Masarweh, *Funding and Expenditures within the Jordanian Family Planning Program. Government and NGO Activities,* Amman: The Futures Group International, 1998, p. 2.

60. Jordanian Association for Family Planning and Protection (JAFPP), the Queen Alia Fund (QAF), Soldiers Family Welfare Association, Arab Women Organis-

ation, and the Noor al-Hussain Foundation (NAF).

61. The clinics managed by those institutions provide and promote modern birth control methods, such as the pill, IUD, condoms, Norplant, and Depo-Provera injections. Female sterilisation can also be performed.

62. Information: NPC and the Ministry of Health co-ordinate information activities (Information and Education Communication) with USAID, UNFPA, JAFPP, the Marketing of Birth Spacing Project and the NAF. Training is provided by Jordan University Hospital, USAID and UNFPA, with the Ministry of Health and JAFPP. Research and evaluation is conducted by the Department of Statistics, Jordan University, and contractors to USAID: Family Health International, the Futures Group International, Georgetown University, Macro International, Pathfinder, the US Bureau of Census, and the University Research Corporation.

63. This method is taken from the works of P. Fargues, cited above. Desired fertility rates are available in surveys on fertility conducted by governements and international agencies from the 1970s onwards in several countries (for Jordan in 1976, 1983, 1990, 1997).

64. This analysis owes much to the analysis provided on Egypt by P. Fargues (1995b).

65. Ibid., p. 3.

66. For example, the type of politico-social dynamics referred to earlier are never taken into consideration. The violent debate that emerged at the Cairo Conference on Population and Development (ICPD) in 1994 has not been analysed in terms of its purely political dimension. Moreover, Islam in the design of the policy,is specifically seen as a force most likely to impede social change, while fieldwork can qualify this perception: C. Underwood, 'Islamic Precept and Family Planning: The Perceptions of Jordanian Religious Leaders and their Constituents', in *International Family Planning Perspectives*, 6 (3 September 2000), pp. 110–17.

67. On the national level, it refers to the political stake of disclosing figures regarding the proportion of Jordanians of Palestinian origin in Jordan (F. de Bel-Air, 2000). On the international level, see the arguments given by Arab State opponents to the Cairo conference, who insisted on the political dimension of attempts to decrease the Arab population, thereby weakening it in front of Israel, among other arguments

68. Hashemite Kingdom of Jordan, *Jordan Population and Family Health Survey (JPFHS) 1997*, Amman: Department of Statistics/Calverton: Macro International Inc., 1998, p. 45.

69. Winfrey and Masarweh, op. cit., p. v.

70. This goes hand-in-hand with other recent attempts to withdraw a certain number of responsabilities from the hands of the patriarchal family, including the implementation of new policies regarding retirement and mandatory universal contributions for health insurance.

THE SOCIAL AND POLITICAL EFFECTS OF TRANSFORMATION PROCESSES IN PALESTINIAN REFUGEE CAMPS IN THE AMMAN METROPOLITAN AREA (1989-99)

Ala al-Hamarneh

Amman is a city of refugees. At the end of the nineteenth century North Caucasian refugees were settled near the ruins of the ancient Roman Philadelphia by the Ottoman administration. Thousands of the Muslim Circassians, Chechens and Dagestanis left their homelands during the second Turkish-Russian war. In short, for more than 700 years there had been no permanent population in Amman but by the beginning of the twentieth century it was a small Circassian centre. The importance of the town grew after 1903 with the new railway station on the Hijaz railway, which connected Istanbul, Aleppo, Damascus and the holy cities of Mecca and Medina, being built near it. Some merchants from Damascus and Nablus appeared in the town thereafter, to be joined by Armenian immigrants, who were escaping from the massacre of their people during the First World War.[1] Prince Abdullah declared the town a centre for his administration after the Great Arab Revolt and later as the capital of the new Emirate. Yet Amman was still a village-like town until the Second World War, with less than 50,000 residents.

In 1948 the first big wave of Palestinian deportees and refugees came to Amman. About 820,000 Arab Palestinians were forced to leave their homeland as a result of the foundation of the state of Israel and the first Arab-Israeli war.[2] About 320,000 palestinian refugees stayed in the West Bank, 210,000 in the Gaza Strip and 180,000 went to other Arab countries. More than 100,000 Palestinian refugees came to the young Kingdom of Jordan.[3] The refugees stayed together in many small and unorganised camps, mainly in the Jordan Valley and near the towns of Amman, Zarqa and Irbid. After the foundation of the United Nations Relief and Works Agency for Palestinian refugees in the Near East (UNRWA) in 1949, four camps were orga-

nised with international help on the territory of Jordan, to accommodate the refugees and to carry out direct relief and works programmes
for Palestine refugees in the Middle East.[4] The camps were planned
as temporary and emergency solutions to the refugee problem and
two of them were built in Amman: al-Wihdat (New Amman Camp),
3 km to the north from the town-centre and al-Hussain, 3 km to the
south. One camp was built in Zarqa and another one in Irbid. Not all
the Palestinians stayed in the camps or even registered themselves
on the UNRWA lists. The Christians, for example, with the help of
the local Christian community and the British administration of the
army, found new housing as well as jobs in other neighbourhoods
and towns.[5]

The second big wave of Palestinian refugees took place in 1967
after the Israeli occupation of East Jerusalem, the West Bank and the
Gaza Strip. This time 388,000 persons had to leave.[6] The majority
of them had received Jordanian nationality after the unification of
East and West Banks in 1951 and were therefore citizens of Jordan.
This is the reason for their classification in the literature as 'Displaced
Persons'. Again, the East Bank, especially the areas of Amman and
Zarqa, were the main locations where they settled down. Six new
camps were organised under UNRWA control: al-Baq'a, Hettin
(Marka), al-Talbieh, Jarash, Suf and al-Huson.

The third wave of the Palestinians to come to Jordan were the so-
called 'Returnees'. These are Jordanians of Palestinian origins, who
were forced to leave the Gulf States, mainly Kuwait, after the Iraqi
invasion and the Second Gulf War in 1990–1. Their number varied
between 300,000 and 350,000 persons.[7] The majority of them had
never lived in Jordan (East Bank) before but had gained Jordanian citizenship through the unification of the East and West Banks in
1951. They then left from the West Bank, to travel directly to the Gulf
seeking work and a better future. When they returned, the Amman
Metropolitan Area (AMA), which covers an area with a radius of 35
km, and a travel time from the periphery of up to 45 minutes into
the centre by public transport, was their main settlement destination.
Beside the Great Amman Municipality, this also includes the cities
of Zarqa, Salt, Ruseifah and Madaba. More than 70 per cent of all
Jordanians live in AMA and the majority of them are Jordanians of
Palestine origin.[8] Not surprisingly, the residents of Amman do not
identify themselves with the city. They are, rather, Circassians or Ar-
menians, from Jaffa, Irbid or Damascus, rather than seeing themselves as 'Ammanis', even though they live in Amman. Modern
Amman started with the railway station and has been fixed in the popular mental horizon as the 'transit stop'.[9] There is a similar problem with

other towns in Jordan that lack a discernible identity. Zarqa started with military camps and an oil refinery and Ruseifah started as phosphate mine. In short, these three cities could not offer a local identity to the people; they offer a residential location but no sense of belonging.

In the years 1968–88, between the second and the third waves of emigration, some 12,000 Palestinians were declared 'persona non grata' by the Israeli occupation authorities, in addition to another 88,000 persons, who could not return to the Occupied Territories because they were not able to renew their Israeli West Bank identity cards or their applications were refused. By 1998 there were 3.2 million 'registered Palestinian refugees' on UNRWA's books, of whom about 1.3 million are living in Jordan. About 320,000 registered Palestinian refugees live in the ten Palestinian refugee camps mentioned above, of which six are situated in the AMA. The general strategy of Jordan has always sought to integrate the Palestinian refugees in the socio-political structure of the country and to integrate the Palestinian refugee camps into municipal planning and construction. Despite the problems of mutual confidence that emerged in the late 1960s and the early 1970s between the Jordanian political elite – which includes a respectable number of Jordanians of Palestinian origin – and the Palestinian political elite (mainly the Palestinian Liberation Organisation – PLO), an unwritten code of coexistence dominated political life in Jordan.

There have been a series of controversial suggestions to solve the refugee problem since the Madrid conference. The vast majority of Israeli officials and academics do not admit Israel's historical responsibility in this tragedy. Since the 1980s, the 'New Historians' group has been trying to throw some light of clarification and correction into the dogmatic official history of the foundation of the Israeli state.[10] Yet, to date, only Benny Morris has satisfactorily explained the double meaning concealed within official orders and the mechanism of deportation as well as the ideology and strategy of 'transfer' developed by the founders of the state to deal with the problem of native Arab Palestinians.[11]

However, even he has never discussed either the present moral and political responsibilities of Israel, or the right of refugees to return to their homes. Shimon Peres, a former foreign minister and prime minister, as well as one of the architects of the Oslo peace process, has discussed the humanitarian problem of individual refugees and the 'population exchanges' in the war years without mentioning Israeli responsibility for the humanitarian problems it has created.[12] Indeed, Israeli plans to deal with this issue are based on the concept of the resettlement of refugees in Arab countries. Israel formally denies any responsibility toward them and merely offers to let a symbolic number of the refugees return as part of a families re-unification humanitarian programme. Even a 'dove' like Sholamit Aloni of the Meretz Party describes the right to return as 'less than a dream'.

On the other hand, Palestinians insist on their basic right to return and on the moral, historical and political responsibilities of Israel. But some senior PLO officials have already admitted that compensation of the refugees will have to play a significant role in the implementation of the principle of the right to return in practice. As Abu Iyad said, in 1990: 'We understand that return will be very difficult but we do not forget what is already established: return or compensation.'[13] These constraints have an immediate implication for the Palestinian refugee camps in Jordan and, in the past decade, fundamental changes have taken place within them. These transformation processes were forced to occur by political and social factors which have dominated the history of Jordan during the same period; the liberalisation of political life in the country, the return of 'Gulf Palestinians' and Arab-Israeli peace negotiations and treaties.

Political integration through Islamic radicalism?

During the riots in the late 1980s, the Palestinian refugee camps remained quiet and tranquil. Some demonstrations took place in al-Baq'a, but they did not match the fervour of the general nationwide movement. PLO chief Yasser Arafat advised his supporters, especially in the Palestinian refugee camps, not to interfere in an internal Jordanian matter. At that point, although not after the departure of the PLO structure and militias from Jordan in 1971, he could legitimately claim to be the leader of the populations in the camps. It was only after King Hussain's official declaration in 1988, which announced the political and juridical separation of the West Bank from Jordan against the background of the *Intifada* there, that Yasser Arafat was eventually able to recover his popularity and political influence in the Jordanian camps.

During the 1980s, the PLO, under Arafat's leadership, had lost much of its image as the vanguard of the perpetual struggle for 'liberation and progress', particularly after the Israeli intervention in Lebanon and the subsequent forced relocation of its headquarters to Tunis from Beirut, or after the later internal struggle within the PLO in Tripoli and official contacts by its leadership with Egypt and Jordan. By then, Yasser Arafat was anxious not to lose his renewed contacts with the political establishment in Jordan and repeat the mistakes of September 1970, especially since no-one knew what the future for the Palestinian struggle would be. By the end of the 1980s, the PLO overall had realised that it could successfully strengthen its positions in the Palestinian refugee camps in Jordan by adopting a pro-Iraqi policy during the Second Gulf War, even though the leadership was more circumspect – albeit to little avail. Nevertheless, since Jordan's population and its Islamic movement, with the tacit support of the government, also adopted such policies, the PLO was not able to claim a monopoly on this issue and thus maximise its local popular support.

In 1989, genuinely free and democratic parliament elections took place in Jordan, the first time that the government had not exerted pressure or intervened directly in the elections since 1956. Some 76 per cent of those registered on the electoral lists went to vote, but in the Palestinian refugee camps only 51–57 per cent of those registered actually voted. This was one of the lowest levels of participation in the elections throughout Jordan. Around half the inhabitants of the camps, recalling Yasser Arafat's advice during the riots in 1970–1, treated the elections as an 'internal Jordanian matter'[12]. Of those who did vote, the majority of their votes went to independent and traditional candidates or longstanding PLO supporters, who had good relations with the Jordanian establishment and with the Muslim Brotherhood – the Islamic Action Front had not yet been founded. The one exception to this pattern was a leftwing Christian candidate, standing for a reserved Christian seat in Zarqa, Bassam Hadadin, who got the most votes in the local refugee camps.

Islamist influence. The drift of the Palestinian refugee camp population toward the radical Islamic movement started during the Second Gulf War and grew on the back of the peace process, given their instinctive support for Iraq and their distaste for the way in which the peace process was organised. The Islamic movement criticised the strategy and the tactics of the peace negotiations on one hand and sought to fill the gap in social service provision in the camps on the other. The PLO had lost Gulf financial support because of its supposed pro-Iraqi position and could no longer sponsor their supporters or the social networks in the camps.

The Oslo agreement was the point after which the camp populations became totally dominated by the Islamic movement. An anti-Arafat and anti-Oslo alliance of Islamists and small groups of leftists and nationalists captured the refugee vote in the camps in the second national elections in 1993. The traditional pro-establishment moderate Islamic candidates were punished for their poor performance in the parliament and the pro-Arafat candidates were punished for Oslo. Up to 63 per cent of those registered to vote in the AMA camps actually voted[14], for the elections were no longer simply an internal matter for Jordanians. The winner was the new political organisation of the Muslim Brotherhood, which was also the most powerful strand in the over all Islamic movement, the Islamic Action Front (IAF). After 1993 the IAF and its allies won majorities on the all elected boards and committees in the Palestinian refugee camps. They controlled youth centres, women's organisations, sport clubs, social foundations and even traditional village leagues. The elections to the executive committees of the camps' youth centres were always one of the best indicators of the political mood in the camps.

Even in the 1980s these elections were relatively free and democratic. Their significance lies in the fact that youth centres play a big role in the daily life of the camps, for they organise workshops, protests, meetings, festivals and public initiatives. 'Jerusalem Day', 'Martyrs Day' and 'Homeland Day' were some of the typical activities with a powerful political significance, which have been organised on an annual basis during the last decade by the youth centres in the camps. Hence, control of these centres provides access to an effective instrument for agitation and political activities under the international cover of UNRWA, so the elections were always a battlefield between the different political factions. An alliance of IAF members and independent Islamic activists has controlled the centres since 1993 in all the camps in the AMA. About 10–20 per cent of the seats in the executive committees are occupied by radical nationalist and leftist parties. It is worth noting, too, that almost every fifth committee member is a woman who is in sympathy with the Islamic movement.

A measure of the strength of the Islamic movement was provided in 1997, when the Islamic Action Front called for a boycott of the 1997 national elections and only 25 per cent of those registered to vote in the camps actually did so. By comparison, nationwide there was a 54 per cent participation rate. Furthermore, the camp vote went to independent radical Islamic candidates and the Islamic movement used every possible legal method to drive out the supporters of Yasser Arafat from the camps, since, through a massive organisational structure for propaganda and welfare work, it had effectively replaced the PLO inside the camps during the 1990s.

This trend also reflected the general radicalisation of the Muslim Brotherhood in Jordan. The radical wing of the movement won 45 per cent of the board seats in the nationwide elections in June 1998.

Their platform of a combination of socio-economic programmes for
more social justice and radical Islamic lifestyles, together with their
anti-peace rhetoric ensured that they defeated the moderate wing, the
representatives of 'cultural Islam', who won only 30 per cent of the
seats. The remaining 25 per cent of the seats went to independent
members, who were nearer to the radicals on the main topics at issue
in the election.[15]

There is today a fundamentally new political situation in the
camps. For the first time since the foundation of the PLO, the refugee
camps are dominated by Jordanian organisations, for the Muslim
Brotherhood is, ostensibly in Jordan, a social organisation with long
and rich traditions and good relations with the establishment.[16] The
Islamic Action Front is an official registered political party that has
formally recognised the constitution and the *Mithaq* (National Charter) and, as such, is an integral part of the political system in
Jordan.

The role of Hamas. Ironically enough, the crises between the Palestin-
ian-based *Hamas* movement, which also has a base in Jordan, and
the government of Jordan in 1999 showed the efficacy and magnitude
of this 'Jordanian' domination of the political scene in the camps.
There were only few uncontrolled protests in favour of *Hamas* in the
camps of the AMA region. The Islamic movement in general was
urged to conform to the rules of the political game and the Islamic
Action Front expressed the views of the camps. The argument, therefore, that the Islamic Action Front and the Islamic movement in general are adopting a pro-Palestinian or pro-*Hamas* agenda and that
they cannot, in consequence, be considered to be purely Jordanian organisations clearly has no base. The fact is that they are indeed local
Jordanian organisations and movements.

There is, however, another question that needs to be resolved and
this is what role the Palestinian issue plays in internal Jordanian affairs. The historical reality is that both the Islamic Action Front and
Hamas are political arms of the wider Muslim Brotherhood but this
does not mean that all three have the same internal logical, functional
and ideological structure nor the same ability for further development,
not least because national branches of the Muslim Brotherhood enjoy
complete political and organisational autonomy. Thus, on a national
basis, issues such as political adjustment, methods of political struggle, political loyalties, personal engagement and civil society caused
great internal discussion and even factionalism. Nor is the Islamic
Action Front the Jordanian arm of *Hamas*. The issue is a very delicate matter but it is the key to understanding the importance of the

political drift towards it that has taken place inside the camps.

In the political history of Jordan, many parties and organisations faced the accusation that they were 'arms' of foreign countries and interests. This was one of the strongest arguments used against political liberalisation in the country after 1957, when it was said that pan-Arab nationalists turned towards Cairo, Damascus or Baghdad and the Left was controlled by Moscow or by PLO. The historical controversy over these matters is not at issue here but there is a danger that it will be manipulated so that, at a time of globalisation and intensive international cooperation between states, firms, organisations and individuals, this extreme conservative, cold-war rhetoric will again dominate political life in Jordan.

Since 1992 the country has had a law on political parties and organisations and this, rather than rhetoric, should govern party politics, even when radical movements chose to act illegally. In Jordan, a legally registered Islamic party challenges society and polity and a theocratic ideology is contrasted with national political liberalisation and modernisation. Yet the movement that does this at least has legal status, and is not militant, integrated Palestinian and Jordanian movement operating within the domestic Jordanian context. As such, it has a legal credibility – whatever the government may think of its views – that *Hamas* could never hope to enjoy and this has an immediate implication for political life in the camps which is increasingly directed towards the Jordanian domestic agenda, as well as its specifically Palestinian concerns.

Spatial development and urban adjustment

Nor are political affiliations the only factor leading towards a degree of integration of Palestinian refugees in the camps into the Jordanian domestic scene. In part this has been accelerated by the return of Palestinian migrants from the Gulf during and after the Second Gulf War, which caused a major expansion in the camps themselves. Indeed, the return of the Gulf Palestinians caused a boom in the construction and the trade sectors in Jordan and more than 85 per cent of the returnees settled down in AMA. Furthermore, the camps and the expansions that had grown up around them were the obvious location for poor and low-income families for residence and to establish businesses. A small number of the returnees had originally lived in the camps before migrating to the Gulf countries and the majority of them had relatives there.[17] The boom in the construction sector in the camps was reflected in the conversion of housing units into commercial spaces – demand for commercial locations increased rapidly

during the 1990s – and in the vertical expansion of buildings, as well
as in the development of the real estate market.

Commercial expansion. In 1999, al-Wihdat camp had more than
1,950 officially registered shops and enterprises, of which some 250
had appeared between 1996 and 1999. In 1989, before the Gulf War,
there had only been 435 shops, although, directly after the war, their
number increased, reaching 976 in 1993. However, it is not only the
number of shops that is impressive but the type and variety as well,
for, at the beginning of the decade, these enterprises were mainly
small, simple, family-owned businesses with a low level of technical
expertise. Today there are jewelleries, electric and electronic shops,
banks, travel agencies, taxi offices and pharmacies together with a
huge number of groceries, clothes stores, fast food outlets and vegetable shops.

The result has been that al-Wihdat camp is now the trade centre
of southern Amman. Of course the geographic position of the camp
was the primary factor that made this rapid transformation possible.
At the same time, however, similar trends have emerged in other refugee camps in the AMA area. In al-Baq'a camp there were 1,040 officially registered shops and enterprises in 1997. In al-Hussain camp
there were 605 and in Hettin camp about 470.[18] Yet, beside the officially registered shops and enterprises, there was also an enormous
number of informal businesses which completed the range of economic activities inside the refugee camps.

This kind of business played an important role in improving the financial situation of low-income families. Although only 2 per cent
of the families in the camps consider such activities as vital for their
survival, about 10 per cent admit their dependence on it. In al-Baq'a
camp, such dependencies were significantly higher at 9 per cent and
18 per cent respectively. The informal sector in al-Baq'a also attracted a large number of poor returnees or their family members. As
elsewhere, children are particularly involved in activities such as
street selling, handcrafts and cleaning. In 1997 there were more than
300 informal-sector shops in al-Baq'a. In the other refugee camps in
the AMA region, the situation is not so critical and the main informal
business there are based on hand-crafted goods produced by women
and some small shops. Adult Palestinian and Egyptian street vendors
were the dominant element in the informal sector in al-Wihdat
camp.

Vertical expansion. The vertical expansion of buildings also reached
unpredictable levels. Fifteen years ago a second floor on a building

was permitted in special cases, with the decision being based on a humane understanding of the needs of the refugees. Today, however, most three- and four-floor buildings are used for commercial purposes and are built to be sold or for rent. About 35 per cent of the units in the camps already have a second floor, except in al-Talbieh where the number is about 10 per cent. In al-Wihdat and Hettin every tenth unit has three or more floors.

Of course, the need for more housing is huge in these refugee camps, for the number of their inhabitants has dramatically increased, far beyond planners expectations, and nobody knows exactly how many people do live there.[19] UNRWA records only registered Palestinian refugees in the camps. The Jordanian authorities have made their own estimates based on a cluster of information sources – electoral register, internal ministry register, general statistics register – but neither estimate includes foreigners and marginal individuals who have simply sought low-price housing there.

The range of available estimates demonstrates the difficulties of obtaining an accurate measure of the real number of refugees housed in the camps. al-Baq'a, for example, is the biggest Palestinian refugee camp, not only in Jordan but also in the Middle East. It was built in 1968 for 26,000 refugees. In 1997 UNRWA, the Jordanian Department of Palestinian Affairs and the local camp director gave wildly different estimates of the number of inhabitants there (85,000, 102,000 and 130,000 respectively), whilst several non-governmental organisations even mentioned a figure of 155,000. The comparable estimates for al-Wihdat varied between 40,000 and 55,000 refugees but also excluded about 8,000 Egyptian workers, Iraqi immigrants and local gypsies. These groups appeared in the camp during the last decade, seeking low-cost housing, work and sometimes merely a secure place, far from the hands of the immigration authorities. It is noticeable that there are no native East Bank Jordanians or Christians in the camps. Many of the low-income families from both these groups have chosen to live near the camps but never inside them, despite the low prices.

The real estate market. This unbelievable concentration of people and business in such small areas (al-Baq'a is 1.4 square km. and al-Wihdat is 0.488 square km.) and the high value location of the camps inside the AMA are the main reasons for the rapidly expanding real estate market there. Despite the fact that selling, buying and renting the units in the camps is officially forbidden by UNRWA it is a common phenomenon, which has also benefited from indirect support from the Jordanian authorities. There are even officially registered real estates agencies in the camps; five in al-Wihdat, three in al-Baq'a and two in each of al-Hussain and Hettin. They are also very busy – about 30 per cent of the properties in the old camps in Amman are already sold. The buyers have mainly been camp-registered refugees who are not always camp residents.

The highest unit prices are in al-Hussain camp (JD11,000: $13,000). These units are generally used for housing. In al-Wihdat the prices are cheaper (JD9,000) and roughly 30 per cent of the units are used for commercial activities. The prices in Hettin and al-Baq'a are around JD7,000 JD per unit. Approximately 18–20 per cent of the units there have been sold. It is not easy today to find a unit to rent in al-Wihdat, particularly if a commercial room in the business area is sought. In fact, 30 per cent of the units in the camp are rented and prices are very high at up to JD100 monthly for a 30 square metre space. The prices for commercial spaces are generally double those for housing units. In the other camps in AMA the rent prices are 50 per cent cheaper and the rent market is smaller – at 10–15 per cent of the units.

Al-Talbieh is an exception. This is the smallest camp in Jordan and the one most distant from Amman city in the AMA region, 30 km. away from the centre. About 11,000 persons live there in miserable conditions with no sewerage infrastructure, defective drinking water supply systems, poor transport connections, bad building standards and an unemployment level of 40 per cent. In such circumstances, there can be neither a real estate market nor meaningful commercial activities and, interestingly enough, no returnees settled or invested there. A few foreign workers live in the camp and work in the nearby vehicle service enterprises on the desert highway.

Returnees and ex-camp inhabitants are the main residents in the extensions to the camps. These new quarters were either built just across a highway, as in al-Baq'a and Hettin, or near the camps on empty plots. The process began in the old camps of Amman in the 1970s as a result of the second wave of refugees and was financed with the first petrodollar remittances from the Gulf. The first development was the al-Nuzha quarter which was established to the north and east of al-Hussain camp and was further expanded in both these directions in the 1990s. The same happened around al-Wihdat camp, to the east and south, of the original site. However, unlike the camps themselves, these expansions are formal areas with official status so that there are no ownership or other juridical problems that will hinder further development and reconstruction as in the original camps themselves.

The camps as new urban centres. The camps themselves, on the other hand, have continued as the centres of social, commercial and political life for the new quarters as well. This is particularly clear in al-Wihdat, Hettin and al-Baq'a, for these camps are today service and trade centres in their own urban zones. The UNRWA schools and clinics as well as the social networks and organisations in the camps strengthen this dominant local position. Commercial streets and areas inside the camps are easy to identify and, opposite to them, are clearly residential quarters, where the new buildings are used for housing purposes and prices are lower.

This unplanned structuring of camp territories is an important and basic factor for their urban integration. In the spatial arrangements of the camps it is easy to mark out different functional zones – the business area, the housing area, slum areas, the administrative centre and the schools. Indeed, the al-Hussain camp has been transformed in the last decade into what is effectively a low-income housing area with evident slum quarters in the eastern and the north-eastern parts of the development. The main street, which serves as a business area, divides the eastern slum area of the camp from the normal housing in the west. The administration and the schools are clustered around the camp entrance to the south.

Another important feature of the camp settlement morphology are the major streets or highways that surround al-Wihdat, al-Baq'a and Hettin camps and which each of these camps to have two business areas. The first is located inside the camp and the second on the surrounding street. Each of these areas has clearly different specialisations: inside the camp area, commerce is generally dominated by food and clothes shops, while in the surrounding area there is a more sophisticated trade structure and service provision, with furniture-shops, electrical shops, fast-food outlets, car service, pet shops and clinics.

The segmentation of the housing areas depends on the financial situation of the inhabitants, as well as on the existence of major groups of 'foreigners' – Egyptians, Iraqis and Gypsies live in the western section of al-Wihdat, while the southern part is a slum housing area. In al-Baq'a there are three housing areas: the north-eastern slum quarters, the expensive western area and the medium-status southern quarters. This structuring of the camp territories is an objective process which will lead to their further urban integration.

The big investments of recent years, especially in commerce and construction suggest that the camps will continue to exist in the future and will develop and adjust to new socio-economic structures. Obviously their future urban form cannot be clearly predicted, even if its continuity is certain. Form, however, depends on the international legal status of the camps in future, the local administrative organisation provided for them, an eventual acceptable solution for the Palestinian refugee problem and the future of city planning in general.

Post-Oslo approaches

The Arab-Israeli peace process – together with the treaties and memorandums drawn up for Oslo Accords, the Wadi-Araba Treaty, the Wye Plantation Agreement and the Sharm al-Sheikh Agreement – played an indirect but very influential role in the changes that have taken place in the Palestinian refugee camps in the AMA. Apart from the political drift from pro-PLO sympathies to pro-Islamic radical positions, there has been a widespread psychological transformation taking place towards realism and pragmatism throughout the populations of the camps – a kind of 'post-Oslo approach'. It is reflected in new approaches to three major issues: living in the camps, the desire to return to Palestine and the acceptance of Jordan and Jordanian citizenship. Changes in attitudes towards these three key issues were explored by the author in 1997–8 in interviews with 370 families in four camps in the AMA – al-Wihdat, al-Hussain, al-Baq'a and Hettin.

The absolute majority of camp residents still insist on their right to return to Palestine and on their right to compensation as laid down in United Nations resolutions. More than half the families questioned (52 per cent) said that they would accept fair, direct compensation. They openly admitted that they did not believe in return to their former homes, either as an issue of choice or as a practical possibility, concentrating instead on life and their individual futures in Jordan. The liberation of the occupied homeland, the foundation of an independent Palestinian state and the right of return are moral and patriotic commitments for them, but they are not a personal option.

The majority of this group belong to the 1948 refugee generation and their children. It contains the third generation that has been born and has grown up in Jordan. Their parents and elders worked hard to build a respectable life and they are not ready to give this up for an unsure future of the kind implied by return. However, they are always ready to help 'the dream to become true' – the phrase most frequently used by people when discussing the issues of return and a Palestinian state. Higher-income families with less active political interests from the 1967 wave of refugees also belong to this group. Some of the poor peasants certainly have better living standards today than in their old homeland. There is only a small group of about 10 per cent who admit that they had no properties at all in Palestine and thus have nowhere to which they can return.

A further 24 per cent of the families interviewed argued that they were ready to accept compensation for family members who were unwilling to return. In effect, this meant that the young generation would not want to return but the members of the older generation might wish to do so and compensation would help both groups. Subsequent discussions demonstrated that older family members wished to return to their 'own' houses, their 'own' fields and their 'own' villages but not to Palestine in general. In other words, their preferences are motivated by nostalgia and, if forced to return to 'new' or 'unknown' places in Palestine, the majority would prefer to stay within easy reach of their children and grandchildren, even if this meant staying outside Palestine.

Only a minority of 18 per cent – 6 per cent did not respond to the question – replied that they would want to return to Palestine, wherever they were settled and that they would never accept compensation if that meant abandoning the homeland. Further discussions showed that many in this group were politically active, educated and enjoyed higher incomes than the average in the camps. They represent the modern socio-economic elite in the camps today and are also children of the 1960s and the youth of the golden years of the PLO in the 1970s. University educated with good social positions and wide connections, they dominate the political discourse in the camps and represent their views as the most objective and the only ones that are free from external influence. Members of this group are trying actively to stop the process of further integration of the camps into the urban, socio-economic and political structures of Jordan. They are playing on the issue of Palestinian identity, even if this means dangerous levels of social isolation within Jordan itself.

The group lost much of its influence in the 1990s. This was not only due to the growing popularity of Islamic political ideology that rejects local and regional distinctions in the name of *al-umma al-islamiyiah* (the nation of Islam), but also because increasing numbers of elite members have left the camps in the past decade.[20] Some of them went to the camp extensions alongside whilst others found new accommodation away from the camps altogether. In general, some 55 per cent of the families interviewed did not consider residence in the camps as a means of guaranteeing their Palestinian identity nor did they see it as an efficient way 'to hold together', in other words, to retain social cohesion. Amongst members of the various elites in the camps, this figure is even higher, at 68 per cent.

In addition, large numbers of former officials of the camps' social and administrative networks, as well as ex-PLO activists feel ignored and cheated as a result of the Oslo Accords. In the past they could have left the camps and found more comfortable accommodation but they stayed because they believed in a common cause and in a promising future. Since the Oslo Accords and the Wadi-Araba Treaty, they have realised that their future is now in Jordan and that their old ambitions have been sidelined. The lesson was driven home when the Palestine Authority was created in the Occupied Territories and they realised how few PLO functionaries were allowed to enter the West Bank and Gaza.

Now they try to make the best of their situation in Jordan for themselves and for their children. They exploit their old networks to make appropriate investments in the camps and co-ordinate their activities with the plans of the international community and its organisations, as well as with the local authorities and non-governmental organisations. They are the new local big players in the camps and are building a new set of public attitudes towards the situation of Palestinian refugees in Jordan – the post-Oslo attitude of dealing with Jordan as a permanent social and political reality. For some of their ex-colleagues and for the radicals in the Islamic movement, they are the new local enemy. For moderate and pragmatic supporters of the Islamic movement in Jordan and for the majority of the residents in the camps, however, they are potential allies against the disappointments of the peace process, as well as being good business partners.

The legal, historical and moral aspects of the Palestinian issue in general and of the refugee problem in particular must not be allowed to dominate the socio-economic and political aspects of the integration of Palestinian refugees into Jordanian society. The survey carried out by the author of this paper confirm Brand's view that the fortunes of the Palestinians in the Arab world have depended on the extent of their involvement in or exclusion from societal participation.[21] The right to return and the right to compensation, as well as the right to a Palestinian identity, should not become a barrier to their comprehensive integration. However they have been citizens of Jordan since 1951 and the political representation of these Jordanians of Palestinian origin should at least reflect their economic and demographic weight in the country – although this is not the case at present. The building of a new national identity, which is acceptable to all citizens of Jordan, no matter what their origins, is the essential basis for the further modernisation and democratisation of Jordanian society, as well as being at the heart of stable peace in the region.

The gulf between the Jordanian establishment and the Palestinians that was created by the tragic incidents in 1970 has to be overcome. Although the PLO and Jordan normalised their relationships a long time ago, the political situation inside Jordan did not significantly improve. Instead, Palestinians formed the economic elite of the country whilst Jordanians dominated the political elite. This arrangement, today, will be inadequate to cope with the necessary and difficult changes that Jordan faces in an era of globalisation and eventual peace in the Middle East.

This pattern of unofficial co-existence between Jordanians and Palestinians has dominated political life since the early 1970s. Its importance is underlined by the fact that, when Hamada Fara'neh won in the 1997 parliamentary elections with the slogan 'The Jordanian candidate of Palestinian origin', he unleashed a nationwide discussion on the topic.[22] The same happened when Adnan Abu-Odeh in 1999 openly criticised the low level of representation of persons of Palestinian origins within Jordan's political establishment.[23] The same discussion erupted once again when the new cabinet of Abu al-Raghib in 2000 was named and up to nine portfolios went to persons of Palestinian origins. The intensity of the discussions made it seem as if the earlier years of political cooperation in government between Jordanians and Palestinians in the 1950s and 1960s had been completely forgotten. That experience was not only a consequence of the political unification of the East and West Banks, but had also involved an ideological vision. The demographic changes in the East Bank after 1967 and the eventual liberation of Jerusalem and the West Bank would have encouraged this cooperation but, unfortunately, the 1970–1 crisis had eliminated this possibility. Now, as the refugee population comes to accept a destiny inside Jordan itself, the country has a renewed opportunity to reorder and to renovate national unity towards a more cohesive and homogeneous society.

The first step in this direction would be to adopt a new Electoral Law. The existing election system generally discriminates against the representation of the AMA in parliament, for the electoral districts were created to discriminate in favour of rural and tribal areas. The cities of Amman, Zarqa and Ruseifah, where there is a clear Palestinian majority, are clearly under-represented in parliament. The 1993 Electoral Law – the 'one person-one vote' law – limited further the potential for active Palestinian participation by minimising the role of the camps in the electoral process.

The second step would be to achieve as soon as possible a comprehensive and permanent agreement on the future of Palestinian refugees, involving all interested parties. The numerous United Nations resolutions on this topic, together with the relevant elements of international law should be the basis of such an agreement.[25] Jordan, too, must play a key role in this issue, given the fact that it is the largest host country for the refugees and has, as a result, a specific demographic structure.

More than 75 per cent of the refugees in the camps are now willing to stay in Jordan, which they now privately acknowledge to effectively be their own country. They have lost their illusions about return and realise that Israel will not permit them to do so. If any refugees ever do return, they will come from Syria or Lebanon, rather than from Jordan. In the AMA region, refugees have learnt to differentiate between rights and possibilities, between principles and opportunities, as far as return to Palestine is concerned, as their political representatives well understand. The continuous assurances by Jordanian and Palestinian officials that Jordan's Palestinian refugees must have the right to return and that there are no plans for their permanent resettlement in the country or elsewhere seem to be designed to encourage greater international diplomatic and financial support for the refugees, as well as to increase pressure on Israel to recognise their collective right to return and, perhaps, increase the numbers of refugees who might eventually do so. In reality, though, the refugees in Jordan know that they will not return.

This realisation is a first, essential step towards their political integration in Jordan, for further political liberalisation there will be less successful if specific social groups are excluded in practice by their identification as alien to the domestic body politic. Alongside the institution of effective rule-of-law through an independent judiciary and effective public accountability and popular participation – issues that have now begun to be addressed since summer 2000 – there must be an effective official and juridical recognition of the pluralistic demographic nature of contemporary Jordanian society. Almost every fifth Jordanian is a registered Palestinian refugee and the most modest estimates of the Palestinian element of the population assumes that 50 per cent are Jordanians of Palestinian origin.

In any case, the Palestinian refugee camps have virtually lost their character as temporary refugee housing and no longer play the role of being political focal points of 'anti-Jordanian Palestinian self-awareness', nor is this likely to re-emerge in the future. The sense of separate identities is certainly deep-rooted in both Jordanian and Palestinian communities,[26] but a constructive sense of Palestinian identity would enrich its East-Jordanian counterpart,[27] thus providing the basis for an integrated common identity and for a successful shared future.[28] The pro-Islamic political orientation of the populations of the camps in recent years mirrors the general political drift in the country and the region.

In any case, the Islamic movement in Jordan is pro-establishment and the role of the Islamic Action Front as an opposition movement has now been accepted by government and monarchy. In any case, the Islamic radicalism of the camps has primary economic and cultural roots, as elsewhere in the Middle East. Charles Maynes pointed out in 1998 that the lack of real democracy and the institutions of civil society, together with demographic growth and poverty in the face of the information revolution will continue to be the main reasons for radicalism in the Middle East, whether in the refugee camps in Jordan or amongst the wider national and regional population.[29] Until those problems are properly addressed, it will continue to flourish amongst refugees and Jordanians alike.

NOTES

1. Y. Ghawanmeh, *Amman, Hadharatuha wa-Tarikhuha*, Amman: Dar Al-Liwa, 1979, pp. 4–37
2. B. Morris, *The Birth of the Palestinian Refugee Problem, 1947–1949*, Cambridge University Press, 1987.
3. E. Zureik, (1996), *Palestinian refugees and the Peace Process*, Washington, DC: Institute for Palestine Studies, 1996, pp. 2–12.
4. UNRWA, *UNRWA, a brief history, 1950–1982*, Vienna: UNRWA, 1986, pp. 3–10.
5. Interviews with Christian Palestinian families in Amman and Zarqa (Nuqol, Haddad, Odeh, Nassar, Hawwa, Matta), 1997–8.
6. A.-T. Jaber, 'The Situation of Palestinian refugees in Jordan', (mimeographed), Amman, Jordan, 1996.
7. Y. Le Troquer, R. Al-Oudat, 'From Kuwait to Jordan: The Palestinians' Third Exodus', *Journal of Palestine Studies*, XXVII, 3 (spring 1999), pp. 37–51.
8. P. Lemarchand and L. Radi, *Israel und Palaestina Morgen. Ein geopolitischer Atlas*, Braunschweig: Westermann, 1997, pp. 61–4.
9. S. S. Al-Tall, *Madinat al-Ward wal-Hajar*, Amman: JCC and Konrad Adenauer Stiftung, 1997, 23–30.
10. See the books by the 'New Historians': S. Flapan, *The Birth of Israel, myth and realities*, New York: Pantheon Books, 1987; I. Pappe, *The Making of the Arab-Israeli conflict, 1947–1951*, London: I. B. Tauris, 1992; A. Shlaim, *Collusions across the Jordan: King Abdullah, the Zionist movement and the partition of Palestine*, Oxford: Clarendon Press, 1998; B. Morris, *The Birth of the Palestinian refugee problem, 1947–1949*, Cambridge University Press, 1987.
11. B. Morris, 'Operation Hiram revisited: a correction', *Journal of Palestine Studies*, XXVIII, 2 (winter 1999), pp. 68–76.
12. S. Peres, *Die Versoehnung*, Muenchen: Goldmann Verlag, 1996, pp. 226–30.
13. M. Kayali, 'Qadhyat al-Laj'in al-Filistiniyin, Asbabuha, Aba'aduha, Muqarabat Siyasiyah li-Haluha', *Samed al-Iktisadi*, 18, 105 (1996), pp. 11–35.
14. All figures on the elections are taken from *Al-Rai*, 10 and 11 Nov. 1997, and *Al-Dustur*, 6 Nov. 1997.

15. *Al-Rai*, 29 June and 16 July 1998.
16. L. Brand, 'The effects of peace process on the political liberalisation in Jordan', *Journal of Palestine Studies*, XXVIII, 2 (winter 1999), pp. 52–67.
17. See note 7.
18. The figures of officially registered shops and enterprises, as well as those on construction are from the local authorities in each camp.
19. For estimates of the number of camp residents see M. Abdel-Hadi, 'Al-Mukhayamat al-Filistiniyah fil-Urdun: Haqae'q wa-Arqam', *Samed Al-Iktisadi*, 18, 106 (1996), pp. 138–54, and K. Manssy, ' Mukhayamat al-Laj'in al-Filistiniyin fil-Urdun', *Samed al-Iktisadi*, 13, 83 (1991), pp. 79–96.
20. S. Tamari, *Palestinian refugee negotiations, from Madrid to Oslo II*, Washington, DC: Institute for Palestine Studies, 1996, pp. 1–58.
21. L. Brand, *Palestinians in the Arab World*, New York: Columbia University Press, 1988.
22. *Al-Rai*, 17 Nov. and 23 Dec. 1997.
23. A. Abu-Odeh, *Jordanians, Palestinians and the Hashemite Kingdom in the middle east peace process*, Washington, DC: USIP, 1999, pp. 1–286.
24. R. Babadji, M. Chemillier-Gendrcau, G. de la Pradelle, *Haq al-awdah lil-sha'ab al-filastini wa- mabadi' tatbiqih*, Beirut: Institute for Palestine Studies, 1997, pp. 3–23.
25. L. Brand, 'Palestinians and Jordanians: A Crisis of Identity', *Journal of Palestine Studies*, 24, 4 (1995), pp. 46–61.
26. S. Al-Tal, 'Al-A'laqat al-Urdunyah al-Filistiniyah', in Rabitat al-Kutab al-Urduniyin (ed.), *Hiwar al-Khiyarat*, Amman: Dar al-Karmel, 1997, pp. 103–31.
27. M. Hamarneh, R. Hollis, K. Shikaki, *Jordanian-Palestinian Relations: Where to? Four Scenarios for the Future*, London: Royal Institute of International Affairs, 1997, pp. 12–21.
28. C. W. Maynes, 'The Middle East in the Twenty First Century', *Middle East Journal*, 52, 1 (winter, 1998), internet edition.

TRIBALISM IN KERAK: PAST MEMORIES, PRESENT REALITIES

Christine Jungen

Many commentators on the Jordanian political scene felt that the legislative elections of 1993 – and, more particularly, those of 1997 – marked the return of tribalism to the forefront of political life in Jordan.[1] In part, they saw this revival of tribal solidarity as being linked to the introduction, in 1993, of a new one-man-one-vote law which encouraged 'primordial' – in other words, tribal – solidarity to the detriment of the political parties.[2] Yet this revival of tribal solidarity also seemed to confirm the vision of a Jordanian society still deeply rooted in its traditional tribal structures, hardly touched by the process of democratisation.

On the other hand, the elections produced the results sought by government; the new Chamber of Deputies elected in 1997 contained fewer Islamist opposition members, as well as a substantial majority of notables traditionally loyal to the government. At the same time, more detailed analyses of the political situation have highlighted the dangers of too superficial a view of the way in which tribal solidarity operates in Jordan's political life, emphasising instead the variety of the reasons that lead to the election of a 'tribal' candidate.[3]

Jordanian tribalism, furthermore, is not solely a heritage from the past, as most Jordanians prefer to believe. Studies by Riccardo Bocco and Joseph Massad have shown how the phenomenon was mainly generated by the Hashemites themselves as they constructed the Jordanian state.[4] The analysis here, however, will not be concerned with the various reasons that persuaded the monarchy to promote the tribe as a social and political model and to encourage a large part of the population, particularly those from Transjordan, to accept such a model. It is more concerned with questioning the nature of tribalism and the representations attached to it. It will also study the way in which these representations are mobilised through political factors at both the local and the national level. The objective is to demonstrate the constant reformulation that takes place in the discourse on the tribe at Kerak and to throw new light on the relationship between tribe and state in Jordan.

The legislative elections revisited: two examples from Kerak

We begin by briefly revisiting the legislative elections, as they occurred in Kerak in 1997. Kerak itself is a medium-sized town in
South Jordan which has always been well-known for the vitality of its
traditional tribal structures and is, above all, a good example of the
political success of the traditional notability. Their victory over opposition forces was particularly striking when the results of the latest
elections are compared with those of the elections which initiated the
democratisation process in 1989. In short, whereas the nine deputies
elected from Kerak in 1989 included five Islamists or Islamist sym-
pathisers as well as a communist, in 1997 the deputies from Kerak
were either members of pro-government parties or were independents. Furthermore, it is impossible not to note the increased presence
of the dominant tribe in Kerak, the Majali. Whereas no Majali was
elected in 1989, Abd al-Hadi al-Majali was elected in 1993 and re-
elected in 1997, along with another member of the tribe, Umjad al-
Majali.

Even if it appears, in terms of the results, that members of the major Kerak families had swept the board, assumptions that voting patterns were solely rooted in tribal solidarity should, however, be
subject to some reservation. To demonstrate this, the way in which
two personalities from Kerak who have subsequently played a role
on the national political scene were elected in 1997 will be studied.
These are Abd al-Hadi al-Majali, who, in the year 2000, was the president of the Jordanian parliament, and Nazih Amarin, who took
one of the two seats reserved for Kerak's Christians in the same
parliament.[5]

Nazih Amarin. Nazih Amarin is one of the two Christian deputies
from Kerak in the Jordanian parliament. The Amarin are linked to
the Halasa tribe, the most important local Christian tribe, both because of its size and because of the political and/or economic success
of many of its members. Nazih Amarin's election took place under
the provisions of the change in the 1993 Electoral Law which introduced the 'one-man-one-vote' system. An observer who has not been
forewarned might see in his election the confirmation that solidarity,
whether tribal or religious, was in good health and had made it possible for the Halasa to have one of their members elected to
parliament.

In fact, two Halasa candidates had stood in the election and the second candidate came from a more prestigious and politically influential
lineage than that of Nazih and had been chosen as tribal candidate in

the internal primary elections. Nazih had refused to give up his candidature and had chosen to present himself as an independent, free from tribal constraints. Even though he had been supported by most of his own kinship group and had been able to count on a significant number of Halasa votes, this did not play the decisive role in his election. His success was also dependent on his own ability to create a client network from his own resources, particularly through his professional work as a doctor practising in Kerak. Nazih had created personal links with his patients and had thus constructed a client network from his professional clientele, mainly through free consultations. In fact, analysis of the vote, district-by-district shows that the majority of the votes that he won had come from voters, whether Christian or Muslim, outside the Halasa tribe.

Abd al-Hadi al-Majali. It is not necessary to recall in detail here the success with which the Majali tribe has penetrated into all levels of the Jordanian state. Suffice it to note that the Majali, who had long been dominant in the Kerak area, supported the Hashemite regime very early on and it was as a result of this support, which was usually considered to be unconditional that its members regularly obtained positions at the highest levels of the state in return. Examples of this success include Haza'a al-Majali, the prime minister who was assassinated in 1960, and Habis al-Majali, the former commander-in-chief of the Jordanian armed forces. Abd al-Hadi, together with his brothers Abd al-Salam (former prime minister) and Abd al-Wahab, now dead, formed the most recent group of Majali to benefit from the Hashemite policy of co-option of local elites.

There is, therefore, at first sight nothing unusual in Abd al-Hadi's personal success which fits within a long tradition of pre-eminence for the Majali, both at the local and the national level. What is more interesting is the fact that Abd al-Hadi's family is, in kinship terms, distant from the hard core of the tribe – the lineage which descends from the Grand Sheikh Muhammad al-Majali[6] and which regarded itself as the leading family in the tribe. Abd al-Hadi and his brothers, however, represented the rise in influence and power of a collateral lineage far removed from the traditional leadership, whose political and social elevation was achieved both against the wishes of the leading lineage and to its detriment. They were able to rise up the social scale as a result of an individual initiative undertaken by Abd al-Hadi's father, especially in providing them with an education. When Abd al-Hadi returned from his engineering studies in Iraq he moved slowly into the Jordanian civil service and then inevitable moved into the army. He completed his military training with the British army and then joined the upper levels of the military command structure until he launched upon a political career in 1993. Whilst his brother, Abd al-Salam, was premier, he then founded a pro-government political party, the National Constitutional Party and was elected deputy first in 1993 and then again in 1997 when he also become president of the parliament.

Because of his closeness to the regime, Abd al-Hadi was able to create his own support-base at the local level. Since he was able to transcend the kinship networks and because he created a support base outside his own kinship network, he also created a local electoral support system. The support-base was created thanks of his access to national resources and was directed against the basic Majali tribal network – the traditional network of the leadership which had been represented in the elections by Umjad al-Majali, the son of the deceased former premier, Haza'a al-Majali. The competition between the two candidates and their respective networks had, furthermore, turned towards open conflict during the electoral campaign and, just before the actual elections, there was a physical clash between the supporters of the two clans. Of course – and as a result of the perceptions of *realpolitik* within the Majali – Abd al-Hadi has now successfully absorbed much of the tribal network into his own support-base. This, however, was only possible once his initial success had been confirmed beyond dispute.

Nonetheless, the tribe does have a political reality, even if it cannot be immediately translated into electoral success. The fact that both our notables come from tribes that are locally important is clearly not an accident; in an undoubtedly complex manner, the tribe has ensured its own interests and it could be argued that there has been a collective appropriation of individual success, insofar as the tribe overall has adopted as its own a success in which, in reality, it had only played a secondary role. At the same time, both examples demonstrate the degree to which individual political success in Jordan can escape from tribal solidarity in its narrow sense. In both cases, success came from the mobilisation of networks that were largely outside the tribal structure. Yet this does not mean that Kerak society is not a tribal society, nor that solidarity at the lineage level is not effective. Perhaps the significance of tribalism, as it manifests itself in Kerak, should be sought elsewhere than in the political sphere.

In fact, it is less the reality of effective political solidarities that matters and more the sense of cohesion which could be seen as imaginary, for, even if, as we have seen in the most recent legislative elections, solidarity hardly extends beyond the lineage, or the restricted family group, the awareness of the role of the tribe, both in daily life as well as in a political context, is clearly present. A Keraki is first and foremost a tribal member and it is as such that he is defined by his own as well as by the outside world. He expects aid and services from every member of his tribe who has been successful in achieving national prominence. This expectation, which is frequently disappointed – as is, for example, the case with many Halasa who criticise Nazih Amarin for neglecting his own tribe whilst they believe that he would never have been elected, had it not been for their votes – is the logical outcome of the principle of obligation within tribal solidarity – in theory, at least, even if rarely in practice.

In fact, another, more implicit discourse is superposed on the universal rhetoric of tribal solidarity. It is constructed around the image of the tribal leader – the *sheikh* in Arab terminology. All those who aspire to a prestigious position within Kerak society must conform as far as possible to the idealised image of the *sheikh*. The example of Abd al-Hadi al-Majali is instructive – his family lives with its wider lineage in the small village of Yarout, less than a kilometre away from the village of Rabba, the fief of the traditional leaders of the Majali. The way in which the village is spatially arranged is immediately striking. On the right of the main road to it are some ruins on the site of the original village. Most of the houses are in its centre, around a brand new school. On the left, slightly distant from the rest are two luxurious villas, one belonging to Abd al-Hadi and the other to its elder brother, Abd al-Salam. Between the two villas and the rest of the village there is a mosque which has only recently been built. Its size and lavish external appearance seem disproportionate with the modest village and its garden houses the graves of deceased members of Abd al-Hadi's family.

From his villa Abd al-Hadi looks after his prestigious reputation. During the week he is in Amman but he tries, whenever possible, to spend his weekends in his village of origin. Nor are the weekends for relaxation; upon arrival he is greeted by the local men who come to celebrate his safe return. The next day – Friday – he takes his place in the *madafa*,[7] which has been specially built for this purpose and anybody can approach him to offer good wishes, ask for a favour or complain about a dispute. Even though he would not take part in any negotiation to resolve such a disagreement, it is certain and he and his brother, Abd al-Salam, would be present during the final stages of its resolution. So Abd al-Hadi is a politician and businessman in Amman but a tribal leader in Kerak, as his regular use of the *madafa*, the focus and symbol of tribal life, makes plain. Thus an implicit strategy of 'sheikhisation' – to coin a new phrase – has been put in place in Yarout. The villagers praise the generosity and authority that Abd al-Hadi and Abd al-Salam manifest. They claim genealogical links with the lineage of Muhammad al-Majali and thus the right to claim a leading position within the tribe. They thus place themselves within the tradition of the great *sheikh*s of the Majala in the past.[8]

Abd al-Hadi, despite the claims of his fraction, is not one of the great figures of the tribe, in the opinion of many. 'Those people in Yarout, they may claim to be major personages but they are small . . . the Majali of Rabba and Qaser, yes, they are great, they are *sheikh*s, but those of Yarout . . . ?' Others condemn what they view as his submission to the heavily criticised government of Abderraouf al-Rawabdeh,[9] who was prime minister until summer 2000.[10] 'He doesn't speak up, he doesn't say anything to Abderraouf . . .' It should be admitted, however, that there is no unanimous support for the current official *shaykh mashayikh*, *sheikh* of *sheikhs*, Sultan al-Majali, who comes from the traditional leadership. In reality, a closer look makes it clear that popular opinion believes that 'true' *sheikhs* no longer exist or, if they do, only in a distorted form which has little to do with the figures of the past. '*Sheikhs*! There aren't any anymore. Yes, there used to be and everybody listened to them. Now they're all dead. Today everyone has to look after himself.'

Tribalism is above all a discourse which cannot be properly understood simply through an analysis of the electoral process. The discourse is focused on the tribe itself and the values linked to it but is still a key point of reference within political culture because it is diffused through the social and political structure of Kerak society. Thus every notable, whether he has newly arisen within the traditional local hierarchy or not, will be judged in terms of his ability to appropriate tribal values and to locate himself within the tradition of the great *sheikhs* – an ability which can, as we have seen, meet with a varied degree of success. It is, indeed, only through a systematic referral to the past, to an ancient golden tribal age, that the tribal discourse and the claim of an inherent 'tribalist' framework to Keraki society can be maintained. Contemporary tribalism is suffused with accounts of the tribal past to which it is innately linked. Thus, to appreciate the role of the tribal discourse, we must examine how the collective memory in Kerak formulates what it considers to have been the glory of the tribal past.

'The reign of the sheikhs': the idealised vision of the tribe

The Keraki vision of its local past is based on the importance of tribal power. It would therefore be useful to consider, first, the historical context of this vision in which tribal organisation is identified as the sole political actor.

In the nineteenth century Keraki society[11] was organised in an autonomous tribal confederation. This confederation, which brought together all the Kerak tribes against external threat, was itself divided into opposed tribal leagues: the *Sharaqah* (the Eastern League) and the *Gharabah* (the Western League). It should be noted from the outset that, although the Keraki confederation internally maintained this apparent egalitarian opposition between the two leagues and the tribes that composed them, in reality, since the beginning of last century, it was primarily under the control of the Majala tribe, who were the leaders of the *Gharabah* and from whom came, on a regular basis, the *sheikh mashayikh* of the confederation throughout the nineteenth century.

Even though Ottoman power in the Kerak region was weak, indeed almost non-existent, up to the end of the nineteenth century, the Porte initiated a policy of centralisation and expansion of Ottoman power to the peripheral regions of the empire from the middle of the century onwards. This policy of progressive incorporation of what is now Jordan into Ottoman administrative control led to the creation of the *mutasarrifiyyah* (governorate) of Ma'an-Kerak in 1893 and to the location of a military garrison in the town.[12] Ottoman rule became an increasing burden on the population through taxation and conscription until, in 1910, the population of Kerak revolted against central authority. The revolt, which was led by Sheikh Qader al-Majali and which was a prelude to the Arab Revolt, was bloodily repressed by the Ottomans. With the advent of a Hashemite state a decade later, the Keraki confederation progressively lost its political importance. Its image, nevertheless, remained vibrant in popular memory and today serves to distinguish between a Keraki and someone who could not lay claim to such an identity – particularly the Palestinian population which has settled in Kerak since 1948.

It is in this historical context of latent or real opposition to state power[13] that the Keraki memory and the corresponding tribal discourse has been formed, with one of the points of pride being the 1910 revolt and, with that, the tribal discourse. Furthermore, it is the absence of, or the opposition to, state power that highlights the great actions of the tribes and their *sheikhs*.

Who were the great *sheikhs* of the past? Each tribe has its own 'great men' whose actions form the narrative thread of tribal memory. They include, for example, Mohammad Qader, Rfefan al-Majali, Hussain Pasha al-Tarawneh, Ibrahim and Odeh al-Goussouss, to name but a few, for the list of those *sheikhs* who filled the local political scene under the Ottoman empire or at the start of the Hashemite state is long. Keraki memory emphasises their struggle for tribal autonomy in Kerak, particularly through the 1910 revolt. The most illustrious example is undoubtedly Qader al-Majali who led the uprising for which he paid with his life. Qader, exalted as the martyr of the revolt, appears as the prototype of the ideal *sheikh*, not only because of his decisive role in the revolt but also because of his charisma, his courage and his contempt for death. This is the best-known and most widely accepted account of his death:

When the Turks made Qader a prisoner, they took him to Damascus. Shortly after his arrival there, they gave him a cup of coffee. A servant came to warn him that the coffee was poisoned. Qader's companion, a lesser *sheikh*, appeared to drink the coffee but, in reality, let it run down his chest. As for Qader, he emptied the cup . . . that's how he died![14]

Behind the history of *sheikhs* stands the image of the 'big man', the archetype of the outstanding leader of men who was able to gather the tribe behind him, despite internal divisions. A more detailed study of the characteristics embodied in a 'big man' of this type reveals a set of special features – rectitude, extreme generosity, physical and moral courage, self-control, the ability to stand above pettiness; in short and in general terms, *sharaf* (honour) and *akhlaq* (moral stature).[15] These attributes of the true *sheikh* as he existed in the past are repeated in the same, unchanging manner to the outside observer until they generate the stereotype of the 'big man' in an image that resembles old daguerreotypes which hang on parlour walls and which recall men of another time, with their imposing moustaches and their *mandils* (headcloths).

At the same time, behind this portrait of a *sheikh*, there emerges another image of the tribe dominated by collective solidarity and consensus behind the leader, together with a capacity to fight and, above all, a determination to remain independent of other tribes in the confederation and of the wider world. Thus the number of guns, the battles, the *razzias* (raids), the political alliances with other tribes and even the conflicts which were sometimes unavoidable are recalled with pride. The tribe is then described as a homogenous body, the guardian of the collective *sharaf* and *akhlaq* of its members, of which the *sheikh* is the public face, re-presenting them to the wider world. This is the body which is the source of authority and which confers such authority on the *sheikh* through a collective consensus.

Furthermore, it is only within the tribal framework that politics appears. Competition for power and access to resources – land and water – can only be expressed through intra- and inter-tribal relations, which are the *sheikhs'* responsibility. The Ottoman empire rarely appears in oral accounts of the tribal period. When it is mentioned, this is either to stress the historical validity of the account[16] or to show how the Ottoman government tried to monopolise political power at the espense of the tribes. Finally, as the 1910 rebellion demonstrates, the tribe only exists in opposition to the state – that is the essence of the message from Kerak.[17] This holds equally true for the early days of the Hashemite emirate as it does for the Ottoman empire – hence the pleasure taken in recounting the episode of Amir Abdullah going to Amman after entering Transjordanian territory and making a halt at Qatraneh[18] in order to ensure the support of the Kerak tribes. He ran up against the splendid indifference of *sheikh* Rfefan al-Majali who did not consider it worth his while to journey to meet the man who would become king of Jordan . . .[19]

The opposition of the *sheikhs*, whether active or passive, to state power is a convention in the accounts of the tribal past. Whilst it is interesting to note that the current tribal discourse refers to this conflictual vision of tribe and state – this is a point to which we shall return – it is even more striking in the context of the historical facts now known about the period in question. Consider only what they tell us about the *sheikhs* of the tribes and their relations with Ottoman power. In fact, it seems that the Ottomans put in place a policy of co-option of local elites even before the *mutasarrifiyyah* of Maʿan-Kerak was created. Thus, for example, Muhammad al-Majali, the *sheikh mashayikh* of Kerak, received Ottoman subsidies as a colonel in the Ottoman army and as governor of Kerak. In return for this, he was charged with collecting taxes on behalf of the Ottomans.[20] It is true that this policy was not always successful, requiring the Ottomans to undertake punitive expeditions in order to extract their due.[21] Nonetheless, it is significant to note that, contrary to the image of Ottoman power as authoritarian and constraining, it could also be seen by the *sheikhs* as a source of revenue, as well as a guarantee of the well-being of the tribes. Indeed, it was because of this that the Ottoman empire was able to make its entry into Kerak; indeed, the administrative centre was placed at Kerak and not at Maʿan, as the Ottomans had intended at the demand of the Kerak notables themselves since they counted on economic benefit as a result.[22] For their part subsequently, the *sheikhs* never jibbed at calling on Damascus, which was the seat of the governorate of Syria, when they needed to, and at the same time assuring the Ottoman authorities of their submission to Ottoman control.[23]

The various accounts of the tribal past therefore mask the Ottoman – and, subsequently, the Hashemite – strategy of incorporating the

tribes and their *sheikhs* under their control, thus ensuring a strengthening of state control over the territory of Kerak. Apart from their financial aid, the Ottomans also played on tribal and religious
divisions to entrench their power, particularly by encouraging the leader of the great tribal rival to the Majala, Hussain al-Tarawneh, as
well as some Christian leaders in the attribution of administrative
posts. Indeed, even if it is clear that the 1910 uprising was mainly motivated by the fear of tax allocations and increases, it must equally
be noted that, amongst the complaints made to the *wali* in Damascus
by the Kerak chiefs some time before the revolt, major attention
was given to the reduction of the subsidies allocated by the state to
the *sheikhs*, as well as the eviction of Majali from the administrative
council created by the Ottomans in Kerak.[24]

It thus appears that the Majala challenge to the Ottoman presence
in the region was also made in the light of their claim to an improved
access to the political and economic resources of the state. Furthermore, other Kerak leaders, such as Hussain Pasha al-Tarawneh and
Odeh al-Goussouss who were more closely integrated into the Ottoman administration than the Majala, played a role which was more
than ambiguous during the revolt, since they did not directly oppose
it initially, as the example of Hussain Pasha shows.[25]

It is therefore necessary to significantly modify the concept of the
sheikhs as sole masters of their decisions, as well as that of an egalitarian tribal structure, independent of, or opposed to, central power.
It could even be suggested that the *sheikhs* did not actually draw their
prestige from their ability to penetrate within the circles of central
authority. Even if the lack of sources makes it impossible to confirm
this thesis, it is clear that the links of the *sheikhs* with the Ottoman
authorities contradict the vision offered by tribal memory. In place of
the image of the tribe outside or against the state, the sources reveal
that the *sheikhs* recognised the state, even if only implicitly. It appears that the ways in which tribal structures were integrated into the
state are not so different from what can be observed today in Kerak
and in the wider context of Jordan.

Nonetheless, tribal memory is engraved with a quite different image of past reality. The super-abundance of accounts of a semi-
mythological tribal past, dominated by tribal values and constructed
to counter state power, means that we should examine the interests
which today lie behind this exaltation of the tribal golden age.

Between myth and reality: the restructured tribal discourse

The concept of tribalism today does play a new role in Jordanian society for it has subsequently been politicised in the current debates which are concerned with the nature of Jordanian society and, furthermore, with the nature of the Jordanian nation. To clarify the context of these debates, it should be borne in mind that the dominant component of the contemporary population of Jordan is of Palestinian origin.[26] Up to the 1970s, as the independent Jordanian state was being constructed, the Jordanian population of Transjordanian origin had fully supported the struggle for the Palestinian cause. The situation changed after the events of Black September and, Jordanians of Transjordanian origin increasingly turned against Palestinians after 1970 because they believed them to be unwilling to recognise their debt to the country that had welcomed them.[27] The gulf between the two populations has got progressively deeper and, today, the fracture between them appears to be complete. Transjordanians regularly accuse Palestinians of disloyalty towards the king and towards the country.[28] There is therefore now a clear distinction made between the 'Palestinian' – a Jordanian of Palestinian origin – and the 'Jordanian' – a Jordanian of Transjordanian origin.[29]

The tribal discourse is now deployed in the context of 'Jordano-Palestinian' tension within Jordanian society. Indeed, it even characterises the distinction between Jordanian and Palestinian when the nomadic traditions of the former are contrasted with the peasant and even urban traditions of the latter. Furthermore, it is in this context, too, that the terms *'asha'ari* (tribal), *watani* (patriotic) and *urduni* (Jordanian) have progressively acquired an equivalence between them. To be tribal, to claim tribal characteristics, to support tribalism thus becomes a way of claiming Jordanian authenticity. At the same time, it also becomes a way of anchoring this authenticity in a tribal epoch which, along with its mythic dimension, extends beyond the event-driven and semi-programmatic way in which the Jordanian state was created. The reference to a tribal past also makes it possible to locate the tribal member within Jordanian territory and one of the most recent developments of this process of territorialisation of the concept of tribalism has been the emergence of the term *sukkan asli* – the 'autochthonous people'[30] – which will now be used to locate the Jordanian-Palestinian opposition within a Jordanian 'territory' which predates the Hashemite state and was occupied by the tribes whose descendants consider themselves to be the 'authentic' Jordanians. In short, if the logic of this position is pushed to the extreme, it means that the Jordanian already existed before Jordan!

The Hashemites have always insisted that Jordanian society – including both Palestinians and Jordanians – was tribal. Does it then follow that the current movement of tribal nationalism, which many

Kerakis support and which excludes the Palestinian community within the country, might eventually challenge Hashemite legitimacy, as Shryock suggests?[31] This question should be posed in light of the apparent incompatibility that exists between the tribal phenomenon and the power of the state and which appears in the accounts generated by tribal memory in Kerak.

It should be recalled here that the ideal types that emerge from these accounts have the primary function of being models, idealised mirrors of a past in contrast with the development of contemporary society. Many people, in fact, regret the end of the *sheikhs*, the end of tribal solidarity, contrasting society today, which is seen as fragmented, individualised and centralised under the state's authority, with the golden age of former times. This vision, which is, in any case, at odds with that of the eternal survival of the tribe and its values, must be taken into account in evaluating the specific nature of tribal ideology. In fact, systematic comparison between 'past' and 'present', between model and reality, requires that the evolution of tribe and tribalism within the Hashemite state be reconsidered.

It was pointed out above that, in Kerak, search for individual prestige requires recognition of the tribal epoch; whoever seeks local status is systematically forced back to the tradition of the great *sheikhs* of the past, with whom he must affiliate himself. At the same time, it was also clear that today's notables are denied the opportunity to achieve a position of prestige equivalent to that attributed to the *sheikhs* of the past. These facts can be explained in many ways; one, proposed by the Kerakis themselves, emphasises the lack of substance of these 'little people' who like to become *sheikhs*.[32] The true *sheikh* is someone who is able to remain 'above' the rest; in other words, he who, whilst being *asli* (to have an origin) – in other words being able to claim a name, a lineage and a tribe – knows how to transcend the limits of kinship. Paul Dresch has shown, in the context of Yemeni tribes, how the *sheikh* links to his lineage base a complementary cliente-list network which is external to the lineage and may even reach beyond the tribe.[33] In the Kerak case, it could be said that such a network is essential for the prestige of a *sheikh* and, without it, he would be reduced to protecting himself from lineage and tribal rivalries not commensurate with his desired status. Thus it is that notables are regularly blamed – despite the reality, moreover, that even the local base itself is often of extra-tribal origins – for only allowing their close kin to benefit from their success.

Another reason that emerges behind popular alienation from the notables is their closeness to the state. In fact – and even though it appears at first sight to be odd in the current context of a powerful and

centralised state where the essential requirement of patriotism is loyalty to the Hashemite monarchy – the Kerakis still refer to the vision
of the tribe and the *sheikh* outside the state when they recreate the
model of the 'big man'. The case of Abd al-Hadi has already been discussed but it applies to several Kerakis who have skirted around central power, whether close in or at a distance. Lacking credibility and
legitimacy in popular discourse because they do not 'speak up to' the
regime, they apparently lose forever the possibility of acquiring the
prestigious status of '*sheikh*' – at least for a time.

As we have seen above, the *sheikhs* of the past, those whose praises
are chanted today, were hardly more independent of Ottoman power
than are today's notables from the Hashemite state. Pierre Bonte
has noted, in his study of the tribes of the Mauritanian Adrar, the link
between segmentary instability and factional fights around central
power.[34] The same analysis could be applied to Kerak if the competition between lineages and tribes over access to state power is reviewed
within these terms of reference. Today's 'little men', probably like
the 'big men' of the past, focus their success into their ability to obtain
access to the interior circles of the regime, thus obtaining prestige
which is reflected back on their close kin and eventually allows the
pattern of lineage and/or tribal hierarchy to be altered. The restructured tribal account can thus subsequently offer its own version of the
tribal ideal by including these modifications within it.

A last example will highlight this pattern of the construction of
the tribal account in terms of the political strategies of tribal leaders.
Rfefan Pasha al-Majali (Qader al-Majali's brother) and Hussain
Pasha al-Tarawneh were two historical emblems who were both local
and national in their scope. In addition, as leaders of the Majala
and the Tarawneh respectively, they symbolised in their conflict-rid-
den relationship, the traditional opposition between the two tribes
and, more generally, between the *Gharabah* and the *Sharaqah*, the
two leagues of the Keraki confederation. Each of the two *sheikhs* followed inverse trajectories – whilst Hussain Pasha supported Ottoman
power, Rfefan very early on established close relations with the Hashemite family whereas Hussain joined the opposition to the emir, later King Abdullah. These links to the Hashemites permitted the
Majali to reinforce their prominence at the local level whilst, at the
same time, the Tarawneh lost part of the leadership they had been
able to establish during the period of Ottoman control. It would be
reasonable to expect that the causes of the rise and fall of tribal leadership, given their obvious linkage to the closeness of central power,
whether Ottoman or Hashemite would be discussed in accounts of
the past. Yet, although the Majali like to discuss the role of Rfefan

alongside Qader al-Majali during the revolt against the Ottomans, his links with the Hashemites are rarely mentioned. On the other hand, Hussain Pasha's role as 'traitor' to the cause of Kerak during the uprising is usually passed over in silence, even by Majalis, whereas his opposition to the Hashemite regime is frequently highlighted. This leads to the question as to whether the inherent contradiction between '*sheikh* against the state' and '*sheikh* within the state' is not in itself a component of the tribal system in Jordan.

From this standpoint, the confrontation between a discourse which describes an ideal-type of tribe and *sheikh*, modelled by memory, and reality takes on a completely different meaning. The tribe then appears, above all, to be a conceptual framework, manipulated at leisure to offer an image of social organisation traced from a mythic past but which, because of the demands of modernity, it can only imitate very imperfectly. This 'traditionalism through an excess of modernity', to use Jeanne Favret's famous expression,[35] which in this case involves a perpetual oscillation between past and present, seems to partly condition Jordanian tribalism. The patterns adopted by contemporary tribal structures are systematically seen as unfulfilled and ineffective compared to a political ideal relegated to a past which cannot be reproduced. It is here that the flexibility of the tribal system within the Hashemite state takes place; expression of a past ideal and a present reality creates a space in which the tribal process and its hierarchies can be renegotiated and restructured, as can be the discourse that accompanies it.

Tribal ideology has been both recovered and promoted by the Hashemite monarchy, within a policy of the tribalisation of Jordanian society. The monarchy has, however, lost some control over the process during the most recent events. In fact, this process has been taken over by a nationalist movement which, as we have seen, puts forward an exclusive and restrictive vision of the Jordanian nation, based on a concept of tribalism and its location in a period before the state was created, on a territory which also precedes the Jordanian state. However, to argue that, in the medium term, this tendency will turn against the Hashemite monarchy which, it should be recalled, is in no way Transjordanian in origin, would be to overlook the way in which the tribal discourse is formulated within the state. The idea of a confrontation between tribe and state as inherent within tribalism itself is only possible if the state itself is recognised as such. Since it is based on a mythical tribal past, the construction of this conflictual relationship within the discourse allows the tribe to be integrated within the framework of the state whilst at the same time allowing the reproduction of the imaginary vision of the tribe. The Hashemite state has certainly played a significant role in the tribalisation of Jordanian society, but the way in which Jordanian tribal ideology, in turn, conceives of the tribal system as generating the Hashemite state should equally be questioned. The following quotation from an interview will serve as a conclusion:

You know that the Hashemites came from the Hijaz, not from here. The truth is that the tribes around here knew that they would never agree with each other; if, for example, a Majali *sheikh* had led Jordan, the Adwan would have immediately asked 'Why the Majali and not us?' The solution, therefore, was the Hashemites – they came from outside, so everybody is happy.

NOTES

1. Jordanian journalists, and analysts, as well as foreign observers, support this view (see J.-C. Augé, R. Bocco, J.-L. Duclos, 'Les élections de 4 novembre 1997. Contexte et prétexte d'une normalisation politique', *Monde Arabe Maghreb-Mashrek*, 160 (1998), pp. 30–49.

2. This law which only allows each elector to have one vote, replaces the previous multi-vote system which had given the voter the right to place on his voting slip a list of names equal to the number of seats available in a particular district. The single named vote system was introduced by the government apparently in order to muzzle the opposition, particularly the Isamist parties, and to ensure the election of traditional notables.

3. See in particular G. Chatelard and A. Al 'Omari, 'Les solidarités primaires et leurs limites. Deux études de cas: les sièges musulmans d'Irbid et le siège chrétien de Madaba', *Jordanies* 5–6, 1998, pp. 273–96.

4. R. Bocco, 'Tribus et Etat en Jordanie', thèse de 3ème cycle, Paris, Institut d'Etudes Politiques; J. Massad, 'Identifying the nation: the juridical and military bases of Jordanian national identity', Ph.D. dissertation, Columbia University, 1995.

5. It should be noted that Jordanian law guarantees special reserved representation for ethnic and religious communities in the parliament. Thus nine seats out of 80 are allocated to Christians and two of the nine are allocated to the Kerak district.

6. Mohammad Abd al-Qader al-Majali, *sheikh* mashayekh ('*sheikh* of *sheikhs*') dominated the Kerak region until his death at the end of the nineteenth century.

7. *The madafa* (literally the 'place of hospitality') is a room or building dedicated to the reception of individuals or tribal groups.

8. Abd al-Salam is more committed than his brother to this reappropriation of the tribal image to his advantage. Thus he liked to wear traditional clothing, and decorates his *diwan* with swords and daggers (brought from Yemen), claiming Bedouin origins. This, however, relates to the process of national 'bedouinisation' which was initiated by the Hashemite monarchy and is outside the scope of this discussion.

9. Abderraouf al-Rawabdeh, quite apart from endless accusations of being personally corrupt, was also blamed by Jordanians from the south of the country for having demonstrated outrageous favouritism towards people from the north of Jordan in allocating governmental and military posts (he himself is from Irbid,

north of Amman).

10. Rawabdeh's mandate ended only shortly before the end of my fieldwork in Kerak.

11. The term refers to the population within the Kerak district, not just the population of the town of Kerak alone.

12. E. Rogan, 'Incorporating the periphery: the Ottoman extension of direct rule over southeastern Syria (Transjordan), 1867–1914', Ph.D dissertation, Harvard University, 1991; E. Akarli 'Establishment of the Ma'an-Kerak Mutasarifiya', *Dirasat*, 13 (1986), 1, pp. 27–42.

13. It was an opposition, moreover, that periodically reappeared, as the most recent upheavals in 1989 and 1995 demonstrate.

14. Although it certainly occurred in curious circumstances, Qader al-Majali actually died after being amnestied by the Ottomans in 1912; see S. Musa, *Tarikh al-urdun fi al-qarn al-'ashrin1900–1959*, Amman: Maktabat al-Muhtasib, 1988.

15. *Sharaf* signifies grandeur and honour in the sense of spiritual fineness; *sharaf*, as understood in Kerak, is generally concerned with masculine behaviour whereas '*ird*, which is also translated as 'honour' is specifically linked to female sexual behaviour. *Akhlaq* (singular *khuluq*) is concerned with ethics and morality in the sense of honesty and moral rectitude.

16. It is, incidentally, interesting to note the historicist role assigned to the state in the context of a tribal period which is implicitly outside time . . .

17. It is, nonetheless, not a message which is specifically Keraki. In this context, see the situation in the Adwan tribe; A. Shryock, *Nationalism and the genealogical imagination: oral history and textual authority in Jordan*, Berkeley: University of California Press, 1997.

18. A small railway station on the Hijaz railway, located some 20 km. east of Kerak.

19. Is this a legend or is it true? Whatever the real situation, it is nonetheless the case that, thereafter, the Majala were always known for their faithful support for the regime. But this is usually discreetly and quietly overlooked, at least by the Majala.

20. A. Amawi, 'State and class in Transjordan: a study in state autonomy', Ph.D dissertation, Georgetown University, 1992.

21. E. Rogan, op. cit.

22. E. Akarli, op. cit.

23. For example, the petition addressed to the Ottomans by the *sheikh* of the Rwala during the drought of summer 1897, a petition which was notably co-signed by the most pre-eminent *sheikhs* of the Kerak tribes. Cited in E. Rogan, op. cit., pp. 146–7.

24. P. Gubser, *Politics and change in Al-Karak, Jordan*, Oxford University Press, 1973.

25. Ibid.

26. The population considered to be Palestinian currently involves Jordanians who had fled or whose parents had fled from Palestine from 1948 onwards. It should be noted that Jordanians of Palestinian origin, but who came to Jordan before 1948, are considered by the community to be fully Jordanian.

27. It should be noted that a significant number of Transjordanians battled alongside the Palestinian *fedayins* during the Black September near-civil war in 1970.

28. There are of course, other views as well but this is a common comment in Kerak.

29. The two terms are used in this sense in the subsequent text.

30. My thanks to Géraldine Chatelard for bringing the increasing use of this expres-

sion to my attention.

31. A. Shryock, op. cit.
32. But are they really so 'little'? If they are denied the status of greatness, does this not imply that they could aspire to it?
33. P. Dresch, 'The position of *sheikhs* among the northern tribes of Yemen', *Man*, 19 (1984), 1 83–99.
34. P. Bonte, 'Donneurs des femmes ou preneurs d'hommes? Les Awlad Qaylan, tribu de l'Adrar Mauritanien', *L'Homme*, XXVII, 102 (1987), pp. 54–79.
35. J. Favret, 'Le traditionalisme par excès de modernité', *Archives européennes de sociologie*, 8 (1967), pp. 71–93.

NEW MUSEOGRAPHIC TRENDS IN JORDAN

THE STRENGTHENING OF THE NATION

Irene Maffi

This analysis will investigate the construction of the national identity and the manipulation of the past in Jordan, focusing particularly on the use of archaeology and of the archaeological and ethnographic museums. It will only, however, focus on museums that have been planned during the last five years of the 1990s since they show the direction in which the Jordanian sense of national representation is evolving. Indeed the analysis of this topic was suggested by the fact that, in recent years, the construction of several new museums had been planned by the Jordanian authorities as well as by different foreign institutions in cooperation with the local Department of Antiquities. This follows from the remarkable tourist development of the kingdom in the last decade. But this explanation is not in itself a complete explanation, because the increasing number of museums is also a symptom of the ideological and political climate characterising the Hashemite kingdom. Though sometimes concealed by the tourist and economic façade, museums have shown that the Jordanian authorities accord considerable importance to their role in relation with the education of the population and over the diffusion of the kingdom's international image abroad. Three different groups of museums and similar institutions will be discussed in order to demonstrate the concepts on which they are based and, in consequence, to outline the main features of Jordan's national representation of itself.

The JICA Museums projects

The first group of museums to be discussed is made up of institutions financed and partially planned by the Japan International Cooperation Agency (JICA) together with the Ministry of Tourism and Antiquities in the frame of a wider plan aimed at developing international tourism in Jordan. Before starting the project, the Japanese agency carried out preparatory studies in order to identify the numbers and the kind of tourists visiting the country, as well as their main destinations. These studies allowed the Agency to identify regions in the kingdom, selected mainly through economic criteria,[1] that were considered 'priority tourism development areas'. In these areas JICA decided to support the construction of four museums which were to form an important element of the planned architectural and historic rehabilitation of the sites chosen. The selected areas were Amman, Salt, Kerak and the Dead Sea. The museums in Salt and Kerak and that of the Dead Sea were to have a local character, because they would illustrate regional or urban history,[2] whereas the museum in Amman will cover the history of the whole kingdom, from the prehistoric period up to the present, and therefore have a national character. JICA has confined itself to control over the various stages of project implementation, whilst private enterprise actually handles implementation, after selection by the Ministry of Tourism and Antiquities. The National Museum, for which Jordan has been waiting for many years,[3] deserves a special mention, because the Royal Palace has taken a direct interest in it and, in November 1999, the Queen herself selected the person to be entrusted with the project.[4]

What, however, are the main conceptual features of these museums? The three museums situated outside the capital, although they will represent the local histories of Salt, Kerak and the Dead Sea region, have been planned in Amman, the political and cultural centre of the kingdom, by enterprises and individuals which are not connected with these locations. These designers are interpreting and staging local histories through the cultural tools available to them, involving multiple sources, from Jordanian secondary and higher education to Western literature and its conceptual models. For instance, Rami Daher, the architect responsible for the Salt Museum, and 'Ali Maher, who is in charge of the Kerak and Dead Sea museums, both live and work in Amman and have studied abroad. The conceptual structure they propose for the museums demonstrates the integration of their Jordanian metropolitan culture with the conceptual instruments they have acquired in the Western world.[5] As a result, local actors – their representations, interests and passions – will be only a subordinate element within the museum projects if, indeed, any attention is paid to them at all.[6] The representation of city history in Kerak, for example, may not mirror the different interpretations that local inhabitants would like to see illustrated in the city museum. Although the representation of local history imposed by the political centre of the country may act as a unifying element at the local urban and national level, this does not allow local voices to speak for themselves. Such an outcome is obviously not the case with the National Museum, since an institution of this kind is expected to represent an official view of national history which is usually not formed from local interpretation, but by governmental representation of national history. Yet, in these projects, centralised planning and design will ensure that the local, regionally-based museums will also reflect the official positions of the Jordanian government, alongside the National Museum.[7] But how are local histories to be articulated within a perspective of a comprehensive national history? In fact, local projects will focus on local historical periods and specific events within the context of official interpretation, as manifest in older museums and in school texts.

The Salt Museum. The project of the Salt Museum does not focus on local political history or on different tribal discourses.[8] Salt history has, instead, been transformed into a folkloric tableau, where the local political and historical distinctiveness disappear behind the integrative uniformity of official discourse. This folkloric approach is certainly a powerful tool for creating a sense of unity and erasing local differences. As Barbara Kirshenblatt-Gimblett points out, 'the proliferation of variation' creates 'the banality of difference'[9] and this conclusion is particularly effectively borne out in the culture section of the museum, where there are a material culture room, a children's room and a domestic life room dedicated to 'traditional' culture. At the same time, it must be admitted that the Salt museum seems to be different from other folkloric museums in the country, since it will include a history section. Though this is not yet clear on what kind of history the museum will focus, nor what point of view will be adopted, it is worth noting that the project aims to illustrate the historical period known as the Golden Age, the period from 1847 to 1918. This will be a very interesting feature of the museum, since the period in question – the end of the Ottoman era – is almost never represented in Jordanian museums. In fact, in the official discourse the Ottoman rule is usually treated as a negative interlude in the history of the kingdom which, according to school texts, consisted merely of military and political domination. For instance, in a textbook which deals with *Al-Tarbyia al-Watanyia al-Madanyia* (civic and national education), for the seventh grade in school, in the section devoted to the history and culture of Salt, we read that the Ottomans *subjugated* the city until 'the forces of the Great Arab Revolt *liberated* it'.[10] These choices of verbs not only reveal the attitudes of the authors of the textbook, but also encourage students to form a negative view of this historical period. The same historical premise determines the exclusion of representations of Ottoman rule in Jordan in museums throughout the country, in which the Ottoman period is almost completely absent. Yet, if the Ottoman period is not included, how does the official discourse locate the beginning of the history of the kingdom? Usually the history of the kingdom begins with the Great Arab Revolt of 1917, so that Jordanian history is identified with Hashemite history. Local history before the appearance of the Hashemite family on the stage of the regional history is given very little attention.

Within this context, the emphasis on Ottoman history in the Salt museum – during which 'most political, social and urban development took place' according to the exhibits – should be seen as a new museographic, perhaps even, ideological trend. Indeed the fact that the official discourse may now be expanded to include historical periods which have been previously ignored may be a symptom of the fact that Jordan no longer fears that some elements of national history may be a threat to national unity. As a consequence, elements that do not necessarily support national cohesion may now be introduced into the national historical tableau. At the same time, the presence in the museum of a section dedicated to the late King Abdullah shows that more traditional modes of display, which focus on national history,[11] mainly the history of the Hashemite family, persist. This is perhaps hardly surprising for, during the last fifty years, at least the Hashemite dynasty has acted as the unifying focus of the nation, the element to which all Jordanians, of whatever origin, can refer to experience a sense of common patriotism. It is of course for this reason that the majority of museums in Jordan often have a separate section dedicated to the history of the royal dynasty.[12]

National museum projects

The second group of museums to be discussed here has a strictly national character, because it results from the internal cultural policy of the Ministry of Tourism and Antiquities, the Ministry of Culture and the University of Al al-Bait. Among the museums in this group, the Museum of Ma'an, the Museum of Political Life in Amman and finally the Samarkand Museum at the University of Al al-Bait will be considered.[13] These museums are addressed, first, to Jordanian citizens and then to tourists and foreign visitors. The purpose of these museums is mainly didactic: they are to teach young generations the history of the kingdom and the crucial role in it played by the Hashemite dynasty. The foundation of Jordan is represented as the result of the Hashemite political and military initiative which was at the

origin of the Great Arab Revolt and the liberation of the Asian pro-
vinces of the Ottoman empire. If the Great Arab Revolt is the founding event in the Jordanian history, the period that followed it
reflects the different reigns of Hashemite monarchs – the reign of Abdullah and the short reign of Talal, which was immediately followed
by that of Hussain.[14] In the official discourse, the reigns of the monarchs constitute the rhythm which characterises national history from
its inception in the Great Arab Revolt.

The Museum of Political Life. An interesting example of the national
institutions mentioned above is the Museum of Political Life, situated
in Amman in the seat of the first Jordanian parliament. This museum,
which is under the jurisdiction of the Ministry of Culture, had originally been planned in 1994[15] and is devoted to the late King Abdullah.
Its purpose is to illustrate the qualities of the kingdom's founder
and to describe the first period of Jordan's history. Although the period of the Great Arab Revolt is not included in the display, its exclusion does not contradict what has been said above since the
descriptive texts accompanying the displays continually remind the
visitor of this event. In fact, in the introductory section of the museum, we read that one of the purposes of the display is to highlight
the allegiance of King Abdullah to the principles of the Great Arab
Revolt – *wahda* (unity), *musawa* (equality), *quwa* (strength), and *ta-
qaddum* (progress).[16] The implication is that the social and political
life of the kingdom is based on the same values and principles, because King Abdullah was the person who 'made Jordan appear on
the political map in 1921'.[17] Indeed he paved the way for democratic
life, political pluralism and freedom of opinion in the kingdom.
Furthermore, in accordance with the principles of Arab unity, he also
'suggested the creation of the Greater Syria' and then declared the
unity of Jordan and Palestine. Another objective of the museum is to
shed light on the personal, political and cultural endowments of the
late king by showing his ability to deal with Jordan's tribes, other
Arab countries and international issues, as well as his poetic and lit-
erary interests.

   This, however, begs a further question related to the development
of Jordan's political life – what of the part played by the rest of the
country, the Transjordanian tribes and families, the Circassians or
the Arab leaders who took part in the Great Arab Revolt and went to
Transjordan with the Emir Abdullah in 1920? The museum does not
seem to have enough space for all these actors, who are relegated to
the backstage. The captions under the photographs and the documents exhibited in the museum, for example, indicate that even the

members of the initial Jordanian Parliaments will be in the background of the displays, even though the exhibition is in the building that they originally occupied. As was noted above, the national version of local history ensures that the monarchy is the political and ideological centre which alone can organise the past in order to guarantee its own existence. In the light of such principles, other actors in national history must play a secondary role, as decided by Hashemite apologists for they have designed the narrative. There is, nonetheless, a special place reserved for those participants in the Great Arab Revolt who were not Jordanian in origin but later became part of the new country. They include those men who played an active role during the Great Arab Revolt, who sought refuge in Transjordan, in order to 'contribute to the growth of the country'.[18] The reason for this is probably not only the fact that the Hashemite dynasty itself came from another country and must thus seek to justify its political power in Jordan, but also the fact that the population of the kingdom is comprised of heterogeneous elements, all of different origins. The emphasis on this group, therefore, is an allegorical personification of the situation of the majority of the Jordanian citizens[19] and of the royal dynasty itself.

The Samarkand Museum. Another recent museum which should be considered as part of the process of evaluating new trends in the kingdom's museography is the Samarkand Museum. The museum is in the University of Al al-Bait and, as the University monthly newsletter reported, 'includes exhibits and elements from Islamic civilisation and culture spanning different eras and places'. It also seeks to preserve, maintain and enrich Jordan's heritage in Islamic civilisation, as well as publish and promote awareness about it, whilst enhancing 'the spirit of cooperation among nations' and at the same time at encouraging 'tourism and national development'. It is worth noting that the museum's philosophy, as reported here, is in harmony with the principles that inform the University of Al al-Bait, which was founded in 1994 under the patronage of Prince Hasan bin Talal, with the purpose of enhancing relationships between and dialogue amongst Islamic countries, in which the Hashemite dynasty would play a central role.[20] The university and the museum also share another feature: both are linked to the development of the Mafraq governorate and the Badia region.[21]

In fact, an important section of the museum is devoted to the archaeological and anthropological study of the Badia region, both in terms of exhibition space and because a group of its researchers has been working in the area since 1996. The thematic approach adopted in the exhibition focuses on three topics related to the Badia: the Hijaz railway, the Al-Fidden traditional village and the Roman road. The reconstruction of a small section of the Hijaz railway and the purchase of a locomotive with some passenger carriages enables the history of the country at the beginning of the century to be illustrated and highlights the importance of regional communication links in the economy. The second thematic exhibition has a more anthropological character since it stages local traditional culture through the reconstruction of Badia 'old houses' and the display of 'ethnographic elements from the local environment'.[22] The third thematic area will be devoted to the reconstruction of a Roman road as an example of the Roman paths still visible in the Badia region. All three themes reflect the interests of the researchers working for the museum – an archaeologist, an epigrapher, a historian and an anthropologist.[23]

Projected and current exhibitions at the Samarkand Museum[24] suggest that the Badia section is expanding at the expense of the Islamic exhibition. One reason for this is, perhaps, the fact that it is quite difficult to acquire objects which would illustrate different aspects of Islamic civilisation.[25] On the other hand, the team running the museum consists of scholars more interested and qualified to study local culture than Islamic civilisation. In any case, it is important to underline that this museum, like the new museums in Salt, Kerak and the Dead Sea, manifests a local character, because the exhibitions are linked with regional cultural and historical development. Yet, even so, the displays in the Samarkand museum, as in other new institutions, do not reflect the narratives of local inhabitants, mirroring instead a metropolitan and centralist official narrative. Thus, the Hijaz railway in the Badia is representative of the whole railway, as it traversed the kingdom. Indeed, it is also echoed in the exhibition in the Ma'an Museum and in the project for the rehabilitation of the station in Amman.[26] The same is true for the traditional houses and the ethnographic objects exhibited in other museums of the kingdom,[27] as well as for Roman remains which form a major part of Jordan's archaeological heritage.

The Ma'an Museum. Local specificity, integrated into the national narrative, is also evident in the museum established in Ma'an in 1998. Ma'an, which was another station of the Hijaz railway, was the city in which King Abdullah stayed for some months after his arrival in Transjordan in 1920. He transformed one of the station buildings into his residence and this has recently been turned into a museum. The decision to restore the Ma'an station has a multiple significance since the architectural complex in itself constitutes part of the national heritage, the location has symbolic meaning linked to the history of the Hashemite family, and the city itself represents the tribes of the south of Jordan. The bonds between the monarchy and the state, on the one hand, and the southern tribes, on the other, find a perfect fusion in the new Maʿan Museum. Although the museum resulted from collaboration between Muʿta University and the Department of Antiquities in Amman, the actual conceptual structuring of the exhibition was decided in Amman,[28] as has happened in the majority of the country's museums.

Yet, despite its location, the museum does not, for example, reflect the genealogical history of the tribes or Ottoman rule in Maʿan. Visitors expecting to find such exhibits will be disappointed because they will, instead, be confronted with an official narrative of national history. In fact, the museum is devoted to King Abdullah and to the foundation of Jordan. The exhibition illustrates early Jordanian history, from the arrival of Emir Abdullah, as he then was, in Transjordan, to the establishment of the kingdom. Whilst the exhibition is very rich in national symbols linked to the personality of Emir Abdullah, local culture is confined to folkloric representations. There are rooms full of domestic objects – old musical instruments, of decorated daggers and rifles, a reproduction of the Bedouin tent or some ancient rugs – but this is all. Yet these kinds of objects can be found in every ethnographic museum of the country and the Maʿan Museum therefore conforms to the powerful influence of folkloric traditions within Jordanian museography, with its capacity to generate 'the banality of difference', as already noted with respect to the museum in Salt. Clearly, this aspect of Jordanian museography reflects a centralist ideology, designed to strengthen national unity and to impose a unique and unified vision of the past. This nationalist and centralist biography of the nation is clearly designed by the state and filtered through a Hashemite filter. Indeed, the only exhibits in the Maʿan Museum that represent the history of the city and which do not depend on folklore are those dedicated to the Hijaz railway. They illustrate the foundation of the station, the construction of the bridge near Maʿan, the names of the donors who helped to finance the construction of the railway and the names of the workers who built it.

Yet there is another aspect which underlines the importance of the Maʿan Museum. It consists in the fact that this museum, like other, similar locations in the kingdom, has been appropriated by the Hashemite dynasty, as it has appropriated Jordan for the sake of the dynasty. This logic of appropriation is designed to transform the soil of Jordan into a significant geographic space filled with locations and structures that recall Hashemite history. It is a way of creating

a national memory and a shared identity, formed by the spatial union
of Transjordan with the Hashemite tradition.[29]

The 'museumification' of space

This appropriation of locations and structures by the Hashemite dynasty in the territory east of the Jordan forms a very important theme
within a national narrative. It embodies the powerful relationship between identity and memory of community and space. Almost a century ago Maurice Halbwachs demonstrated the role played by spatial
references in sustaining group identity. Landscape and buildings as
physical objects give 'a sentiment of order and stability',[30] needed by
any group of people if it is to sustain its identity. Since space is transformed and adapted by individuals, 'every aspect, every detail of [a]
place has a meaning which can be understood only by the members of
the group, because every part of the space it occupies corresponds respectively to the several aspects of the structure and the life of their
society'.[31] In a reciprocal fashion, the modification of space and of
the meaning ascribed to it may also influence the social and cultural
organisation of the community involved. In other words, the relationship between space occupied by a specific group and its identity provides, in itself, an opportunity for its manipulation. With Jordan's
national territory, the fact that location recall a shared national memory is less important than the fact that such places are related to
Hashemite history. Such locations are more significantly linked with
the history of the royal family than with the past of the inhabitants of
Transjordan. Thus Jordanians exist and can be defined as such only
through this reference to the Hashemite past.

Biblical itineraries. The ascription of a particular meaning to space
– its semantic significance – plays a crucial role in two activities related to museograpy which have been promoted by the Jordanian
authorities during 1999 and 2000. The first consists of the identification of biblical sites on the territory of Jordan. This is a phenomenon
that, though enhanced and publicised during 1999 and 2000, has already a long tradition in the kingdom. In fact, since the end of the
1950s and in the 1960s, the tourist and international image of Jordan
has been closely linked to Biblical history. During that period, such
an identity was much easier because the West Bank and Jerusalem, as
key components of the Holy Land, were still part of the kingdom.[32]
Brochures, books and postcards referred to this Biblical history and
reminded Western visitors of the sacred nature of the kingdom's soil.[33]
Despite the Israeli occupation of the West Bank and the subsequent

disengagement announced by King Hussain in 1988, the advent of the Christian Jubilee in the year 2000 revived the biblical significance of Jordan. Beside the undoubted tourist value of this development, there are also other meanings. A short quotation from the tourist brochure *Biblical Sites of Jordan* helps to clarify what is in effect the 'museumification' of the territory of Jordan.

Jordan is a modern country, a holy river and an ancient culture – a timeless physical and spiritual panorama of prophets miracles and human faith. For a religious pilgrimage or a touristic visit to the holy land of Jordan, the Bible is more than a document of faith – it is also a gazetteer and a virtual road map of ancient places, people and events associated with this serene and spiritual land.[34]

Interestingly, such Biblical references do not appear to contradict Jordan's Islamic character. Indeed, the lives of the prophets of the Old Testament and the story of Jesus are also narrated in the Qur'an, so that Islamic tradition considers them prophets who anticipated the revelation of Muhammad. Thus the brochure presenting the holy sites of Jordan, where we read that Jordan is 'the River and the Land of the Baptism', also states that Muhammad was the last of the prophets, through a long tradition which starts with Abraham. It is evident that the Jordanian authorities seek a compromise between such a Christian identity for the territory and the essential Islamic character of the Hashemite monarchy. In order to understand the multiple significance of this image, it is essential to appreciate that the Hashemite dynasty aspires to a role as mediator between the Christian world and the Arab Islamic world,[35] and that Jordan has its own Christian minority, which identifies with the Christian past of the kingdom.[36] In the official narrative, therefore, the Biblical sites of Jordan are transformed into a common historical arena with which western tourists, the local Christian minority and the rest of the population can identify.

In reality, there are several common elements that could be shared by believers of both religions – ancient history, the spiritual and sacred character of the land and the veneration of specific sites. The representation of the land as spiritual and sacred, for example, involves a duplicated significance for Muslims and Christians alike. On the one hand it is clear that Jordan's history and territory are narrated and recreated through the Biblical text, in order to make them immediately familiar to a Christian pilgrim going to the Holy Land. On the other hand, Jordan is the 'gateway of the Arab-Islamic conquest' as it is often described in the official narrative,[37] since the Byzantine army was defeated near the River Yarmouk and many companions of the Prophet, who fell during this military campaign, were buried in the soil of the kingdom. Furthermore, since the Hashemites, whilst in Mecca, were considered for many centuries to be the guardians of the sacred places of Islam,[38] they have also been able to claim to be the protectors of many sacred sites in Jordan linked with Arab Islamic history.[39]

Ancient history is another important element that contributes to the creation of Jordanian identity and that could become a common point of reference for both Muslims and Christians. In fact, the 'religions of the Book' – Judaism, Christianity and Islam – accept a considerable part of the events narrated in the Old Testament that took place within the geographical region covered by Jordan. The archaeological sites and remains dating back to events narrated in the Bible thus also confirm the antiquity, the consequent status and the importance of modern nations that can claim direct links with such important precursors,[40] although, interestingly enough, the Israelites and the Jewish religion are never mentioned in this narrative of Biblical history and locations, despite their central role in the events that constitute the narrative itself!

The example which demonstrates most clearly the political significance of national antiquity and of its link with the Biblical narrative has been the struggle between Jordan and Israel over the identification of the site of the baptism of Jesus.[41] Both countries have identified their own site for the place where John the Baptist baptised Jesus. As far as Jordan is concerned, the site is located in the ancient remains of Bethany, to the east of the River Jordan, on the Wadi Kharrar, opposite Jericho. The cultural and political importance of the identification of the Baptism site to Jordan was made explicit by the publicity given to its restoration during 1999, through conferences, newspaper articles, postcards, postage stamps[42] and even a special website. Moreover, in order to achieve international recognition of the Baptism site, Jordan has sought to include Bethany beyond the Jordan in the UNESCO World Heritage list, together with Petra and Quseir 'Amra.[43] In other words, the Jordanian state considers that its national identity is represented at the international level by a Nabatean city and an Umayyad castle, as well as by the Baptism site with its direct link to Biblical history.

Umayyad pathways through Jordan. In short, the cultural process of ascribing particular significance to territory through history may be used to express a multitude of meanings simultaneously, so that the Biblical significance of Jordan is only one among other possible linkages. This principle becomes clear when a second example of 'museumification' of Jordanian territory is considered. This is the creation of an exhibition trail under the theme 'The Umayyads: The Rise of Islamic Art'. The project has been promoted by the European Union since 1997, as part of the process of Euro-Mediterranean co-operation, and seeks to create Islamic art and history itineraries in Mediterranean countries. The Jordanian Department of Antiquities chose five itineraries that include archaeological sites from the Umayyad period of the history of Transjordan. The reasons for the choice seem quite straightforward; although there are many examples of buildings dating back to other Islamic periods, the Umayyad desert castles are among the oldest and most beautiful Islamic remains in the country. In addition, during the seventh and eighth centuries, when they were built, the territory of modern Jordan was in the centre of the expanding Arab empire, since Damascus was the seat of the Caliphate.

Moreover, this is not the only Umayyad site of importance in modern Jordan. During Umayyad times, the ancient city of Amman was an important administrative and political centre, as the recently excavated and restored Islamic citadel in the city demonstrates. From the point of view of national ideology, the recent restoration of this complete Umayyad citadel is of considerable importance, because it allows the Hashemite dynasty to give historical depth to the capital of the modern kingdom and to establish a significant link between the modern monarchy and the Umayyad caliphate. Indeed, subsequently the Abbasid dynasty moved the capital to Baghdad and the ancient city of Amman fell into obscurity and decadence which lasted till the twentieth century, when it once again became the capital of the new Emirate.[44] Thus for more than one thousand years Amman played no important role and was almost forgotten. In short, the choice of another historical period for the inineraries would have downplayed the role of Amman and of Jordan, because it would have reminded visitors of a period during which Jordan was at the periphery of the Islamic world.

The restoration of the Umayyad citadel in Amman is also very significant because it facilitates the establishment of a supposed genealogical and political relationship between the Hashemite monarchy and the Umayyad dynasty, a theme which appears very often in official discourse. Thus, if the Islamic citadel of Amman constitutes an historical antecedent to the modern Jordanian capital, the Umayyad caliphs are, in some sense, the ancestors of the Hashemite monarchy. This ideological centrality of the site, together with the fact that the tourists usually start their journey around the country from Amman, explains why the first itinerary of the Jordanian exhibition trail is the Umayyad citadel located in the kingdom's capital. Ironically enough, the desert castles that, before the importance of the citadel in Amman was established,[45] were considered the most important Umayyad monuments in Jordan, are now included only in the third itinerary.

Visitors might be puzzled by the second and the fourth itineraries, since they are dedicated to non-Islamic sites. In fact, the second itinerary goes to Byzantine archaeological sites in and around Madaba, and the fourth itinerary visits the cities of the Decapolis in the northern part of the kingdom. The inclusion of these sites in the Umayyad exhibition trail is, however, justified on two grounds. First, since the populations of the Hellenistic and Roman cities of the Decapolis are considered to be of autochthonous origin, the fact that they were first polytheist and subsequently Christian is considered to be less important than the fact that they are the ancestors of modern Jordanians. Secondly, after the Islamic conquest life in these places continued in the same way as it had under Byzantine rule. Indeed, during the Umayyad period Christian cities and the churches were not destroyed and their inhabitants were allowed to keep their faith.

Thus if in general the emphasis on continuity in local culture is an important element in the official discourse on modern Jordan, because it shows that the country has an ancient and rich history and, in consequence, a strong sense of national identity, this insistence on cultural continuity during this particular period also has a specific function. It helps to strengthen national unity, since the Christian minority of Jordan is an integral part of the nation, and it also highlights the traditional Jordanian tolerance towards the Christianity and other cultures. This is an important component of the international image of the kingdom and of the role to which the Hashemite dynasty aspires in the political and religious panorama of the Near East. Last but not least, the second and the fourth itineraries of the Umayyad exhibition trail help to make Western tourists feel at ease, since they involve Hellenistic, Roman and Byzantine sites – evidence of those civilisations that are considered as the precursors of modern European and American culture.

The fifth itinerary leads to the southern part of the kingdom, along the old roads that, since ancient times, have crossed the land to the East of the River Jordan. Here, too, the link with the Umayyad period is indirect. Although the inclusion of these roads among the itineraries is justified in terms of history because they were still used during the Umayyad period, the literature accompanying the itinerary does not provide precise information about the reasons for their inclusion. All that is said is that the fifth itinerary reveals 'caravan

stations and trading routes', and that 'the southern cities have a commercial significance', since 'they served as centres of business activities and stations for pilgrims and traders.'

Yet, in reality, the purpose is to reinforce the theme of continuity
and of the intrinsic relationship between the Umayyad period and the
Roman and Byzantine era. Indeed, the linkage is made explicit when
the textual material points out that the itinerary provides an opportunity to make a comparison between the structure of Islamic cities
and Roman military camps built along the *limes*. Indeed, the visitor
is left with the impression that this reaffirmation of the continuity of
Western influence on Umayyad architecture and art is also a way of
creating a strong relationship between the supposedly dominant civilisations of the past and the culture of the Arab-Islamic world. In
other words, Jordan has achieved the unusual objective of inheriting
and integrating Arab Islamic Umayyad culture, as well as the elements of Western civilisation, both past and present, for it is, as the
fifth itinerary demonstrates, a place of cultural, commercial and religious encounter, with the cultural richness which is the consequence
of its geographic location at the cross-roads of culture.

NOTES

1. See Ministry of Tourism and Antiquities, *The Study of the Tourism Development Plan in the Hashemite Kingdom of Jordan*, 1996. Executive Summary.
2. The local history represented in these museums does not coincide with the version that local inhabitants may narrate but rather with the interpretation of central government. Thus, for instance, the museum in Kerak will describe the ancient history of the city, from prehistoric times to the Islamic period but will omit any account of the events of the nineteenth century and the beginning of the twentieth century even though they play a crucial role in the definition of the identity of lo-cal citizens. For more detail on the local version of the past produced by the inha-bitants of Kerak, see the chapter by Christine Jungen in this volume.
3. Since the end of the 1970s a committee formed by archaeologists, university pro-fessors, members of the royal family and important personalities in the kingdom, had been working on the constitution for a National Museum without success. Only in 1999, thanks to Japanese aid, did the situation change and the project has now finally been financed.
4. In July 1999 a project for the National Museum had been presented to JICA and the Ministry of Tourism and Antiquities, which was very similar to the conceptual organisation of the Museum of Jordanian Heritage, located at Yarmouk Univer-sity.
5. Among western concepts adopted in museum projects is the concept of the eco-museum, used in the context of the rehabilitation of the old city of Salt. The con-cept of a museum itself is a Western institution which was first introduced at the end of the nineteenth century by European colonisers in the Middle East as well as in other parts of the world.
6. Though Rami Daher has paid great attention to the impact that the museum

and the planned tourist trail will have on the inhabitants of Salt, the way the project has been conceived and implemented, will probably not allow them to play an active role. On this subject see also R. Daher, 'Gentrification and the Politics of Power, Capital and Culture in an Emerging Jordanian Heritage Industry', *Traditional Dwellings and Settlements Review*, X, 11 (spring 1999).

7. The role of the local inhabitants is referred to in a special paragraph about the project, where it is said that local participation must be encouraged. But what kind of participation does it suggest the project requires? We read that the inhabitants of Salt should be trained in museum curation, offer guided tours, perform traditional activities and donate the ancient objects they possess. However, although the attention paid to local participation is a new and important idea in Jordan, the kind of approach suggested in this project can still be improved. In fact no voice is given to the local inhabitants during the design phase of the museum display. They may become active actors only once the museum has been established, since it needs a staff and the objects to function.

8. For instance, Dr Abu 'Ayash, the chief of the Tourism Sector Development Project, who is in charge for the project in Salt, is aware of the problem (interview with the author, October 1999).

9. B. Kirshenblatt-Gimblett, 'Objects of Ethnography' in I. Karp, S. D. Lavine, (eds), *Exhibiting Cultures: The Poetics and Politics of Museum Display*, Washington, DC: Smithsonian Institution Press, 1999, p. 433.

10. Ministry of Education, *Al-tarbiya al-watanyia wa al-madanyia, a-saf al-sabi'* (National civic education for the seventh class) Amman, 1999, p. 129.

11. When I use the term 'national history' I refer to the history of the Jordanian people as an entity that already existed before the advent of the Hashemite dynasty to the throne. Indeed before 1921 and the establishment of the unified emirate of Transjordan, it was not possible to identify a Jordanian people, since under the Ottoman rule the country did not constitute a unitary administrative region, although it was considered a part of the bigger cultural and economic unity of Bilad al-Sham. Consequently national history in Jordan coincides primarily with the history of the Hashemites and starts with the unification of the country. For more details on the history of pre-Hashemite Jordan, see E. Rogan, 'Incorporating the Periphery: The Ottoman Extension of Direct Rule over Southeastern Syria (Transjordan), 1867–1914', PhD dissertation, Harvard University, 1991.

12. There are many museums in the country devoted entirely to the history of the Hashemite family: the Martyr's Memorial, the Museum of Abdullah mosque, the museum inside the Raghadan palace in Amman, the museum of Ma'an, the museum in Zarqa. The creation of these Hashemite museums dates back to the 1980s, with the exception of the Martyr's Memorial, which was founded in the 1970s.

13. These are only some of the new museums in the kingdom, since currently a new archaeological museum is being founded in Irbid, a new military museum is going to be constructed in Amman and a new visitor centre will be opened in Jerash. Small visitor centres have been opened also in Iraq al-Amir and in the region of the desert castles during the closing months of 1999.

14. The new museums will probably include a section devoted to King Abdullah II.

15. See the project of Hazim al-Rifa'i, *The Museum of Political Life* (in Arabic).

16. It is interesting to compare this section of the project with a chapter in the textbook for the seventh grade about the world's ancient civilisations (*tarîkh hadarât al-'alam al-qadîma*), devoted to life in Mecca and Medina during the pre-Islamic period, because it casts light on an ideological feature of the official historical narrative. In this section, the period where the Quraish, the ancestors of the Hashemite

family, ruled in Mecca is represented as a kind of democratic government (pp. 30–2). Considering the well-known relationship between the Quraish and the Hashemites, this image is clearly linked with the discourse on the Great Arab Revolt and hence of the foundation of Jordan.

17. See *Project for the Museum of Political Life* (in Arabic), 1999, p. 1.

18. Ibid., 3.

19. Over the issue of the Jordanian nationality see R. Bocco and T. Tell, 'Frontières, tribus et état(s) en Jordanie orientale à l'époque du Mandat', *Maghreb-Mashrek*, 147 (Jan.–March 1995), pp. 42–3.

20. 'Al al-Bait University Law', article 5, *Al-Zahra*, IV, 18 (August 1997), p. 12. For the importance of the role of the Hashemites in the promotion of the interfaith dialogue, see also G. Châtelard, 'Interfaith dialogue in Jordan: a display of Hashemite moderation', Jordanies, 4 (December 1997), Amman: CERMOC.

21. Badia has been the object of a research programme for almost a decade, under the patronage of Prince Hasan Bin Talal, under the title of the 'Badia and Research Development Programme', which was established in 1992.

22. A. Mahmoud, 'Samarkand Museum', *Al-Zahra*, IV, 18 (August 1997), p. 25.

23. The team also includes a photographer and an artist, who are to produce a photographic and pictorial documentation of the Badia region.

24. The museum was still not finished in 1998 when the author of this paper visited it.

25. For more details see F. Zink, A.-C. Janke-Zink, *Proposal of the Setting up of the Museum*, 1994.

26. See R. Daher, 'The Resurrection of the Hijaz railroad line', in *Studies in the History and Archaeology of Jordan*, Amman: Department of Antiquities, 1995.

27. The Museum of Jordanian Heritage in Yarmouk University displays another example of a reconstructed traditional house.

28. Interview with Nasmieh Rida, an employee of the Department of Antiquities in Amman (1998).

29. As early as the beginning of the twentieth century Maurice Halbwachs showed how memory can reconstruct and thus appropriate space, in his book *La topographie légendaire des Evangiles en Terre sainte*, Paris: PUF, 1941. On this issue see also U. Fabietti, and V. Matera, (eds), *Memorie e identità. Simboli e strategie del ricordo*, Rome: Meltemi, 1999.

30. M. Halbwachs, *La mémoire collective*, 130 (author's translation).

31. Ibid., 133.

32. We must underline the fact that in the most recent tourist brochure devoted to Biblical sites of Jordan, the West Bank and Jerusalem are still represented in the map of the kingdom as a part of it:, Jordan Tourism Board, *Biblical Sites of Jordan*, Amman, 1.

33. See for example K. Katz, 'Jordanian Jerusalem: Postage Stamps and Identity Construction', *Jerusalem Quarterly File*, 5 (1999), Institute of Jerusalem Studies.

34. Ibid., 2.

35. This traditional attitude of the Hashemite dynasty is clear in the importance attributed to the visit of Pope Paul VI to Jerusalem in 1964 and in the emphasis placed on the journey of John Paul II to Jordan during March 2000.

36. Identification with the ancient Christian civilisations of the country, despite the fact that they were Greek and Roman, seems to be a recent phenomenon in Jordan, since the Christian minority preferred to identify with Arab culture and local tribal traditions. Nor should we forget that, for example, the Ghassanids, who led an important kingdom in the centuries before the Islamic conquest of Transjordan, were Arab and Christian. The identification with Hellenistic and Roman

civilisations has been promoted by the official Jordanian discourse which is trying to integrate all past civilisations, in order to forge the historical depth the nation needs to legitimate its existence.

37. See for example *Al-tarbiyia al-watanyia wa al-madanyia, a-saf al-sabi'* , 10.

38. The Hashemites still claim to have a special role in Jerusalem and in the West Bank. In fact, until agreements were signed between the Palestinians and the State of Israel, the Jordanian ministry of religious affairs and endowments continued to pay the salaries of staff in religious institutions in the Occupied Territories. The same principle explains why the late King Hussain personally financed the last restoration of the Dome of the Rock.

39. For the official point of view about the issue of the sacred nature of Jordanian soil see also (1996), *Holy sites of Jordan*, Amman: TURAB, a book which describes the sacred places of Islam and Christianity in Jordan.

40. See for examples the articles of Rami Khouri published in the *Jordan Times* under the series 'Our ancient heritage', which are dedicated to the Biblical sites.

41. in 1997 the minister of tourism, when speaking about the issue of the Baptismal Site, said that 'While the [Israeli] site is an artificial one, Jordan has the unique potential provided by a real and credible product ... historically and religiously authenticated', 'Ministry announces plans to develop Jesus baptism site to encourage religious tourism', *Jordan Times*, 24 December 1997.

42. In 1999 and 2000 special series of stamps and postcards were produced to illustrate the Biblical sites.

43. Of great importance was the recognition by the Vatican of Bethany as an official place of pilgrimage for the year 2000.

44. As early as the two last decades of the nineteenth century, some groups of Circassians settled in the Amman region, because they found there an uninhabited location rich of water which was suitable to agriculture. Amman also became a station of the Hijaz railway in 1903. For more details see: E. Rogan, 'The Making of a Capital', op. cit.

45. See for example the article 'The great congregational mosque of Umayyad Amman has been identified', *Jordan Times*, 11 October 1997.

Part IV. JORDAN'S ECONOMY IN THE 1990s

TRANSITION TO DEVELOPMENT?

Oliver Schlumberger

This chapter analyses Jordan's economic transition since 1989. After more than a decade of policy reforms, the time seems now ripe to take stock of Jordan's economic development in the 1990s. Finding out where the Jordanian economy stands today and assessing the challenges ahead is obviously a rather complex task.[1] For an interpretation of the process itself and an explanation of its results until today, it is necessary to select some of its crucial aspects – and, invariably, relegate others to the background – in order to be able to address them in some depth.

Revisiting the process of liberal reforms in Jordan in the 1990s reveals that, after having undergone a successful stabilisation process, Jordan today strives at a thorough transformation of its economic order which is not yet completed. At the same time, performance during the second half of the 1990s neither matched the hopes and expectations tied to the reforms by large parts of the population, nor did it correspond to the intensity and profoundness of efforts at restructuring the economy, which numerous successive governments have undertaken for a considerable span of time. The question to be addressed is therefore: why is that so? As is shown below, we can reasonably assume that a multitude of variables account for this finding, and, again, only some of the obstacles to sustainable development which are at work can briefly be hinted at (section 3). The socio-political dimension of economic reform is chosen here for further discussion because, firstly, it is all too often neglected in economic reflections on developmental policies, liberalisation and market reform. There is, however, a much stronger case to be made: this dimension represents an aspect of the transition which influences each and every effort for reform, regardless of the sector concerned, and is therefore even more essential to understanding the successes and failures of market-oriented reform in Jordan than any purely economic variable. A cautious outlook on future trends or trajectories to a functioning market order concludes the chapter.[2]

The transformation of a semi-rentier economy

Jordan's economic transition was triggered by an acute fiscal crisis of the state in 1988–9. Jordan, a typical semi-rentier system,[3] was an indirect victim of the structural decrease in oil prices which had reached a peak in 1981, but have fallen ever since until the end of the decade: Jordan's economy heavily depended on private remittances by expatriate workers employed mainly in the Gulf, as well as on official assistance from the oil-rich Gulf countries. When sharp reductions of international capital transfers to the country threatened the rentier mode of development in the 1980s, Jordan resorted to external (commercial) and domestic borrowing to finance budgetary deficits. Thereby, 'income and consumption at levels that exceeded those that could be expected from the available production capacity in the domestic economy'[4] could be maintained in the short run, but at considerable long-term costs: the country soon found itself confronted with a huge debt burden[5] because the regime continued to cling to rentier-type policies of resource allocation.[6] Towards the end of the 1980s, Jordan had accumulated such a high level of international indebtedness that it had become unable to meet its debt-service obligations. With per capita debt levels of more than $1,900 (in 1988), Jordan had become a victim of the 'debt trap', and the regime ultimately had no choice but to call in the International Monetary Fund (IMF) for comprehensive debt rescheduling and the initiation of a stabilisation programme.[7] The World Bank, too, stepped in with financial help, most notably with an 'industrial and trade policy adjustment loan'.[8] As usual in such cases, resources made available by the Bretton Woods institutions were dependent on economic policy reforms as conditioned by the donors. 1989 therefore marks the starting point of a fundamental reorientation of Jordan's economic policies and is taken as a point of departure for the purpose of this chapter. It is worth bearing in mind that economic liberalisation was not the regime's voluntary choice but a direct result of the economically unproductive allocative policies typical for rentier-states. These had been pursued as long as possible; only after the economy had collapsed did the kingdom initiate liberal reforms. For analytical purposes, macroeconomic stabilisation (first phase) can be distinguished from structural adjustment (second phase) within the transitional period.

The first phase: successful stabilisation

In order to identify those areas where the most radical changes were implemented or initiated, and to separate them from other aspects where structural continuities determine the picture today, a discussion of the macroeconomic stabilisation of Jordan's economy in the early 1990s is necessary.

The first agreement Jordan concluded with the IMF entered into force in February 1989. Two months later, the government had introduced the first steps of the programme as prescribed by the Fund, which was strongly resisted by the population: a 30 per cent increase of fuel prices resulted in riots in the southern city of Ma'an which quickly spread to other major towns in the country. In the light of this legitimacy crisis, King Hussain, aware of the economic situation, avoided an outright cancellation of the programme. He nevertheless reacted by dismissing the then prime minister Zayed Rifai, and by giving the green light to first steps of political liberalisation.[9] Soon after, however, the programme was thrown off course by the Gulf War: Iraq's isolation following its lost war against the US-led coalition meant the virtual disappearance of Jordan's single most important trading partner.[10] Moreover, Jordan had to cope with refugees from Iraq and with over 300,000 Jordanian migrant workers who were forced to return from their host countries in the Gulf.[11] Economic hardship continued and a second agreement with the IMF was signed in 1992.

However, many of the returnees had managed to liquidate their assets before leaving their host countries, which caused a massive, yet temporary increase in private remittances to Jordan. These resources quickly generated an economic boom – especially in the construction sector, but, as a consequence, also in the service and financial service sectors.

This was the main cause for high rates of gross domestic product (GDP) growth during the early 1990s: GDP growth in 1992 was well over 11 per cent in real terms, and continued at a relatively high levels through 1994 (7.6 per cent) and 1995 (3.9 per cent). These figures have sometimes been attributed to the positive expectations associated with Jordan's decision to make peace with Israel, or, as another version of the same error, they have been interpreted as the success of the government's economic reforms.[12] However, both assumptions hold true to a limited degree at best, and tend to lead to misunderstandings: if the high growth of the early 1990s had been correlated to the Jordanian-Israeli peace treaty and the corresponding expectations, it would remain totally unclear why growth rates had peaked in 1992 with no peace treaty in sight, and declined ever since until 1995 when the first benefits of these developments – if tangible – could in fact have become visible in economic indicators. Another erroneous interpretation of the high growth during these years is attributed to

Jordan's reform efforts. This overestimates the success of the structural adjustment programme, which had, until then, been implemented rather reluctantly. A different view can easily be reached when
looking at the development of net foreign direct investments (FDI), a
more reliable indicator for the investment climate than GDP growth,
which had attained a level of no more than $16 million as late as
1996! Thus, the temporary boom of the early 1990s cannot be considered a consequence of structural economic reforms.

The problem with this temporary boom was that it worked to
further postpone reforms in important areas such as public sector reform and privatisation. Ultimately, a boom caused by the sudden influx of unexpected capital was to end in renewed stagnation soon,
and the corresponding rise in unemployment was to reveal its longer-
term implications. However, these remittances, as well as the *ad hoc*
introduction of a tax on cars brought in by returnees, worked to improve domestic savings and bolstered foreign exchange reserves, and
thus did help to make stabilisation in Jordan a success.

The most pressing issue were Jordan's immense external debts,
which stood at around twice the size of GDP in 1989. The IMF's involvement in Jordan's reform process created renewed confidence
among the country's bilateral creditors: The Paris club rescheduled
Jordan's debts in 1989, and again in 1992, 1994, and 1997, the same
years in which Jordan renewed the terms of its cooperation with the
IMF. The London Club, too, agreed to reschedule commercial debts
in 1993; in that year, Jordan was already able to reduce its debts to
foreign commercial banks through cash buybacks. Furthermore, with
the help of large discounts, Jordan managed to buy back official debts
from creditors such as Brazil or Russia. Thirdly, as Syria had done
before, Jordan managed to reduce debts incurred with the former Soviet Union through a barter arrangement involving commodity exports.[13] These developments eased the country's external debt
situation, even though the remaining levels were still high.

Austerity measures, which were implemented in parallel, could
now begin to show their impact. The government pursued tight
monetary and fiscal policies throughout the early 1990s: financing
through domestic borrowing from the central bank was reduced, public sector wages were temporarily frozen, and subsidies on basic consumer goods and services such as food, transport or fuel, which had
put untenable strains on the budget, were cut.[14] Overall expenditure
restraints are estimated to account for roughly two thirds of the fiscal
consolidation achieved until 1994.[15] The prior pegging of the Jordanian dinar to the US dollar, of course, was a pre-requisite for such a
consolidation, and helped to bring down inflation from more than 20

per cent in 1989 to slightly above 3 per cent in 1993.[16] After two deva-
luations of the dinar in the late 1980s, inflation remained low at levels
2–4 per cent throughout the decade.

Table 1. JORDAN'S ECONOMIC TRANSITION: SUCCESSFUL
MACROECONOMIC STABILISATION

Indicator	1989	1990	1991	1992	1993
Real GDP (% change to previous year)	–10.9	1.9	1.8	16.1	5.8
Debt-service ratio (debts as % of exports)	24.9	23.2	38.7	22.4	19.9
External public debt (as % of GDP)[1]	157.0	188.8	163.9	128.9	118.8
Current account (as % of GDP)	–2.5	–19.1	–17.0	–14.4	–11.6
Budget deficit (excl. grants, as % of GDP)	20.6	18.3	12.9	3.4	5.6
Consumer price inflation (% change)	25.7	16.2	8.2	4.0	3.3
Foreign currency reserves (in US$m.)	48.0	221.0	824.4	588.4	431.2[2]

1 Figures in this line are given by the IMF staff report of 1995; however, actual rates may be
   higher since in most calculations, the IMF staff exclude undisbursed loans from their
   calculations.
2 Foreign exchange reserves at the central bank had decreased in 1993, but due to a revaluation
   of the gold reserves, net assets still grew positively that year.

Sources: World Bank; World Trade Organisation; IMF, *Jordan – Background Information. Staff
Country Report No. 95/97*, Washington, DC, 1995; Economist Intelligence Unit, *Country Profile
Jordan*, London, various years.

On the revenue side, tax and non-tax revenues both rose moderately,
but steadily since 1989, so that the budget deficit could be reduced
from over 20 per cent of GDP into the low one-digit range, as is
shown in Table 1. Even though the share of grants in total government revenues had decreased from over 10 per cent in the late 1980s
to a mere 3.4 per cent in 1994, largely because of the discontinuation
of transfers from the Arab Gulf countries, Jordan managed to bring
its fiscal situation under control within five years.

Table 1 shows the development of some of the relevant macroeconomic indicators during these first years of Jordan's transitional period; they clearly demonstrate that the efforts to stabilise the economy
were not in vain. Through continued austerity, and with the help of
large capital inflows from the Gulf returnees, growth had resumed –
albeit temporarily. The agreements with the IMF enabled Jordan to
handle its debt problems and restored Jordan's access to international
capital markets. At the same time, the government was able to re-

build a solid base of foreign exchange reserves, which had fallen to an all-time low of $48 million only during the crisis: After a tenfold increase during the stabilisation phase, foreign reserves stood at roughly $2 billion, or over five months of imports at the end of the 1990s. The overall picture emanating from these observations leaves no doubt: the first phase of Jordan's transitional period from 1989 until 1994 was characterised by successful macroeconomic stabilisation.[17] Stabilisation, however hard to achieve, was but a first step on the road to a much more profound transformation of Jordan's economy: structural adjustment, which always entails deeper institutional and legislative changes to the economic order, followed suit.

The second phase: incomplete structural adjustment

After the economy was set on track again and the acute danger of an economic collapse of the country had been averted, more far-reaching reforms were implemented. The general aim of Jordan's structural adjustment programme was to enhance competitiveness in order to be able to benefit from opening the economy to a globalising international environment and to gain access to new markets. Exports were envisaged by both the international financial institutions and the government to become the cornerstone of sustainable growth on which the economy should in the future rely. For this purpose, it seemed clear that state influence on the economy proper had to be reduced since many of the public sector entities worked inefficiently and produced losses the budget could no longer sustain. Cutting down the state was to be achieved mainly by privatisation and expenditure restraints, which would at the same time generate resources to be employed otherwise.[18] Deregulation and the liberalisation of the trade regime were a second pillar which was hoped to create a surge in private investment and exports. Indeed, the structural reforms Jordan has been undergoing until 2000 were of such comprehensive nature that hardly any sector of the economy was left out. A look at some of the changes in economic legislation may best serve to illustrate how far-reaching the nature of reforms became during the second half of the 1990s.

In an effort to achieve a badly needed increase in domestic revenues, the replacement of the former consumption tax with a general sales tax (GST) in June 1994 was one of the first measures of this phase and a response to the kingdom's hitherto quite inefficient system of taxation.[19] From its introduction to the end of the decade, annual revenues generated by the new tax rose steadily and were estimated to have doubled by 2000,[20] when plans became concrete to replace the GST with a fully-fledged value-added tax (VAT).[21]

A new Investment Promotion Law (no. 16/1995) was designed to attract more foreign and domestic investment through generous incentives like long-term tax holidays and duty exemptions. Important institutional changes came along with the introduction of the law: the Investment Department, formerly a low level department at the ministry of industry and trade, was promoted into a fully fledged corporation under the direct supervision of the prime minister. The law also called for the establishment of a 'Higher Council for Investment Promotion',[22] chaired by the prime minister and attended by other key ministers, the governor of the central bank, the presidents of the chambers of commerce and industry and, not least, by three private sector representatives which are appointed for two years. Discriminations against foreign investors were abolished and equal treatment of Jordanian and non-Jordanian investors was put into law.

The investment climate was further improved by the establishment of so-called 'qualifying industrial zones' (QIZ), an idea which was first discussed in late 1996 and then realised in 1997, and which soon arose the attention of national as well as international investors. QIZ products meeting certain requirements are allowed duty-free and quota-free access to the American market.[23] A wide range of other business laws and regulations aimed at enhancing private sector development has been introduced in the second half of the decade; since it would take far too much space to discuss them in detail, suffice it here to mention the new Companies Law (no. 22/1997) as the single most important one.[24]

Reform also included efforts at revitalising the Amman Financial Market (AFM; Financial Market Law no. 23, 1997), where a securities commission was established as an independent regulatory body competent to issue by-laws, and thereby eliminating the need to pass laws through parliament. The intention was to achieve greater transparency in the financial market by introducing, *inter alia*, stricter penalties for insider trading and strengthening the rules on reporting. In order to become more attractive to non-Jordanian investors, a rule which limited foreign ownership of stocks to 50 per cent was abolished in late 1997.

Apart from such legislative steps aimed at enhancing the business environment, two other areas stand out due to their importance for the economy as a whole. These are the privatisation issue and the liberalisation of the movement of goods and capital, corresponding to the export orientation Jordan was aiming at. After years of discussions and hesitations, the privatisation programme finally gained momentum towards the end of the 1990s with the (partial) sale of formerly state-owned companies or their restructuring for privatisation in the sectors of telecommunications, transport and energy, as well as in the cement industry and in water management; preparations for privatising the postal service were under way in 2000. The Jordan Investment Corporation (JIC), too, began to sell some of the shares it held in dozens of industrial ventures, banks and service companies, and yet another new law with a view to providing a framework for the treatment of privatisation proceeds (against unsustainable increases in government expenditure) was in the pipeline at the time of writing.

While the pace of reforms had noticeably slowed down in 1998 compared to the previous year, the young King Abdullah II quickly gave new life to the reform process after his succession to the throne. His determination to accelerate Jordan's economic transition became apparent in 1999 and 2000, when a series of difficult tasks were tackled, including new legislation in a wide variety of areas. From the first days of his reign, King Abdullah has been giving high priority to economic policies and the reform process continued from then on at a speed which probably no Arab country has witnessed to this day.

External trade was one of the main targets. From the beginning of the transitional period, measures to liberalise the trade regime were implemented successively. Licence requirements for imports were abolished, quota on certain goods lifted, and import tariffs were reduced step by step. The maximum import tariff rate reached 35 per cent in early 2000,[25] and the one for intermediate goods was set at 10 per cent as an indirect protection of infant industries. In 1998, a new customs law was introduced for the purpose of simplifying procedures. This proved to be but a prelude to a whole series of new laws passed through parliament in 1999; they mainly related to intellectual property rights, but also to arbitration and anti-monopoly regulations. In December of that year, Jordan's bid for membership in the World Trade Organisation (WTO) was accepted.[26] This was a second major step towards the integration into the global economy after the country's participation in the so-called Barcelona Process within the frame of the Euro-Mediterranean Partnership Initiative (EMPI), which envisages free trade with the EU for manufactured goods by 2010.[27]

With a focus on Jordanian economic policy-making, the main events of 1999 and 2000 were, first, King Abdullah's installation of an 'Economic Consultative Council', a majority of which consists of young liberal business people not so closely associated with the old state bourgeoisie of the rentier period. In 2000 an unprecedented private-sector initiative was launched under the motto 'Jordan Vision

2020' with the ambitious goal of raising per capita income to JD2,200 (roughly twice its present level), by 2020.[28] Both initiatives reflect the new hopes for restored growth and sustainable development; they both contributed to the creation of highly optimistic expectations. Maybe the single most important factor for the positive atmosphere at the beginning of the new century is the King himself: a sympathetic figure, he proved professional in marketing Jordan on the international scene with his widely acknowledged speech at the World Economic Forum in Davos. However, it is not at all guaranteed that the current optimistic atmosphere can in fact be translated into real development. Although the widely disliked Premier Rawabdeh was ousted in 2000, resistance to the new rules of a possible new era is far from being broken.[29]

This brief review of Jordanian economic policies is, by necessity, incomplete and leaves out more than it can discuss, given the limitations on available space. However, what has become clear is that, apart from successful macroeconomic stabilisation, Jordan is currently undergoing a deep transformation of its entire economic system: the policies implemented during the past decade have touched on virtually each and every aspect of the national economy: the fiscal area and monetary policies, the tax system, investments in industry, agriculture, tourism and transport, international business cooperation, banking and financial markets, foreign trade and tariffs, administration and the public sector[30] through institutional reforms and privatisation. They have created an economy hardly recognisable when compared to the one of the early 1980s. Yet, this transformation is far from being accomplished and the new Jordanian economic order is still in the making. It remains to be seen what type of economic order this will once become.[31] Today the rentier character of Jordan's economy no longer exists in its previous form of the 1970s and early 1980s.

Performance

The government and international financial institutions agree that Jordan's implementation of the structural adjustment programme (SAP) is a success story: in a 1996 statement on Jordan, an IMF representative spoke about the 'impressive progress' Jordan had made, reflecting the 'appropriate macroeconomic and structural reform policies', while the economy was 'well poised to continue on the path of high growth, increased employment opportunities and improved living standards'.[32] In retrospect, the words quoted here sound almost cynical.

High growth was not experienced since the inflow of capital brought in by returnees from the Gulf countries in 1991, and came close to zero (or maybe even below; see Table 2 below) in 1998; real per capita GDP has remained negative since 1996. Unemployment remained essentially unaltered at high rates of an estimated percentage somewhere between 20 and 30 points.[33] For most of the decade, real wages continued to fall and a 1999 study by the World Bank[34] shows that poverty was alleviated only marginally; the absolute number of poor people had remained constant in comparison to 1992.[35] The 1996 riots in Kerak – a result of the government cutting down bread subsidies – were a clear signal of the precarious standard of living of large parts of the population.[36]

A high number of poor and the deterioration of living standards for the middle classes are often dismissed as 'temporary adverse social effects' of structural adjustment. However, as the Latin American experience shows, where Gini-indices are today among the highest in the world, such effects may well perpetuate. These findings do not sound all too promising. Table 2 shows the development of some selected indicators to approach the question of how far the objectives of the reform were achieved.

The data presented here do not give much reason for enthusiasm.

Table 2. STRUCTURAL ADJUSTMENT: AMBIGUOUS RESULTS

Indicator	1995	1996	1997	1998	1999[x]
Real GDP (% change to previous year)	3.9	1.0	1.3	2.2^a / -1.0^b	1.5^c / 1.3^b
— per capita (% change)	0.3	–2.5	–2.1	-1.2^a / -4.6^b	n.a.
Government Expenditure (in % of GDP)	37.3	38.5	35.9	38.8	35.6
Exports (excl. re-exports; in % of GDP)	22.0	22.1	21.6	20.0	n.a.
Imports (in % of GDP)	56.7	64.6	58.8	51.9	n.a.
Net FDI (in US $ millions)	13	16	22	d	n.a.

x: preliminary
y: budgeted
a: official figure, same figure as officially estimated beforehand
b: EIU estimate
c: government estimate
d: Sources differed so greatly that this box was left blank (figures for 1995–7 are taken from The World Bank, *WDR* 2000).

Sources: Central Bank Jordan, *Monthly Statistical Bulletin, May 2000* (Amman: CBJ); CBJ, *Annual Report* (Amman, 1999); EIU, *Country Profile Jordan, 2000/2001*, 2000; Marto, Michel and Zaid Fariz, *Letter of Intent to the IMF, 28 Aug. 1999* (*www.imf.org/external/np/loi/1999/082899.HTM*); Ministry of Finance, *Government Finance Bulletin, Amman, February 2000*; World Bank, *World Development Report 1999 / 2000* (Oxford University Press), 1999.

First, curbing the state has not taken place to the desired extent: government expenditure as a share of GDP has remained continuously at the same levels, and was budgeted for 2000 at the same percentage as in 1995. Government services also remained one of the largest single contributors to GDP, with 21.6 per cent, only exceeded by financing, business and real estate services (22.1 per cent).[37] It is quite obvious that the state has not been sized down to the expected extent in the course of transition.[38] The volume of foreign trade has not increased when seen in relation to GDP, which is a sign that the economy has not – or not yet – become as liberalised and outward-oriented as was hoped by the advocates of the reform process. Thirdly, reform policies have not brought about any substantial change in Jordan's chronic trade deficit: Jordan's heavy dependence on imports for industrial inputs and energy cannot be overcome in the foreseeable future. Thus, in order to make export-oriented policies a successful development strategy, Jordan must necessarily find alternative export sectors in which its products have significant comparative advantages in order to reduce its trade deficit structurally. Given the current economic structure of the country, their identification will be difficult. From the evolution of the composition of exports, it is obvious that until now, such niches have not been found, let alone been exploited. Export earnings continue to depend on the mineral resources sector (mainly phosphates and potash) and a few related downstream products of the chemical industry such as fertilisers or detergents.[39] Although the continuous rise of imports was stopped in 1997 and in subsequent years the trade deficit narrowed, current developments indicate a further increase by over 30 per cent during the first four months of 2000, compared to the corresponding time span in 1999.[40] The underlying problem is that only few industries are competitive enough to become viable export earners, and that most of the economy consists of family-run small and medium scale enterprises without any substantial potential for export.[41] The potential to increase revenues generated by tourism and the bright prospects of information technology notwithstanding, the King's 'great hopes for the future' and expectation 'that we are bound to reap the fruits of our efforts in the coming year [2001]' neglect these structural obstacles to development. The 'real leap in social and economic conditions' he speaks of[42] has neither taken place during the 1990s nor is it likely to do so in the early years of the new decade.

It was only towards the end of the decade that voices were raised suggesting that Jordan could and should promote the IT (information technology) sector because of its huge potential for growth.[43] King Abdullah has announced his personal interest in promoting the

industry and brought leading international IT companies to a conference at the Dead Sea. Given the size of the Arab market and the skilled
labour force Jordan possesses, this could in fact become a future focus
and should be promoted by the government. However, Jordan is not
the first country to discover the possibility; Egypt is one neighbour
which has already had some success with focusing on the computer
industry and some of the Gulf countries, too, are in the business.[44]
Jordan will surely secure its share in the regional market. But for the
period observed here, one must note that new and competitive sectors
for increasing exports have not been found or sufficiently expanded.

Although investment incentives in Jordan did improve and FDI increased in absolute terms, Jordan could not manage to catch up with
other Middle East and North African countries, let alone with other
developing regions, when looking at FDI in relation to GDP. Portfolio investments, too, have not yet become an attractive alternative
for investors: total trading volume at the Amman Financial Market
in 1998 (JD413.6 million) was below 1994 levels (JD430.3 million).
More recently, the Market saw a decline in non-Jordanian net investments during the first five months of 2000, down to JD5.3 million
from JD12.4 million during the same time span in 1999,[45] which is no
great sign of international investors' confidence in the shares traded.
Activity at the Market remained limited well into 2000, when 165
shares were listed, but where a few large institutional (and sometimes
even state-owned) share-holders such as the Social Security Corporation or the Jordan Islamic Bank dominate it and therefore no great
fluctuations occur.

This inspection of Jordanian economic development in the 1990s
demonstrates that Jordan's reforms indeed deserve to be labelled
'structural' since virtually all aspects of the national economy have
been targeted and fundamentally reshaped, especially during the second half of the decade in the context of accelerated privatisation.
However, it is also clear that the Kingdom faces enormous developmental challenges. Most of the goals of economic reform in Jordan
have only partially been achieved. Many hopes have not materialised,
although, as has also been shown, Jordan has been more determined
in achieving a transition of the rentier economy than maybe any other
Arab state. However far-reaching Jordan's attempts at reform were,
performance clearly falls short of what would be expected as the results of such enduring efforts at liberalisation; even though growth
in 2000 was higher than in 1999, today nothing indicates a developmental take-off. What obstacles to development are at work to reward such strong policy efforts with such a modest success? It may
be helpful to cast an eye on some of the factors which are to blame

for the lacklustre performance the economy has displayed during the second half of the 1990s.

Obstacles to development

Since performance has not improved at the same pace as reforms have been implemented and since Jordan's economy suffers from largely similar problems as at the beginning of the transitional period, it seems plausible to search for variables which have remained, by and large, constant since the late 1980s and which might cause the less than satisfying results of the transition process. What possible impediments to successful economic transition have remained in place and continue to exert their influence on economic performance, in spite of all structural changes? The obstacles to sustainable growth and development in Jordan are numerous and only a few issues can be mentioned here. However, three points seem of paramount importance: external political and economic factors,[46] scarcity of resources and the domestic socio-political environment

A brief explanation of what is to be understood by these factors follows.

External political and economic factors

As Benjamin Navon wrote, 'The careful observation of Middle Eastern economic development shows that it is not solely determined by economic policies of governments and other economic variables, but also by political realities.'[47] The regional political climate as determined by the progress or setbacks of the peace process and its implementation comes to mind in this connection. After all, in recent years, the perception of the Mashriq in Western media was largely determined by incidents such as suicide bombings by militant Islamist groups, by the murder of Yitzhak Rabin and, until 1999, by an Israeli administration which left the prospects of regional peace stagnating at best. This evidently created negative spill-over effects which hit the Jordanian economy. It left FDI (in per cent of GDP, 1997) at an extremely low 0.32 per cent,[48] a similar level as in Syria, which has implemented economic reforms only half-heartedly. The remaining political difficulties in the core area of what for decades was the Middle East conflict[49] undoubtedly continue to exert their influence, even though violence associated with the peace process does not normally occur in Jordan. In the long run, there is no alternative to greater regional economic cooperation and integration, possibly including all states in the Levant. But as long as no Syrian-Israeli peace is achieved

– and, thus, Lebanon, too, is not integrated – such a scenario refers to some uncertain future.

A second point directly resulting from regional political events are the constraints on Jordan's external trade arising from the United Nations' sanctions on Iraq. Apart from the food-for-oil deals, Jordan's single most important trading partner before the 1991 war had virtually been cut off from Jordan. Exports to Iraq had roughly halved during the 1990s when compared to the pre-war years, and dropped further in the late 1990s. Furthermore, greater economic openness makes Jordan more vulnerable to global economic developments, as had become evident during the global financial crisis which had originated from East Asia.

Scarcity of resources

With the exception of the small port of Aqaba, Jordan is a landlocked country; due to the absence of a comprehensive regional peace agreement, access to the geographically close ports of the Mediterranean remains costly. A net importer of petroleum, Jordan is endowed with only little natural resources. Phosphates, potash and some other minerals are virtually the only exploitable mineral resources. At the same time, the small size of both the economy and the local market prohibits an import-substituting industrialisation strategy. However, Jordan has not managed to substantially increase the exports-GDP ratio (see Table 2), due to the lack of a diversified and globally competitive industrial base.[50]

Even more importantly, water scarcity is *the* major natural barrier to development: with less than 10 per cent of the national territory being cultivable, there are no reasonable prospects for large-scale agro-business.[51] In spite of its minor importance in GDP generation, agriculture currently consumes over two thirds of the country's water supplies.[52] As a service-based economy with considerable investments in industry and an expanding tourism sector, Jordan cannot afford to maintain such distributional patterns – even more so since ground water resources are depleting rapidly and population growth remains high at an estimated 3.6 per-cent per annum. Current water usage elevates opportunity costs since agriculture in Jordan hardly possesses expansive prospects. Furthermore, the lack of water imposes limits to the expansion of tourism for ecological reasons, as well as to industrial development. Other problems such as the influence of world oil prices on the performance of the economy or the continued reliance and dependence on external assistance as well as the heavy dependence on labour markets abroad could be added to this list, but it is beyond the scope of this chapter to deal with these issues in detail.[53]

The domestic economic environment

While Jordan has made great efforts at modernising and improving the domestic economic environment, the most striking fact about Jordan's economic transition from 1989 to 2000 is that this is not reflected in performance. The main reason for this finding (apart from the factors already mentioned which can hardly be changed by 'good policies') is that economic reform does not only consist of legal and institutional change, but that reforms can attain their desired effects only to the degree they are actually implemented. All efforts at reform are in vain if implementation does not follow suit and the crucial point is the *mode* of implementation.

Business and donor institutions agree that actual implementation of the institutional and legislative reforms is lagging behind. The Economist Intelligence Unit analysis argues: 'Although changes have affected customs, taxation, companies law and the financial market, foreign and local business have tended to find that much of the legislation exists on paper only'.[54] It is noteworthy that even a cabinet member at the time, in assessing the current situation after over a decade of policy reforms, highlighted a 'lack of clear rules regarding all necessary permits' and a 'lack of specific guidelines on the documents and processes required for obtaining them' as regards the start-up of companies. With respect to the tax administration, he finds that 'tax assessment is the outcome of a negotiation process' and 'damaging to business incentives and the investment climate'. Customs procedures are analysed as 'cumbersome' and 'onerous', with 'inconsistent application of customs rules' allowing officials 'to make discretionary decisions about tariff rates and applications',[55] even though a green line for accredited importers was introduced.

These are only examples for the overall discretionary leeway bureaucrats have retained in spite of all the new institutions and legislation. Granting and searching for non-market privileges establishes preferences among buyers and sellers alike; it heavily distorts the costs of economic transactions[56] and has strongly adverse developmental impacts. To summarise, competition (and, more specifically, access to the market) is restricted in many ways, even though on paper the economy seems to have become much more liberal. The rule of law is to a large part ruled out due to officials' discretionary power of an arbitrary application of rules and regulations.

The underlying problems are less in the economic sphere or in economic policies than in the social and political arenas. Just like the geographical factors and those of a problematic external environment, they belong to the variables which have remained largely constant during the transitional period: There is nothing new in the statement that Jordan's system of political rule, albeit parliamentary, is strongly neo-patrimonial in nature and heavily reliant on patron-client relations:[57] Decision-making is characterised by informality and hierarchical relations, with patronage being a prevalent feature. But far from being restricted to politics alone, informality, patronage and the use of *wasta*[58] are much wider phenomena among the population at large.[59] This, too, is no new finding with regard to Jordan.[60] But in economic analyses, it is often left out either with the argument that *wasta* cannot be measured numerically, or by acknowledging the fact of its existence, but focusing on more 'economic' issues.

Obviously, it is easier to lower a tariff rate than to tackle the issue of patronage and *wasta*. The problem is, however, that any formally adopted economic policy initiative and any newly established formal institution (such as, for example, the Telecommunications Regulation Corporation, or the Anti-Corruption Unit at the General Intelligence Department which came into being in 1996) will be penetrated by the informal nature of patronage networks, which are likely to determine the 'what' and, equally important in Jordan, the 'who' of that institution.[61] It is obvious that patronage, societal rent-seeking and the use of *wasta* directly affects the entire economic process and performance. Therefore, it deserves closer analysis.

The socio-political dimension of economic transition

The issue addressed here may sound vaguely familiar, however, confusion prevails as to the usage of terminology. Patronage, *wasta*, rent-seeking, corruption: they all describe interpersonal relations of a discrete nature. While patronage and *wasta* are analytical concepts derived from political science and sociology, rent-seeking and corruption have their origin in economics. What they have in common on the socio-political side is the informality they rely on. Such relations are therefore difficult to identify since they are assumed to be mutually beneficial for those involved and essentially depend on discretion.

As regards the Jordanian case, our finding of a seemingly arbitrary implementation of laws and the wide-spread use of discretionary power accumulated among bureaucrats at all levels can be traced back to the societal predominance of precisely these phenomena. Rent-seeking, *wasta* and corruption are also alike in that they involve non-market individual gains, but create losses on a macroeconomic level. This is the reason why *wasta* is widely considered a form of corruption,[62] even though both are by no means synonymous.[63] *Wasta* and rent-seeking both relate to value systems which are different from the capitalist one as described by Weber[64] since rewards or profits are de-linked from merit or capability: not one's competence, knowledge, work or product, but the closeness of personal relations to the one who extends benefits to others determines whether the strife for benefits (material or immaterial) is successful or not. Hence, *wasta* and rent-seeking can be described as the mechanism by which patronage works. Hisham Sharabi aptly describes *wasta* as 'the lubricant of the patronage system'.[65]

While rent-seeking, by definition, is opposed to productivity, this is not synonymous with 'inefficiency'.[66] Because rent-seeking is efficient in a rentier-state, the past decades have strongly contributed to spreading and fostering rent-seeking behaviour in Jordan. What all of the terms discussed here have in common is that, first, they are patterns of informal social interaction. Therefore, they mostly go unrecognised or are disregarded in economic analyses which focus on formal and measurable indicators: laws, institutions and organisations, the transfer of ownership of economic establishments and companies, trade flows, and the like are easier to measure than the prevalence of *wasta*.

But because of their informal nature, patronage and *wasta* pervade formal institutions and, by de-linking capability from reward, they undermine the authority of formal institutions and laws. The above quoted finding that much of the new legislation 'exists on paper only' is a symptom of the socially prevailing norm that the person does make a difference in economic and political decisions, as well as in the application of laws. Obviously, 'the primary problem is not public versus private, the problem is excessive intercessory *wasta*, which distorts costs.'[67]

The use of *wasta* and/or rent-seeking greatly increases transaction costs, since all material and immaterial costs which are employed in these activities raise the costs of the desired outcome, no matter if this concerns the establishment of a factory, attaining a certain certificate, or getting a position. The more people are involved in *wasta* and rent-seeking, the more time, money, energy, 'gifts' and so on, will be invested in these activities, so that overall resources spent on *wasta* and rent-seeking can be assumed to be immense. Additionally, it may be that the investment needed to achieve the desired results rises as more individuals commit themselves to rent-seeking. At their heart, rent-seeking and the use of *wasta* constitute a collective action issue:[68]

although microeconomically rational, to act as a rent-seeker or to
use *wasta* generates less optimal outcomes on a macro level and thus
results in overall welfare losses. Numerically, the losses created by
the prevalence of rent-seeking and *wasta* are hard to measure since
the costs of investing time and other resources can hardly be assessed
quantitatively (e.g. the obligation to do favours in exchange to someone who has been doing a favour to oneself or on whom one expects
to rely in the future).[69]

Thus, *wasta*, if predominant, creates significant overall losses in
any given society. Such remarks are frequently dismissed on grounds
of their presumed insignificance to economic performance. Those
few studies that have tried to address the issue in a scientific way
usually try to give anecdotal evidence from a possibly wide variety of
areas to underpin how widespread the phenomenon is. Yet this was
not enough to convince many of the need for further inquiry.

In Jordan, however, the first quantitative survey on *wasta* ever
was carried out, and despite debatable methodological shortcomings,
it does provide quantitative results: of all respondents, over 65 per
cent said that they would look for *wasta* when they 'need to get something done at a government office, a company or organisation'. Even
more startling, 90 per cent responded that, with reference to their past
experience, they would now be ready to use *wasta* for either some or
even all of their dealings. Strikingly, after twelve years of policy reform, when asked whether the need for *wasta* as a general tendency
would decrease, remain as it is, or increase in the future, 39 per cent
thought it would remain as it is, and more than half of the sample assumed it would even increase, while less than 7 per cent thought the
need for *wasta* was bound to decrease.[70] This clearly indicates that
structural economic reforms in Jordan have not sufficiently – if at all
– addressed the socio-political environment which strongly influences
economic performance.

Respondents were chosen from both public and private sectors,
from all age groups, various educational standards and job positions.
Hence, the pervasiveness of the phenomenon can not be attributed
to limited social segments. In the context of economic transition
geared towards private-sector development, it has to be pointed out
clearly that the socio-political phenomena discussed here are not the
problem of some unwilling and inefficient bureaucrats only, as is often assumed. Even privatisation, which has long been approached
very reluctantly because of its immense political importance and the
interests at stake, cannot be thought of as alleviating the developmental problems associated with the prevalence of *wasta* and rent-seeking:
'Privatisation neither eliminates *wasta* nor, in the absence of other

factors, leads to development.'[71] The distribution of resources and power to influence the market is often handled just as discretionary in the private sector as it is in the public sector. Liberal economic policies open the door to public-private partnerships, true, but this also opens the door for new (quasi-)monopolies and oligopolies to emerge, so that market distortions may continue despite a transfer of ownership.

Several steps have been taken during the reform process which seem to point in the opposite direction. Examples are the establishment of the Anti-Corruption Department, or the anti-trust legislation passed in 1999 in order to be accepted as a WTO member. At the inauguration of the new Abul-Ragheb government in June 2000, King Abdullah is quoted as having told the new prime minister 'to introduce meritocracy as the guiding principle of public services' and that the government should 'establish a code of honour to put an end to *wasta*, favouritism and cliques'. He demanded that 'we should put an end to monopoly and re-examine the system of choosing government representatives in the companies' boards of directors.'[72] Yet powerful interests are at stake which may well involve more of Jordan's political and economic elites than is commonly thought. Secondly, a social norm cannot be wiped out as if it was a stain on the carpet: 'No amount of external criticism can change the inner structure of patronage system, for wherever patriarchal relations exist [. . .], patronage *dominates*.'[73]

It is evident that the currently prevailing patterns of social interaction are an important impediment to development in Jordan. The optimistic scenario King Abdullah and others, including international organisations, hope for, is not realistic because it fails to take into account this socio-political context. Minor ups and downs in GDP growth notwithstanding, as long as *wasta* is adequately described as the 'societal rule',[74] the relation of productivity and profit will continue to be undermined from within. New institutions can be established, but they will come like a new slide on top of one already projected: the second one appears, but the contours of the first will not vanish.

In this case, in assessing the nature of Jordan's economic transition, a second, albeit closely related aspect needs to be addressed: when Jordan's economy is moving away from the past system of rentierism, what will the new system then be? Virtually all observers agree that 'economic transition' in Jordan is in the direction of a market economy. In formal terms, this cannot be denied, but when speaking of market economies, we invariably think of liberal capitalist economies as they emerged from bourgeois revolutions in the aftermath of the

enlightenment in Europe or North America. In the Jordanian context, the question is: what market economy do we mean?

Hitherto, Jordan has undergone an incomplete transition. Some
of the rentier structures of the past have vanished, but the socio-
political norms fostered by rentierism remain predominant within society. Patronage, *wasta* and rent-seeking, however, are not compatible with a market economy in the sense used here. Where personal
ties determine the access to the market, to information, to licences
etc., we cannot speak of competition, which, by definition, is the single most important fundamental of a market economy.[75] Secondly,
the rule-of-law is essential for an economy to be called a market system. Property rights, contract security, the issuance of a license or registration of a company are no subject for bargaining in a market
order. To invest resources, whatever they may consist of, for things
one is legally entitled to, is not compatible with a 'market economy'.
There is a structural contradiction between the social norms of rent-
seeking and the employment of *wasta* on the one hand, and the most
basic prerequisites of a functioning market order. Thus 'any effort
aiming at a mere shift in economic policies and the legal or institutional framework in which economic agents operate is highly unlikely
to significantly alter the predominant socio-political patterns of interaction'.[76] For all that, it is premature to speak of a market economy
in Jordan today. Loyalties remain based on family, clan, or informal
groups and characterise not only private life, but also politics and
economic behaviour. Therefore, the orthodox economic course Jordan has adopted in terms of policies is not today built on the principles of open competition, open markets, or the rule of law.

Today, Jordan's economic system is characterised by the duality
of informal social patterns related to a rentier economy and formal
institutions pertaining to the concept of a market economy. Strict
hierarchies of power and personal relations continue in many cases to
determine the success or failure of economic activity. The marketplace is, of course, nowhere a neutral sphere where the price only
reigns, as some economists would have it.[77] But in Jordan, the present
patrimonial relations in politics as well as in society at large, characterise the market too. Therefore I would like to call today's economic
order 'patrimonial capitalism'. With this term, it is possible to grasp
the hybrid combination of informal socio-political remnants of a
former rentier economy which coexist in structural contradiction
with the formal institutions and policies associated with a market
economy.

The groups which benefit most from patrimonial capitalism are
those that possess the resources to diversify their economic activities

and have the potential for export. This is precisely the relatively narrow stratum of the urban rich who benefit from their ties to the political establishment (or are members of both the political and economic elite), and thus enhance their personal interests at the expense of the public welfare. It cannot be assumed that these agents share any interest in opening up markets to new competitors or in abandoning their privileges by calling for an equitable application of laws. Given the prevalence of *wasta* and patronage in the domestic environment, it is unlikely that this group would act as the spearhead of new market-oriented economic behaviour in Jordan. As long as individual gains can be perceived as increasing through the use of *wasta* and clientelism, the principle of maximising gains will remain the predominating ethos.

What economic order? What are prospects for development?

In the course of the 1990s, Jordan gradually lost some of the attributes commonly found in rentier states and which had characterised its economy for decades. The share of external revenues to the budget structurally decreased and Jordan has abandoned much of the economic policies associated with rentierism in the past: a good deal of the legislation passed in the 1990s aims at reducing state intervention. Taxation has become an increasingly important sources of government revenue. Large-scale public prestige projects are a feature belonging to the past just as an excessively protective trade regime. And the state's direct control over the economy, though still existent, has also been reduced in some core areas. In the early 2000s, this continues as the privatisation process expands to include new sectors. While large external capital inflows accruing directly to the state are still essential for the economy's survival, rentierism figures no longer among the salient features of Jordan's economy. The Jordanian case provides convincing evidence that semi-rentier economies can be stabilised and reformed through liberal economic policies.

However, economic transition in Jordan has not led to the emergence of a market economy. While the transition of the 1990s lead away from the semi-rentier economy Jordan was known as, this analysis has also shown that the 'point of arrival', at least for the foreseeable future, is not an open market economy. Instead, an economic order which displays some elements of a liberal market economy has emerged: most of the legislative framework and parts of the institutional environment are in fact so similar to the traditional market systems of the West that it is hard to distinguish between them and the Jordanian system.

Jordan in the new century possesses the *formal* institutions of a market system, but this frame works along the *informal* lines of socio-political action and interaction inherited from the previous rentierist system: the prevalence of societal rent-seeking, the widespread use of intercessory *wasta* and patronage networks. Relying on private capital accumulation, but at the same time determined by patrimonial socio-political relations, this hybrid economic order can best be grasped as *patrimonial capitalism*.[78]

For the time being, patrimonial capitalism can certainly survive economically. Due to conducive international trends (such as a high oil price), performance prospects for the immediate future were quite bright at the time of writing. Also, the economy suffers less serious problems today than it did a decade ago. Yet a sustainable developmental take-off, resulting in improved living conditions for the population at large, is hardly possible with the present economic system. A commentator in a local newspaper intuitively grasps the point made here with precision: 'Until such a time when people reach positions, stay in positions, and perhaps more importantly, do not stay in positions, judged upon ability, not connections, family name, heritage or social status – until such a time, Jordan will not move a stagnant economy forward. The kingdom will not be competitive in a global market-place, and injustice and unfairness at a social level will prevail'.[79]

It may be that this economic order proves to be a transitory phenomenon, an interim which will ultimately be replaced by a liberal market economy. The international environment, most notably through Jordan's WTO membership and the Euro-Mediterranean Partnership, increasingly exerts pressure and reduces possibilities for rent-seeking and the use of *wasta*. However, political and economic elites in Jordan have proven to be extremely flexible and highly capable of adapting to changing local, regional or international circumstances.

The questions discussed here are long-term issues: attitudes and values which were individually rational in a rentier economy will take more time to change than does the introduction of a Privatisation Law. In fact, they may well take a generation to change as profoundly as they have to in order for a 'market economy' as defined here to take hold. Even then, a market economy is only one of many possible alternatives which may emerge. Therefore, today's system will remain in place, at least for the short- to medium-term future.

NOTES

1. An earlier version of this chapter was presented at the seventh conference of the International Association of Middle Eastern Studies, 4–8 October 2000, in Berlin. A research grant from the German Academic Exchange Service (DAAD) is gratefully acknowledged. Thanks are due also to André Bank, Kerstin Eberle and Rolf Schwarz for great research assistance and proof-reading. In numerous discussions on the topic and/or on earlier versions of this chapter, Holger Albrecht, André Bank, Arwa Hassan and Markus Loewe greatly helped me clarify my views. The author, however, claims full responsibility for any remaining errors.

2. The two final sections of this chapter draw strongly on O. Schlumberger (2000), 'Competition, the Rule of Law, and Non-Market Transition. The Socio-Political Dimension of Economic Reform in the Arab World', paper prepared for the Seventh Annual Conference of The Economic Research Forum for the Arab Countries, Iran and Turkey (ERF), held in Amman, 26–29 October 2000.

3. The role and characteristics of rentier *states* in political economy (governments acting as international rent-seekers) is the subject of H. Beblawi and G. Luciani (eds), *The Rentier State*, London: Croom Helm, 1987. For the concept of rent-seeking in economics see A. Krueger, 'The Political Economy of the Rent-Seeking Society', *American Economic Review*, 64, 3 (June 1974); pp. 302f. M. Ricketts, 'Rent-Seeking, Entrepreneurship, Subjectivism and Property Rights', *Journal of Institutional and Theoretical Economics*, 143 (1987); pp. 457–66, presents a critical overview of rent-seeking as a concept in (micro-) economics.

    Rentier states are defined as systems that depend on substantial inflows of international rents for economic survival. In the past, such rents to Middle Eastern states have mostly accrued directly to the respective governments. Official transfers from the oil-rich Arab Gulf States to the non-oil economies like Jordan allowed similar patterns of development to emerge even in these comparatively 'poor' states; a regional sub-system labelled 'petrolism' thus emerged, consisting of ideal-type rentier states and so-called rentier states of second order or 'semi-rentiers'. These latter ones do possess some industries, as well as a domestic tax base, but due to external capital inflows monopolised by the governments, states grew to become the largest and most powerful agents by far in all Arab countries; they were able to dominate and exert control over their national economies. It is worthwhile mentioning that this holds true regardless of the political nature of the respective regimes (conservative, monarchical vs. progressive, revolutionary or nominally socialist). Evidence for this point is given by B. Glasser, 'External Capital and Political Liberalisations: A Typology of Middle Eastern Development in the 1980s and 1990s', *Journal of International Affairs*, 49, 1 (summer 1995); p. 48.

    Rents need not necessarily be reinvested in the production process, but can be disbursed domestically. As historical evidence confirms, in Middle Eastern countries this has happened according to political priorities for the purpose of enhancing the regime legitimacy rather than in economically efficient ways. This has taken on various forms, ranging from broad support of the population at large (such as through free or inexpensive health and educational systems, subsidies on basic consumer goods, job creation in ever-expanding bureaucracies, and so on) to the specific alimentation of strategically important societal groups (for example, local entrepreneurs) which could thus be acquiesced and coopted.

4. IMF, *Jordan – Background Information on Selected Aspects of Adjustment and Growth Strategy*, Staff Country Report no. 95/97, Washington, DC, 1995, p. 4.

5. It is beyond the scope of this contribution to deal with the developments of the 1980s in detail. For figures and analyses of that phase, see G. Feiler, 'Jordan's

Economy, 1970–1990: The Primacy of Exogenous Factors' in J. Nevo and I. Pappé (eds), *Jordan in the Middle East: The Making of a Pivotal State*, London, 1994, pp. 45–60, and F. Khatib, 'Foreign Aid and Economic Development in Jordan: An Empirical Investigation' in R. Wilson (ed.), *Politics and the Economy in Jordan*, Routledge, 1991, pp. 60–76.

6. This has been observed in virtually all semi-rentier systems; for comprehensive reflections on that point see G. Luciani, 'Resources, Revenues, and Authoritarianism in the Arab World: Beyond the Rentier State?' in R. Brynen, B. Korany and P. Noble (eds), *Political Liberalisation and Democratisation in the Arab World*, vol. 1: *Theoretical Perspectives*, Westview Press, 1995, pp. 211–27. An excellent theoretically based contribution to the debate is P. Pawelka, and C. Schmid, 'The Modern Rentier State in the Middle East and its Strategies of Crisis Management', paper presented at the 22nd annual conference of the MESA), Los Angeles, 2–5 November 1988, which typologise and discuss the options of rentier states when facing economic crises.

7. For figures see Economist Intelligence Unit (ed.), *Country Profile Jordan, 1998–99*, London, 1999, p. 10.

8. For details, see World Bank, *Jordan – Industrial and Trade Policy Adjustment Policy Loan, Report No. 14772 of 06/30/95*, Washington, DC, 1995.

9. Political parties, for instance, were legalised, and in November 1989, the first general elections to the lower house of parliament were held after several decades. What is more: these elections were considered free and fair by virtually all observers. In December, the first post-election government introduced a further series of political reforms, including the release of political prisoners, and abandoned several other means of political repression such as giving greater freedoms to the media. See R. Brynen, 'Economic Crisis and Post-Rentier Democratisation in the Arab World: The Case of Jordan', *Canadian Journal of Political Science*, 25, 1 (spring 1992), pp. 73–92, for a discussion of the connection between the economic crisis of the rentier state and the liberalisation of the political sphere.

10. Of course, since 1995 Jordan did benefit from the food-for-oil deals as permitted by the UN Security Council, but this could not offset the trade volume lost by the closure of borders. Even the value of exports realised through that programme has declined in subsequent years from JD 138 m (1998) to JD 70 m (1999) and JD 50.3 m (2000). See Jordan Focus (ed.), *J-Biz Newsletter*, London, 22 Aug. 2000.

11. IMF, *Jordan – Background Information*, 2.

12. See, for instance, The World Bank, *Jordan – Industrial and Trade Policy Adjustment Loan; Report no. 14772*, Washington, DC, 30 June 1995, World Bank ; 2 (ad. 7), which reads: 'Domestic investment and growth responded vigorously to the improved incentives. This achievement was all the more impressive considering the adverse external environment during the ITPAL [Industrial and Trade Policy Adjustment Loan] period [from 1989 to 1992], reflecting the strong commitment of the government to adjust'. The report goes on to speak of a 'sharp surge in private capital inflow, as a response to higher domestic interest rates', which, too, seems a somewhat illusionary interpretation of economic developments in the aftermath of the Gulf War.

13. For details, see P. Alonso-Gamo and A. Mansur, 'External Debt Strategy', in E. Maciejewski and A. Mansur (eds), *Jordan – Strategy for Adjustment and Growth*, IMF Occasional Paper no. 136, Washington, DC, 1996, pp. 49–52.

14. Food subsidies alone had mounted to 3.5 per cent of GDP in 1990, but were reduced to less than half in absolute terms by 1994, when they had been curbed to about 1 per cent of GDP. Cf. IMF, *Jordan – Background Information*, 1995, p. 115.

15. E. Challatay and A. Mansur, 'Public Debt Dynamics and Fiscal Policy' in E. Maciejewski and A. Mansur (eds), *Jordan – Strategy for Adjustment and Growth*, 1996, p. 25.
16. IMF, *Jordan – Background Information*, 1995, p. viii.
17. Of course, during this time, first steps were taken not only to stabilise, but also to re-structure the economy. Yet, for analytical purposes we shall distinguish this first phase of successful stabilisation from a second phase of the transition period, starting in 1995/96 which is discussed below.
18. Although the Jordanian economy is traditionally private sector-oriented, the public sector's impact on the economy is larger than its GDP shares suggest. For details on this point, cf. T. Kanaan, (1999), 'The Business Environment in Jordan' in S. Fawzy and A. Galal (eds), *Partners for Development. New Roles for Government and Private Sector in the Middle East and North Africa*, Washington, DC, World Bank, 1999, pp. 58–64.
19. This, too, met with some resistance, but although introduced in mid-1994 at a 7 per cent level, it was increased in 1995 to the initially planned 10 per cent. A further increase of the tax became effective through royal decree in July 1999, with the GST now reaching 13 per cent.
20. Cf. Central Bank of Jordan, *Annual Report, 1998*, 1999, p .153, and Ministry of Finance, *Government Finance Bulletin* Feb. 2000, p. 10.
21. At the time of writing, the draft VAT law had not yet passed parliament.
22. The regulation is in Art. 11 of the law.
23. The main condition is that at least 35 per cent of the value added of the product be generated from operations within the QIZ, and that, secondly, a minimum of 8 per cent within these 35 per cent be contributed by the Jordanian producer, with another 8 per cent stemming from an Israeli producer. For further details, see P. Dougherty, 'Special Report Jordan', *Middle East Economic Digest*, 30 April 1999, p. 12, and P. Dougherty, 'Special Report Jordan', *Middle East Economic Digest*, 29 May 1998, p. 12. Cf. also the information given on the Investment Corporation's homepage at www.jordaninvestment.com/5.htm.
24. For details, cf. H. Hourani and L. Saqqaf (eds), *Business Laws of Jordan*, London: Kluwer, 1998.
25. Compared to over 300 per cent at the beginning of the reform process!
26. For Jordan's access to the WTO and the expectations and challenges associated with that, see Rateb Sweiss' contribution to this volume.
27. On the implications of the Euro-Mediterranean Partnership for the Arab Countries, see O. Schlumberger, 'Arab Political Economy and the EU's Mediterranean Policy: What prospects for Development?', *New Political Economy*, 5, 2 (summer 2000), pp. 247–68.
28. S. Ma'ayeh, 'Jordan Vision 2020 sets course for unified national economic strategy', *Jordan Times*, 11 June 2000. See also Jordan Vision 2020 (ed.), *Jordan Vision 2020: An initiative of leading Jordanian business associations*, Amman, 2000.
29. On the resistance to reforms and its breakdown, from a more actor-oriented perspective, see Hamed El-Said's contribution to this volume.
30. For this important aspect of Jordan's economic transition, see A. Kassay, 'Administration and Efficiency – Bureaucratic Reform. The Case of Jordan', *Mediterranean Politics*, 3, 3 (autumn 1998), pp. 52–62.
31. We shall return to the question of economic order in the conclusions.
32. IMF (1996), *IMF Statement on Jordan by Mohamed El-Erian, News Brief 96/5* (21 August 1996), www.imf.org/external/np/sec/nb/1996/NB9605.HTM.
33. Considering the growth rates during the 1990s, and knowing that an average an-

nual rate of some 6 per cent would be needed only to absorb the annual new entrants to the job market, it is hard to gain great confidence in an unemployment survey conducted in 1999 by the Department of Statistics which places the total unemployment rate at only 10.2 per cent. Results of the survey are published on the Department's internet homepage: www.dos.gov.jo/dos.home/press.130799.htm

34. The World Bank, *Poverty Alleviation in Jordan in the 1990s: Lessons for the Future*, October 1999.
35. For a fuller assessment of the development of living conditions, see the Norwegian study by J. Hanssen-Bauer, J. Pederson and Å. Tiltnes (eds), *Jordanian Society: Living Conditions in the Hashemite Kingdom of Jordan*, Oslo: FAFO Institute for Applied Sciences, 1998.
36. For details on the events, see P. Dougherty, 'Les émeutes du pain à Kerak. Une réponse au programme d'ajustement structurel en cours en Jordanie (un aperçu général)', *Jordanies*, 12, 2 (1996), pp. 95–9. For a comparison between the April 1998 events and the 1996 riots, see C. Ryan, 'Peace, Bread and Riots: Jordan and the International Monetary Fund', *Middle East Policy*, 6, 2 (October 1998), pp. 54–66.
37. CBJ, *Annual Report 1998*, 21.
38. This, of course, is also one of the most difficult tasks in the economic transition of an economy where vested interests have been firmly entrenched to serve the personal interest of incumbents and their families rather than the public, and where, secondly, public sectors widely functioned as 'employers of last resort'. For an analysis of this aspect, see the contribution to the debate by J. Waterbury, 'The Heart of the Matter? Public Enterprise and the Adjustment Process' in S. Haggard and R. Kaufman (eds), *The Politics of Economic Adjustment. International Constraints, Distributive Conflicts, and the State*, Princeton University Press, 1992, pp. 182–220.
39. In fact, production of these commodities has increased more than other manufactured products during the second half of the 1990s. But in themselves, they are no sufficient means to reduce the trade deficit, let alone a pillar on which to build development.
40. R. Awwad, 'Foreign trade expands in year's first four months', *Jordan Times*, 8 June 2000.
41. For an analysis of this point, see T. Piro, *The Political Economy of Market Reform in Jordan*, Lanham, MD: Rowman and Littlefield, 1998, pp. 38 ff.
42. In a speech on Jordanian Television on the occasion of the 'Army Day', as quoted by the London-based Jordan Focus (ed.), *Jordan Focus* (online newsletter), issue 075, 15 June 2000.
43. A 1999 USAID-financed study estimated that the sector could generate up to 30,000 new jobs and earn as much as US$550m annually in exports by 2004. See P. Dougherty, 'Special Report Jordan', *Middle East Economic Digest*, 9 June 2000, p. 12. See also REACH Initiative 'Launching Jordan's software and IT industry. A strategy and action plan for H.M. King Abdullah II, March 2000', unpublished document prepared for presentation to King Abdullah, Amman, Jordan.
44. For a review of the Jordanian IT sector, cf. Ibid.
45. T. Ayyoub, 'Non-Jordanian net investments in ASE decline in the first five months', *Jordan Times*, 12 June 2000. Rather, it seems as if the foreign investors' interest in Jordanian stock markets decreased to 1996 levels, when net foreign investment stood at JD4.8 million only.
46. The chapter by Markus Bouillon in this volume analyses Jordan's foreign policies from the Gulf Crisis to the Peace Process and beyond.

47. B. Navon, *Comment on Ali Anani's 'Recent Adjustment Steps in Jordan: Breaking Old Structures or Paying Lip-Service to External Investors?'*, Munich: Research Group on European Affairs, August 1996, p .24.

48. Author's calculation from data given in The World Bank, *Global Development Finance 1999*, Washington, DC, vol. 2, 5, and CBJ, 1999, *Annual Report 1998*, 9 and 52. For comparison: The average ratio in the MENA region in 1997 was below 1 per cent, compared to 4 per cent in East Asia and 3 per cent in Latin America. See World Bank, *Global Development Finance*, vol. 1, 1999, p. 163.

49. This area is mostly perceived as including Israel, Jordan, Palestine, Syria and Lebanon.

50. Industry today accounts for only about 17 per cent of GDP, and since 1995, GDP shares of all commodity producing sectors have continuously fallen. Cf. Central Bank of Jordan, (1999), *Annual Report 1998*, 1999, pp. 20–1.

51. The sector's share in GDP was less than 5 per cent in 1998, with oligopolistic structures determining the market.

52. Cf. EIU *Country Profile Jordan, 2000/2001*, p. 6. Strikingly, in 1998 industry used less than 4 per cent, and households some 28 per cent of total supplies.

53. Much has been written on the problems mentioned here. On the question of foreign aid, cf. for example T. Piro, *The Political Economy of Market Reform in Jordan*, 1998. On labour migration, see O. Winkler, *Population Growth and Migration in Jordan*, Sussex Academic Press, 1997.

54. EIU (2000), *Country Profile Jordan, 2000/2001*, p. 10.

55. Quotations are all taken from: T. Kanaan, 'The Business Environment in Jordan', pp. 73–5.

56. For a more detailed discussion of the adverse impact of these phenomena on transaction costs, opportunity costs and costs associated with the inefficient allocation of resources in Schlumberger, 2000, 'Competition, the Rule of Law, and Non-Market Transition'.

57. The concept of 'patrimonialism' dates back to M. Weber, *Wirtschaft und Gesellschaft*, Tübingen: Mohr, 1947. It has since been further developed by S. Eisenstadt, *Traditional Patrimonialism and Modern Neo-Patrimonialism*, Beverley Hills: Sage, 1973, and others. See also E. Gellner (ed.), *Patrons and Clients in Mediterranean Societies*, London: Duckworth, 1977, and S. Eisenstadt and R. Lemarchand (eds), *Political Clientelism, Patronage, and Development*, Beverly Hills: Sage, 1981.

58. The Arab term for intercession on behalf of a friend, relative, business partner, etc. describes informal personal relations with the purpose of mutual benefit. Whoever is in a position to grant privileges (scholarships, licences, permits, or other 'favours' of all kinds) extends *wasta*, knowing that this may one day become a reciprocal relation when he is in need of 'getting something done'. Also, it is considered normal (in the sense of 'according to the norm') to extend *wasta* to family members who can be helped. It is inherent in the nature of this kind of social relationships that loyalty is primarily to the small and informal group and/or to the family rather than to office, country or the constitution.

59. A classical introductory reading is J. A. Bill and R. Springborg (1994), *Politics in the Middle East*, New York: HarperCollins (4th edn), chap. 3 and pp. 150–75.

60. F. Czichowski, (1988), "Ich und meine Vettern gegen die Welt...". Migration, 'Wastah', Verteilungskoalitionen und gesellschaftliche Stabilität in Jordanien', *Orient*, 29, 4 (winter 1988), pp. 561–78, was the first to assess *wasta* as a dominant social phenomenon with a specific focus on Jordan. R. Cunningham and Y. Sarayrah, *Wasta. The Hidden Force in Middle Eastern Society*, Westport, CT: Praeger, 1993, also concentrates on Jordanian examples for *wasta*.

61. A recent case in point is the dismissal of Yussuf Mansur from his post as director general of the Telecommunications Regulation Commission (TRC) in May 2000, although he excelled in his job, increasing the TRC's revenues from less than JD2 million in 1998 to over JD25 million in 1999. As the then Minister of Posts and Telecoms, Abdallah Touqan, said: The TRC board wanted 'a more technical person'. The minister had admitted that Mansur had done 'a great job', but 'those things aren't always the yardstick [by which to judge]'. Quotation from A. Henderson, 'Minister defends dismissal of Mansur', *Jordan Times*, 23 May 2000. The suspicion could be raised that the meaning of 'more technical' may really be 'less political', and that Mansur's work ethics were an obstacle to some private interests – although, according to the Telecommunications Law of 1995, the TRC is supposed to be an independent body. In practice, it is certainly not, as long as the minister concerned is on the board and the public sector still in possession of a company in this field (the JTC).

62. In a survey of the Arab Archives Institute, when asked 'Do you think that wasta is a form of corruption?', more than 85 per cent of the sample responded with yes. See Arab Archives Institute (2000), 'Al-wasta fi-l-Urdun' (Wasta in Jordan), paper presented at the conference 'Towards Transparency in Jordan', held in Amman, 22 May 2000, p. 9.

63. Corruption is a term of Western origin which denotes a form of behaviour against social norms, values and rules in Western societies. As a matter of fact, corruption is regarded a crime and can be prosecuted. Wasta, however, is a term which, in its region of origin, refers not to a crime but to a socially predominant pattern of social interaction, which is regarded a value in itself: Any incumbent of an official post, when able to help a family member through his position, would be expected to do so, and it would rarely be understood if he refused to do so. Corruption and wasta should therefore not be used interchangeably since they refer to an exactly opposite social behaviour: The former means acting against the social norm, the latter means acting according to it.

64. M. Weber, *Protestant Ethic and the Spirit of Capitalism* (transl. T. Parsons), Los Angeles: Roxbury, 1998.

65. H. Sharabi, *Neopatriarchy. A Theory of Distorted Change in Arab Society*, New York: Oxford University Press, 1998, p. 45.

66. In rentier economic systems, rent-seeking is microeconomically rational since the gains one can derive from it are considered higher than those from productive activities. Thus, individual rent-seeking can be extremely efficient – though not in the Weberian sense usually thought of in the West. This semantic problem is discussed in O. Schlumberger, 'Arab Political Economy'.

67. R. Cunningham and Y. Sarayrah, *Wasta: The Hidden Force*, 1993, pp. 178 f.

68. For the analytical concept of 'collective action problems' see M. Olson, *The Logic of Collective Action: Public Goods and the Theory of Groups*, Cambridge, MA: Harvard University Press, 1965.

69. However, there *are* estimates about the welfare losses of rent-seeking in a given society; see, e.g., D. Laband and J. Sophocleus, 'The Social Cost of Rent-Seeking: First Estimates', *Public Choice*, 58 (1988), pp. 269–75.

70. Arab Archives Institute, *Al-wasta fi-l-Urdun*, 2000.

71. R. Cunningham and Y. Sarayrah, *Wasta: The Hidden Force*, 179.

72. *Jordan Focus*, issue no. 77 (20 June 2000).

73. H. Sharabi, *Neopatriarchy*, p. 47 f. Italics in the original text.

74. R. Cunningham and Y. Sarayrah, *Wasta: The Hidden Force*, 36.

75. For the 'constitutive principles', as he calls them, of a functioning market order, see W. Eucken, *Grundzüge der Wirtschaftspolitik*, 6th edn, Tübingen: Mohr, 1990.

76. This aspect has been discussed with a background giving more economic theory to support the argument in O. Schlumberger, 'The Arab Middle East and the Question of Democratisation: Some Critical Remarks', *Democratisation*, 7, 4 (winter 2000), pp. 104–32.

77. For this aspect, cf. G. White, 'Towards a Political Analysis of Markets', *IDS Bulletin*, *23*, 3 (1993), pp. 4–11.

78. The developmental potential and other traits of patrimonial capitalism as distinct from both rentier economies and market systems are discussed in detail in: O. Schlumberger, 'Competition, the Rule of Law, and Non-Market Transitions'.

79. Comment 'Weighing Wasta', *Jordan Times*, 23 May 2000 (author's name not given).

THE POLITICAL ECONOMY OF REFORM IN JORDAN

BREAKING RESISTANCE TO REFORM?

Hamid El-Said

In April 1985 the late King Hussain appointed a new cabinet headed by Zayed Rifai. The main task of the new government was to 'reinvigorate the economy from its sluggishness' and to enhance growth rates, efficiency and productivity. The strategy which the king himself recommended in order to achieve this goal was one based largely on increasing the role of the private sector, both foreign and domestic. It called for facilitating investment procedures and complex bureaucratic measures, enacting a new Tax Law, providing more financial incentives, giving equal treatment for foreign and local investment, and, more important, the sale of the public sector enterprises to private investors.[1]

Jordan's reform efforts were supported by a series of agreements with the International Monetary Fund (IMF) and World Bank in 1989, 1992, 1995 and 1999. These agreements called for a more far-reaching reform measures than the ones envisaged in the 'spontaneous' programme of the mid-1980s, including stronger stabilisation, trade liberalisation, financial deregulation and privatisation. Yet despite the impetus of the pressure from without, the pace of reform until the end of 1998 remained frustratingly disappointing. Little was done to promote market reform in most sectors and progress was virtually non-existent in areas like privatisation. Where some advances occurred, as in fiscal and monetary policies and macroeconomic stabilisation, countervailing actions by the government vitiated the benefits of reform.[2]

Yet a different picture emerges after 1998, when the pace of reform picked up dramatically. One indication of the rapid pace of change was Jordan's speedy and in many ways unexpected, admission to the World Trade Organisation (WTO) in early 2000. This process required a strong record of compliance with the conditions stipulated in the agreements signed by the Jordanian government with the IMF and World Bank since 1989. In addition to stronger trade liberalisation and a privatisation drive, the latter included new rules and regulations pertaining to intellectual property rights (IPRs).

In the interim, however, two significant political developments had occurred. The first was the re-introduction in 1989 of parliamentary elections and the lifting of the martial law, in force since the late 1950s. This process accompanied the first agreement with the IMF and World Bank in 1989 and aimed at facilitating reforms by sharing and pooling responsibilities and blame for its outcome.[3] Second, in February 1999 Jordan experienced for the first time since 1953 a change in regime when King Hussain died and was succeeded by his eldest son, Abdullah II.

Did the process of political liberalisation produce a credible parliament, accountable to its constituency and keen to push forward with badly needed economic reform? In other words, was the parliament responsible for the positive change in the pace of reform after 1998? The fact that progress in implementation occurred ten years after the first elections were held in 1989 suggests that the answer to this question is negative. The process of political liberalisation has not changed the fact that Jordanians and their representatives in parliament continue to have no say whatsoever over the selection of their prime minister, cabinet members, or any other high state posts, including the future king. In fact, since the 1993, when the Electoral Law was changed to the 'one man one vote' system, the parliament has become a 'rubber-stamp', 'dominated by tribal elders fiercely loyal to the king'[4] and 'running on local issues rather than the grander questions of peace with Israel or Jordan's IMF's-driven economic policies'.[5] The available empirical evidence suggests that a change in regime, by severing links between the previous ruling elite and powerful domestic interest groups in favour of the *status quo*, can facilitate reform. Waterbury argues that the emergence of 'a change team' is a precondition for successful economic reform.[6] At first sight, this seems to provide a good explanation for the improved implementation record in Jordan after 1998. During its 'honeymoon' period, King Abdullah's new regime seemed capable of inaugurating bold economic measures without being handicapped by past compromises or history of previously failed policies.

There are grounds to believe that King Abdullah is far more committed and ideologically attuned to market-oriented reforms than was his father King Hussain. In a speech at the World Economic Forum in Davos in early 2000, King Abdullah said 'We have taken the initiative to make free markets the only norm of resource allocation'.[7] The new king even went further to assure Jordanians that he would solve all of their economic problems in two years, 'promis[ing] that

Jordanians will reap the fruits of his drive for economic reform in 2001'.[8]

However, bold reforms actually started shortly before King Abdullah took office in February 1999. More precisely, they started in October 1998 when the Tarawnah cabinet sold the first 33 per cent of its equity in the Jordan Cement Factory Corporation (JCFC). The remaining 12 per cent were sold three months after the King came to power.[9] King Abdullah, it would seem, maintained the impetus for reform, but he was not its initiator.

How, then, can we explain progress with implementation in Jordan after 1998? Why was reform so slow in the pre-1998 period? What accelerated the pace of reform in the post-1998 period? What factors influenced the degree of compliance with the IMF and World Bank loan conditionality throughout the whole period? To what extent have the policy conditions attached to the IMF and World Bank agreements been implemented? In answering the questions posed above, it will be argued here that the change in the position and mix of domestic vested interests in favour of some degree of reform has been largely responsible for the improved implementation record in Jordan after 1998. It is not the aim of this paper to evaluate the performance of the Jordanian economy under the IMF and World Bank programmes. Several 'exogenous' factors, which had nothing to do with the IMF and World Bank programmes, strongly affected the performance of the economy during 1989–9. These included the 1990–1 Gulf crisis, the forced return of more than 300,000 Jordanians with their life savings from the Gulf and the peace treaty with Israel in 1994 and its 'dividend' of increased aid, debt relief and debt-rescheduling on extremely generous terms. It is impossible to isolate the real impact of the IMF and World Bank programmes under these circumstances.[10] Instead, the paper will focus on Jordan's compliance rate, that is, what has and has not been implemented out of the key loan conditionalities attached to the IMF and World Bank agreements since 1989. Within this framework, however, the impact of the above cited 'exogenous' factors on the political economy of implementation in Jordan cannot and will not be neglected.

Instead, this paper revolves around the role of the interest groups in shaping and influencing the economic decision process in Jordan. It is important therefore to identify from the outset those interest groups that have traditionally influenced policies in Amman. This should be set against Jordan's reform efforts since the mid-1980s, highlighting the slow pace of reform between 1985–8 and documenting progress in implementation after 1998. The main developments in Jordan's political economy since the late 1980s and early 1990s are also important because of their impact on reform implementation and the rate of compliance.

The origin and evolution of interest groups in Jordan

The roots of Jordan's main interest groups can be traced back to the late nineteenth century when several merchant families from Palestine and Syria were attracted to Transjordan by the political stability provided by the Ottomans, following the introduction of *Tanzimat* (reforms) in the second half of the century and later by the establishment of the British Mandate and the creation of the Emirate in 1921. These merchants soon established strong relations with the Emir (Abdullah I), high-ranking state officials, bureaucrats and British officers in Transjordan. For the Emir, the merchants became a ready source of finance, providing him with cash whenever his allowances from the British government fell short of his expenses. In return, he bestowed on them influential positions in the state apparatus and endowed them with economic and financial benefits, including import licenses, tax exemptions and state land.[11] Their close relations with the palace and other state officials paid off during the shortages of the Second World War. Thanks to their monopoly over import licenses, some thirty merchants, nicknamed the 'quota coterie', accumulated enormous amount of wealth. Amawi argues that the shortages of the mid-1940s and the state policies not only dramatically altered the fortunes of the merchants in Transjordan, but also 'transformed them into a wealthy, cohesive class closely connected to the state'.[12]

In 1946 Jordan gained political independence. King Abdullah I was assassinated in 1951 and following a short interval under King Talal, King Hussain I was crowned in 1953. In no way did the change in regime from Abdullah to Hussain undermine the position of the ruling coalition. Hussain's regime was a continuation of Abdullah's, not a revolutionary regime that sought to weaken and eliminate the traditional business groups for their collaboration with the colonial power. In fact, during the 1950s and 1960s the 'merchants' began diversifying their activities into other sectors, particularly industry. They were responsible for initiating most of the projects in this period, including the largest three projects, namely, phosphates, cement and oil refinery, all of which were established on the basis of public-private partnership. This diversification process was encouraged by the state itself, which played a minimal role in the economy, only interfering to facilitate and protect private investment.[13]

Following a series of Arab summits (1969 in Khartoum, 1974 in

Rabat and 1979 in Baghdad) Jordan as 'frontline state' in the confrontation with Israel was allocated a large amount of financial assistance by the oil-rich Gulf States. Foreign aid receipts totaled JD615 billion ($2 billion) annually between 1974 and 1978, rising to more than JD1 billion in 1979–83.[14] Contrary to general expectations,[15] however, the inflow of foreign funds weakened, rather than strengthened, the developmental capacity of the Jordanian state. Hussain's personalised style of rule was largely responsible for this outcome. Rather than focusing on creating a strong and productive domestic economy, Hussain began greatly expanding an old but, in terms of political control, effective system, namely patronage politics. Members of the loyal families, from both East and West Banks, were co-opted into influential state positions.[16] The aim was to widen the regime's domestic base of support and at the same time to prevent young, intellectual Jordanians, of both Palestinian and Transjordanian origin, from turning to opposition politics,[17] particularly following the upheavals of the second half of the 1960s.[18] Some of the most prominent families to hold key state positions were Rifais, Badrans, Tuqans, Talhunis, al-Qasims, al-Masris, Abu Odas and, most important in the 1990s, particularly following the severing of 'economic and legal ties' with the West Bank in the late 1980s, the al-Rawabdehs, al-Majalis and al-Kabarities. Other prominent beneficiaries include members of the Royal Family, notably Zayed Ibn Shakir (King Hussain's cousin) who served as commander-in-chief of the Jordanian army in 1976–89 and later as chief of the Royal Court and prime minister.

While the elite group benefiting from state patronage included figures from both banks of the Jordan, East Bankers were more reliant on family and tribal ties than Palestinians. Following the footsteps of their master, Jordanian officials also practiced patronage politics in filling positions in institutions of state with relatives, members of their extended family and region. In all cases appointments were undertaken on the basis of loyalty, not competence.[19] Thus, a division of labour developed in Jordan between Palestinians and Jordanians. The former came to dominate the private sector, while the latter formed the majority in the public sector.[20]

Moreover, encouraged by the 'rotational' nature of politics in Jordan and also by the fact that 'King Hussain had a blind spot towards' corruption, several high ranking state officials invoked their political power to enrich themselves and their cronies.[21] Corruption became widespread, not only among top state officials, but also among lower level bureaucrats whose wages and salaries were too low to support a decent standard of living. In the words of the former health minister,

Dr Malahs, the state sector became 'Mafias' and 'whales', each using the resources of the state for their own personal interests.[22] Under these circumstances, businessmen realised that, by learning what the neo-classical economists call the 'art of rent-seeking', they could bolster their profits and control market entry. 'Corruption and bribery [in Jordan] became one of the major diseases of the government sector'[23] and it became a new survival strategy for civil servants in Jordan to accept bribery and other material benefits in return for bending, neglecting and overlooking rules and regulations.[24] Many businessmen strengthened their position and relations with the ruling elite through commercial and business relations and also through inter-marriages.[25]

The reform programmes

An established pattern of alliances thus emerged in Jordan, cementing a coalition of businessmen and bureaucrats who benefited from the *status quo*. It led to the emergence of what Niblock has called the 'bourgeois-bureaucratic state . . . in Jordan . . . built on the linked interest of the state bureaucrats and the commercial bourgeoisie [with no] strong interest in the transformation of the economy'.[26] This alliance, which was established and consolidated its power during the boom years, eventually came to influence the implementation capacity of the Jordanian state until the late 1990s, when a slight shift in the composition of the vested interests it represented created a new momentum for reform. This period is best divided into three main parts: the period of 'spontaneous reform' in 1985–9 without co-operation with the IMF and World Bank, the period of halting reform in 1989–8 under the auspices of the IMF and World Bank and the period of more determined implementation in the post 1998 period.

'Spontaneous' reform without the IMF and the World Bank, 1985–89. There was a good economic case for reform in Jordan in the early 1980s when the economy began experiencing a slowdown in its activities and growth rate. The country's external environment was deteriorating rapidly as a result of the decline in international oil prices and the reduced ability of the oil-rich Gulf States to provide Jordan with the $1.25 billion agreed on during the 1979 Arab summit in Baghdad. Regional recession undermined both Jordanian exports to the Gulf and threatened remittances from Jordanians working there. It also caused many Jordanians to lose their jobs in the Gulf and thus to return to Jordan where the unemployment curve was already

moving upwards. Iraq, Jordan's main trading partner, had its financial position weakened as its war with Iran dragged on longer than expected and it too reduced its imports from Jordan. Finally, Jordan also experienced a deterioration in its terms of trade, as the international price for its main export item (phosphates) collapsed.[27] The upshot was a mounting current account deficit and declining rates of growth (see Table 1).

Internal factors also failed to adjust to the changing external environment and therefore compounded Jordan's economic malaise. Even before Rifai' was appointed as prime minister in 1985, a fierce internal struggle had taken place between the anti- and pro-reform groups. The former emerged the winner. The government thus ignored the advice of its 'local economists calling for austerity for the past four or five years'.[28] Jordan was also rowing against the tide of, not only its local economists, but also of some international financial institutions, like the IMF, who similarly advised the government to adopt austerity measures. But 'Jordan . . . in the early 1980s [chose to] ignore the IMF recipes'.[29]

Under Rifai', however, whose cabinet included several ministers who were drawn from the private sector, the government followed an expansionary policy which was based on running down reserves and foreign borrowing. Rifai's cabinet also increased protection for domestic industry via tariffs and non-tariff barriers at a time when the rational economic policy response was pointing to the other direction, as the economy was already suffering from waste and inefficiency caused by the lack of competition. The government even went further in the mid-1980s and initiated a slight revaluation of the already artificially overvalued Jordanian dinar (JD).[30]

The response of the Rifai's cabinet to the 'intense lobbying' by local businessmen, many of whom were cabinet members with strong connections to the private sector, was detrimental to the treasury and economy as a whole.[31] Revenues from trade represent the main source of domestic income. Therefore, raising protection to a prohibitive level aggravated the budgetary deficit. Strong protection also encouraged further waste and inefficiencies in the economy. Revaluation of the currency, aimed at protecting local industry by reducing the price of imported raw materials, exacerbated the current account deficit by encouraging imports and discouraging exports. Continued reliance on expansionary policies to increase growth rates increased foreign debt to an alarming level. Foreign debt rose from less than $1 billion in 1978 to around $3.4 billion and $9 billion in 1986 and 1989, respectively (see Table 1). In early 1989, Jordan's economic slowdown, which started in 1982, culminated in an economic and financial crisis. The government began defaulting on its foreign debt for the first time, and the crisis peaked shortly thereafter, when the value of the Jordanian dinar fell by almost 50 per cent overnight.

SOME MACROECONOMIC INDICATORS IN JORDAN, 1975–89
(*$ million*)

	Public deficit	Trade deficit	External debt
1975	95	589	0.327
1976	440	837	0.400
1977	560	1150	0.617
1978	581	1141	0.834
1979	916	1449	1.038
1980	989	1684	1.241
1981	969	2491	1.634
1982	940	2717	1.947
1983	985	2788	2.255
1984	975	2741	2.443
1985	1120	2130	2.985
1986	1366	2148	3.391
1987	1032	2298	3.696
1988	2142	2107	8.044

Source: Central Bank of Jordan, Yearly Statistical Series (1964–89), Amman: Department of Research and Studies, October 1989.

The failure to undertake significant reform at this time reflected the strength of the 'bourgeois-bureaucratic' alliance in Jordan, although the strength of this alliance was tested during the recessionary period of the 1980s. In contradiction to the 'statist' views of Jordan's political economy, led most notably by Brand, the Jordanian 'bourgeois' appeared to have more political clout than is generally expected.[32] Their calls for more protection and government spending at a time of economic slowdown appealed to those at the highest level of the executive authority, particularly to 'those around the palace . . . many of whom derive economic benefits from their roles as commission men or as traders with privileged access to those with political influence, and some of whom use[d] public office for private gain'.[33]

It was thus not surprising that hardly any of the key policies envisaged by the 1985 'spontaneous' programme were implemented. The 1985 privatisation programme, for example, called initially for the divestiture of the Telecommunication Corporation, the Royal Jordanian Airlines, the Transportation Corporation, later to include the Cement and Phosphates Corporations, known in Jordan as the 'big-five' state-owned enterprises.[34] But privatisation threatened the perks and privileges of bureaucrats and high state officials. It was thus virtually non-existent. Rather than encouraging trade liberalisation and foreign investment, which would have threatened the profits of local businessmen, a tighter system of industrial licensing was used effectively to block new entry into the market.[35]

Halting reform under IMF and World Bank auspices, 1989–98

In April 1989 Jordan was forced to sign its first structural adjustment agreement with the IMF and World Bank as a means of correcting internal and external imbalances. Prescriptions for reform revolved around the typical IMF and World Bank recipe. To restore internal imbalance, a stabilisation programme that targeted fiscal and monetary policy was recommended. Measures included cutting public expenditures and subsidies, imposing a new sales tax and expanding and improving the tax base in addition to credit ceilings on public borrowing. To improve efficiency and productivity, a strong trade liberalisation, financial deregulation and a more aggressive public administrative reform in addition to 'promoting privatisation more seriously' were among key conditions of the World Bank's structural adjustment programme.[36] However, the 1989 adjustment programme was suspended as a result of the outbreak of the Gulf War in August 1990. The agreement was renewed in 1992, following the end of the crisis. Jordan's reform efforts since then were further supported by a series of agreements with the IMF and World Bank in 1995 and 1999.[37]

In all fairness, significant changes did take place during this period. For example, food subsidies were gradually and painfully reduced, if not entirely eliminated. Some trade liberalisation occurred as well, as tariffs were reduced and in many cases replaced quantitative restrictions. Interest rates were also raised and made positive in real terms. Some *infitah* (economic opening) was also permitted, allowing some businessmen to acquire new assets, particularly in the services sector, for example telecommunications, education, finance and tourism. The government also franchised public bus routes in the Amman area and sold its majority shares in the Jordan Hotels and Tourism Company in 1994.[38]

These changes, however, were far from creating a fully liberalised economy. For instance, although the Jordanian government reduced food subsidies, it also provided a series of wage and salary raises to civil servants and bureaucrats to compensate them for the decline in subsidies in direct violation of the agreement with IMF and World Bank. It also established the National Aid Fund to provide direct, cash assistance to the poor and most vulnerable. By the late 1990s, the Fund increased its assistance to more than JD23 million ($32.9 million), an amount which exceeded the savings to the treasury from lower subsidy. It is not clear how effective the Fund has been in combating poverty in Jordan, which has actually increased to include one-third of the total population by the late 1990s.[39]

As with regard to tax reform, the imposition of a new Sales Tax (ST) was delayed until February 1994, following fierce opposition from powerful domestic interest groups. The latter not only deprived the treasury from the revenues promised by the new tax for well over two years, but also succeeded in extracting major concessions from the state in return for the introduction of the ST in 1994. Thus, the rate of the ST was reduced from the 10 per cent originally demanded by the IMF to 7 per cent. The list of domestic products exempted from the new tax was also enlarged considerably and in addition the government was forced to reduce the corporate income tax. More importantly, interest groups managed to modify the Tax Law in a way that 'prevents the government from imposing any additional taxes or duties without parliamentary approval'.[40] This suggests a change in the old, informal style of lobbying used before the introduction of parliamentary elections in 1989 to a more formal one.

Distortions also remained in the trade sector despite a general reduction in the levels of protection. Reductions occurred only in areas where domestic production did not exist. Countervailing actions, like increasing taxes and surcharges on competing imports while exempting domestic firms undermined further the benefits of trade reform. As a special World Bank Report on Jordan put it:

Important distortions remain in the trade regime, some as a result of trade interventions, others as a result of domestic policies. There is still considerable variance in the tariff structure ... [which] remains biased against exports. Tariff exemptions undermine the legal tariff and surcharge structure in a non-transparent way. It appears also that the customs regulations increase the base price of those goods that do pay duties by about 24 per cent ... taxes on some imports appear to be higher than on domestically produced goods.[41]

Reform was weakest in the area where it was needed most, namely, the public sector. Despite strong rhetoric and repeated calls to privatise, to trim and clean up the corrupt bureaucracy, hardly any of these areas was touched at all. Privatisation, apart from sales in the hotel company, was virtually non-existent despite the fact that the process had officially began as far back as the mid-1980s. As a local columnist wrote in early 1999, 'Jordan's privatisation programme looks much as it did one year, two years, or even five years ago – a half-hearted effort with rhetoric far exceeding action . . . .Jordan's privatisation drive has hardly left the starting block'.[42] The most impressive achievement in this area was the sale, in October 1998, of 33 per cent of the government's shares in the Jordan Cement Factories Corporation (JCFC).

In August 1998, nine months prior to the May 1999 stand-by agreement, the Jordanian government washed its hands of the previous agreement which it had signed with the IMF in 1995 and unilaterally 'froze' all of its policies due to their failure to improve economic growth rates.[43] This reflected the fact that compliance with the IMF and World Bank loan conditionality was very weak during 1989–98. In summarising progress in implementation during this period, Al-Fanik, Jordan's leading economic columnist, wrote:

> There is a consensus [in Jordan today] that the process of economic adjustment has not been completed . . . and the process of structural re-adjustment did not happen except unless we consider changing the names of some public enterprises into companies an important thing. Privatisation did not even start despite repeated talks about implementation as the government has missed all the privatisation dates which it committed itself to, particularly privatisation of the Royal Jordanian Airlines, the Telecommunication Company and the Aqaba Railway.[44]

High compliance: 1999–2000

On 7 February 1999 King Hussain was succeeded by his eldest son, King Abdullah II. Following the end of the forty-day mourning period in March, Abdullah immediately appointed a new cabinet headed by the veteran politician Abd al-Ra'uf al-Rawabdeh, nicknamed 'the bulldozer'. In his first parliamentary speech, the 'bulldozer' 'promised to reform the administration, fight corruption and press on with Jordan's long-delayed privatisation drive'.[45] During its first nine months in office, al-Rawabdeh's government completed the sale of 45 per cent of equity in the in the JCFC to a French consortium company. A strong trade liberalisation drive was launched in August 1999, involving big cuts in customs on a number of imported products, including cars, computers, all type of phones, shaving machines, clocks, cameras and other electrical equipment. At the same time, subsidies on basic food products were reduced further and the price of petrol, public transportation, water and electricity were raised. Another large round of tariff-reduction took place in April 2000 that further reduced protection on the items cited above. A new Value Added Tax was introduced in late 1999, replacing and raising the former ST to 13 per cent. Privatisation of public sector enterprises finally took off under the new regime. A 25-year operating concession for the indebted Aqaba Railway Corporation was agreed with an American-led consortium. In early 2000, the government sold 40 per cent of its stakes in the Jordan Telecommunications Company (JTC) to a French company, Telecome. Even the sale of Royal Jordanian Airlines achieved some progress and the airline shed several of its non-core businesses, including the duty free shop, aircraft maintenance, its engine overhaul, catering and training. New privatisation and intellectual property right laws were introduced, clearing the way for an early entry to the World Trade Organisation (WTO) in early 2000.[46] The speed with which these reforms occurred caught the eye of the American ambassador in Jordan, William Burns, who commented during a speech at Jordan's First IT Forum in March 2000:

I have been deeply impressed by the economic changes which have been achieved over the past year. A year ago, if you had asked most observers, myself included, if Jordan had a real chance to join the WTO, they would have said no. A year later not only has Jordan won accession to the WTO in record time, it has also completed several major privatisations, streamlined its customs system and transformed its intellectual property rights regime.[47]

On the surface at least, there seems to be in this vignette a classic vindication of the argument that a change in regime is a necessary condition for successful implementation. However, a deeper analysis of the main developments in Jordan's political economy since the late 1980s and early 1990s gives a somewhat different picture.

The Political Economy of Implementation, 1989–2000

In 1989, Jordan had signed a painful adjustment agreement with the IMF and World Bank. The agreement was fiercely resisted, not only by members of the private sector, but also by Jordanians as a whole, who dominate the public sector and are therefore more economically dependent on the state. Although viewed as the regime's bedrock of support, some Jordanians, particularly in the southern part of the country, represent, along with the Palestinian refugees, the poorest strata in the society. Unemployment and poverty in 1989 were already higher in the south than in other parts of the country. The southerners' opposition to the adjustment programme, which called for lifting of food subsidies and raising the prices of public services, was violently expressed in widespread riots that immediately followed the announcement of the agreement with the IMF in 1989.[48] When the Gulf War erupted in August 1990, the regime must have been relieved to suspend the programme, albeit temporarily.

Following the end of the Gulf crisis in 1992, the agreement with the IMF and World Bank was renewed. But in 1992, Jordan was in an invidious position. The soft tone which the regime had adopted towards the 1990 Iraqi invasion of Kuwait had not gone down well either in Washington or the Gulf. American and Arab aid was cut off and the Gulf States went further, closing their markets to Jordanian products and labour, expelling more than 300,000 Jordanians who had previously worked in Kuwait and Saudi Arabia. As a result Jordan's population jumped by approximately 10 per cent overnight, and poverty and unemployment rose dramatically all over the country. This was no time for austerity. Implementing reforms under these circumstances, particularly privatisation and cutback in public sector, represented 'a great gamble' for Jordan's leadership.[49]

In 1994, Hussain intensified negotiations with Israel, leading to the Wadi Araba peace agreement in November of the same year. It was hoped that a 'peace dividend' would provide sufficient financial rewards to procrastinate on bold reform measures, or perhaps to avoid them altogether and at the same time to enable the regime to continue to buy 'loyalty and support' of its main constituencies, which is 'based on their economic dependence on the state'.[50] Peace did bring some dividends. The American government restored its aid programme to Jordan, with an annual package of $150 million in military and economic aid. It also wrote off $700 million of Jordan's foreign debt and lobbied the Paris and London Clubs for softer loans and rescheduling terms.[51] It is doubtful whether Jordan could have managed to obtain such favourable treatment in terms of debt rescheduling and extension of further loans and grants without the Wadi Araba Agreement.

Despite these short-term benefits, Hussain's peace treaty with Israel brought insufficient 'dividends' to solve Jordan's deep economic and financial problems. Just to stay solvent – and judging from the level of financial assistance it used to receive during the 1973–82 period – Jordan required more than $150 million annually and $700 million debt relief. Unlike Sadat of Egypt, Hussain failed to negotiate a massive, unconditional aid package as a prerequisite for achieving peace with Israel. As Al-Fanik put it,

Jordan volunteered in 1994 to sign a comprehensive peace treaty with Israel after hasty one-day negotiations at the top level, which took only a few hours, without American mediation and for free. For some unknown reason,[52] Jordan opted to make the cheapest peace treaty in the history of the region, making no demands [in return] whatsoever.[53]

Jordan, after the treaty, found herself in the same position as she had been before: financially insolvent and forced to press on with implementing painful reform. Abdul Salam Al-Majali, then Jordan's prime minister, had to break with tradition and deliver a parliamentary speech before the minister of finance presented the budget for the new year (1995) to remind MPs and Jordanians in general that they had no option but to comply with IMF and World Bank demands:

We should realise that those nations with surplus funds and able to offer economic and financial assistance . . . want to know how the aid will be spent. They refuse to offer financial aid unless they are sure that the aid is connected with economic endeavours and are convinced of these efforts.[54]

The prime minister was simply telling his audience that his government had conceded a great part of its sovereignty to the IMF and World Bank, an approach which departed from the model implemented in what the IMF called 'advanced' and more 'successful reformers' in the region, such as Turkey, Tunisia and Morocco.[55] The government of each of these countries insisted publicly that the ideas behind reform were 'indigenous', designed by local bureaucrats and state officials to serve national interests. Jordan's main interest groups seized the opportunity left by the regime's hesitation. Through the Chambers of Industry and Commerce, they organised a massive campaign against reforms, including national conferences, drawing opposition parties and professional associations. They held public meetings and fully exploited the press and media to manipulate public opinion against the IMF and World Bank. In an open letter to the prime minister, businessmen, along with the Professional Associations, argued that 'an international conspiracy . . . is imposed on our government as part of a series of measures by foreigners in the IMF and is not part of any national programme . . . The project impinges upon the sovereignty of Jordan and its people'. They called upon all Jordanians, including bureaucrats and state officials, to resist IMF and World Bank policies.[56] Accordingly, 'the calls for reform fell on deaf ears, particularly among public sector employees and high state officials. Jordanians [looked to] King Hussain as their rescuer, and they believed that he would somehow pull them and the country out of the economic crisis no matter how deep it was'.[57] Of course, bureaucrats and high state officials had their own, selfish reasons for opposing reforms. They feared losing their perks, privileges and traditional dominance over the public sector. Their fears were intensified in the 1990s by the fact that most of the returnees from the Gulf were of Palestinian origin, and that a largely Palestinian private sector stood to gain most from some reforms, particularly divestiture.[58]

In order to defuse opposition to his peace treaty with Israel, Hussain successfully lobbied the American government for further aid, which rose in late 1997 to $225 million. Increased American aid further muted reform efforts.[59] This was clearly manifested in both increased fiscal deficit, from 5.4 per cent in 1995 to 8.1 per cent in 1999 and foreign debt from $7.8 billion in 1995 to $9.3 billion in 1999.[60]

In the last decade of King Hussain's life, however, his 'system was already creaking, hit by several external [and internal] shocks'.[61] By 1999 a third of the population were living under the poverty line and the unofficial, but recognised, unemployment rate rose to 27 per cent.[62] Jordanians took to the streets in 1996 and 1998 in violent protests against economic austerity that coexisted with widespread corruption among state officials. The United Nations embargo on Iraq dramatically reduced commerce with Jordan's main trading partner from more than $2 billion before the embargo to only $857 million in 1999.[63] Jordan's trade with the West Bank, expected to rise to the pre-1967 level, was crippled by Israel governments' obsession with security issues. Increased American aid, though helpful, could not compensate Jordan for the loss of commerce with Iraq. Multilateral donors began 'chafing at the slow pace of reform [and were] reluctant to concede much more until Jordan adopts a more vigorous' approach and implemented far-reaching reform measures.[64]

Moreover, the king's health deteriorated rapidly in the second half of the 1990s. He spent the last seven months of his life in the Mayo Clinic in the United States being treated for cancer. His younger brother Hassan, the Crown Prince and Regent, was in effect running the country. 'Prince Hassan was more attuned to the kind of market-oriented policies preached by the IMF and World Bank and had for long 'made economics his special concern'.[65] With Hussain's imminent death, interest groups, both inside and outside the state sector, calculated that 'change is inevitable' and Hassan, once in power, would proceed with reforms even if he had to crush the anti-reform groups.[66] In fact, one reason for the eventual humbling of Prince Hassan was that while acting as regent, reforms and 'changes', as King Hussain himself put in a letter which he sent to Prince Hassan from his bed in Mayo Clinic a few days before death, 'had been insisted on'.[67]

The looming prospect of change brought a shift in business attitudes to reform. Some, but not too much, liberalisation was now seen as desirable and beneficial, reducing criticisms against the anti-reform group, making the 'businessman [appear to be] shouldering his civic responsibility . . . being a good corporate citizen', yet without reducing his share of the economic pie.[68] When the American government,

towards the end of King Hussain's life, began pressing for the implementation of bold reform measures, particularly those pertaining to
the WTO where major violations for IPRs were costing some American businesses millions of dollars, business opinion in Jordan felt that
'if we don't join the WTO now, more and more conditions will be imposed on us as time goes by . . . The longer we wait to join, the more
burdens we will have to face in joining'.[69]

As a result, one should also look more carefully at what kind of reforms have so far been advocated and how they affect various powerful vested interests in Jordan. The new ST, for example, which
almost doubled from 7 per cent in 1994 to 13 per cent in 1999, is paid
by consumers, not producers. It is also a 'regressive tax' that favours
merchants and large businessmen, and is therefore a socially unjust
tax that disproportionately impacts on the poor.[70] In return for the
imposition of the new tax, however, businessmen were offered further
concessions from the state in terms of lower corporate income and
also lower taxes on inputs.

Similarly, the impact of trade liberalisation has been ambiguous.
Due to lack of domestic resources, Jordanian producers rely almost
completely on imported raw materials, intermediates and other inputs for their operations. Reduction in tariffs and non-tariff barriers
on imports reduce their production costs and hence increase their
profits. Trade liberalisation also provided a better export potential,
particularly with the establishment of several free zone areas in Jordan in addition to the privileged access Jordanian producers have in
the European Union (EU) and American markets, as a result of the
Euro-Mediterranean Partnership Initiative and the Free Trade Area
agreement which Jordan signed with the American government following the 1994 peace treaty with Israel.[71]

The threat of increased foreign competition in the domestic market, however, is still contained by a closely-knit grid of corrupt ties
between bureaucrats and high state officials, on the one hand, and
some members of the private sector, on the other. Evidence suggests
that, despite a recent surge, foreign investment in Jordan remains
much lower than expected, hampered by the rise in corruption, red-
tape measures and even complex licensing system which increased noticeably under the panel of liberalisation.[72] Bureaucrats and high-
ranking state officials also managed to preserve the 'Jordanian touch'
and East Bank prominence in the public sector. The imposition of
the new tax not only increased the state's revenues, but also made bureaucrats and state officials, on the surface at least, look more efficient,
as if they had 'done a service to the country', while hiding their inefficiencies and enabling them to continue their old habit of employing

members of their families, tribe and region.[73] Abdullah II's first cabinet, headed by 'the bulldozer', had the smallest number of Jordanian-Palestinians since 1989 and was determined to preserve Jordanian dominance over the public sector. Al-Rawabdeh thus personally opposed economic reforms, impeded foreign investments, set up new standards for bribery and corruption, in addition to putting efforts into appointments 'based not on the promised competence, efficiency and integrity, but on birth in [his] home town'.[74]

Privatisation, despite progress, remains partial and limited by regional and international standards. The state has sold less than fifty per cent of its shares in two of its largest enterprises, namely, the JCC and TCC. It thus remains the largest shareholder in the privatised enterprises. While enacting the new Privatisation Law in 1999, the parliament 'stipulated that the government should retain the so-called golden share which entitles it to veto decisions made by the board of directors ... of any privatised company'.[75] The government, while selling shares in some public enterprises, also 'clearly stipulated that no ... employees would be dismissed in the next two years ... after that period, the performance of each employee would be assessed and his career advancement would depend on his productivity and diligence'.[76]

Only fourteen months before his death, King Hussain himself admitted that interest groups both outside the state and inside it, including 'many Jordanians [have] become the main obstacle in' the path of economic and political reform.[77] The ability of these groups and individuals to influence and shape the state's economic policies, including policies prescribed by the IMF and World Bank, is the outcome of Hussain's personalised style of politics employed since the early 1970s. Rather than fundamental change under King Abdullah II's regime, it would seem that the dominant coalition of merchants and bureaucrats had adjusted to the new realities brought about by a decade of external and internal pressures and changes. Since then, the composition of those groups underwent important changes. A refashioned business elite had emerged to take advantage of the new opportunities that arose in the 1990s from the *infitah* policies set in motion in the mid-1980s. The new groupings played an important role in modeling the path of economic restructuring. As Wils has noted, 'The economic reform process of the 1990s [was supported by] the emergence of new actors on the economic scene ... demanding a further liberalisation of the economy, but it is not in favour of more open competition which would endanger its privileges.'[78]

One faction of the new business grouping includes some of the returnees from the Gulf who brought back with them their life savings and invested a great deal of them in Jordan.[79] Another group includes some investors from the Arab World: the Egyptian businessman Ghayth Suwaris (who recently bought approximately 60 per cent of the shares in the Jordanian Fast Link Company); the Saudi tycoon Khalid Ibn Mahfuz (the biggest single shareholder in Jordan's second largest bank, the Housing Bank); the Saudi billionaire and nephew of King Fahd, Prince al-Walid Ibn Tala (who controls 60 per cent of the $50 million new hotel being built on the Dead Sea in addition to stakes in at least one other hotel still under construction); and the Iraqi Nazmi Awji (the main shareholder in the JD120 million Royal Tower Project). The final set of actors and – those most relevant to this study – includes the progeny of the former state officials on whom King Hussain relied during the 1970s and through to the 1990s. They include members of the old East Bank tribal elite such as the Majalis, notably Shadi, the son of the former prime minister Abdul Salam and the only holder of the license for the pay telephone company 'Allo', and his cousin Sahl, son of a former army chief of staff and current speaker of the Upper House, Abd al-Hadi, who was involved in Jordan's first and so far only mobile company, Fastlink, which obtained a four-year monopoly that ended in September 2000. Other actors include Imad Badran, the son of the long serving prime minister and former Mukhabarat chief, Mudar Badran; Said Abu Odeh; the son of the former minister of information, chief of the Royal Court and for a time King Abdullah's political adviser, Adnan Abu Odeh; Laith al-Qasim, the son of the former chief of the Royal Court, Marwan al-Qasim; Shakir Ibn Shakir, the son of the former commander-in-chief of the Jordanian Army and later chief of the Royal Court and Prime Minister, Zayed Ibn Shakir; and the former prime minister and later chief of the Royal Court himself, Abdul Karim al-Kabariti. The departure of Hassan and Hussain has also empowered the younger members of the royal family, such as Prince Hamzeh (the new Crown Prince), Prince Ali (King Abdullah's private bodyguard) and Prince Talal and Prince Ghazi, King Abdullah's cousins, the former his military secretary and the latter his adviser on tribal affair.

This chapter has examined the pace of reform in Jordan since its inception in the mid-1980s. It noted the limited progress in implementation until 1998, and recorded the improved compliance and implementation rate thereafter. Several factors have affected the pace of reform and degree of compliance in Jordan in the 1990s. They include the lingering effects of severe economic crisis and the growth of popular feeling against the *status quo*, external pressure from donors and multilateral financial institutions and a change in regime. One more factor, however, has been particularly prominent in influencing compliance rate in Jordan. That is, change in the composition and position of different factions of Jordan's ruling coalitions who came to favour some degree of reform.

It is not unique or unusual to see a change in the stance of interest groups towards reform, or even their readiness to incorporate efficiency and productivity criteria into their calculations of loss and profit. Interests of various groups in a society may undergo considerable change in response to changing economic and political circumstances and their position is not fixed in perpetuity. In his seminal work on interest groups, Olson argues that in order to enlarge their share of the economic pie and protect their current interests, various interests groups may be interested in adopting a more long-term attitude in which efficiency is incorporated into calculations of self-interest.[80]

This argument is applicable in Jordan, where the bureaucracy is riddled with interest groups, and where competition is rife both inside and outside the state. A dominant coalition of 'bureaucratic-bourgeoisie' coalition opposed reforms for a long time and managed to postpone it until the late 1990s, shortly before Abdullah II succeeded to the throne. For more than a decade after 1985, this grouping displayed a tremendous ability, not only in deciding the time and pace of reform, but also a skill in shaping its outcome.

As Jordan's economy moved from rentier boom to economic stagnation and crises, there has also been an important change in the composition of the main interest groups that affect the economic decision process in the country. In addition to the members of the old 'merchant class', a new business elite has emerged with even stronger connections with bureaucrats and high state officials. The members of the new business elite are the progeny of the men who served, or continue to serve in some of the highest state posts, including the army and security. Their economic interests are thus more linked with the interests of bureaucrats and state officials than the old members of the 'merchant class'. Unlike members of the old class, the roots of most of the new business elite lie in Transjordan. They are either of an East Bank origin, or were born and raised in Jordan and, thanks to the long record of service and loyalty of their fathers to the Hashemites, see themselves as even more Jordanians than the indigenous East Bankers themselves.

The relationship between the new and old business elites in Jordan is not free of competition or conflict and further progress in reform will largely depend on the outcome of the continued competitive struggle between the old and new elites on the one hand, and between the anti- and pro-reform groups, including the IMF and World Bank, on the other. Despite progress in implementation after 1998, the role of the state in Jordan is still strong and distortions remain in the domestic economy. Privatisation, for example, is still limited and partial, taxes and surcharges still biased in favour of domestic businessmen and foreign investment is hampered by a strong network of corrupt links between the bourgeois and bureaucrats and high state officials.

Finally, it is worth noting an important analogy between Jordan and many other countries in the region, particularly the 'more advanced' and 'successful reformers', like Morocco, Tunisia and Egypt after 1992. Economic reforms there have also been occurring within the context of the emergence of new groups and individuals with strong connections to bureaucrats and high state officials.[81] This leads us to the conclusion that far-reaching reforms, even in countries where they have been stalled for a long time, are possible. But they are only possible with the context of the rise to influence of new beneficiaries that have strong links with the state. However, the path of reform will be moulded and shaped by the interests of those competing groups and individuals. The outcome will be less than a completely free market economy.

NOTES

1. M. Al-Quaryouty, 'Prospects for Privatisation in Jordan', *Journal of Arab Affairs*, 8, 2 (1989), pp. 159–90.
2. J. Harrigan, and H. El-Said, 'Stabilisation and Structural Adjustment in Developing Countries: The Case of Jordan and Malawi', *Journal of African Business*, 1, 3 (summer 2000), pp. 63–110.
3. D. Pool, 'The Links Between Economic and Political Liberalisation' in T. Niblock, and E. Murphy (eds), *Economic and Political Liberalisation in the Middle East*, London: British Academy Press, 1993.
4. 'Jordan: Musical Thrones', *The Economist*, 30 January 1999.
5. 'Jordan Drifting Apart', *The Economist*, 8 November 1997.
6. J. Waterbury, 'The State and Economic Transition in the Middle east and North Africa' in N. Shafik (ed.), *Prospects for Middle East and North African Economies: From Boom to Bust and Back?*, London: Macmillan, 1998, p. 164.
7. Quoted in F. Ciriaci, 'In an Address from the World Economic Forum in Davos', *Jordan Times*, 31 January, 2001.
8. *Jordan Times*, June 2000.
9. S. Hattar, 'Government Takes Decision to Negotiate with France Telecome for Stake in JTC', *Jordan Times*, 22 November, 1999.
10. Harrigan and El-Said, 2000; H. El-Said, 'The Political Economy of Foreign Direct Investment in Jordan', *UCLA Journal of Middle Eastern Studies*, 14 (1996) pp. 1–20.

11. E. Rogan and T. Tell (eds), *Village, Steppe and State: The Social Origins of Modern Jordan*, British Academic Press, 1994; R. Abu-Jaber, *Pioneers over Jordan: The frontier of settlement in Transjordan 1850–1914*, London: I.B. Tauris, 1989; P. Gubser, *Politics in Al-Karak Jordan*, Oxford University Press, 1973; A. Abu-Odeh, *Jordanians, Palestinians and the Hashemite Kingdom in the Middle East Peace Process*, Washington, DC: United States Institute of Peace Press, 1999.

12. A. Amawi, 'The Consolidation of the Merchant Class in Transjordan During the Second World War' in E Rogan, and T. Tell, (1994) (eds), *Village, Steppe and State: The Social Origins of Modern Jordan*, London: British Academy Press, 1994, p. 167.

13. Z. Sha'sha, 'The Role of the Private Sector in Jordan's Economy' in R. Wilson (ed.), *Politics and the Economy in Jordan*, London: Routledge. It is important to note here that a group of nationalist bureaucrats emerged in the 1950s and 1960s which challenged the position and policies advocated by the merchants. But due to lack of capital, the bureaucrats had to rely on the merchants. They thus gave them more concessions and special privileges, including monopolies and import licenses, in return for participation in developmental projects. This strengthened the position of the merchants in the economy. See O. Wils, 'Competition or Oligarchy? The Jordanian Business Elite in Historical Perspective' in H. El-Said and K. Becker (eds), *Management and International Business Issues in Jordan: The Potential of an Arab Singapore?*, New York: Howarth Press, 2001.

14. Wils, 2001, p. 13.

15. Particularly those of the rentier-state theory, which finds a correlation between financial autonomy and political autonomy. See H. Beblawi and G. Luciani (eds), *The Rentier State*, London: Croom Helm, 1987.

16. This process was mainly confined to the public sector and ministerial posts. The top brass of the army and security remained dominantly controlled by Jordanians, traditionally seen as regime's bedrock.

17. S. Bar, 'The Jordanian Elite – Change and Continuity' in A. Susser and A. Shmuelevitz (eds), *The Hashemites in the Modern Arab World*, London: Frank Cass, 1995, p. 224: V. York, *Domestic Politics and Regional Security: Jordan, Syria and Israel: The End of an Era?*, Sydney: Gower, 1988.

18. This period started with the challenge posed to the regime by the birth of the PLO in 1965, the loss of the West Bank to Israel in 1967, continued border skirmishes with Israel soldiers throughout the late 1960s, a fierce battle with the Israeli troop known in Jordan as the *Karama* battle of 1969, and a bloody military conflict with PLO fighters in 1970–1.

19. R. Cunnigham, and Y. Sarayra, *Wasta: The Hidden Force in Middle Eastern Society*, New York: Praeger, 1993, p. 10.

20. Brand, L., Jordan's Inter-Arab Relations: the Political Economy of Alliance Making, New York: Columbia University Press, 1994.

21. R. Satlof, *From Hussain to Abdullah: Jordan in Transition*, Washington, DC: Washington Institute, research memorandum no. 38 (April 1999), 4.

22. A. R. Malhas, *al-Fasad al-Qanuni* (Legal Corruption), *Al-Ra'i* (5 May 1993).

23. F. Al-Fanik, *'al-Sahafa al-Urdunia Wa Qadaya al-Iqtisad Wa al-Fasad*' (The Jordanian Press and Economic and Corruption cases), *Al-Ra'i* (30 September 1994), 48.

24. *Al-Ra'i*, 7 March and 28 December 1994.

25. H. El-Said, 'Jordan: the Political Economy of Industrialisation in a Rentier Economy', PhD thesis, University of Manchester, 1996, chapter 4.

26. T. Niblock, 'International and Domestic Factors in the Economic Liberalisation Process in Arab Countries' in T. Niblock and E. Murphy (eds), *Economic and Po-*

litical Liberalisation in the Middle East, London: British Academy Press, 1993, 57–8 and 84.

27. B. Bichara and A. Badran (eds), *The Economic Development of Jordan*, London: Croom Helm, 1987.

28. P. Dougherthy, 'Jordan Goes Down the Path of Austerity', *Middle East Economic Digest*, 18 November 1988, 5–6.

29. I. Harik and D. Sullivan (eds), *Privatisation and Liberalisation in the Middle East*, Bloomington: Indiana University Press, 1992, p. 4.

30. See El-Said, (1996).

31. S. Chitale, 'Industrial Growth and Employment Creation: The Role of Small and Medium-Term Enterprises in Jordan' in M. Buhbe and S. Zreigat (eds), *The Industrialisation of Jordan: Achievements and Obstacles*, Amman: Friedrich-Ebert Stiftung, 1989, 57. Also see J. Anani, 'Adjustment and Development: The case of Jordan' in S. El-Naggar (ed.), *Adjustment Policies and Development Strategies in the Arab World*, Washington DC: International Monetary Fund, 1987, pp. 124–49.

32. Brand (1994), for example, argues that the lack of democratic institution in Jordan in the pre-1989 period created an autonomous state not subject to any pressure from or influence by society.

33. V. Yorke, *Domestic Politics and Regional security*, Sydney: Gower, 70.

34. Al-Quaryouty (1989).

35. H. El-said, 'Waiting for Privatisation in the Arab World: The case of Jordan', *Journal of Transnational Management Development*, 6, 1 & 2 (winter 2001).

36. Central Bank of Jordan, *Annual Report 1993*, Amman: Department of Research and Studies, p. 136. Also see F. Al-Fanik, *The Structural Adjustment Programme 1992–1998*, Amman: Al-Fanik Corporation, 1992.

37. E. Maciejewski and A. Mansur, *Jordan: Strategy for Adjustment and Growth*, Washington DC: IMF Occasional Paper no. 136, 1995.

38. Ibid.; Harrigan and El-Said (2000); H. El-Said, 'Waiting for Privatisation in the Arab World', op. cit., 2001.

39. Maciejewski and Mansur (1995); Harrigan and El-Said (2000).

40. El-Said (1996), p. 327.

41. *World Bank, Peace and the Jordanian Economy*, Washington, DC, 1994, p. 23.

42. G. Taher, 'Privatisation – sitting in idle', *Jordan Times*, 24 June 1999.

43. F. Al-Fanik, 'Ahala Abwab Barnamaj Jhadeed' (On the doors of a new programme), *Al-Ra'i* (29 April 1999).

44. F. Al-Fanik, 'Mustaqbal Burnamage al-Tasheh' (The future of the adjustment programme), *Al-Ra'i* (31 August), 1998, 26.

45. 'Jordan: New King, Old Courtiers', *The Economist* 10 July 1999, 64.

46. World Trade Organisation, *Draft Report of the Working Party on the Accession of the Hashemite Kingdom of Jordan to the World Trade Organisaton*, Geneva, 1999.

47. W. Burnes, 'Remarks by the US Ambassador to IT Forum, US Information Service', Amman, 24 March 2000.

48. L. Brand, 'Economic and Political liberalisation in a Rentier Economy: the Case of the Hashemite Kingdom of Jordan' in I. Harik and D. Sullivan (eds), *Privatisation and Liberalisation in the Middle East*, Bloomington: Indiana University Press, 1992, 167–87.

49. O. Abu Shair, 'Privatisation and Development: Insights From A Holistic Approach with Special Reference to the Case of Jordan', PhD thesis, University of Salford, 1994, pp. 460–1.

50. Ibid.

51. J. Anani, 'The Sociology of Jordan: the Map of Gains and Pains' in H. El-Said and K. Becker (eds), *Management and International Business Issues in Jordan: The Potential of an Arab Singapore?*, New York: Howarth, 2001.
52. Satloff (1999) argues that, unlike Egypt, Jordan is not seen by the US government as a strategic partner in the region. Therefore, peace dividends were much lower in this case than in the case of Egypt.
53. F. Al-Fanik, 'We Made Peace with no Dividend', *Jordan Times*, 14 August 2000.
54. *Jordan Times*, (December 8–9) 1994, p. 7.
55. E. Maciejewski, and A. Mansur. 1995.
56. *Al-Ra'i*, 7 March 1994: *Al-Ra'i*, 28 December 1994, p. 17: Amman: *Shehan Weekly Political and Social*, 26 March 1994, p. 15.
57. Anani, 2001, p. 28.
58. Ibid.
59. O. Wills, 'Foreign Aid Since 1989 and its Impact on Jordan's Political Economy: Some Research Questions', Jordanies, 5/6 (1997), pp. 1–10.
60. Central Bank of Jordan, *Monthly Statistical Bulletin*, Amman: Department of Research and Studies, June 2000.
61. *The Economist*, 10 July 1999, p. 64.
62. Satloff, 1999, p. 3.
63. R. Awwad, 'PM Expects 3.5% Growth Rate', *Jordan Times*, 29 August 2000.
64. *The Economist*, 10 July 1999, p. 64.
65. *The Economist*, 30 January 1999.
66. 'Jordan's New King', *The Economist*, 13 February 1999.
67. Satloff (1999), p. 17.
68. Z. Baharuddin, 'Dr. Fuad Zayyd Ready to Help Investors get Down to Business', *Jordan Times*, 2 November 2000.
69. S. Hattar, 'Marto Projects Healthy Growth for the Economy in Fiscal Year 2000', *Jordan Times*, 5 April 2000.
70. Y. Mansur, 'Only Taxing the Poor', *Jordan Times*, 12 June 2000.
71. Satloff (1999).
72. El-Said (1998); World Bank (1997), *Promoting Foreign Direct Investment in Jordan: Policy, Strategy and Institutions*, Washington, DC: World Bank, November 1997.
73. Y. Mansur, 'The Privatisation Paradox', *Jordan Times,* 9 June 2000.
74. *The Economist*, 10–16 July 1999, p. 64.
75. D. Hamdan, 'Lower House Starts Debate on Draft Privatisation Law', *Jordan Times*, 25 May 2000.
76. S. Hattar, 'France Telecome-led Consortium Acquires 40% of Jordan Telecom', *Jordan Times,* (24 January). Also see Anani (2001) and F. Al-Fanik, '*Alhessa Al-Thahabia Wa al Hessa Al-Khashabia*' (The Golden Share and the Wooden Share), *Al-Rai*, 8 March 2000.
77. 'Jordan Without its King For a Time', *The Economist*, 1 August 1998.
78. O. Wils, 'Competition or Oligarchy? The Jordanian Business Elite in Historical Perspective' in H. El-Said and K. Becker (eds), 'Management and International Business Issues' in *Jordan: The Potential of an Arab Singapore?*, New York: Howarth Publications, 2001.
79. An example here is Dr. Fuad Abu Zayyad, for example, who established the Inter-Arab Investment Fund with an estimated $120 million total investments in agriculture and industry.
80. 'The State, Interest groups and Structural Adjustment in Zimbabwe', *Journal of Development Studies*, 29, 3 (April 1993), pp. 401–28.

81. See N. Shafiq (ed.), *Prospects for Middle east and North African Economies: From Boom to Bust and Back?,* Macmillan Press: S. Nsouli, S. Eken, V. C. Thai, J. Decressin, F. Cartiglia and J. Bungay *Resilience and Growth Through Sustained Adjustment: The Moroccan Experience*, Washington, DC: IMF; H. Lofgren, 'Economic Policy in Egypt: A Breakdown in Reform Resistance?', *International Journal for Middle Eastern Studies*, 25 (1993), 407–21: D. Vandewalle (ed.), *North Africa: Development and Reform*, New York: St Martin's Press.

SECTORAL ACTORS IN THE JORDANIAN ECONOMY

Nasim Barham

Private sector economic actors are becoming increasingly important in Jordan as a result of economic change, but they have been relatively neglected in the academic literature and therefore deserve specific academic attention. There are, in addition, four major reasons that make this timely and necessary. First, the decline of the role of the state in national economies is an international trend as the emergence of the private sector as an alternative to government in economic matters is becoming increasingly common. Second, most Arab countries, including Jordan, have, as a result, initiated privatisation processes for state economic assets. The success of such processes depends on the size and effectiveness of the business class. Third, Jordan itself has very limited natural resources, so it must depend on its human capital and its economic actors, in particular, as its utmost vital economic resource. And fourth, Jordan has had to realise that its past economic policies, which were directed towards the exploitation of material assets, were inadequate. Large investments have been allocated to infrastructure development in the past, without there being a concomitant improvement in economic performance. As a result, Jordan must now redirect policies towards a recognition of the important role played by entrepreneurs.

Jordanian analysts have come to accept that overall development and high growth rates in the so-called 'golden era', between 1975 and 1984, was related, to a great extent, to external rents, a dependence which was thrown into sharp relief with the decrease of both main sources of such rent – Arab financial aid and the remittances of Jordanian migrants, mainly in the Gulf region. This realisation was a major reason for Jordan's acceptance of the economic reform programme suggested by the World Bank in 1988 which included *inter alia* the devaluation of the Jordanian dinar (JD), the shift from inward- to outward-oriented economic policies and the decline of the government's role within the economy, mainly through privatisation.

In this context, the development of new economic actors, including entrepreneurs, becomes a national necessity if such reforms are to achieve their objectives. There has, indeed, been a grassroots response to the new economic climate created in Jordan over the past decade. Since 1990, a large number of formal, government-encouraged and spontaneous informal activities designed to promote such changes in professional attitudes and to encourage the development of new economic actors have emerged in Jordan, including research programmes as well as societies and associations involved with entrepreneurs. The best-known initiatives of this kind include the Young Entrepreneurs Association and the Jubilee School which trains technocratic elites.

Many scholars have recently identified the importance of the role of new economic actors in dynamising neo-liberal economic reforms – accepting, in effect, that the Washington Consensus of purely economic measures is unlikely to achieve significant, permanent and positive economic change without the appropriate actors, particularly in terms of entrepreneurial expertise. Hadad,[1] for example, has discussed the issue of the relationship between entrepreneurship and development in the context of the history of entrepreneurship in Egypt and in other Arab countries. She highlighted the role of the state, which tended to focus on investment in large-scale industries, for example, leaving small-scale enterprises to the private sector. The consequence has been that small-scale enterprises dominate the private sector in most Arab countries, a development that has often been encouraged by legal regimes. The legal framework in oil-rich states, for example, have forced foreign investors to accept joint ventures with local citizens who hold a minimum 51 per cent majority share in projects, even though they usually make no other input and act merely as 'sleeping partners'.

Amawi[2] has taken a more historical approach, stressing the impact of political conditions in Jordan and in the region as the framework for the consolidation of the merchant class – as a crucial first step towards modern entrepreneurship – between the two world wars. Her analysis focused on the social, political and economic environment of the region in which a merchant class was consolidated. She demonstrates that, once the new class was established, it was able to exploit its environment to create an appropriate legal framework in which to further their class interests. By doing this they laid the basis on which a modern entrepreneurial elite would subsequently be able to build.

After the start of the Middle East peace process, a wave of new studies on the potential for entrepreneurial elites was conducted in view of the widespread belief that economic consolidation along neo-liberal lines was an essential prerequisite for permanent peace. Although

French scholars focused on Palestine entrepreneurs in the diaspora, most studies sought to evaluate the possibility of constructing a new social and economic basis for the development of Palestine. Typical of these approaches is the work of Hanafi,[3] Blin[4] and Bahout.[5] Most of these studies dealt with the attitude of entrepreneurs towards peace and their willingness to invest in Palestine, concluding that caution was their main response to the new environment created by the peace process.

The Jordanian case

Most research into the behaviour of entrepreneurs focuses on the socio-economic environment in which they operate and on the personal and professional characteristics that allows them to act as they do in such an environment. Such an approach has also been applied to Jordan in order to establish the links between environment, individual characteristics and specific circumstances in conditioning an entrepreneurial approach.[6] In this particular study, use has been made of research on private enterprises in Jordan which was sponsored by the 'FORAREA – Bayerischer Forschungsverbund Area Studies' – research programme which was carried out between 1996 and 1998, together with some more recent work on the tourism sector. The results were derived from interviews with more than 130 entrepreneurs active in all sectors of the national economy, with a particular emphasis on tourism. The research was concentrated mainly on large private enterprises – those with capital investment of at least JD1 million or employing at least 100 workers. However, given the concentration of large businesses in Amman, Zarqa and Aqaba exceptions to these criteria were made in the smaller urban centres of Jordan, in order to provide an adequate geographic and sectoral spread.

Table 1. ECONOMIC ACTIVITIES AND FREQUENCIES

Economic activity	*No. of enterprises*
Agriculture	5
Trade	40
Industry	49
Trade and Industry	12
Construction	11
Tourism	9
Other Services	5
Total	131

Source: research survey

The key to any investigation of this kind is the meaning to be attached to the term 'entrepreneur'. It clearly involves a series of ideal characteristics connected to commercial activity of one kind or another and is usually considered to be distinguished from other commercial and economic actors by features such as creativity and a penchant for innovation and risk-taking. Kuratko and Hodgetts[7] listed forty-two features associated with an entrepreneur, making the point that entrepreneurship is a form of economic behaviour and not an occupation. In the Jordanian case, such commercial actors also act under opaque and difficult objective conditions because of regional political instability and an unpredictable and changeable national legislative climate. Such actors, therefore, have to place a high premium on risk-taking on a long-term basis, not simply during the initial phase of an activity, thus underlining the need for entrepreneurship to be seen as a mode of behaviour within a specific environment, rather than as simply a professional activity. Indeed, risk-taking is probably a more important characteristic than innovation or creativity in this context, for as Schumpeter has pointed out more generally for the developing world, Jordan's stage and level of development excludes any premium being put upon such qualities yet. Nonetheless, creativity and innovation are intimately associated with risk-taking and commercial experience in the Jordanian case, so the definition of 'entrepreneur' that will be used here is:

The owner and manager of a relatively large-scale commercial enterprise. He is able to take effective decisions and to consider the norms of his environment but is also in the position to introduce innovations. The word entrepreneur, business man and actor will be used as interchangeably in the discussion that follows.

Furthermore, if risk-taking is such an important part of the entrepreneur's behaviour-pattern, the environment in which he does this is of increasing importance. This is certainly true in the case of Jordan and, in addition, the interaction of Jordan with its surrounding region also forms part of that environment and the framework in which the entrepreneur acts. As Burns points out in a quotation by Johnson,[8] the social environment is crucial: 'It is not the consciousness of men that determines their existence, but on the contrary, it is their social existence that determines their consciousness'. To what extent, therefore, is the Jordanian environment appropriate for the creation of entrepreneurs?

The business environment in Jordan

On the eve of Jordan's creation as a state in 1921, the economy was solely agricultural, with dry farming and livestock as the main economic activities of the majority of the population to ensure its self-sufficiency. Very few urban centres – mainly old Jordanian cities like Ajloun, Salt and Kerak along the western part of the plateau that forms the backbone to the country – acted as contact points between sedentary farmers in the west of the country and in Palestine and the nomads in the east. These centres engaged in limited trade of agricultural products and imported goods, brought in through ports in Palestine. Their populations contained a high proportion of migrants from the main trade centres of the Levant, such as Damascus, Nablus, Hebron and even Beirut.

The new government of the Emirate, together with the British mandate authorities, created new employment opportunities, especially in security, such as the police and the armed forces, as well as other public sector activities, which were to have a profound effect on population mobility and urbanisation in Jordan. One of the most important aspects of these changes was the policy of centralisation of political life and economic activity within one urban centre, Amman. This led to massive urban drift into the Amman-Zarqa complex and the situation after the creation of the state of Israel in 1948 and the influx of hundreds of thousands of Palestinian refugees. The main features of this pattern of development involved the following factors that stimulated economic development.

The demand for housing, from internal immigrants and from displaced Palestinians opened a new investment niche – construction. This is why housing construction played and still plays a vital role in the economy of Jordan. Given the high population growth rate and high levels of urban drift, housing construction was never a risky option, nor did it require entrepreneurial creativity, simply because of the constant demand. Thus those actors engaged in the sector did not really develop either characteristic and the consequent innate caution and lack of enterprise has continued to be a severe problem in the evolution of the entrepreneurial spirit in Jordan ever since.

The need for construction materials such as cement and iron required large manufacturing plants to achieve the necessary economies-of-scale and this requirement came to dominate the overall production paradigm. The investment demands of such plants meant that state aid was an absolute necessity and the same approach has been subsequently applied to the extraction of Jordan's limited natural resource base, dominated by phosphate and potash. One by-product of this approach to manufacturing and processing has been a clear delimitation of the public and private sectors since the 1950s whereby the state promoted large enterprises and the private sector was restricted to small-scale initiatives.

The state itself, as was the case with many rent-seeking states in the region, provided welfare services and employment to the population at large, irrespective of qualification or need. Furthermore, such benefits were differentially accessible through patronage and influence, as a result of persistant social and political traits – the well known *wasta* system.[9] The system, which dominated whole sectors of the Kingdom's political and economic life, severely restricted the opportunities open to qualified and creative people. The system certainly provides the state with an effective means of control and influence but it undermines all economic or even managerial efficiency. Unfortunately this feature of Jordanian collective life is an irreversible fact that hinders all attempts at economic and social restructuring and entrepreneurs have to cope with the system but cannot change it. Subsequent developments in Jordan and in the Middle Eastern region have tended to entrench these characteristics, at least up to 1990.

The civil war in Lebanon in 1975 forced a new wave of immigrants to Jordan, which led to massive growth in the number and quality of hotels and restaurants in the country. Lebanese cuisine and lifestyles became very popular and Jordanians imitated this success by establishing a large number of such economic activities in the suburbs of Amman and near to tourist sites. Lebanese-style restaurants and hotel services have become the backbone of the Jordanian tourist sector. Furthermore, by 1999 fully 12.5 per cent of all industrial joint ventures in Jordan involved the participation of Lebanese immigrants in the kingdom.

The Iraq-Iran war powerfully stimulated the development of Jordan's transport sector. Imports to Iraq passed through the port of Aqaba for onward land transport to Iraq itself. More than 19,000 trucks and semi-trailers transported these goods between Aqaba and Baghdad. This growth in transport activity was accompanied by major Jordanian private sector investment in transport, import-export agencies and industrial joint-ventures with Iraqi partners.

The effect of the Second Gulf War in 1991was particularly experienced through a new wave of migrants, consisting of Jordanians forced to return from Kuwait, Saudi Arabia and other Gulf States. The returnees and local entrepreneurs who copied their success, developed a new style of urban services for Jordan. Fast food outlets, computer services centres, import and export agencies, publicity and advertising companies, together with similar businesses have spread throughout the major cities. It is as if the Jordanian private sector has been Americanised, at least as far as service industry is concerned. The government has recently tried to capitalise on this trend and has put resources into the information technology sector as a future pivot of national economic development in the kingdom. Specialised actors have found new opportunities in both software and hardware. In addition, the embargo on Iraq has raised the level of Iraqi investment in Jordan. Today 75 per cent of wholly-owned foreign industries and 26 per cent of industrial joint-ventures in Jordan are in Iraqi hands.

The effect of the Middle East peace process on the landscape of entrepreneurship in Jordan was quite different, however. Tourism became the major activity and those already in this sector enlarged their enterprises both horizontal and vertically whilst newcomers, whether qualified or unqualified, entered the sector enthusiastically. Jordanian entrepreneurs in other economic fields fell prey to uncertainty and decreased investment to a minimum, so their economic behaviour became dominated by extreme caution. The result has been that the Jordanian economy has faced significant stagnation and even decline during the last five years. Jordan has, in short, been transformed during the past decade from being a transit country and a 'frontline state', with all the diplomatic and military rents associated with such status, into an isolated state with little obvious economic opportunity.

This is the economic structure which has conditioned the economic environment in which Jordanian economic actors must operate. The main characteristic of this environment is uncertainty which itself arises from unpredictable and unsettled diplomatic and political circumstances. Yet entrepreneurs are also driven by personal motivation and an ability to spot niche opportunities, even in an environment as unpromising as that in Jordan so that, despite the constraints, a new generation of entrepreneurs has emerged.

Development of entrepreneurship

The number of entrepreneurs prior to the foundation of the Jordanian state was small. In essence, a few Palestinian merchants from Nablus, Jerusalem and Hebron migrated, initially seasonally but then increasingly on a permanent basis, to Salt and Kerak and later to Amman. Once there, they started commercial contacts with the neighbouring countries of Syria and Palestine. As the pioneers of the entrepreneurial spirit in Jordan, most of their descendants today dominate the mercantile and industrial sectors in the country. In the mid-to-late 1920s, these pioneers were joined by Syrian merchants and some artisanal producers, particularly in Amman, where they set up businesses in these fields. The role of the family in financing and running these businesses was and still is critical to success. The Second World War provided this new merchant class with new opportunities.[10]

The development of Jordan's economic actors occurred in five separate phases which themselves reflected political and economic conditions in the Middle Eastern region. In the first phase, the period before 1960, only eighteen companies investigated or 13.8 per cent of the research base had been established. Most of these initiatives were concerned with trade, with far fewer being in manufacturing industry. The entrepreneurs were, nonetheless, innovative, introducing automobiles into the country and establishing plants to produce vehicle batteries and plastic articles. It is worth noting that the industrialisation of Jordan was the result and not the cause of urbanisation; thus, population centres, such as Amman and Irbid, were the location of the major commercial and manufacturing sites. During the 1960s – the second phase – the number of enterprises in the current study declined to fifteen units, just 11.5 per cent of the number investigated. This was one of the consequences of the 1967 Arab-Israeli war and the Jordanian economy only started to recover during the third phase, in the second half of the 1970s, when the total rose to 24 units – 18.5 per cent of the research base. The peak of economic activity occurred during the 1980s, the four phase, when 47 businesses investigated (36.2 per cent of the research total) were inaugurated. In the final phase, from 1991 until the end of 1998, only 26 (20 per cent) of the total number of the enterprises studied were founded.

It is worth noting that enterprise growth coincided with improvements in the national economy, which implies that actors follow economic growth but not tend to cause it. Government calls to invest in times of recession have simply fallen on deaf ears. In such crucial moments, actors look for alternative activities, as was demonstrated in the mid-1980s when Jordan suffered a severe economic crises and the Jordanian dinar had to be devalued. The country lacked hard currency to pay for imports and the purchasing power of the population was weakened. This was the proper time for entrepreneurs to shift into manufacturing, with merchants establishing their new industries to manufacture the goods in which they trade – thus creating a new class of entrepreneur engaged simultaneously in trade and manufacturing. The continuous tradition of business in Jordan since its inception does not, however, imply that its economic actors are always so specialised and flexible. Instead, professional survival has depended on family networks, so that the family can be mobilised in times of crisis. Most business families have created close-knit relations with each other and with politicians both through common interests and through marriage links, to strengthen their position.

Characteristics of entrepreneurs

Jordan's entrepreneurs share some common characteristics in personal terms, particularly in the contexts of education, age and mobility – all crucial factors in determining the elite's eventual success.

Education. Jordan boasts a literacy rate of 82 per cent because the kingdom has placed a high priority on human capital. More than fifty colleges provide two-to-three-year courses specialising in most academic and related disciplines and sixteen universities – both state and private – offer a full range of subjects for study in BA, MA and PhD programmes to more than 100,000 of domestic students, in addition to the thousands of young Jordanians who complete their studies abroad. Jordanian entrepreneurs show a high standard of education – 81.6 per cent of them obtained the level of General Secondary Certificate or above and 52 per cent of them possess a university degree. They also invested in their children. Male children go to European countries or to the United States to gain their higher education and mainly take courses related to the family business. The dominant influence of both countries is at its apogee today, for eleven members of the Economic Consultative Council formed by King Abdullah on 13 December 1999 received their university education in the United States and another in Britain. Their female children usually go to Arab universities in Cairo or in Beirut. One university in the Arab world is particularly deeply rooted in Jordanian society – the American University in Beirut (AUB).

Engineering, business administration, management and accounting are the most common specialisations for the new generation. Their knowledge of foreign languages, particularly English, is excellent and they make much use of it in business. The language used in the meetings of the Young Entrepreneurs Association (YEA), for example, is English. This well-educated new generation has benefited from the parental generation's traditional economic bazaar-style linkages, on which the new generation has created an international and modern network. Furthermore, the children from the political elite have followed a similar pattern but also enjoy the patronage of the state.

There is, interestingly enough, a spatial differentiation in educational levels for, whilst 73.3 per cent of entrepreneurs in Amman have obtained a university degree, the proportion doing this declines to 37.5 per cent in Aqaba and to as low as 31.2 per cent and 21.4 per cent in Zarqa and Irbid respectively. It is zero in other Jordanian cities, such as Ma'an or Kerak. As mentioned above, there is a high correlation between education level and kind of businesses. Businesses tend to be more specialised in Amman with its advanced education than, for instance, in Zarqa. In the case of Aqaba, most large enterprises are in tourism, where high educational levels are required.

Those entrepreneurs who are involved in several economic sectors, such as trade and industry, tend to be better educated than those who are only involved in a single sector and there are variations in education level according to the kind of economic sector in which a particular entrepreneur is involved (Table 2). In modern sectors such as industry and tourism, 75 per cent and 66.7 per cent of entrepreneurs respectively have university-level educational attainment. In the construction and farming sectors, the rate was 50 per cent and it declined to only 26.2 per cent amongst merchants. The figures for farming, which seem, at first sight, to be atypical, reflect the fact that the farms concerned are sophisticated modern dairy operations in Wadi Dhuleil, to the north east of Zarqa. Entrepreneurs involved in the construction sector depend more on capital and experience than on high educational levels. For medium-to-large projects they hire engineers to handle the technical aspects of the operation. In any case, most of them are self-employed and cannot undertake large-scale projects which are left to foreign firms.

Table 2. EDUCATION LEVEL AND ECONOMIC ACTIVITIES

Activity/education	Illiterate	Elementary	Secondary	College	University
Agriculture	–	1	–	1	2
Trade	3	13	13	2	11
Industry	1	1	9	2	33
Trade and industry	–	1	2	1	6
Construction	–	3	3	–	6
Tourism	–	1	2	–	6
Services	–	–	1	1	1
Total	4	19	30	7	65
% of total	3.2	15.2	24.0	5.6	52.0

Source: research survey.

Age. In developing countries, for many people capital is the vital constraint on their ability to start a business as they need more time than elsewhere to amass it. Jordanian entrepreneurs start in business at an average age of 38 years – compared with an average age of 32

years in Lebanon and 28 years in India – so their business experience
is necessarily short. Two explanations have been proposed for this
late starting date. The first is the fact that young people have to emigrate, to Gulf States for example, to earn money for their families
and for themselves as a first stage towards developing a capital base.
Only when these prior needs are met, can they start to save capital
on their own account for future investment. The only exceptions to
this rule are those entrepreneurs who join their father's business or
who take such a businesses over – and, in any case, they are often too
young to be successful. The second explanation reflects the innate
caution that characterises Jordanian entrepreneurs. This means that
they only decide to take risk very slowly because of the intense inse-
curity and hesitancy they feel before they can cross the Rubikon towards investment and risk-taking.[11]

There are also differences in the actual entrepreneurial starting
age depending on education level, outside those with only elementary
education, where the age distribution was evenly spread through all
age groups. By comparison, 42.8 per cent of entrepreneurs with secondary education start their business between the ages of 30 and 39
and 32.1 per cent of them are less than 30 years old. The number of
entrepreneurial initiatives thereafter decreases with age over 40 years
old, provided the education level remains constant. For example,
only 10.7 per cent of entrepreneurs begin in either the 40–49 or the
50–59 age group. It is very rare in Jordan for entrepreneurs to start
their own businesses if they are 60 years old or more.

On the other hand, 37.5 per cent of businessmen with community
college education start their businesses when they are less than 30
years old. The same figure applies to the 30–39 age group. For other
age groups with community college education, the distribution was
equal amongst the age groups. The picture is very different for persons with university-level education, for 45.7 per cent of them start
their enterprises at ages below 30. Many in this group belong to the
second generation of entrepreneurs who enjoy access to professional
life through the family. Only 28.8 per cent of this group start in business between the ages of 30 and 39 and a further 23.7 per cent in the
40–50 age group, with only 10.2 per cent taking the plunge at more
than 50 years old. In short, it seems that with higher educational levels
self reliance and confidence increases and individuals are thus prepared to start their own business at younger ages.

Mobility. Mobility in traditional societies is generally very limited,
for individuals tended to be isolated from external influences, especially when information transfer was impossible or, at the least, very

difficult. This is revealed by the vernacular language, for the word '*khatar*' in colloquial Arabic is used for trip or travel, although its true meaning is 'danger'. In short, any kind of mobility could involve danger or the threat of danger and was therefore avoided, if at all possible. Economic stagnation was the inevitable concomitant of such isolation.

After the Second World War, the new traffic network and emigration removed this social isolation as did internal urban drift. Labour migration to the Gulf States, to Europe and to the United States, all of which began in the 1950s, improved emigrant income, as well as that of their families through the remittances they sent back. As the dream of young people migration also conferred considerable social status. Yet migration caused not only spatial change but also value and attitudinal change, as well as creating individual opportunities for movement and personal freedom. This, in turn, upset traditional status patterns,[12] thereby broadening attitudes of mind, creating the conditions for social transition and stimulating the emergence of entrepreneurs. Migrants were the first persons to established banks, in Jordan, as was the case with Muhammad Shuman, the founder of the Arab Bank, who is one of the best-known examples of this kind of activity. Young engineers who studied abroad were the pioneers in establishing national industries Indeed, in a recent study on joint-ventures in Jordan, it was established that 26.3 per cent of Jordanian entrepreneurs met their foreign partners though emigration. Large-scale Arab investment also entered Jordan through such partnerships.

In fact, the majority of entrepreneurs in Jordan are Palestinian origin. In this study, the origins of 116 leading entrepreneurs in Jordan were established, showing that 48.3 per cent of them were born in Palestine and, although 12.9 per cent of them had been born in Jordan, their families had originally immigrated into Jordan from Palestine. The second largest group – 30.2 per cent of the total – were of Jordanian origin but had immigrated into major cities such as Amman, Zarqa, Irbid and Aqaba. Immigrants from other Arab countries with Jordanian nationality comprised only 8.6 per cent of the sample and, in any case, half of them were Palestinian too. In short, two-thirds of Jordan's entrepreneurs are Palestinian in origin, a figure which reflects the role of the Palestinians in the Jordanian economy.

No other country in the region has had to host entrepreneurs from abroad as Jordan has had to do. Palestinian entrepreneurs have been flooding into the country since the end of the nineteenth century. Jordan was the destination for migrants of Syrian origin after the political shift towards socialism under Arab nationalist and Ba'ath regimes from the 1950s onwards. In the past twenty years, hundreds of Lebanese and Iraqi businessmen have invested in Jordan because of the political tensions in their countries of origin, so that, today, 64.5 per cent of industrial joint ventures in Jordan have Iraqi, Syrian or Lebanese partners.

Yet for the Jordanian government this influx of entrepreneurial talent has been a political, not an economic, issue and such immigrants have not been integrated into the Jordanian social community or polity. Since Jordan was only a host country, the moment that conditions in their countries of origin improved, they returned home, taking their skills and investment with them. Today they seek to move to Egypt, Canada, the United States or even Europe.

How entrepreneurs act

Quite apart from their origins and educational achievements, entrepreneurs in Jordan also have to consider objective factors in determining their willingness to undertake risk in investment. These can include factors such as the location of an enterprise, its size and the role of informal networks that support its activities within the specific context of Jordanian society.

Locational choice. The development of Amman as the largest urban centre in Jordan has attracted Jordanian entrepreneurs as a factor in itself in choosing it as location for their businesses. Amman is, after all, the largest market due to the large proportion of the total population resident there – about 1 million in 1994. Interestingly enough, the advanced stage of development of Jordan's infrastructure and services has decreased to some extent the importance of location in making investment decisions since this reduces the effect of distance between market and production on cost. Indeed, in Jordan it could be argued that the effective national infrastructure reduces transport costs to a negligible factor in investment decision. In fact, 21.3 per cent of the respondents in the study mentioned the availability, quantity and quality of sites as the primary factor in their investment decisions, with the issue of market access and size as a secondary factor – it was the dominant concern for only 17 per cent of the respondents in the study. Amman inevitably remains, therefore, the main location for businesses, despite Jordan's regional development polices which offer generous state incentives to invest outside the capital.

The success of the Amman Industrial Estate in Sahab, south of the capital, where more than 360 plants have 13,000 employees reflects the importance of both these factors of proximity to market and agglomeration economies. Indeed, 10.6 per cent of the entrepreneurs questioned also placed services and agglomeration considerations as the main reasons for their investment choices. Of course, there are many other factors that affected businessmen in decisions over business location, such as open spaces, city zoning plans, investment incentives, or quality and modernity of residential areas and services. The latter factors were important for particular businesses that depended on their immediate environment for a significant part of their markets, businesses such as information technology concerns, automobile salespoints and supermarkets

Enterprise size. Most Jordanian entrepreneurs tend to start on a small scale, not simply because of a lack of capital or because they adopt strategies to minimise risk, but because of the limited size of the local market and the weakness of purchasing power of the majority of the population. Those who start up with medium-to-large-scale enterprises are often forced later to reduce them in size. In addition, in many cases, businessmen will prefer to engage in small-sized enterprises in order to avoid official and legal requirements concerning social obligations towards employees. Enterprises with more than ten employees have to pay social insurance for their employees and have to join chambers of commerce and industry. Table 3 demonstrates the consequences of these considerations on the size of enterprises in Jordan.

Table 3. Size of Enterprises in Jordan

No. of employees	No. of enterprises	%
5–9	2,949	53.5
10–24	1,599	29.0
25–49	429	7.8
50–99	218	3.9
100 and above	319	5.8
Total	*5,514*	*100.0*

Source: Department of Statistics, Employment Survey, Amman, 1993.

If enterprises with between 5 and 25 employees are defined as small-sized enterprises, then 82.5 per cent of all enterprises in Jordan would fall within this category. Medium-sized enterprises with between 25 and 50 employees comprise only 7.8 per cent of the total and, given their key role in economic growth, their relatively small proportion of the total reflects a crucial bottleneck in Jordan's economic performance.[13] The link between education levels and business size is also significant in Jordan, for the educational levels of small-scale entrepreneurs are poor – 22 per cent of entrepreneurs in this category only have elementary education, 12.5 per cent have secondary education and just 3.2 per cent have university-level education. In large-scale enterprises, however, the majority of entrepreneurs have completed their university studies (Table 4).

Table 4. EDUCATION LEVEL AND SIZE OF ENTERPRISES

No. of employees	Illiterate	Elementary	Secondary	College	University
Less than 5	–	4	3	1	2
5–9	2	7	4	1	9
10–24	–	5	9	5	12
25–49	2	1	3	–	13
50–99	–	1	3	–	16
100 and more	–	–	6	1	10
Total	4	18	28	8	62

Source: research survey.

The geographic distribution of the different categories of enterprise size is also important. Most large enterprises are located in Amman with Zarqa and then Irbid coming far behind, although Irbid also has a larger number of medium-sized enterprises. In the south of the country dominate small-scale private enterprises dominate, alongside large state and parastatal enterprises. In other words, entrepreneurs whose plants generate large-scale outputs seek large cities as a production base, no doubt because of the proximity of an adequate local market or the availability of appropriately skilled labour. In the final analysis, however, size is dominated by the state sector, for the largest enterprises remain in the hands of the state which controls 49 per cent of all enterprises and employs 56 per cent of the labour force. It is also worth noting that Jordanian entrepreneurs in the manufacturing sector tend to invest in labour-intensive industries in order to benefit from the available supply of cheap labour. Salary policies in Jordan are evidently still biased towards the employer, not the labour force, for low salary levels are deemed to be part of Jordan's comparative advantage.

Partnership and role of the family. Jordanian entrepreneurs place a high value on independence and look for partners only if really necessary. Conditions that make partners necessary are usually related to access to capital, rather than to managerial or technical concerns. Even in the industrial sector, where technology transfer is badly needed and could be achieved through partnerships and joint ventures, entrepreneurs are relatively indifferent to such possibilities. In fact, Jordanian manufacturing industries generally avoid processes where advanced technology is required.[14] The result is that partnerships are generally short-lived, for Jordanians place such a high premium on independence.

Individualism is so deeply rooted in the Jordanian social psyche that it almost amounts to selfishness. Nor is such behaviour consonant with Arab culture or with Islam. It has emerged as a result of the absence of trust throughout society and the institutions within rent-seeking states. A former Jordanian prime minister, Sa'd Jum'ah,[15] once published a book with the title *The Society of Hate* in which he discussed this problem and underlined the damage that such behaviour does in countering progress.

The main form of ownership in Jordan is the general partnership company which is used in 2,017 firms (36.6 per cent of the total). The sole proprietorship company involves 1,949 commercial and industrial establishments (35.4 per cent of the total) and the limited liability company format has been adopted by a further 11.7 per cent of the total. The balance, presumably, have no legal protection in this respect.

In all three forms mentioned above, however, the patronage-clientage system and the innate distrust that characterises Jordanian society continue to operate. The owners of these companies are either individuals or family-based partners. The rate of businesses involving partnerships generated through inheritance practices, as shown by the study was very high, reaching 65.4 per cent of the total. In essence, businessmen in Jordan tend to employ their own relatives in their enterprises. The proportion of such procedures reached 81.4 per cent of the total in the industrial sector, 23 per cent in commerce, 50 per cent in agriculture and 90–100 per cent in dual sector activities, such as trade and industry. Its incidence in cooperative companies and public shareholdings is limited to 0.5 per cent and 2 per cent respectively.[16]

The following examples illustrate many of the points made above.

Example I

Six brothers migrated from Palestine to the Gulf States in 1962 and worked in various fields. One of them was employed in a transport company and had, therefore, good relations with German car dealers. He became self-employed and started a business trading in used cars. His brothers provided the necessary funding. Because of enormous profits another brother was able establish a construction company in Kuwait. At the end of the 1980s, the car dealer came to Jordan and founded a textile manufacturing company together with a German businessman who owned a transport firm in Germany. Shortly afterwards they also established a vegetable oil plant.

Jordan had stopped the import of apples at the end of the 1980s in order to promote the cultivation of this fruit domestically. As there was a good opportunity to acquire cheap land in South Jordan, fit for apple cultivation, the car dealer took it up and bought 3,000 dunums (300 hectares) with capital from his brothers. Then, in 1996, the pharmaceutical industry in Jordan generated very good profits and experts and banks advised him to invest in this sector, which he did. By now the administration of his companies required adequate office space, so an office building with a floor area of 6,000 square metres was built and partly leased. This entrepreneur, who has no academic background, was able, in the space of ten years, to move into textiles, edible oil processing, fruit production and construction. Not surprisingly, his son is currently studying business administration in the United States. He considers himself to be successful because his business has a solid financial basis. He attributes his success to his strong family bonds as well as to his approach toward business risk. He manages his companies himself and maintains a constant and thorough oversight of what occurs within them.

Example II

The second example also involves a Palestinian, who had migrated from Hebron to Amman. Because he had no profession nor, indeed, any education, he was forced to work as a porter in the vegetable market there. He then improved his situation by manufacturing wooden boxes and selling them. He invested his savings in an agricultural premise and cultivated summer vegetables. In the midst of the 1970s, land prices increased dramatically, so he sold his property for a large profit. This made him realise what a good business real estate trading was. Within several years he was able to amass a considerable capital base.

He sent three of his sons to study in Yugoslavia, whilst a fourth studied in Amman. Only the fifth son left school without going into higher education, working instead as a broker in the vegetable market. All four sons who did go into higher education studied agriculture or water technology. Because the father felt responsible for his sons, he planned their future – he saw himself as the 'incubator' for his children's future success which, he believed, would be based on variety and dependency. For each of his sons, he created a company and for each company a different partner was chosen. The father explained his anxiety that each of his sons should have a business partner as follows. The partner would enable his sons to make use of specialised knowledge which was not available within the family; the company would gain access to additional capital without turning to banks, because the father was very religious and considered bank interest as immoral; and the partners would be chosen from within the extended family – the partners are all sons-in-law – thus ensuring the support of relatives who would otherwise not be in a position to set up their own enterprises.

The range of businesses thus created ensured that each son was autonomous and that the family as a whole was able to weather market fluctuations. Although the sons managed their own enterprises, they did so under the tutelage of their father who himself continued to run his original business. After his death, his sons became wholly independent but his business remained within the family, as a symbol of family unity, with the sons taking it in turn to run it. Here caution and the importance of family structure are the two characteristics that dominate the entrepreneurial ideal.

How the Jordanian entrepreneurs face crises. The two examples, together with the earlier discussion, underline the fact that most entrepreneurs in Jordan, except for merchants, are more imitators than innovators who respond to crisis in a traditional manner, although their behaviour varies in terms of educational level, economic branch and business size. Yet this leaves unanswered the crucial question of how they deal with risk and respond to crisis. The survey on which this analysis is based attempted to deal with this question and every entrepreneur interviewed was asked about the most severe problems he had faced. Some 211 different problems were listed, with most – 39 per cent – coming from the industrial sector. Furthermore, not surprisingly, the type of problem faced and the importance accorded to it in terms of ranking varied from economic sector to economic sector. In general, the most severe problems involved government procedures (28 per cent of the total), market changes (19 per cent) and labour performance (15.2 per cent), although the behaviour of the Jordanian consumer, high production, capital and service costs were also mentioned.

The responses to such situations varied, often in terms of enterprise size but were marked, not surprisingly, by caution. Owners of large-scale and longstanding enterprises tend to spread risk by investing in different types of businesses at the same time. They secure their income and presence in the marketplace through a compensation strategy by not putting all their eggs in a single basket. The impact of such behaviour on innovation, specialisation and creativity is, however, negative and this kind of strategy originates from what entrepreneurs perceive to be an insecure business environment. Agricultural production, for instance, is never secure because of farmers' dependence on rainfall. Furthermore, political and even economic life throughout the region are never secure as far as entrepreneurs are concerned because of the lack of effective institutions.

Yet entrepreneurs do possess capital and are able to seize lucrative opportunities, particularly in an opportunistic fashion, as such opportunities occur, rather than according to a preconceived strategy – as example 1 above demonstrates. Indeed, this seems to have been the way in which enterprises in Jordan have traditionally evolved. Yet educational levels do provide some guide as to how Jordanian entrepreneurs will respond to crisis, if not always to opportunity. University-educated entrepreneurs in industrial enterprises tend to react to crises immediately and, in some cases, they even take preventive action. They look for new markets, take bank credits and diversify their products or pricing strategies. Less educated entrepreneurs tend to reduce production, lower quality and reduce labour force size. In the late 1990s, in the tourism sector then facing crisis, three types of strategies could be identified:

Entrepreneurs with high educational levels who were in charge of large-scale enterprises anticipated change at the international level and responded globally, joining international hotel chains.

Medium-sized entrepreneurs were pro-active in their responses. They looked for new markets and clients, upgraded the quality and management of their hotels and offered competitive prices.

The third group of entrepreneurs with low levels of education and less professional experience tended to respond reactively. They reduced the quality of their services, reduced labour force size and looked to the government to solve the problem.

The most striking aspect of these different strategies of response to crisis was that there was no attempt at finding a collective response. This conclusion underlines the role of distrust within the entrepreneurial realm in Jordan as a result of the lack of a tradition of professional cooperation, as well as the lack of professional organisations that could counter such tendencies. It is also a response to the actual differentiated nature of the entrepreneurial experience in Jordan, itself a socio-cultural response to the nature of the Jordanian polity and society. For in Jordan the ideal-type entrepreneur rarely, if ever, exists. Instead, the private sector is dominated by strategies of dependence on government or dependence on family, all cemented together by patronage-clientage networks implicit in the *wasta* system. Only in a few specialised branches does this not apply and then it is the international market that beckons.

NOTES

1. N. Hadad, 'Entrepreneurship in small industries in the Arab countries' in ESCWA, *Proceedings of the expert group meeting on creation of indigenous entrepreneurship and opportunities for small-and medium-scale industrial investment*, Damascus.
2. A. Amawi, 'The Consolidation of the merchant class in Transjordan during the Second World War' in: E. L. Rogan and T. Tell (eds), *Village, steppe and state – the social origins of Modern Jordan*, (London, New York), pp. 162–87.
3. S. Hanafi, 'Les Entrepreneurs Palestiniens en Syrie' in L. Blin and P. Fargues (eds), *The economy of peace in the Middle East, Vol. 2: Palestine entrepreneurs and enterprises*, Luisant, 1995, pp. 299–307.
4. L. Blin, 'Les Entrepreneurs Palestiniens' in Blin and Fargues (1995), pp. 285–99.
5. J. Bahout, 'Les Entrepreneurs Syriens et la Paix au Proche–Orient' in Blin and Fargues P. (1995), pp. 307–27.
6. N. Barham, 'Characteristics of entrepreneurs: a portrait of Jordan' in ESCWA, *Proceedings of the expert group meeting on creation of indigenous entrepreneurship and opportunities for small- and medium-scale industrial investment*, Damascus, 1993.
7. A. B. Kuratko, and R. M. Hodgetts, *Entrepreneurship: a contemporary approach*, Chicago, 1989.
8. G. M. Robinson, *Methods and techniques in human geography*, New York, 1998.
9. F. Czichowiski, *Jordanien: International Migration, wirtschaftliche Entwicklung und soziale Stabilitaet*, Hamburg: Deutsches Orient-Institut, 1990.
10. A. Amawi, 'The consolidation of the merchant class in Transjordan during the Second World War' in Rogan and Tell, (1994), pp. 162–87.
11. D. Fricke, (1999), 'Die Gruendung der Unternehmung' in Forarea Konferenz. *Unternehmertum im regional-kulturellen Kontext*, Erlangen, 1999.
12. M. U. Deshpande, *Entrepreneurship of small industries*, New Delhi.
13. B. Kilby, 'Breaking the entreprenurial bottleneck in late-developing countries: is there a useful role for government?' in H. Leibenstein and D. Ray (eds), *Entrepreneurship and development*, New York: United Nations.
14. N. Barham, 'Productzyklus and Industrieentwicklung – am Beispiel Jordanien', *Festschrift für Wigand Ritter zum 60. Geburt*, Nürnberg: Nürnberger Wirtschafts- und Sozialgeographische Arbeiten, 1993.
15. S. Joma'h, *The society of hate* (in Arabic), Amman, n.d.
16. Hashemite Kingdom of Jordan, Department of Statistics, *Employment surveys*, Amman, 1994.

THE EFFECT OF THE WORLD TRADE ORGANISATION ON THE JORDANIAN ECONOMY

Rateb Sweis

As we begin the new millennium, the world economy is undergoing a number of fundamental changes. International markets are growing rapidly and capital mobility has increased tremendously. World trade continues to grow and companies are becoming global in their structures and operations. This situation creates a need for closer co-operation amongst nations in a world of growing market interdependence, globalisation and liberalisation. At the centre of globalisation is the World Trade Organisation (WTO). The WTO is defined as the legal and institutional foundation of the multilateral trading system[1] and was the outcome of the Uruguay Round negotiations of the General Agreement on Tariffs and Trade – the precursor to the WTO – which were concluded in 1994 and ensured that trade relations between countries evolve through debate, negotiations and adjudication. This chapter seeks to answer two questions: what are the requirements for Jordan's accession to the WTO? And if these requirements are met, will the effect on Jordan's indigenous industries be sufficiently large and its impacts significant enough to warrant the initiation of public policies to promote WTO-related awareness programmes for Jordanian institutions? The first section of this analysis presents an overview of the WTO agreement. The requirements for Jordan's accession to the WTO are presented in the second section. The third section discusses the major impacts of WTO membership on the Jordanian economy emphasising its role in attracting foreign investment, creating an environment conducive to long-term economic growth and promoting construction activity.

World Trade Organisation agreements

On 15 April 1994 the WTO was formally created by the Marrakesh Declaration, in order to provide the common institutional framework for the conduct of trade relations among its members. The WTO agreements are lengthy and complex because they are legal texts covering a wide range of activities but the multilateral trading system they define is based on two major principles: (1) Most-Favoured-Nation (MFN) – that countries cannot normally discriminate between their trading partners – and (2) National Treatment whereby imported and locally produced materials should be treated equally – in other words, others should be given the same treatment as one's own nationals.

Functions of the WTO

According to Article 3 of the Marrakesh Agreement[2] the WTO shall perform the following functions:

– facilitate the implementation, administration and operation and further the objectives and shall provide the framework for the implementation, administration and operation of the Plurilateral Trade Agreements;
– provide the forum for regulations among its members concerning their multilateral trade relations;
– administer the Understanding on Rules and Procedures governing the settlement of disputes;
– administer the Trade Policy Review Mechanism;
– with a view to achieving greater coherence in global economic policy-making, cooperate, as appropriate, with the International Monetary Fund (IMF) and the World Bank (WB) and its affiliated agencies.

Major Agreements of the WTO

Three of these agreements are relevant here and are outlined below.

Multilateral Agreements on Trade in Goods. This agreement includes, besides the General Agreement on Tariffs and Trade 1994 ('GATT 1994'), agriculture, application of sanitary and phytosanitary measures, textiles and clothing, technical barriers to trade, trade-related investment measures, pre-shipment inspection, rules of origin, agreement on import licensing procedures, subsidies and countervailing measure and safeguards.

General Agreement on Trade in Services (GATS). This agreement applies to members carrying out trade in services. The general obligations and disciplines for members are:[3]

Most-Favoured-Nation treatment, transparency, disclosure of confidential information, increasing participation of developing countries, economic integration, labour markets integration agreement, domestic regulations, recognition, monopolies and exclusive service suppliers, business practices, emergency safeguard measures, payments and transfers, restrictions to safeguard the balance of payments, government procurements, general exceptions, and subsidies.

Agreement on Trade-Related Aspects of Intellectual Property Rights (TRIPS). The purpose of this agreement is to reduce distortions and impediments to international trade and promote adequate and effective protection of intellectual property rights. TRIPS articles include the following but are not limited to them:[4]

Copyright and related rights, trademarks, geographic indicators, industrial designs, patents, layout designs of integrated circuits, protection of undisclosed information, and control of anti-competitive practices in contractual licences.

Joining the WTO: The accession process. To join the WTO, a country must submit an application and this goes through four stages:

– The government applying for membership must submit a memorandum describing all aspects of its trade and its economic policies that have a bearing on WTO agreements. The memorandum is examined by the working party dealing with the country's application.
– During this stage, bilateral talks begin between the prospective new member and individual countries. The purpose of the negotiation is to allow the prospective new member to work out with the rest of the members individually what it has to offer in terms of tariff rates and specific market access commitments.
– Once the bilateral market access negotiations are complete, the working party produces a draft membership treaty ('Protocol of Accession') and a list of the joining member's commitments.
– The WTO Council of Ministerial Conference votes on the protocol and list of commitment. If a two-thirds majority of WTO members vote in favour, the applicant is free to accede to the organisation.

Since 1995 Jordan has been working towards joining the WTO by attempting to conform to WTO agreements.[5] According to the WTO, significant legal and policy reform remains to be implemented in order for Jordan to fulfill current WTO requirements for membership. Jordan had to reform its foreign trade regime by amending many of its existing laws, enacting many new laws and changing many of its trade policies by the end of 1999 or at the latest in early 2000. However, since Jordan missed this target, its accession to the WTO has been delayed.[6]

Major impacts of WTO membership on the Jordanian economy

The development of industrial stimulus policies in Jordan has been heavily influenced by the policies of the International Monetary Fund (IMF).[7] Such policies are aimed largely at the fiscal stability of the country, but they have significant impacts on the latitude available to small developing countries for adopting stimulus packages. Creating tax incentives, credit easing or the establishment of any form of protectionism for indigenous industries runs counter to IMF liberalisation policies. Mandating participation of indigenous firms on governmental or internationally financed projects would also be discouraged if such mandates raised the cost of the project.

In assessing approaches to encourage indigenous industries in Jordan, the dilemma posed by globalisation is clear. The liberalisation of trade and the free flow of capital when coupled with greater political stability will certainly stimulate industrial activity. With this greater activity comes greater competition at a time when small indigenous firms cannot compete. A recent IMF position paper stated that, 'Increased trade, capital and labour movement, and technological progress have enabled greater specialisation and the dispersion of specialised production processes to geographically distant locations.' Although the observation was made with respect to manufacturing, it is appropriate to consider its relevance to other industries as well.

Currently the WTO has 134 members including eight Arab states Djibouti, Egypt, Kuwait, Mauritania, Morocco, Qatar, Tunisia and the United Arab Emirates and thirty-six other countries including Jordan, Saudi Arabia and Sudan are negotiating accession. Members of the WTO account for about 90 per cent of total world trade in goods and services and is currently 83 per cent of Jordan's foreign trade is with countries that are WTO members.[8] It is therefore imperative that Jordan does not remain isolated from WTO activities; by doing so, Jordan might risk serious negative economic consequences on its economy, both in the medium and long term. The following section analyses in some detail the major impacts that may result from Jordan's membership in the WTO.

Attracting foreign investment

The world economy today is undergoing a number of fundamental changes. Capital has achieved a great degree of mobility and international financial markets are not only closely interconnected but also are growing exponentially. Countries that are unable to participate in the expansion of world trade or to attract significant amounts of private investment run the risk of being marginalised by the global economy and those countries that can manage to establish a better investment environment will have higher potential to attract investment.

When investors make decisions to invest in a specific country, a number of key factors must be taken into account. Are trade and investment rules in line with internationally accepted rules and principles? Is the investment environment stable, predictable and attractive? Do the country's products and services have open access to the outside world? Does the country respect intellectual property rights?

Developing countries, in general, possess many characteristics, such as low standards of living, political instability, unemployment and under-employment and low levels of productivity which are unattractive to investors. Furthermore, the fluctuating demand, tied to political and economic volatility,[9] makes it extremely difficult to forecast economic performance. These phenomena, along with financial and other business risks, hinder the flow of foreign investment into such a country. However, by conforming to the various agreements of WTO (GATT, GATS and TRIPS), the government of Jordan will be creating an environment that is attractive, protective of intellectual property rights and open to the markets of 134 – soon to be 170 – countries around the world.[10]

The impact on exports. As noted above, a WTO member should grant non-discriminatory Most-Favoured-Nation (MFN) and National Treatment to products imported from another WTO country. Currently, Jordan has no control over how other countries treat its exports and other countries may impose import duties, quotas and internal taxes on Jordanian exports thereby making Jordanian goods and services non-competitive in international markets. Jordan's accession to the WTO would provide an effective tool for Jordan to secure advantages and fair treatment for its exports in at least 90 per cent of world markets. However, Jordan must not ignore or minimise the fact that it needs to improve the quality of its products and services to the levels of other member countries, if it is to compete effectively in international markets. Jordanian industries will probably encounter some short-term difficulties in adapting to the new WTO system of trade because of deficiencies in these areas.

Domestic industry participation in economic growth. In both developed and developing countries, the construction industry plays a major role in the economy by contributing significantly to Gross Domestic Product (GDP), employing a sizable portion of the working population, accounting for about half of the capital formation, and interacting strongly with other sectors of the economy.[11] Thus, a healthy construction industry is considered both a result of and a prerequisite for economic development. Adding to the importance of the construction industry is its pivotal role in infrastructure development. Infrastructure can be the foundation of both economic and social development but often becomes instead a bottleneck to economic expansion in developing countries.[12] In view of these factors, the past performance of the indigenous construction industry as a

Figure 1. GROWTH OF JORDAN'S CONSTRUCTION INDUSTRY, 1980–94

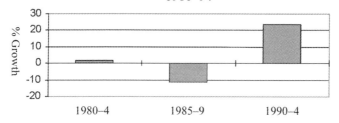

leading sector in the Jordanian economy will be evaluated. The participation of Jordan's indigenous construction companies as a percentage of total construction activity in the past is shown in Figure 1 which illustrates five-year rates of growth of construction over the period 1980–94.

Past periods of expansion in construction activity in Jordan suggest the conclusion that indigenous construction activity may not grow at a rate proportional to overall growth. If total construction activity in Jordan is examined between 1990 and 1995 (encompassing the last cycle of expansion and contraction), a number of observations are relevant to any assessment of the way in which Jordan's indigenous construction industry is likely to participate in any new growth cycle. Figure 2 shows the total activity carried out by indigenous firms. In 1990 and 1991, the foreign share of the total market was quite small at 1 per cent. This percentage grew to 14 per cent in 1993. Foreign

Figure 2. TOTAL, INDIGENOUS, AND JOINT VENTURE ACTIVITY IN
JORDAN, 1990–4

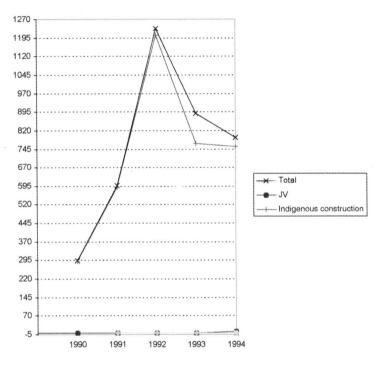

Figure 3. SHARE OF FOREIGN FIRMS IN PUBLIC SECTOR
CONTRACTS, 1990–4

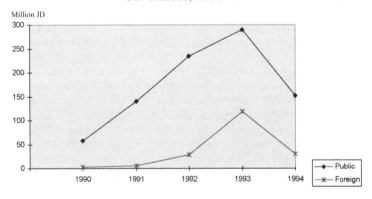

market share follows the trend in public sector construction much more closely than private sector activity. Figure 3 shows the foreign construction activity relative to public sector financed construction.

Although the data is sketchy, some conclusions can be drawn. The first observation is that the market as a whole is highly volatile, growing by 300 per cent in two years, only to contract to almost half this level within the next two years. This volatility is not conducive to long-term investment in equipment or any fixed investment by indigenous firms that operate only in Jordan, for they are generally smaller and have more limited access to capital markets than foreign competitors.

The public sector market, while not as volatile as the private sector, seems likely to favour foreign firms during periods of expansion. From 1991 to 1993, public sector activity expanded by JD150 million; foreign construction firm activity expanded by JD 90 million. When the public sector activity contracted sharply in 1994 by JD140 million, foreign construction contracted by nearly JD90 million. The low level of joint venture activity throughout this period (as presented in Figure 2) would lead to the conclusion that public sector contracts are prime targets for foreign firms and that the government has not developed an approach, at least during this period, that would use public sector contracts to assist either in the long-run expansion of indigenous firms or in reducing the volatility of construction activity levels.

The percentage of public sector activity to total construction ranged from 20 per cent to almost 30 per cent over this period. If the 1990–4 market share with respect to public sector/private sector and indigenous/foreign market sizes remains a valid criterion, 75 per cent of total growth would occur in the private sector and indigenous companies would absorb it. It would be expected that this activity would encompass smaller, less complex projects, requiring lower amounts of capital equipment. Public sector activity, representing perhaps 25 per cent of total growth, would be subject to foreign participation.

The actual level of foreign participation would depend on a variety of factors, such as the complexity of public sector opportunities, the enforcement of joint venture regulations in Jordan and the capacity or willingness of indigenous construction firms to embark on longer-term capital expansion plans, as well as their access to capital.

Other impacts. Once Jordan's accession to the WTO is complete, it is likely that Jordanian production and exports will increase, imply-ing increases in corporate income which could be used to further corporate investment. Furthermore, the projected increases in corporate revenues are likely to strengthen the fiscal revenue base. Foreign investors would probably no longer need tax incentives to invest in Jordan thus leading to an additional increase in fiscal revenues.[13]

Whilst there is great potential for the expansion of the country's fiscal revenues, the negative impact of tariff reduction and, ultimately, the removal of most restrictions on trade, might offset the projected increase in fiscal revenues. In addition, projected increases in private sector investment are not necessarily going to be channeled to small indigenous firms. The more general economic problem is that Jordan – like many developing countries – faces the unpredictability of future events and the possibility of critical developments in its socio-political environment. Thus, while accession to the WTO might create a great potential for the expansion of economic activity in the country, the continuing perception of instability may provide a difficult environment for the largely small-sized indigenous companies without the implementation of government policies stimulating expansion. On the other hand, one of the most notable aspects of Jordan's accession to the WTO is that Jordan would have access to the WTO Dispute Settlement Body (DSB). DSB, in turn, will facilitate resolution of any trade dispute that Jordan may have with its trading partners. This system of dispute settlement is, supposedly, significantly superior to mechanisms that resolve trade disputes on a bilateral basis, especially with a more powerful trade partner.

On the evidence provided above with respect to the construction industry, an effective, if not conclusive case can be made to justify Jordan's accession to the WTO. The expected benefits could be high, for the WTO plays an essential role in international trade development that is critical to the sustainable development of any country. WTO agreements promote the utilisation of a broad spectrum of skilled and unskilled labour available in member countries. In countries such as Jordan, the forecast of overall economic growth due, in part, to an expected improving political climate, will provide opportunities for the growth of its export sector – if Jordan is in a position to take advantage of such opportunities. It seems clear that accession to the WTO would be adequate to achieve meaningful stimulation of the Jordanian economy. However, based upon the analysis of the Jordanian case, two shortcomings to the accession process may be identified. First, many of the agreements may have the impact of stimulating overall industrial activity but will not necessarily be targeted towards indigenous industries. Secondly, the accession agreements do little to reduce the overall market volatility for indigenous firms. Such volatility is particularly high in developing countries and is a disincentive for long-term investment in capital equipment or for productivity-enhancing investment.

The conclusions proposed can only be tentative in nature, however, for the World Trade Organisation is a relatively new phenomenon. More preliminary information and established data on single-country experiences with the WTO is needed if a more complete understanding of this subject is to be developed. Furthermore, only a general assessment was attempted here, in the context of the relevant articles of the WTO agreement. A full evaluation of the agreement's effect on the stimulation of the economy of Jordan would require considerable additional information, such as the full definition of Jordan's industrial sector. Such a definition would include details such as firm size, past activity levels, linkages with other sectors, information on market segmentation, pricing policies, and productivity measures – yet much of this information is not available. However, without such information, assessing reactions to any stimulus policies aimed at the indigenous industry will be difficult.

NOTES

1. B. Hindawi, 'The WTO's General Agreement on Trade in Services and the Insurance Sector in Jordan', Ministry of Industry and Trade, Jordan, 1999.
2. Ministry of Public Works and Housing, Jordan, Government Tenders Directorate Year Book, 1995.
3. World Trade Organization, *Introduction to the WTO*, Geneva, 1994.
4. Ministry of Planning, Jordan, Five-Year Plan for Social and Economic Development 1993–1997, Amman, Jordan, 1993.
5. United Nations Conference on Trade and Development, *Trade and Development Report*, New York, 1996.
6. World Trade Organization, *The Results of the Uruguay Round of Multilateral Trade Negotiations*, Geneva, 1999.
7. R. Sweis, 'A Model to Assess Alternative Strategies to Promote the Construction Industry in Developing Countries', Northwestern University, Evanston, IL, 1999.
8. World Trade Organization, 1999, op. cit.
9. F. Moavenzadeh, 'The Construction Industry and Economic Growth', *Asian National Development*, June/July 1984, pp. 56–60.
10. World Trade Organization, 1999, op. cit.
11. P. Hillebrandt, 'Economic Theory and the Construction Industry', Macmillan, London, 1984.
12. World Bank, *World Development Report*, New York: Oxford University Press, 1993.
13. World Trade Organization, 1999, op. cit.

DEVELOPMENT STRATEGIES AND THE POLITICAL ECONOMY OF TOURISM IN CONTEMPORARY JORDAN

Matthew Gray

Tourism has emerged as a pivotal economic sector in Jordan, especially in the 1980s and 1990s, as previous sources of foreign income and economic sustenance have diminished and the Kingdom has been forced to look towards new sources of income and employment creation and, more profoundly, new models of economic development.[1] This analysis charts the course of tourism policy in Jordan, up to and in particular during the 1990s, from a political economy perspective and especially as an investigation of the broader role of tourism in the economic development strategies of the Jordanian leadership. It argues that tourism policy and its manifestations have been founded on a bipolar strategy of, first, linking tourism to the wider-ranging process of economic reform and restructuring and second, of linking tourism to Jordan's role in the Middle East and especially in the Arab-Israeli peace process. It begins by outlining the historical evolution of tourism in Jordan and the impacts of this on the current standing of tourism in the Kingdom's political economy. It then progresses to a detailed analysis of the bipolar structure of tourism in contemporary Jordan, with an account of the place of tourism in the economic liberalisation process and the peace process and vice versa. The discussion concludes by considering the unique aspects of Jordan's tourism sector and the features that set it apart in the region.

The evolution of tourism in Jordan to 1991

Jordan has only recently begun to target tourism as a major source of economic development, although tourism as such is nothing new. In the nineteenth and early twentieth centuries, Western tourists and travellers to the Middle East confined themselves largely to the main urban areas of the Holy Land and Egypt; a handful of people visited Petra, but the first Western visitor was the Swiss traveller Johann

Ludwig Burckhardt in 1812.[2] However the difficulty (and often the physical danger) of visiting Petra, the lack of major cities and infrastructure in Transjordan, and the allure of the religious and other historical sites elsewhere in the region meant that most travellers bypassed Jordan, at least until the 1920s.

In the 1920s, the government of Transjordan introduced or upgraded a number of facilities throughout the countryside, including roads, communications and power, in order to increase its political reach and effectiveness and to restrict the power of tribal groups. As a result, tribes, which had often long been hostile to foreign travellers, lost much of their ability to disrupt the nascent tourism industry around Petra and in the countryside. The 1920s also saw archaeological interest in Petra and other areas increase dramatically and the establishment by the Thomas Cook Company of a small hotel at the entrance to the site.[3] The changes during this period increased the comfort for tourists, as well as their actual ability of undertake the journey to Petra, while archaeological digs caught the attention and imagination of potential travellers. Nonetheless, at this time only the wealthiest of foreign travellers could afford the time and money that a visit to Petra or other areas such as Wadi Rumm required; a situation that remained until well into the 1950s.

The small size of tourism industry and the fact that tourism operators at major sites rarely used local labour limited the economic and development importance and impact of tourism during the period from the 1920s to the 1940s. Workers at Petra and other tourism sites were typically Egyptians. An early example of 'guest workers', they were brought to tourism sites for six or eight months a year, chosen as guides and employees because of their ability to speak European languages and for their knowledge of Western customs and social norms.[4] During and especially later in this period, Transjordan benefited from the West Bank, especially East Jerusalem, which it possessed until the Arab-Israeli War of 1967. Jerusalem had long since become a centre of Christian, Muslim and Jewish pilgrimage. Again, the Thomas Cook Company had been instrumental in forming and developing a tourism industry there, linking Egypt and the Holy Land and offering tourists the additional option of visiting the east bank of the Jordan River.

Jordan's first direct effort at attracting tourists was made in the 1950s, with the advent of direct air links between Jordan and Europe and as tourists began travelling in increased numbers to Egypt, Israel, and Lebanon. A tourism department was established by the Jordanian government in 1953, to regulate hotels, tourism assets and sites, and to register guides and travel agencies.[5] The following year, an advertising campaign was undertaken in the United States to encourage visitors for Easter that year. However the tourism sector was unable to accommodate all those who visited as a result of the advertisements, which highlighted the inadequate infrastructure for tourism at the time. This led the government to pay greater attention to the development of facilities such as hotels, restaurants and road and transport links, as well as to the training of staff in languages and other tourism-related fields.[6] This was followed by the formation of Royal Jordanian Airlines in 1963. The decision to form an airline was made by the government, but its establishment and management was left to Ali Ghandour, an external and relatively independent manager brought in from Lebanon.[7] Although Royal Jordanian was initially very small, it developed rapidly into a major regional carrier, with an average annual growth rate of 18.8 per cent during the 1960s and 1970s.[8]

Table 1. THE 1967 ARAB-ISRAELI WAR AND TOURISM TO JORDAN

Origin of tourists	Tourist numbers (1967)	Tourist numbers (1968)	% change
Arab World	262,943	279,400	+6
Middle East/Asia	79,079	75,572	–4
Europe	53,458	15,026	–71
Americas	24,039	3,605	–85
Other	6,114	1,829	–70
Total	425,633	375,432	–11

Source: Hashemite Kingdom of Jordan Official Statistics, quoted in Kameel Majdali, 'Christian Visitors to Jerusalem: Pilgrims, Tourists, Lobbyists?', *Journal of Arabic, Islamic and Middle Eastern Studies*, 1, 2, 1994, p. 49 (Table 3).

Whereas the period from the 1950s to 1967 witnessed a solid expansion in the size and value of the tourism sector in Jordan, the loss of the West Bank to Israel as a result of the Six Day War in 1967 caused a dramatic reversal of this trend. In particular, the loss of East Jerusalem and Bethlehem, with their important historical and religious sites, meant that Israel gained a large proportion of the tourism that had previously gone to Jordan.[9] The war 'stripped Jordan of 90 per cent of its tourism assets'.[10] After 1967, largely as a result of the loss of the West Bank, the Jordanian government changed the goals of its tourism policy towards attracting shorter-term 'stop-over' tourists, and began selling Jordan as a 'gateway' to the Middle East. Hotel facilities and tourist sites throughout the country were upgraded and expanded.

In a strange twist to the Arab-Israeli conflict, tourism links between Jordan and Israel after 1967 were rarely severed and in fact at times

flourished. The King Hussain/Allenby Bridge crossing on the Jordan
River remained open for much of the period 1967–94 and although
it was virtually impossible for Israelis to visit Jordan and vice versa,
third-party tourists travelled remarkably freely between the two
states much of the time. Although Israel occupied the West Bank
after the 1967 war, Jordan continued to view it as Jordanian territory.
As a result, tourists in Jordan were required simply to obtain a West
Bank travel permit to cross the Jordan River and, once across, Israel
considered such tourists to be in Israel. Despite periodic closures of
the bridge during periods of tension, a number of travel agencies
maintained branches in both Amman and Jerusalem[11] and quite
openly marketed Jordan and the West Bank simultaneously to foreign tourists.

The development of tourism in Jordan, especially in the 1970s,
was aided by the general economic growth and expansion in Jordan
and the Middle East region during this period, as well as by the marketing of Jordan as a 'stop-over' destination. The economic boom of
the 1970s found its origins in the dramatic rise in Jordanian workers'
remittances from abroad, especially the Gulf, which grew strongly
in the period 1976–80, were at a peak in the period 1981–5, but which
then declined markedly in the years following.[12] Much of the remittances went into unproductive investments such as residential housing and consumer goods, however some also went into private sector
businesses such as transportation and tour companies. As a percentage of Gross National Product (GNP), the tourism sector in the period 1976–80 increased in value from 10.57 to 12.56 per cent, a rise
of almost 20 per cent.[13] Much of this growth was attributable to increased private sector activity and investment in tourism, such as a
dramatic rise in hotel and tour company investments,[14] but some was
also the result of increased government spending, most notably the
construction of Amman's Queen Alia airport[15] and an increase in
government spending on transportation.[16]

As a rentier economy with a strong expatriate workforce in the
Gulf and elsewhere, Jordan also relied for income on the export of
tourism-related labour. Jordanian training facilities for hotel, airline
and tour staff expanded along with the boom in the economy, largely
training people for work in the tourism sectors of other states rather
than in Jordan. The training facilities owned by Royal Jordanian Airlines, for example, trained pilots and cabin crew for a number of airlines in the developing world.[17] A large number of Jordanians with
English language skills were (and remain) in demand in many parts of
the Arab World for positions as hotel staff and in other tourism-
related work. The training of Jordanians for employment abroad was

very profitable throughout the 1970s, as these workers typically returned in value several times the cost of their training as repatriated
funds.

In the 1980s, however, Jordan entered a serious economic recession
and so began to look more closely to the development of its own tourism sector as a method of achieving economic development and employment creation. The recession was the result of several economic
changes, including a fall in workers' remittances, an expanding trade
deficit, a decline in foreign aid and other international assistance
and low levels of productive investment. The rentier structure of the
economy made it very difficult politically for the government to create a taxation base or to introduce austerity measures in response.
The attempts to expand and develop tourism in response to the recession took several forms, with the logic of choosing tourism as a pallia-
tive the result of its labour-intensive and foreign-income-generating
nature. Not surprisingly, the development of tourism required a major restructuring of the sector and considerable government resources
and therefore it did not deliver immediate economic results.

The emphasis after 1967 on attracting transit and short-stay tourists had created certain characteristics to the Jordanian tourism sector. It had, over the previous fifteen or so years, been structured
around two main types of foreign visitors, neither of which could easily be transformed into longer stay tourists who would spend more
money. The first category of visitors was transit passengers travelling
on Royal Jordanian Airlines. Some were Europeans travelling to the
Gulf, but most were Arab tourists flying between Baghdad or the
Gulf, to Cairo or destinations in North Africa or Europe. When
Queen Alia airport was designed in the late 1970s, an enormous number of transit passengers was assumed. The number peaked in 1982
at 2.56 million, however the recession which began at that time, combined with the Iran-Iraq war, cut heavily into the number of transit
passengers stopping in Jordan. With declining numbers, transit passengers could not be converted into an overall increase in longer stay
tourists.

The second group of visitors was business travellers. Again, the
Iran-Iraq war dealt a blow to the number of transit business travellers, as did the expanding size and improving reputation of the airlines of the Gulf, which competed with Royal Jordanian Airlines by
offering direct services to the Gulf States which were as safe and comfortable as the Jordanian carrier. The additional problem, of course,
was that business travellers focused on saving time rather than
money, and were therefore more inclined to choose direct air services
rather than flights requiring a stop-over or change of aircraft. The

time constraints on business travellers and their preference for direct flights meant that they proved difficult to convert into tourists.

A combination of economic recession, a lack of internal tourism, Jordan's geographic centrality in the region and the limited success of concentrating on stopover tourism, led the Jordanian government to begin aggressively marketing Jordan as a tourist destination in and of itself in the late 1980s.[18] Full-scale tourism development became a strategic economic focus of the Jordanian government. A change in circumstances assisted Jordan in partially developing the status of a tourism destination in its own right. One change was the strong numbers of European and North American tourists, attracted to Jordan for its historical sites and its geographical centrality in the Levant. By the mid-1980s, Jordan's tourism infrastructure was in place and was of good quality and Petra had been developed into a major Middle East attraction, Aqaba had become a resort of international reputation, the springs and castles around the countryside were being marketed internationally as important attractions, and nearly all the major cities and towns had adequate numbers of quality hotels and restaurants.

As well as providing assistance with the structural improvements mentioned above, the government was also closely involved with the regulation and deregulation of tourism activity and with the marketing of Jordan to potential foreign tourists. In the late 1980s the Jordanian government combined its resources with the private sector and Royal Jordanian Airlines to spend about US$1 million on international marketing.[19] The core markets of Europe and North America were given particular attention, but the Gulf States, with the potential to supply large numbers of people seeking refuge from the summer heat of the Gulf, were also targeted. It was at around this time that Royal Jordanian began expanding its services to include North America and the Far East. This coordinated marketing campaign stressed the major attractions of Petra, Jarash and Aqaba, and also introduced new types of tourism, especially conference and incentive travel, both of which promised considerably higher financial value than group or individual tourism.[20] At the end of the 1980s, the Jordanian government also began to tighten the rules governing tour guides, who until this time had operated relatively freely and often without adequate qualifications. After 1990, new rules were implemented which required guides to have a university qualification and experience and to have passed an examination on a foreign language and an examination on the sites where they would be authorised to work.[21] Guides were no longer allowed to work throughout the country as they wished; different categories of licences were created for

Table 2. Jordan – Visitor Arrivals and Tourism Revenue, 1989–98

	1989	1990	1991	1992	1993	1994	1995	1996	1997	1998
Arrivals (× 1,000)	644	577	439	669	775	858	1,074	1,103	1,127	1,256
% annual change		−10.40	−23.92	52.39	15.84	10.71	25.17	2.70	2.18	11.45
Receipts (JD million)	314.6	339.8	216	314.3	390.2	406.4	462.5	527.2	548.8	604.7
% annual change		8.01	−36.43	45.51	24.15	4.15	13.80	13.99	4.10	10.19
Receipts (US$ million)	443.59	499.51	317.52	546.88	561.89	581.15	661.38	743.35	773.81	852.63
% annual change		12.61	−36.43	72.24	2.74	3.43	13.80	12.39	4.10	10.19

Source: Statistics Section, Jordan Ministry of Tourism, retrieved electronically from the website http://www.mota.gov.jo/TOPIC7.HTM on 24 April 2000 at 1215 GMT.

various areas.[22] Prices for a tour guide licence were increased, but also set, by the government.

From the mid-1980s onwards, Western tourists increasingly spent a week or more in Jordan, with a side-trip of a few days to Jerusalem, and less the reverse situation that had been more common in the 1970s. To a certain extent, the growth of tourism in the late 1980s can be attributed to 'a long period of stability, combined with improved infrastructure and sustained international marketing efforts',[23] especially given the limited economic reforms in the tourism sector at the time.

However, the Iraqi invasion of Kuwait on 2 August 1990, and the subsequent Gulf War of January-February 1991, threatened to undo most of the growth of tourism and to worsen the troubles bedevilling the economy more broadly. The 1990-1 Gulf War affected Jordan more than most Middle East states. It could not have come at a worse time for Jordan and its King: the economic problems of the past decade and the growing political activity of both Palestinians and Islamists, placed King Hussain in an unenviable position – perhaps his weakest position since the upheaval of Black September two decades earlier.

Beside the political challenge for King Hussain of balancing international condemnation of Iraq with popular support for Saddam Hussain on the streets of Jordan, the 1990-1 crisis further damaged Jordan's already frail economy. Aqaba had become a transit point reliant on Iraq's foreign trade and subsequently lost much of its income as the international sanctions against Iraq caused a 66 per cent decline in Aqaba's trade between 1989 and 1992.[24] The Gulf War also caused a massive decline in international trade with, and foreign aid and assistance to, Jordan. Workers' remittances also fell, as Jordanians working in Kuwait and Iraq were repatriated.[25] Unemployment, already at 15 per cent before the invasion of Kuwait, reached 40 per cent in early 1991.[26] The cost of the Gulf War to Jordan, in the year after hostilities ceased, was estimated by the Jordanian finance minister at $2.144 billion, or 'the equivalent of 63 per cent of GNP'.[27] The wider regional economic losses associated with the Gulf War also had a strong impact on Jordan and its economic situation: a decline in inter-regional and intra-regional trade, a plummet in investment in the region and economic instability brought about by the uncertainty of the crisis. The regional losses from the War included approximately $12 billion in lost output from Middle Eastern countries and $5 billion in lost income,[28] which further damaged Jordan's interdependent economy.

Further, in common with most states in the geographical vicinity of the crisis, Jordan's tourism sector suffered an immediate and drastic decline as a result of the crisis; almost immediately the tourism sector 'all but disappeared'.[29] Even before the Allied attack on Iraq on 16 January 1991, most European airlines had either suspended operations to Jordan, or had greatly reduced services.[30] Royal Jordanian Airlines suffered average losses of $12.5 million per month in the September to December 1990 period, after losing not only tourists to Jordan, but also transit passengers, cargo, charter flights and valuable routes to Iraq and Kuwait.[31] Royal Jordanian's only growth service at this time – which was short-lived – was the evacuation of foreign workers from Iraq and Kuwait in late 1990.[32]

But despite the manifold negative impacts of the Gulf War on Jordan, a number of which still remain as a burden on the Kingdom, the period since 1991 has been one of economic recovery.

The economic liberalisation of tourism in the 1990s

The Jordanian government continued the process of economic reform in the 1990s, despite the added economic and political constraints that stemmed from the 1990–1 Gulf War and the unpopular nature of many of the reforms that were implemented. Unlike in other states of the region, such as Egypt, the liberalisation of tourism during the 1990s has been implemented with a strong role for the government; a realisation by the Jordanian government, perhaps, of the negative consequences of the 'over-liberalisation' of tourism, as has been the case in some aspects of Egypt's tourism sector (more on which later). The 1990s have therefore witnessed an increased emphasis by the government on the economic liberalisation of tourism, but mixed with a strong government role in the management and development of the sector. The government's role in the economy, tourism included, had been gradually increased between the 1940s and the 1970s and its retreat from the economy, starting in the 1980s, has been equally gradual, marked by caution and, at times, hesitation. Although under pressure from the World Bank and the IMF, King Hussain made it clear that economic reform would move at a pace with which Jordan was comfortable and which would minimise the problems associated with economic change. This drew some criticism that it was very 'slow to open up [to foreign investors]'.[33]

Such gradualism is not without its benefits. In contrast with Egypt, where economic liberalisation in the past few years has been poorly planned and often chaotic, the measures which have been included in Jordanian liberalisation have generally offered positive results, and have been undertaken with fewer problems and negative impacts as a result of such caution. Although the indicators for Jordan's tourism sector have fluctuated slightly in the late 1980s and early 1990s, they have nonetheless shown an overall positive trend. Beyond the government's caution, furthermore, a number of major economic reforms have been undertaken, including many in the tourism sector. The dominant feature of economic reform has been the government's attempts at macroeconomic and budgetary reforms, linked with attempts at improving its economic management. Rather than particular watersheds in economic liberalisation, the 1990s have been characterised by more subtle reforms and attempts by the government to increase gradually the role of the private sector. However, engaging and expanding the role of the private sector in economic development has obviously required some significant policy shifts, especially in laws pertaining to investment, foreign exchange, international trade, taxation, customs and immigration.

In the early 1990s, the view was widely held that, had it not been for the economic downturn associated with the 1990–1 Gulf War, the Jordanian tourism sector would have grown rapidly after the boom of the late 1980s. Therefore the government continued to market Jordan as a primary destination, as opposed to a stopover destination or a one- or two-day side-trip from Israel or Egypt. The emphasis on resort tourism to Aqaba also continued, after the success achieved in the late 1980s. Aqaba, especially with its nearby attraction of Wadi Rumm and closer to Petra than Amman, drew large numbers of European visitors in the late 1980s who stayed for a week or longer.[34] The construction of hotels and tourism infrastructure continued after the Gulf War at Aqaba as well as at Petra, where an expansion of about 500 hotel rooms had been planned for in 1990, before the 1990–1 Gulf War.[35] The rapid expansion of hotel and other tourism infrastructure in Petra was frozen by the government in 1994, in an attempt to preserve the Petra site, but by this stage Petra had already suffered the environmental side-effects of nine major hotels (with a total of 1,151 rooms) as well as a number of illegal hotels and guesthouses in the nearby town of Wadi Mousa.[36] The emphasis on regional cooperation in tourism also continued, with Jordan remaining reliant on Egypt, Israel and Syria to provide many of its tourists. Further, there was an increased emphasis on the role of the private sector in tourism investment, development, and service delivery. Finally, there was a more focused marketing campaign, with coordination between the government, the private sector and Royal Jordanian Airlines, which presented a 'slick'[37] image in Jordan's tourism marketing.

As well as the continuation of the above strategies for tourism, government policy also expanded to include some new plans for tourism development. The emphasis from the 1980s on marketing Jordan as a tourism destination in the United States and Europe continued, but with a stronger focus on marketing coordination between sectors in Jordan. Despite some friction between the Ministry of Tourism and the private sector – particularly over the amount of money spent by the government on tourism development[38] – coordination between the public and private sectors did increase after 1991. The private sector, which preferred campaigns focused on a single country or group of countries (rather than a thinly-spread global campaign), encouraged the government to establish more focused marketing programmes. Thus in the early 1990s, Jordan initially targeted three countries per year (for example, Spain, Germany and the Netherlands in 1994), and then undertook individual projects in certain countries in subsequent years, such as the Netherlands in 1995 and Japan and the United Kingdom in 1996.[39] The 1990s also saw new types of tourism gain attention in Jordan's strategic plans; in particular, cultural tourism, health tourism and incentive and conference tourism were given a renewed emphasis by the government, perhaps in recognition that some limits did exist in the typical areas of guided tours and stop-over visits.

In the 1990s the government also developed regional tourism sites. In part, this was designed to spread tourism throughout the country, since the majority of Western visitors were spending most of their time in Aqaba and the southern areas of Jordan. Greater emphasis was placed on sites in the north and east of Jordan such as the Dead Sea, the desert castles east of Amman and the towns of Madaba, Azraq and Umm Qais.[40]

In terms of reform policy, the Investment Law of 1987, which had represented a step towards the liberalisation of foreign investment, underwent a number of amendments in the early 1990s to improve its efficacy and the attractiveness of Jordan to investors, especially from other Arab states. The law was ultimately overhauled in 1995 and passed through parliament as the Investment Promotion Law of 1995. The laws aimed at attracting investors not least in tourism, which had begun a period of growth in 1992 but was restricted by a number of inefficiencies and, in some areas, an under supply of appropriate facilities to cater for a rapid expansion of the sector. A further economic reform in the 1990s was the dismantling of government monopolies in key areas, a continuing policy of macroeconomic and budgetary stabilisation and a number of smaller liberalisation initiatives. It is important to note the changing emphasis of the Jordanian government and yet its continued gradualist approach to economic liberalisation. Despite the enormous financial losses and problems associated with the Gulf War, Jordanian liberalisation in the 1990s has been characterised by a series of reforms, which have balanced the need for change with the short-term costs and disruptions associated with liberalisation.

In an attempt to encourage private sector involvement in the tourism sector, the government began to dismantle barriers to private sector entry and operation in tourism. Most notable was the cessation in 1995 of some public sector monopolies in tourism, especially that previously enjoyed by the government-owned Jordan Express Tourism and Transport Company (JETT). JETT's monopoly on internal bus services in Jordan had been unpopular with the private sector, even though, starting in 1980, JETT had contracted out some of its services and had entered agreements with private sector firms to offer additional services such as catering and accommodation.[41] The removal of JETT's monopoly, furthermore, was not a complete liberalisation of the transport sector: new firms were required to have JD10 million in capital and at least 50 buses,[42] a requirement which did little to encourage smaller-scale competition with JETT.

Another example is the ongoing debate over the privatisation of Royal Jordanian Airlines. When the privatisation debate began in 1986 and 1987, Royal Jordanian was one of the first firms considered for (partial) sale. The airline had expanded considerably in the 1970s and 1980s, but had also had several years during the 1980s in which it registered a financial loss; in 1983 and especially in 1984, while in 1985 it managed to avoid a deficit only through asset sales.[43] The original plan was to offer 30 per cent of the airline to the public and 10 per cent to its employees in late 1987, followed in 1988 by a further sale of between 20 and 30 per cent to Arab and Jordanian investors. The aim was for the government to retain about 15 per cent of the carrier, combining that with at least 36 per cent private Jordanian ownership to keep the majority of the company in Jordanian hands.

The fact that Royal Jordanian was not privatised as planned highlights the ways in which political and economic instability have a direct impact on the liberalisation process in the tourism sector. After the privatisation announcement in 1987, Royal Jordanian registered in 1988 one of its worst financial years on record – a loss of JD11.7 million (US$16.97 million) – due almost exclusively to a drastic devaluation of the currency in 1988.[44] The currency devaluation was a result of Jordan's rapidly deteriorating financial position and especially of its foreign debt, which was consuming a large percentage of its export income. Although a devaluation of the dinar might have increased the income from a sale of the airline, the resulting loss eroded any potential gain and the sale was shelved. Before the airline had re-covered from its losses in 1988, the 1990–1 Gulf War occurred, dis-rupting Royal Jordanian's operations and causing a 19.9 per cent decline in its carriage of passengers.[45] Routes to both Baghdad and Kuwait were lost and other regional routes were badly affected by a regional slump in tourism during late 1990 and 1991. Only in 1992 did the airline return to the passenger loads and profitability of the mid-1980s, at which time the privatisation preparations were again commenced. However, largely as a result of poor performance and poor management in the late 1980s and early 1990s, by 1992 Royal Jordanian was carrying an enormous debt, costing about $40 million a year to service, which eroded profits and reduced the potential sale value of the airline. By late 1998 the Jordanian government was still talking about the privatisation of the airline and two years later had only just begun the privatisation process.[46]

Other reforms with a direct impact on tourism included the crea-tion of free trade zones and special areas of land dedicated to tourism development projects such as hotels and resorts. Set up in 1973, Aqa-ba is the oldest, but others include the Zarqa zone near Amman, and plans for a free zone at Queen Alia International Airport. The free zones are aimed both at liberalising the transit of goods and at in-creasing the level of foreign investment in Jordan.[47] The most impor-tant case of dedicating land to tourism has been the sale of land along Jordan's southern coast by the Aqaba Region Authority, aimed at developing resort tourism in the Kingdom, especially since the neighbouring Israeli port and resort of Eilat has almost four times the hotel room capacity of Aqaba.[48]

The Peace Process and the political economy of tourism

Concomitant with economic reform, the development of tourism in Jordan has been aided by the role of the Kingdom in the region and relations with its neighbours, especially Israel. One of the pivotal events of the 1990s for Jordan – certainly the event which has cap-tured the most attention – was the signing by Jordan of a peace treaty with Israel on 26 October 1994. The treaty was, in a sense, an exten-sion of a broader Arab-Israeli peace process, which began after the Gulf War with the Madrid conference in October 1991 and then led, on a different track, to the signing of the Declaration of Principles be-tween Israel and the PLO in September 1993. However the motives behind Jordan signing an treaty with Israel were very different to those behind the PLO's Declaration.

Despite the uncertainties of peace with Israel, Jordan had strong economic motivations for pursuing the agreement of October 1994 and for opening its economy to trade and investment with Israel. Both the PLO and Jordan stood to make substantial economic gains from a closer political relationship with Israel and a dismantling of the economic barriers which had previously existed between Israel and its neighbours (apart from Egypt, which had made peace fifteen years earlier). In the case of Jordan, however, the potential gains were greater and more immediate and there was less pressure on Jordan than there was on the PLO, given the PLO's need to integrate the return of land into its agreement with Israel. Further, given the nature of Jordan's economy and its geographical position in the region, the development of closer ties with Israel seemed to carry far fewer risks and less possibility for a failure of the peace treaty.

Among the sectors of Jordan's economy most likely to benefit in the shorter term was tourism. One study gives the seemingly pedantic, but in fact quite important, example of airfares from Jordan to Europe and the United States, which fell after the peace treaty was signed because Royal Jordanian Airlines was able to fly over Israeli airspace and save about 18 minutes in flying time.[49] More broadly, of course, peace with Israel allowed Israeli tourists to visit the Kingdom, which they did in far greater numbers than Jordanians visited Israel. The more general economic benefits of economic ties with Israel – regional economic integration, Israeli and other foreign investment, more open trade and the like – also promised to deliver economic benefits to Jordan. The initial tourism arrival figures for Jordan after the 1994 treaty signalled a strong boom in tourism, circumstantially indicating enormous benefits for tourism as a result of Israelis being able to visit the Kingdom.

However the introduction of Israeli tourists to Jordan has not been without controversy or problems. The statistics suggest that tourist arrivals prior to the 1994 peace agreement fluctuated and showed little overall growth trend. They then show not only that more than 100,000 Israelis per year since October 1994 were spending money in Jordan, but also that the peace treaty led to a great overall increase in tourist arrivals: the result, perhaps, of the common perception that peace and stability make tourists more inclined to visit a country or region.[50]

It is impossible to argue that no economic benefit has come from the increase in tourism numbers from Israel, however there have been some unexpected, unpopular and less than positive outcomes from the introduction of Israeli tourists to Jordan. The first point in this respect is that both Israeli tourists and other tourists travelling from Israel, as a whole spend less time in Jordan than tourists who are visiting Jordan only or who base themselves, during their vacation, in another Arab country rather than Israel. The average length of stay for a tourist to Jordan in 1995 was 3.75 nights, including 4.49 nights for European tourists overall, 4.99 nights for Arab visitors[51] and as much as six nights or more for some European nationals.[52] However the reputation among Jordanians of Israeli tourists is that they visit Jordan for a very brief stay, often only for the day, and that they 'bring everything, including sandwiches and water, with them from Israel.'[53] This led the Jordanian government to drastically increase the entry fees into popular sites such as Petra, in order to ensure that some income was earned from 'day trip' tourists from Israel. It was not only Petra which failed to gain all the benefits of tourism links with Israel. The port of Aqaba, immediately next to the much larger and better equipped Israeli port of Eilat, had expected to benefit from the opening of the border with Israel. Instead, many tourists stayed in Eilat and visited Aqaba briefly if at all. In late 1994, Eilat had 5,500 hotel beds compared to 1,413 in Aqaba and also had more restaurants and more experience in tourism. After the opening of the border between Eilat and Aqaba, hotel occupancy rates in the latter were lower, not higher, than before and it appeared that the larger city of Eilat, with its numerical and qualitative advantages in tourism facilities, would dominate over Aqaba.[54]

For these reasons, and perhaps also because of the enormous numbers of Israelis which suddenly appeared on the streets of Jordan, there was considerable popular resentment by Jordanians towards Israeli tourists. The Jordanian Ministry of Tourism and Antiquities quickly placed a cap on the number of Israeli tourists allowed into Jordan, at 900 per day.[55] This was more than the daily average who visited, but was designed as much to appease popular concerns as to restrict Israeli arrivals. The popular concept that tourism creates greater understanding between peoples and that it would cement the peace treaty between Israel and Jordan, appears to have limited validity in this case.

There have been some notable benefits for Jordanian businesses after the peace treaty. A considerable number of new investment projects, financed by both domestic investors and foreign sources, have been undertaken since 1994. In particular, a spurt of tourism infrastructure development has occurred since the development of tourism links with Israel. Nine major hotel projects were authorised by the Jordanian Ministry of Tourism for 1996 and another twenty-one were underway from previous years.[56] Of these nineteen were in Amman, three in Petra, three in Aqaba, two in Kerak and three elsewhere in Jordan.[57] This commercial expansion, concomitant with the introduction of Israeli tourists to Jordan, partly reflects the need to meet a growing demand, while also indicating an increasing commercial and international confidence in Jordan's stability and economic future. Further, many companies have expanded or have been created to cater for Israeli tourists and tourists based in Israel who also visit Jordan. These include all levels of tours, from short one day visits to major eight day tours of several of Jordan's main sites.

The main theme which comes from Jordan's recent tourism and economic ties with Israel is that relations with Israel have had only a marginal positive effect on Jordan's tourism sector. Peace with Israel has delivered limited benefits to Jordan, but the pervading assumption, which looked very persuasive in 1994, that Jordan's tourism sector would 'boom' after a peace treaty with Israel has proven to be only partially true. A view, not without merit, developed among some analysts that King Hussain had 'oversold the peace process'.[58] Former Jordanian Prime Minister Abdel Salam al-Majali in September 1994 made the interesting prediction that 'the short-run fiscal impact of peace [with Israel] is likely to be negative for Jordan'.[59] While not completely borne out by recent experience, the prediction nonetheless contained an element of accuracy, including in the case of tourism.

The most important has been the disparity in economic power between the two states, the dominance of Eilat over Aqaba being a manifestation of this in the tourism sector. A key link between economic and political liberalisation and tourism is evident from the problem of wealth disparity between Israel and Jordan, especially in terms of the public policy debate over how Jordan might best compete with Israel on an even economic footing. One view calls for Jordan to integrate and economically liberalise its economy, in cooperation with neighbouring Arab states. This view argues that Israel's Arab neighbours would compensate for lower per capita income and spending power by organising a numerical advantage; in essence, this view is the economic counterpart of the popular Arab strategic approach to the Arab-Israeli conflict, that a quantitative advantage could be used to compete with Israel's qualitative advantage. By extension, and also in many cases ostensibly, this argument calls for economic liberalisation in the Arab states which would cooperate to compete with Israel. Others have called simply for economic liberalisation in Jordan, regardless of whether it enters into some formalised trade and economic cooperation with its neighbours. The magazine *The Middle East* quotes a Jordanian economist, Dr Riyadh al-Momani, as saying that 'Jordan's ability to benefit from peace depends on "its impact on ordinary Jordanians by raising their standard of living. This will require internal reforms and elimination of all forms of administrative corruption and other problems"'.[60]

Regional economic integration, however, whether in competition
or cooperation with Israel, is not without its dangers. In the case of
tourism and related areas such as international private investment
and open borders, integrated states and economies mean that instability in one state has a greater impact in the other states. While
Jordan could potentially benefit from closer tourism ties with Israel,
or with other Arab states, this may deepen the negative consequences
on Jordan from, say, domestic instability in Israel or Egypt. This is
typically the case in Middle Eastern states bordering Israel anyway,
regardless of the state's relations with Israel, but has been felt particularly strongly in Egypt during the 1980s and 1990 and in Jordan since
1994. In particular, in situations where tourists are based in Israel
and travel to Jordan as a side-trip, international instability will have a
strong affect. During Israel's 1996 'Grapes of Wrath' operation in Lebanon, for example, the tourism sector in Jordan suffered a short
but sharp decline in visits by Western tourists, tourists travelling from
Israel and Israeli tourists.[61] Although Jordan was a considerable distance from the conflict in Lebanon, tourists were deterred by the remote threat of a broader regional conflict and by the anti-Israel
sentiment in the Arab world created by 'Grapes of Wrath'.[62] Direct
violence against Israelis, or foreigners thought to be Israeli, has been
very limited in Jordan, but serious events have occurred. The 1997 attack on an Israeli school bus by a Jordanian soldier, for example,
was widely reported in Israel and throughout the world. Less sinister,
but no less important, have been periodic reports by the media in Israel of cases where Israelis have been poorly treated or discriminated
against while travelling in Jordan.

Tourism and economic development in Jordan

The Jordanian government's gradualist approach to economic liberalisation, so as to minimise the political costs and maximise the benefits of reform, has occurred simultaneously with the peace process
since 1994. Recent experience would indicate that economic liberalisation and the peace process are not completely aloof of each other.
As with the broader attempt in the 1980s to use tourism growth to al-
lay the need for economic liberalisation and restructuring, the Jordanian government appears to be using the peace process, at least to
some extent, to boost the economy and to limit the need for more extensive economic liberalisation. The importance of tourism in Jordan's trade and economic relationship with Israel would seem to be
indicative of this. Furthermore, there are several unique features of
tourism strategy in Jordan.

One interesting feature of its tourism strategy, in contrast with Egypt, is the strong role that the state has played in tourism development and management. In many other states in the Middle East – Egypt, Tunisia, Turkey, Morocco, for example – the state has minimised its role in tourism to the extent possible, as an aspect of its more general retreat as manager of the economy. In the case of Jordan, the state's strong role may prove to be a positive factor in the development of tourism: in many other Middle Eastern states, the self-destructive nature of tourism, especially the problem of overly rapid tourism expansion, threatens to undo many of the tourism development policies that have been introduced. For example, the negative aspects of the over-development of tourism on rural coastal Egypt have been documented by Soraya Altorki of the American University of Cairo.[63] Altorki studied the affects of tourism on Marsa Mutrah, which has expanded dramatically as a result of tourism growth. The study argued that the benefits from tourism, such as increased employment, construction and economic activity, have been overshadowed by problems such as economic inequality, agricultural decline, greater local resentment of tourists and social problems such as alcoholism and prostitution. Such problems are not unusual to tourism, but to the tourism sectors of developing economies in particular. In Jordan, the government seems to be taking the guiding role that appears so necessary for the smooth growth and development of tourism and appears to be addressing some of its negative impacts. It has retained control over key areas of the tourism sector, such as resort and hotel development, labour laws, and the like. In a less positive example of the state being reluctant to reduce its role as manager of the economy, political concerns have had a strong impact on the privatisation programme. Privatisation often enters Jordan's economic agenda (and its leaders' political lexicon), but is yet to be seriously implemented. The earlier example of Royal Jordanian Airlines is particularly indicative of this.

The main link between economic liberalisation programme and tourism in Jordan is that tourism has been used to cushion some of the financial hardships caused by liberalisation. This has been a common feature of the strategies of the states of the region: governments are attracted to the labour-intensive nature of tourism, and the hard currency that foreign tourists provide for the economy. Further, tourism is not a complex sector to develop and does not usually rely on large injections of capital or expertise. As a sector that has expanded most dramatically only in the last decade or so, it carries with it few political risks, either to the government, its leadership and its allies, or to the stability of the country more generally. In large part, this accounts for the juxtaposition in the 1990s of tourism and economic reform as pivotal aspects of Jordan's political economy.

The peace process with Israel offers Jordan further opportunity to develop its tourism sector. Many visitors to Israel, who would have otherwise not visited Jordan at all, are now able to include Jordan in their itineraries. And Israeli tourists themselves are also able to visit Jordan. This presents a mixed blessing, of course, as many Jordanians want the money that Israeli tourists bring, but do not want the tourists. Some of the concerns about closer ties with Israel do have some validity, especially given the discrepancies in wealth and economic size between Jordan and Israel. The fear of being swamped by the Israeli tourism sector is a very real one for the Jordanian tourism sector. This issue highlights a unique facet of the liberalisation of tourism. The government has been willing to promote tourism by Israelis and others arriving from Israel, but under the pressure of political opposition to such a strategy, the government has cunningly responded by appearing to limit its liberalisation efforts, while in fact introducing measures with little, if any, impact. That a limit was placed on the number of Israelis that could visit Jordan, but that this limit was considerably higher than the actual numbers, represents both a clever political trick and, more importantly, indicates the unwillingness of the government to be associated with unpopular aspects of reform or change.

But in light of the above, it must also be remembered that Jordan faces a unique tourism structure, with its potential perhaps more limited than many of its neighbours. In this context, the steps that have already been taken are more ambitious and bold than they may initially appear and the tourism sector's performance has been, overall, remarkably positive given the geographic, political and economic position in which Jordan finds itself.

NOTES

1. For a political and economic overview of Jordan in the 1980s and early 1990s, including its attempts at political and economic liberalisation, see Laurie A. Brand, 'Economic and Political Liberalisation in a Rentier Economy: The Case of the Hashemite Kingdom of Jordan' in Sullivan, J. Denis and Iliya Harik (eds), *Privatisation and Liberalisation in the Middle East*, Bloomington: Indiana University Press, 1992, pp. 167–88.
2. John Shoup, 'The Impact of Tourism on the Bedouin of Petra', *Middle East Journal*, 39, 2 (spring 1985), 279.
3. Ibid., 280.
4. Ibid., 281.
5. International Bank for Reconstruction and Development, *The Economic Development of Jordan*, Baltimore: Johns Hopkins University Press, 1961, p. 249.

6. Ibid., pp. 249–50.
7. 'A Third World Airline Takes Flight', *South*, special survey 'Jordan', 25 (November 1982), p. 41.
8. Ibid., p. 41. In the period 1963–83, in only one year – 1967 – did the airline not register a positive growth rate.
9. For example, in the mid-1960s, about 600,000 Christian pilgrims visited Jerusalem annually. A similar number after 1967 went instead to Israel. See Kameel Majdali, 'Christian Visitors to Jerusalem: Pilgrims, Tourists, Lobbyists?', *Journal of Arabic, Islamic, and Middle Eastern Studies*, 1, 2 (1994), pp. 45–58.
10. Jim Auty, 'New Tourist Horizons', *South*, special survey 'Jordan', 25 (November 1982), p. 43.
11. Ibid.
12. Christopher McDermott, 'Macroeconomic Environment and Factors Underlying Growth and Investment' in Edouard Maciejewski, and Ahsan Mansour (eds), *Jordan: Strategy for Adjustment and Growth*, Washington, DC: IMF, 1996, p. 14 (Table 3.2).
13. Derived by the author from statistics presented in Bichara Khader, 'Targets and Achievements of Jordan's Last Five-Year Plans, 1976–1980 and 1981–1985: A Summary' in Bichara Khader and Adnan Badran (eds), *The Economic Development of Jordan*, London: Croom Helm, 1987, p. 181 (Table 10.4).
14. Auty (1982), p. 43.
15. Khader (1987), op. cit., p. 179 (Table 10.2).
16. In particular, the rapid expansion of Royal Jordanian Airlines and the Jordan Express Transport and Transportation Company (JETT).
17. 'A Third World Airline Takes Flight', op. cit., p. 41.
18. Rami G. Khouri, 'Tourism: Developing All-Round Attractions,' *Middle East Economic Digest*, special report 'Jordan' (9 February 1990), p. 14.
19. Ibid.
20. Author's interview with a hotel marketing manager, Amman, 25 June 1996.
21. Author's interview with a registered Jordanian tourist guide, Amman, 26 June 1996.
22. Ibid. Three categories of licence were established. Category A allowed a guide to work in all 12 tourism districts, category B in nine districts, and category C only in a certain tourism region or area. Special courses were introduced to qualify guides for specialised tourism, such as scientific or archaeological tourism.
23. Khouri (1990), op. cit., p. 14.
24. Peter Feuilherade, 'The Long Arm of the Embargo', *The Middle East*, March 1993, p. 39.
25. Adam Garfinkle, 'Jordanian Policy from the Intifada to the Madrid Peace Conference' in Robert O. Freedman (ed.), *The Middle East after Iraq's Invasion of Kuwait*, Gainesville: University Press of Florida, 1993, p. 308.
26. Ibid.
27. Yahya M. Sadowski, *Scuds or Butter? The Political Economy of Arms Control in the Middle East*, Washington, DC: Brookings Institution Press, 1993.
28. Ibid., p. 20 (Table 2–1).
29. Simon Edge, 'Jordan's Fate Hangs in the Balance', *Middle East Economic Digest*, 18 January 1991, p. 4.
30. Lufthansa, KLM Royal Dutch Airlines, Swissair, Air France and Alitalia all suspended or reduced services to Jordan. See ibid., p. 4.
31. Pamela Dougherty, 'Coping in the Most Adverse of Conditions', *Middle East Economic Digest*, special report 'Aviation', 18 January 1991, p. iv.
32. Ibid.

33. Pam Dougherty, 'Adjusting to More Sober Expectations', *Middle East Economic Digest*, special report 'Jordan', 21 April 1989, p. 9. Also on the cautious nature of economic reform in Jordan, see Kirk Albrecht, 'Now the Business Begins', *The Middle East*, December 1995, p. 16, and the examples of cautious reform in Peter Feuilherade, 'Implementing Checks and Balances', *The Middle East*, (January 1996, p. 19–20.

34. Khouri (1990), p. 14.

35. Ibid.

36. 'Special Feature: Petra', *Middle East Land and Development*, April 1996, pp. 5–7.

37. Author's interview with a tourism consultant, Bahrain, 30 June 1996.

38. Simon Edge, 'Getting Back on the World Tourist Map', *Middle East Economic Digest*, special report 'Jordan' (28 May 1993), 13.

39. Author's interview with a registered Jordanian tourist guide, Amman, 26 June 1996.

40. Ibid. See also Edge (1993b), p. 13.

41. Shoup (1985), op. cit., p. 282.

42. Pam Dougherty, 'Peace Pays an Instant Dividend,' *Middle East Economic Digest*, special report, 'Jordan', 21 April 1989, p. 16.

43. Pam Dougherty, 'Jordan Aims for Sharper Commercial Edge', *Middle East Economic Digest*, 30 May 1987, p. 31.

44. Simon Edge, 'RJ Flies Out of the Clouds', *Middle East Economic Digest*, special report 'Aviation', 11 June 1993, p. 16.

45. Percentage figure calculated from statistical data presented in ibid.

46. See Pam Dougherty, 'Cement Sale Fiasco Masks Progress on Privatisation', *Middle East Economic Digest*, 1 May 1998, pp. 2–3.

47. On the free trade zones, see the brochure published by the Free Zones Corporation, *Investor's Guide to Free Zones in Jordan*, Amman: Free Zones Corporation, 1995.

48. In 1995 Eilat had 5,500 hotel beds compared with Aqaba's 1,314, and a greater variety of hotels and restaurants. See Dougherty (1995b), p. 16.

49. Abdel Jaber Tayseer, 'Key Long-Term Development Issues in Jordan', *Economic Research Forum for the Arab Countries, Iran & Turkey (ERF)*, (Working Paper 9522), Economic Research Forum for the Arab Countries, Iran & Turkey (Cairo); p. 11.

50. This is a common argument in the tourism sector, and was the premise used by Shimon Peres, to state that peace would bring immediate and sizeable economic benefits to Middle East tourism. See Shimon Peres, with Arye Naor, The New Middle East, New York: Henry Holt, 1993, pp. 149–51.

51. Preliminary tourism figures obtained by the author from the Jordanian Ministry of Tourism, Statistics Section, Amman, Jordan, June 1996.

52. Ibid.

53. Ben Wedeman, 'Lukewarm Reception,' *The Middle East* (December 1994), p. 34.

54. Ibid., p. 34.

55. Dougherty, 'Peace Days an Instant Dividend', p. 16.

56. Preliminary tourism figures obtained by the author from the Jordanian Ministry of Tourism, Statistics Section, Amman, Jordan, June 1996.

57. Ibid.

58. Ilene R. Prusher, 'Despite Peace, Jordan Sees Tourist No-Show', *Christian Science Monitor*, 14 August 1996; retrieved electronically at http://www.csmonitor.com.

59. Wedeman (1994), p. 34.
60. Ibid., p. 34.
61. Author's interviews with a registered Jordanian tourist guide, Amman, 25 June 1996, and a Ministry of Tourism official, Amman, 26 June 1996. A similar decline in the case of Egypt was expressed to the author in several interviews in Egypt, April and May 1996.
62. Ibid.
63. Soraya Altorki, (1996), 'Tourism Development on Egypt's Desert Northwest Coast', speech to the Third AUC Research Conference, Sustainable Development in Egypt, American University in Cairo, 22 April 1996.

MAPPING THE LANDSCAPE OF THE 'NEW MIDDLE EAST'

THE POLITICS OF TOURISM DEVELOPMENT AND THE PEACE PROCESS IN JORDAN

Waleed Hazbun[1]

When Jordan and Israel signed a peace treaty in 1994, it not only marked an end to a state of war but it also set in motion the formation of links of economic cooperation and interdependence. These links, it was hoped, would begin to transform the map of the war-torn Middle East. One day, borders would no longer be militarised frontiers but stop-over points along trans-regional highways transporting people and goods to new markets and destinations. Proponents of this so-called 'New Middle East' vision argued that such a model would help promote Arab-Israeli peace by demonstrating that it could generate mutual economic benefits and would then solidify closer relations by forging shared material and strategic interests between the governments and their respective private sectors.

Promoting regional tourism development was widely viewed as the critical first arena across which regional linkages would be formed and economic cooperation would begin. This viewpoint is summarised by Patrick Clawson in a 1994 report assessing the prospect for tourism development and economic cooperation in the New Middle East:

Tourism offers a wide variety of opportunities for the economic development of the Levant. More importantly from the perspective of the international community it holds the prospect of demonstrating the material rewards of Arab-Israeli peace. Many of those rewards will come automatically, as a more peaceful environment encourages more visitors and stimulates private sector investment in tourism facilities. In addition, there are a variety of ways in which government action and donor assistance could further encourage tourism.[2]

A few years after the triumphant signature of the Wadi Araba Treaty, though, it became apparent to most Jordanians that the expected economic benefits of peace would prove meager. Regional trade and economic cooperation across the Jordan River have since remained limited and steps towards the normalisation of relations with Israel continue to face vocal opposition from elements in Jordanian society. As one former peace negotiator declared, 'The model of peace to which we aspired would achieve improved living conditions, mainly through increased trade with our neighbours. This hasn't happened, and this is why the anti-peace camp is now having a heyday.'[3]

The failure of the peace process to 'achieve improved living conditions' in Jordan is most evident in the tourism sector. A few years after the boom and bust cycle, which was experienced immediately after the treaty was signed, few in the tourism industry still looked at economic cooperation with Israel as the answer to the sector's woes while most expressed disappointment about the meager economic benefits generated by peace. The experience of tourism between Israel and Jordan in the wake of peace represents a challenge to the theory that peaceful relations between states can be promoted through projects of economic cooperation which generate mutual material gains, foster personal contact between peoples and increase links of interdependence. While external factors, such as political events in Israel or the frugal spending habits and improper behaviour of Israeli tourists in Jordan, are often blamed as the cause of the failure of economic cooperation in the tourism sector, such arguments overlook the domestic political factors which shaped tourism development patterns in Jordan.

This chapter argues that while tourism development in the wake of peace offered opportunities for some entrepreneurs in Jordan, the economic benefits of tourism did not 'come automatically' as Clawson and other advocates of the New Middle East vision had suggested they would. Tourism development has been difficult to sustain in the context of an increasingly complex global tourism economy without adequate public and private institutions for its promotion. This analysis contends that, nevertheless, the state's ability to represent the peace process as leading to a tourism development boom which could readily provide material benefits for broad segments of the Jordanian population helped King Hussain move rapidly towards making peace with Israel in 1994 in the face of much potential domestic opposition. Without the ability to represent tourism as a vehicle for generating material rewards from peace, political opposition to the treaty and the government would likely have developed sooner and spread more widely throughout the population. Through a close reading of the official discourse surrounding the peace process and Jordan's specific tourism development plans, the analysis will show that this misrepresentation of the dynamics that govern tourism economies contributed to inadequate state policies for tourism promotion and led to misguided entrepreneurial strategies by much of the private sector. In

particular, it led many Jordanians to seek to exploit short term opportunities by rapidly commodifying Jordanian geography and cultural heritage while being unable to build institutional mechanisms
for monitoring and promoting the demand for their products within
the global tourism economy.

Imagining the 'New Middle East'

In the wake of the 1992 Oslo Accords between Israel and the Palestinian Liberation Organisation a new expression began to enter the diplomatic lexicon. Politicians, political analysts and think-tank policy
papers began to re-imagine the political economy of the Middle East
through the lens of the 'New Middle East'. This vision was most em-
phatically articulated by Israel's foreign minister and peace negotiator Shimon Peres. In a 1993 book, *The New Middle East,* Peres laid
out a far-reaching plan for the future of regional integration and economic cooperation across the Middle East.[4] He called for 'a New
Middle East following a European plan: economic cooperation first,
followed by increasing, ongoing political understanding until stability
was achieved'.[5] This form of economic cooperation was expected to
lead to a remapping of Middle Eastern political identities. Replacing
the antagonistic nationalist identities of Arab and Zionist, Peres argued that the Middle East now has 'a common enemy: poverty' which
is 'the father of fundamentalism'.[6] Peres sought to forge a new regional post-nationalist logic for Middle East politics defined by supporters of 'peace' and the New Middle East on one side and, in his
view, by fundamentalists and terrorists on the other side.

In Peres's vision, tourism played a key role as a means to begin
stitching the economies of the Middle East together. 'Tourism', he
writes, is 'one of the most important resources of the sun-soaked
Middle East'.[7] He called for the building of an expansive tourism and
recreation infrastructure along a 'Red Sea to Dead Sea canal', joint
regional tourism projects and a major airport along the 'Gulf of Eilat'
serving Israel, Jordan, Egypt and Saudi Arabia. Claiming that 'violence' had been the main barrier to tourism development in the region, he stretched his enthusiasm for tourism to suggest that 'A
flourishing and stable tourist industry is also good for stability –
equal in importance to an international police force.'[8] He went even
further: 'Today, more than ever, the measure of a country's strength
is not how many troops it has but how many tourists.'[9] Most critical
to the argument presented below, Shimon Peres confidently noted that
tourism 'is an important industry, which can, *in a relatively short time,*
generate profits and create employment opportunities'.[10] Even Arabs

who were sceptical of the other elements of Peres's vision often agreed with this one last point.

The logic of the peace treaty in Jordan

The logic of the New Middle East looked different from the other side of the Jordan River. Having alienated itself from its former Gulf allies and with Iraq remaining under siege, Jordan in the early 1990s was seeking to reposition itself in the emerging regional order dominated by the United States and its eastern Mediterranean allies, Israel and Turkey.[11] The King's choice to conclude a peace treaty with Israel rapidly was most likely driven by the desire to maximise Jordan's future strategic interests in this emerging environment. Peres's New Middle East vision from this perspective might be read as a liberal gloss over a realist alliance framework through which Jordan sought increased military support and economic payoffs from the United States.

Following Laurie Brand's argument that, for Jordan, 'budget security' is often the defining motivation behind foreign policy choices, most commentators on the peace treaty have emphasised how the potential economic rewards of peace shaped Jordan's interest in the treaty.[12] These views suggest that Jordan's expectation of economic rewards in the wake of peace made the option of peace more attractive and made the selling of peace easier domestically. However, the critical question in assessing the influence of economic incentives on the peace process is to ask where the economic gains were going to come from and how they were going to be disbursed. Jordan's quickest material rewards from a peace deal were expected to consist of aid and debt relief from the United States, but while a peace with Israel was generally understood as the American condition for these, 'both sides publicly deny there was a *quid pro quo*.'[13] The Jordanian government could not publicly defend the treaty by pointing to concrete material rewards from a definite source. Furthermore, under International Monetary Fund (IMF) imposed austerity measures and pressures for economic privatisation and liberalisation, debt relief and aid would not have enabled the state to expand public sector employment, increase consumer subsidies and rebuild and sustain the old political patronage systems.

Thus, while aid and debt relief were critically needed by Jordan's fragile economy, the political implication of the expected economic rewards of peace played out in a more complex way. In his effort to craft a constructivist reading of Jordan's foreign policy, Marc Lynch faults what he terms 'rationalist' readings of Jordan's foreign policy which assume Jordan's national interests are objective and fixed. He argues that such analyses ignore '. . . the importance of identity and public deliberation in producing state interests.'[14] In this vein Lynch suggests that the choice of the peace option was not determined by an economic calculation but that '. . . the economic rewards were more of a public sphere justification strategy than a major cause' of the peace treaty.[15] By this he means the public discourse over the economic rewards can be viewed as part of an effort to publicly redefine Jordan's national interests and identity. In particular this meant a disengagement from Arab nationalist and Palestinian concerns and an embrace of closer integration into the global economy. Additionally, the official public discourse supporting the New Middle East vision can be understood as an effort to evoke a 'substantive change in norms and institutions' in Jordan. 'As Prince Hassan often explained', Lynch notes, 'a Middle East Market could allow Jordan to break its dependence upon foreign aid and turn its particular combination of human capital, close ties to Israel, and poor natural endowments to its long term economic advantage.'[16]

Along with this reconstruction of Jordan's political economy which would redefine its identity and interests, Jordan's support of the New Middle East vision developed as part of a process of reformulating the regime's political survival strategy. In the late 1980s Jordan began a controlled political opening which was widely viewed as driven by declines in rentier incomes such as remittances and aid from the Gulf.[17] Political liberalisation was used, in part, as a means to temper the critical political reaction to the imposition of economic austerity measures. In the 1990s, though, operating in a context of more open political discourse the King's policy of pursuing a rapid peace treaty with Israel risked fostering domestic political opposition which now had a more open press and parliament as vehicles for dissent. Jordan's entry into the peace process signaled another shift in the state's survival strategy, this time de-emphasising political openness[18] and focusing on broad-based national economic development as a basis of political stability and regime legitimacy. What was most critical for the government about the expected economic rewards from peace was that the New Middle East model would establish the foundation for a new economic development strategy for the kingdom which would provide material benefits to wide segments of the population.

Selling peace, tourism and the 'New Middle East' in Jordan

While not highly publicised at the time, it was understood in many quarters that the material rewards from the treaty would not come quickly and even debt relief and aid from the United States might be drawn out over a few years. These would be inadequate to publicly justify the peace, especially in the short term. For example, delivering a speech written by Prince Hassan to the Middle East Policy Council in Washington, Dr Jawad al-Anani, a key figure in both the peace process and economic development issues in Jordan, acknowledged that indeed, according to a World Bank report,[19] Jordan's national income and state revenues would probably drop in the first years after a peace deal. Liberalising trade, for example, would mean lowering tariffs and this would mean a decrease in government revenues and in most sectors Jordan's economy was far outmatched by Israel's. The World Bank report even notes that Jordan's underdeveloped tourism facilities would make it very difficult to compete with Israel and Egypt. Dr. al-Anani thus suggested that Jordan would first have to invest heavily 'in roads and infrastructure and hotels and restaurants' before the gains could be realised.[20] His remarks, though, also demonstrate how many officials thought that Jordan would be able to depend on the tourism sector to get through the difficult transitional phase: '[So,] what we're doing, we're doing like sometimes shopkeepers [do], looking for things which can generate cash, like encouraging tourism, you know. There is ready money there.'[21]

With few other options, the prospect of a boost in national income initiated by expansive tourism development in Jordan became the linchpin for the state's 'public sphere justification strategy.' This strategy was bolstered, as noted above, by the widely held view in the international community that 'Tourism . . . holds the prospect of demonstrating the material rewards of Arab-Israeli peace.'[22] This view became manifest in the large contributions of American, European and Japanese aid to support tourism development planning and antiquities preservation. Most critically, the tourism sector was envisioned as being able, *in the short term*, to provide the national economy with tangible economic benefits from the peace. Thus not only would peace bring the state additional debt relief, aid, hard currency and tourist fee revenues, but by linking the expansion of tourism so closely with the advance of the peace process in the official public discourse, peace could be represented as offering benefits broadly to anyone willing to take advantage of the opportunity. Tourism, furthermore, was thought to be one of the few economic activities that, under the new regime of economic liberalisation, the Jordanian state could centrally manage as a sector of the national economy. Additionally, state-owned national resources such as coastal land and national heritage sites could provide new sources of state revenue. Allowing the state to control and direct the economic benefits of tourism would increase the state's bureaucratic powers and secure its supply of hard currency.

The arguments for realising the economic gains of peace through tourism development were expressed early in the peace process. On 23 November 1993 in a speech to the parliament concerning the peace process broadcast on Jordanian TV, King Hussain stated that the government would support the development of tourism facilities. He noted: 'This should increase economic returns in a manner that would support the balance of payments, replenish the treasury's hard currency reserves, augment the economic growth rate and ex-pand the gross national product.' He made particular reference to the private sector which 'would have a major role to play in tourist development' and would be encouraged 'through incentive expanding investment, streamlined procedures and tourist development legislation'.[23]

In addition to the announcement of the opening of border crossings with Israel the Jordanian government pledged a massive tourism in-frastructure plan and began drawing up a series of tax incentives for foreign and local investors in the sector.[24] To promote investment nu-merous press conferences were held announcing the expected growth of tourism in the country. For example, in August 1994 at the Dead Sea the Minister of Tourism with his Israeli counterpart announced a plan for twenty new investment projects as he predicted a prosperous tourism industry in the coming years. 'You know', he said, 'tourism is a peace industry, [it] flourishes always within a peaceful environ-ment that is based on stability and security. And we believe that all parties in the region . . . will benefit greatly once peace is achieved.'[25] Tourism planning documents spelled out in detail the state's visions for tourism development on a massive scale and explained: 'The 6.3 per cent annual growth in hotel rooms over the past 10 years is pre-dicted to increase dramatically, along with the average occupancy rate of 65 per cent and the current average daily room rate of $86.'[26] More dramatically, the Jordan Valley Authority's *Dead Sea Master Plan* (1994, revised 1996) explained that based on projected tourism flows:

This set of potentialities places the development planning approach in the po-sition of [a] 'supply strategy'; in other words, the essential parameters [for planning tourism development growth] stem rather from the Study Area bearing capacity, within, naturally, 'a sustainable development concept', than from any potential market appraisal![27]

The official effort to publicly promote tourism investment gained its great-est exposure with the plans prepared by the Ministry of Planning and pre-sented under the eyes of the world media at the 1994 and 1995 Middle East and North Africa (MENA) summits in Casablanca and Amman. In addition to an Aqaba 'Peace' airport, numerous fantastic, coordinated Jordanian-Israeli projects were officially announced at these meetings and other press conferences. Driven by international investment, the realisation of Peres's New Middle East vision would leave the Israeli-Jordanian border across the Wadi Araba and the Jordan River as well as the Gulf of Aqaba dotted with deluxe hotels, amusement parks, and even a multifunctional John the Baptist baptism pool and conference center. These developments were all to be connected by super highways across the desert and concrete promenades along the shores.[28]

In the wake of peace

Soon after the border crossings with Israel were opened there was a massive flood of Israeli as well as North American and European tourists. Driven by curiosity and the almost mythic aura that Petra had acquired, Israeli tourism expanded from officially zero before 1994 to over 100,000 in 1995. European and American tourist arrivals grew by 75 per cent from 204,000 over the whole of 1993 to 359,000 over the course of the year 1995. Most notably, package tourism shot up from 440,000 to 1,141,000 over the same period while total visitors to Petra rose from about 40,000 during 1991 Gulf War ebb to 200,000 in 1994 and then jumped to 330,000 in 1995 and to 414,000 in 1996.[29]

The explosion of tourism visitors in 1994 and 1995 led to previously unheard levels of overbooking at hotels while all other aspects of the industry, such as bus lines and rental car agencies, quickly faced acute shortages. The occupancy rate of hotels classified as 5-star deluxe went from an average of 42 per cent in 1993 to 66 per cent over the course of 1995. Well-established hotels like the Inter-Continental in Amman were often experiencing occupancy rates of over 90 per cent.

In the midst of this tourism boom, local investors were quick to expand, often haphazardly, Jordan's tourism capacity. These new opportunities stirred the Jordanian private sector at all levels. Tourism development was being promoted as a means to stimulate national growth, not simply to benefit the firms already working in the sector. The economic potential of tourism development seemed to hold out potential opportunities for almost anyone regardless of skill, profession, or even capital endowment while avoiding the question of the limits or distribution of these gains. Everyone interested, it seemed, could imagine a way to profit from the new influx of tourists. The wealthy merchant and banking families could exploit these new opportunities as could the tribes of Wadi Musa, the former workers in the Gulf now driving cabs in the wealthy sections of Western Amman and the souvenir hawkers in the poorer areas of Amman's downtown. In particular, the rural Transjordanian regions in the south and along the Jordan River in the north, which were badly hurt by the austerity programmes, were expected to benefit by direct government efforts at fostering regional development schemes centered around tourism. Tourism was also thought to be able to benefit most segments of the Palestinian population which dominated the private sector from the assimilated bourgeoisie elites to the lower middle class shop owners. Unlike other forms of private sector development, it seemed the benefits of tourism could potentially be spread widely down the class ladder and regionally across the whole imagined national community of Jordan.

Whilst most local smaller investors in the tourism sector, as well as a few larger ones, had little previous experience in the industry, Jordanian investments in tourism were soon spurred by growing confidence in the future of the tourism market. Few relied on previous experience or direct knowledge of the international tourism market in making their investment choices. As more and more Jordanians began to open tourism-related businesses this led others to rush to get their facilities built in order to beat their competitors to the profits. At a time when the economy was weak and there appeared to be few other opportunities, news stories about the Jordanian economy in both the local and international press singled out tourism as, for example, '. . . the one industry that is expected to see a major boom in the next five to ten years.'[30]

As a result of these investments from 1993 to 1996 the number of hotel beds in Jordan expanded 68 per cent from 13,500 to 22,700. Over the same period the number of rental car offices expanded from only 75 in 1993 to 237 in 1996, while the number of rental cars tripled as nearly did the number of tourist guides in the country. The area around Petra experienced some of the most rapid and extensive changes. In just days after the peace treaty many residents were at work converting their existing apartments into make-shift hotels. Soon big developers from Amman were buying up expensive plots of land with grand visions of tourist palaces. At a cost of $70 million to $80 million in the two years after the peace treaty the hotel capacity in Petra/Wadi Musa had quadrupled to 2,000 rooms while land values skyrocketed.

This boom, though, was not to last. As soon became clear, the general public greatly misjudged the effects of peace on the tourism economy. Even without the turn to the right in Israel and the continued siege of Iraq, the tourism explosion was unlikely to keep up this radical pace for long even though government commissioned plans and the few investors who drew up feasibility studies often assumed that it would. While tourism receipts in 1995 and 1996 grew by over 14 per cent (in nominal terms), in 1997 they grew only 4 per cent. Hotel occupancy rates for all hotels went from 46 per cent in 1995 back down to 38 per cent in 1997. In Petra, combining a drop in tourism with an expansion of capacity the highs and lows are more extreme, going from almost 62 per cent in 1994 then dropping to 31 per cent in 1997. Furthermore, open borders with Israel, which allowed for package tours to easily travel from Israel to Jordan and back, had an unexpected result. As borders literally fell off the tourism maps,[31] most Western tourists experienced 'regional tourism' in the Middle East by visiting Jordan as adjunct day trip from Israel. As a result, while Petra saw more visitors, Jordanian hotels, tour operators, and airlines were often by-passed. Overall the average length of stay for package tours decreased from five nights in the 1989–94 period to 3.7 nights in the 1995–7 period.[32] As one Jordanian economist put it 'Hotels, tourist buses and travel agencies are real and sad examples of how parts of the economy went on an investment binge in 1995, only to come down to earth with a thud a year later and then start to wallow in a depression which continues.'[33]

We should note here that tourism did not die out in Jordan and in recent years government figures have shown renewed growth in the number of tourist arrivals. But these numbers do not reflect the changing value of the tourism product and the economic costs of tourism development efforts which took place in the immediate wake of the peace treaty. The over-development of similar products and the high fluctuations in tourism inflows has led to destructive competition, downward price spirals and wasted resources, not to mention dashed hopes. For many in the hotel sector the over-capacity of supply and the desperate quest for revenues has made paying back loans impossible while eroding their efforts to improve the quality of their products and services. This has also prevented the development of robust linkages to the small and informal businesses associated with tourism. After a law eliminated the government monopoly in the tour bus sector, the number of tour buses expanded greatly. But with the downturn in tourism, tour bus operators began facing such ruinous oversupply that they formed a cartel to keep a floor on prices. This cartel system has since become a subject of anti-trust legislation in parliament. As for travel agents and tour operators, many have had to shut their doors a few years after opening while the ones that remain face stiff competition. The impact is even being felt by outgoing Jordanian tourists, the *Jordan Times* reports, since 'strained economic conditions seem to be compelling some tour operators to skip on their promises to their clients'.[34]

Rethinking tourism development

Tourism development in the wake of the peace process resulted in the unsustainable over-commodification of the tourism landscape where creating tourist products (such as hotel rooms, handicrafts and cultural experiences) proved easier and more accessible to local entrepreneurs than attempting to coordinate and ensure demand for such products. This was made possible by the promotion of a strategy of national tourism development – beginning with the negotiation of the peace deal and represented in tourism development plans – where firms were encouraged to imagine potentially unlimited markets for tourism products and to invest considerably to meet those markets. The state, in the process of selling the peace deal, became the central marketer of information for these firms. In granting licences for hotel developments and announcing infrastructure projects the state was presenting the private sector with a certain type of 'market' information. At the same time, the state was producing tourism figures, projections and plans which touted tourism as the new 'oil' on the national economy.[35] Driven by unwarranted optimism and the political imperative of over-promoting tourism development as a means to capture the economic rewards of peace, state agencies and state plans lacked an accurate vision of what the tourism economy would look like from the vantage point of the individual private firms in the tourism sector.

It is useful to contrast these experiences with an example of a tourism firm which has been able to develop mechanisms to coordinate and ensure the demand for such products. Some of the larger tourism firms in Jordan, such as those owned by Zara Tourism Investments, use hotel management companies (such as Movenpick, Inter-Continental and Hyatt) which allow their hotels to draw on the vast marketing networks of these global corporations. Carefully constructed management contracts often require these hotel operators to attain a certain total gross revenue in order to earn their management fees. Additionally, Zara has created its own backward and forward linkages by starting, for example, an engineering consulting firm specialising in building hotels, as well as a Dead Sea products company which stocks the gift shops in Zara-owned hotels. Such linkages are often viewed by tourism planners as vital mechanisms through which the economic benefits of tourism are able to spread to other sectors of the economy. But often, instead of generating opportunities for independent entrepreneurs, these linkages are formed through vertical and horizontal integration within complexes of tourism firms owned by the same set of investors. This limits the scope of the economic benefits gained from tourism and shuts out those who lack the capital and skills to conduct such strategies. This result is the reverse image of what the peace process was suppose to produce. Instead of providing an engine of national economic growth which leads to increased standards of living throughout the population, this process has led to the development of luxury tourism enclaves governed by a narrow tourism elite. The irony is that this 'tourism bourgeoisie' is often derided as a parasitic 'rentier class' but in fact they benefit not by capturing rents but because they have the skills, capital, and access to market information which most smaller firms lack.

What can the state do to assist smaller firms to better understand and adjust to market conditions? One attempt at an answer is the Jordan Tourism Board (JTB) as envisioned in the early 1990s by the United States Agency for International Development (USAID). Even before the peace process was completed USAID had drawn up plans to establish the JTB as a privately run (but partly government-financed) organisation to market Jordan as a tourism destination overseas. The tasks of the board were to include, among other things, the development of market intelligence capabilities in order to monitor trends and developments in the international tourism market. It was to serve as a link between international markets and local tourism firms. It was to help these firms with theme promotion, brochure development and market interruption strategies.[36] The formation of the JTB, though, became mired in politics. The USAID, the ministry of tourism and various private sector representatives spent years sorting out the funding and governance mechanism of the JTB. USAID preferred that the JTB have joint private and public funding but be privately managed. In the end, though, the Jordanian authorities fearing that it would become a slush fund for private agents, refused to give it this sort of decentralised autonomy. After a series of unsuccessful meetings USAID abruptly pulled out of this project as well as all their other tourism development efforts. The ministry of tourism eventually established the JTB on its own terms. But without the funding, strong private sector leadership and skilled staff originally envisioned by the USAID plan, the JTB for years was able to do little more than represent Jordan at tourism trade fairs. While the JTB has vastly expanded its capabilities and functions since, this came too late to help the sector through the boom and bust cycle in the wake of the peace treaty.

In order to best translate future tourism inflows into broad-based economic development, agencies such as the Jordan Tourism Board and the Jordan Hotel Association should work towards helping firms acquire the market knowledge and technical skills needed to find and exploit links to appropriate markets. Doing this does not require large-scale master planning which often proves problematic in such a volatile tourism economy, but does require a 'firm-centred' approach where the different needs and abilities of a diverse range of firms are catered for.

There is, though, another method for public agencies to help firms find such market opportunities which does not require these agencies to possess superior market knowledge. Drawing on Albert Hirschman's theory of 'unbalanced growth' Charles Sabel suggests a method for public agencies to help firms find such market opportunities by inducing what he calls *disequilibrium learning*. In this model, the state, 'instigates the firms to set goals with reference to some prevailing standard so that shortfalls in performance are apparent to those with the incentive and capacity to remedy them – [that is] the firms themselves – and new targets are set accordingly.'[37] In other words, in exchange for committing to this process of self-improvement leading to producing goods that are competitive in the international market the state offers various forms of inducements, subsidies, or protection such as providing access to public land or providing public goods to these firms.

One ongoing example in Jordan which comes close to this model is the Royal Society for the Conservation of Nature's (RSCN) ecotourism project at Dana Nature Reserve. The RSCN was given management authority over a protected area of government land. While the objective of the Dana Reserve was primarily the preservation of biodiversity, as part of the project the RSCN developed a tourism unit which built a low impact camp site with tents, a guest house and a number of walking trails. The objective of this project was to generate income and jobs for the local community including people displaced or who had their livelihoods impinged upon by the establishment of the nature reserve on their grazing land. Such a project would not have been possible without the state granting the land and authority to the RSCN and without the World Bank granting funding. But these resources were granted conditionally. The project has been required to show progress on certain performance standards (economic, social and environmental) in order to retain World Bank funding and government support. After a few years of operation the tourism unit has steadily increased its self-generated income stream to the point of covering 100 per cent of the reserve's running costs. Critical to the project's success was institutional capacity building efforts which established procedures for task design, implementation, and evaluation. The project developed links to tour operators interested in eco-tourism as well as drew on the local tourism market. By linking the eco-tourism project to the local production and national marketing of items such as jams and handicrafts they even created a 'brand' name which is used to promote their products by associating these handicrafts and jams with the cause of environmental awareness and nature appreciation represented by 'the Dana logo.' This project has genuinely created a new market in Jordan for a previously little known commodity, nature tourism, and turned a biodiversity project into a viable business model with exemplary organisational and operational methods.[38]

Such a strategy could work in the rest of the tourism sector where access to land, building licences, skill training, tax breaks and market information can be exchanged for state monitoring of firm performance on a number of indices. In doing so, the state could seek to limit rent-seeking, over-capacity and low quality standards in the tourism sector. This would require limiting entry into the market of firms unwilling or unable to seek to match a set of rolling performance standards as well as helping firms which exhibit the ability to improve themselves over time. Along with this, other criteria – such as upholding environmental standards or requiring the local hiring and training of employees – could be enforced by giving firms positive incentives. Politically, though, this would have been difficult in the context of the selling of New Middle East vision as a means to quickly reap material rewards from the peace. Instead of simply opening borders and then attempting to extract rents from day tourists (such as through the high Petra gate charge), Jordan could use similar disequilibrium learning techniques to regulate international and Israeli tour operators. Regional cooperation could be reestablished by implementing such regulatory institutions and techniques on a regional basis. As tourism firms across the Middle East develop equivalent standards and methods of operation, tourism would flow better across borders as would market information and, more critically, firm-to-firm ties would increase leading to mutual economic gains.

NOTES

1. Research for this project was funded by the American Center for Oriental Research in Amman, Jordan. The author also thanks Michelle Woodward for a careful reading of this chapter.
2. P. Clawson, 'Tourism Cooperation in the Levant', *Washington Institute Policy Focus*, Research Memorandum no. 26 (May 1994), p. 7.
3. See A. Henderson, 'Jordanian-Israeli peace treaty: Mixed bag of success, failure',

Jordan Times, 30 November 1999.

4.   New York: Henry Holt.
5.   Peres, *The New Middle East*, p. 11. Exclaiming that 'the Middle East needs a Jean
     Monnet approach today' (p. 71), Peres explicitly modeled his vision after post-
     World War II visions of Europe which led to the formation of the European Eco-
     nomic Community. His vision echoes the thinking of the liberal 'integration' the-
     orists of the 1950s and 1960s. See D. Puchala, 'The Integration Theorists and
     the Study of International Relations' in C. W. W. Kegley Jr and E. R. Wittkopf
     (eds), *The Global Agenda: Issues and Perspectives*, New York: Random House,
     2nd edn, 1998, pp. 198–215.
6.   Peres, *The New Middle East*, p. 72.
7.   Ibid., p. 149, see also pp. 150–3.
8.   Peres, *The New Middle East*, p. 74.
9.   S. Peres, *Battling For Peace: A Memoir*, New York: Random House, 1995, p.
     199.
10. Peres, *The New Middle East*; p. 74 (emphasis added).
11. See M. Mufti, 'Jordanian Foreign Policy: State Interests and Dynastic Ambi-
     tions', a paper presented at the '*Politique et Etat en Jordanie, 1946–96*', confer-
     ence, Institut du Monde Arabe, Paris, 24–25 June 1997, pp. 19–20, and C. Ryan,
     'Jordan in the Middle East Peace Process: From War to Peace with Israel' in Ilan
     Peleg (ed.) *The Middle East Peace Process: interdisciplinary perspectives*, Albany:
     State University of New York Press, 1998, pp. 162–6.
12. L. Brand, *Jordan's Inter-Arab Relations: The Political Economy of Alliance Mak-
     ing*, New York: Columbia University Press, 1994, pp. 295–7; C. Ryan, 'Jordan
     in the Middle East Peace Process'; pp. 166–7; and S. Zunes, 'The Israeli-Jordanian
     Agreement: Peace or *Pax Americana*?', *Middle East Policy* 3,4 (April 1998).
13. Zunes, 'The Israeli-Jordanian Agreement', pp. 60–1.
14. M. Lynch, *State Interests and Public Spheres: The International Politics of Jor-
     dan's Identity* , New York: Columbia University Press, 1999, p. 167.
15. Ibid., p. 179.
16. Ibid., p. 180.
17. L. A. Brand, 'Economic and Political Liberalisation in a Rentier Economy: The
     Case of the Hashemite Kingdom of Jordan' in I. Harik and D. J. Sullivan (eds),
     Privatisation and Liberalisation in the Middle East, Bloomington: Indiana Uni-
     versity Press, 1992, pp. 210–32, and R. Brynen, 'Economic Crisis And Post-rentier
     Democratisation in The Arab World: The Case of Jordan', *Canadian Journal of
     Political Science*, 25, 1 (March 1992), pp. 69–97.
18. Laurie Brand argues that the developments in the peace process led directly to re-
     treats in the political liberalisation process, see 'The Effects of the Peace Process
     on Political Liberalisation in Jordan', *Journal of Palestine Studies* 28, 2 (winter
     1999), pp. 52–67.
19. *Peace and the Jordanian Economy*, Washington DC, 1994.
20. El Hassan bin Talal, 'Jordan and the Peace Process', *Middle East Policy* 3, 3
     (1994), p. 39.
21. Reported by the Federal News Service, 26 September 1994. The transcript is rep-
     rinted in a slightly altered form in *Middle East Policy* 3, 3 (1994), p. 39.
22. Clawson, 'Tourism Cooperation in the Levant', p. 7.
23. BBC Summary of World Broadcasts, 25 November 1993.
24. See Hashemite Kingdom of Jordan, 'Tourism Infrastructure', and Industrial Pro-
     motion Corporation, 'Investment Promotion Law' no. 16 for 1995, Regulation
     no. 1 of 1996, and Regulation 2 of 1996.
25. Radio Jordan broadcast in English, 17 August 1994, transcribed in *BBC Sum-*

mary of World Broadcasts, 19 August 1994.

26. Hashemite Kingdom of Jordan, 'Tourism Infrastructure', 1995.
27. Jordan Valley Authority, *Tourism Development Project of the East Coast of the Dead Sea (SPy)*, part 4: *Market Evaluation & Assessment, Suweimeh & Zara Development Areas*, Amman, 1996, p. 22.
28. The following documents are revised versions of the official government schemes presented at the 1994 MENA summit in Casablanca: Government of Israel, *Development Options for Cooperation: The Middle East/East Mediterranean Region: 1996 Version IV*, Chapter 7 (Ministry of Foreign Affairs, Ministry of Finance); Ministry of Planning, *Jordan: A Winning Business Destinatioy*, Amman: Tourism Sector, 1995.
29. Tourism statistics were gathered from the Ministry of Tourism and Antiquities, Statistical Section. Figures have been rounded off.
30. M. Shahin, 'Defining a nation', *The Middle East*, January 1994, p. 33.
31. See R. L. Stein, 'National Itineraries, Itinerant Nations: Israeli Tourism and Palestinian Cultural Production', *Social Text* no. 56 (fall 1998), pp. 95–7.
32. Cited in N. Barham, 'Tourism in Jordan: Development and perspective', *Jordanies* 5–6 (June–December 1998), p. 132.
33. R. Khouri, 'Bandwagon economics lead nowhere', *Jordan Times*, 23–4 July, 1998.
34. S. Ma'ayeh, 'Shady travel agents cloud meant-to-be sunny holidays', *Jordan Times*, 1–2 September 2000.
35. Ministry of Tourism and Antiquities, Hashimite Kingdom of Jordan and Japan International Cooperation Agency, *The Study on the Tourism Development in the Hashimite Kingdom of Jorday: Final Report*, February 1996, abstract page.
36. USAID, 'Technical Feasibility Studies V Project: Tourism Marketing Strategy' (prepared by Chemonics International, 28 September 1993), p. V-13.
37. C. F. Sabel, 'Learning by Monitoring: The Institutions of Economic Development', in N. Smelser, and R. Swedberg (eds), *Handbook of Economic Sociology*, Princeton, NJ: Sage, p. 149.
38. RSCN 'Conservation of the Dana Wildlands and Institutional Strengthening of the RSCN', Final Report, Amman: The World Bank/UNDP, 1997; K. Irani, and C. Johnson, 'Making it pay: Can community based biodiversity conservation programmes be sustained through market-driven income schemes?' (RSCN), paper prepared for World Bank conference on Community-Based Natural Resource Management, Washington, DC, 10–14 May 1998, and RSCN, *Socio-economic Development for Nature Conservation*, Amman USAID, 2000.

SOCIAL ADAPTIVE CAPACITY TO WATER CRISIS

THE CASE OF JORDAN

Eugenia Ferragina

This chapter seeks to analyse the recent evolution in Jordanian water policy, with an emphasis on the features of persistence and innovation in water management strategies pursued in this sensitive sector of the economy. During the 1960s, the increase in water demand in Jordan – which, apart from natural growth, was also connected to the wave of Palestinian refugees in 1967 – was satisfied by the implementation of huge water projects. Supply management policy also involved the use of non-renewable water resources. Jordanian water policy during this period can best be analysed on the basis of theories proposed by Allan and Karshenas, which link the degree of stock exploitation of environmental resources to the level of economic development.

Towards the end of the 1970s, water policy turned out to be both ecologically unsustainable and economically inefficient. Resource scarcity as a result of increasing demand, emerged as a major problem, leading to the situation which Allan has called importation of 'virtual water'. From the beginning of the 1980s, Jordan was forced to intensify initiatives aimed at improving efficiency in the use of water resources by means of water saving technologies. In recent years, the need to reallocate water from agriculture to service and industrial use has come to be of crucial importance. The water crisis affecting the country calls for radical measures, which the government finds difficult to implement.

Given assumptions of an increase water deficit, the Ministry of Water and Irrigation has planned a comprehensive strategy oriented towards an integrated approach in water resources management. The government is also experimenting a Private Sector Participation Program, which is designed to achieve higher efficiency. The objective in this analysis will be to focus attention on the social and institutional factors that enable Jordan to cope with a situation of water scarcity by introducing the concept of 'social resources scarcity'.

Water resources and supply-demand disparity

Jordan suffers from a particularly unfavourable situation in terms of water resources stock as, given the country's global surface area of 92,500 million square metres, 90 per cent of the territory has less than 200 millimetres of rain per year. The average amount of rainfall per year is about 8,500 million cubic metres, 90 per cent of which evaporates, 5 per cent is lost in surface run-off and only 5 per cent recharges the underground water systems through seepage. As a result of these agro-climatological characteristics, the area for rain-fed agriculture does not exceed 5 per cent of the total surface area.

Jordan can be divided into fifteen surface water drainage basins whose discharges are subject to remarkable seasonal and inter-annual fluctuation (Figure 1).

In 1997 surface resources comprised 328 million cubic metres that is to say 38 per cent of the global water balance of the country, which amounts to 875 million cubic metres (Table 1). The main rivers are the Jordan and its tributaries, the Zarqa and the Yarmouk. Possibilities for the enhancement of the flow of the River Jordan flow are limited because of the massive withdrawal of Lake Tiberias water by Israel. As a result, this reduces the water-flow in the river coming from Lake Tiberias, so that it becomes saline and cannot be used in agriculture.

The Yarmouk River, representing 40 per cent of global surface water, is the main source of surface water in Jordan. In the last few years, as a result of water projects launched by Israel and Syria, the exploitation of this resource by both countries has significantly increased. Jordanian draw-off of Yarmouk water does not exceed 120 million cubic metres per year.

Underground resources are the main source of the country's water provision. It is possible to define twelve main ground water basins, two of which comprise basins with non-renewable (fossil) water (Figure 2). The main fossil water reserve is the groundwater held in the Disi aquifer in the southern area of Jordan's Southern Desert.

In the last years, water exploitation has gone far beyond safe levels for the protection of the groundwater resources. Nowadays, seven ground basins experience over-pumping ranging from 135 per cent to 225 per cent of safe yield levels, while in four others the extraction levels equal safe yield levels.[1] The over-pumping of wells causes a decline in the water table which, in turn, has several adverse effects. It increases the pumping costs and the amount of energy needed for pumping. Moreover, a lowering in water tables reduces pressure in the aquifer with the concomitant danger of polluting fresh water.

Figure 1. JORDAN'S SURFACE WATER BASINS

Source: 'Water Resources Management Policy Reforms for the Hashemite Kingdom of Jordan', *Second Regional Seminar on Policy Reform in Water Resources Management Middle East/North Africa/Mediterranean (MENA/MED) Water Initiative,* The World Bank, Amman, 8–11 May 1999.

Figure 2. JORDAN'S GROUND WATER BASINS

Source: As for Figure 1.

Environmental costs, which are linked to the excessive exploitation of the ground waters, are enormous because they cause a qualitative degradation of the resource and threaten the whole ecosystem.

A classic example of environmental degradation is the oasis of Azraq, which is 80 km. at the south-east of Amman, in the heart of the Azraq basin. The oasis was famous for its palm trees and dates and provided an important habitat for migratory bird species.[2] The area also had a great potential for eco-tourism because of opportunities to develop bird-watching activities, and its links with the Arab Revolt – at one time it was the headquarters of T. E. Lawrence – as well as its closeness to the Umayyad desert palaces were a further attraction.

The exploitation of ground water there, which started in the 1960s, expanded until 1990 in order to satisfy the increasing demand for water in Jordan's capital, Amman, causing, in consequence, the drying up of the springs that fed the wetland.[3] In 1990 the Jordanian government fixed a maximum limit for ground water exploitation there and the Global Environmental Fund of the United Nation Development Program (UNDP) allocated $3.3 million for five small-scale projects over a three year period. UNDP opted for water harvesting projects – the building of small dams for water storage where the land is permeable so as to supply the ground water resource. The aim was to stop the environmental degradation and to exploit the water resources of the basin by preserving the oasis and the unique bio-diversity that characterises the area on a long-term basis. However, as often occurs, the damage caused to the ecosystem is largely irreversible. In spite of the interventions designed to restore the ecological balance, ecological conditions have continued to deteriorate. Unlicensed wells have continued to cause an excess abstraction of ground waters near the oasis and, in addition, the projects launched by UNDP did not achieve the expected results.[4]

The use of treated wastewater is now very important for the national water balance. The first treatment plant was constructed in Amman in 1968. Since then, fourteen other wastewater treatment plants have been established in the country. Wastewater is not directly used for irrigation, but is mixed with irrigation water before use, mainly in the Jordan Valley. Treated wastewater volumes reached 60 million cubic metres in 1997 and very large increases are expected in future.

A weak element in Jordan's water situation is the lack of storage basins on its territory. These are vital for collecting water during wintertime, for use in summer.[5] Another factor contributing to the current water emergency is the lack of inter-connection between those areas where ground waters are located and those where there is a high

Table 1. Jordan's Annual Water Budget, 1985–97

	Municipal		Industrial		Irrigation		Livestock		Total
	(MCM)	%	(MCM)	%	(MCM)	%	(MCM)	%	(MCM)
1985	116.00	18.2	22.00	3.4	496.85	77.8	4.00	0.6	638.85
1986	134.70	21.8	23.00	3.7	456.24	73.7	5.00	0.8	618.94
1987	150.40	20.2	23.50	3.2	565.46	76.0	5.00	0.7	744.36
1988	164.70	20.2	39.22	4.8	607.91	74.4	4.77	0.6	816.60
1989	169.77	20.4	36.30	4.4	618.35	74.5	5.92	0.7	830.34
1990	175.57	20.2	36.64	4.2	652.03	75.0	5.26	0.6	869.49
1991	173.23	20.8	41.83	5.0	613.19	73.6	4.82	0.6	833.05
1992	206.64	21.7	34.78	3.7	700.47	73.7	8.84	0.9	950.73
1993	213.54	21.7	33.25	3.4	726.44	73.9	10.35	1.1	983.58
1994	215.82	23.7	24.45	2.7	655.25	72.1	13.32	1.5	908.84
1995	239.85	27.3	32.57	3.7	596.33	67.9	9.46	1.1	878.21
1996	236.36	26.8	35.76	4.1	597.87	67.8	11.79	1.3	881.77
1997	235.63	26.9	37.24	4.3	597.87	67.6	11.11	1.3	875.66

Source: 'Water Resources Management Policy Reforms for the Hashemite Kingdom of Jordan',
*Second Regional Seminar on Policy Reform in Water Resources Management Middle East/North
Africa/Mediterranean (MENA/MED) Water Initiative*, The World Bank, Amman, 8–11 May 1999.

level of water consumption. The Disi water basin – the main ground water reserve in the country – is located 300 kilometres away from the Amman conurbation and this has a considerable influence on the transport costs of water.[6]

The only possibility for Jordan to cope with its water supply imbalance, both over time in terms of location, is to create a major storage basin for Yarmouk river water. This was the national objective originally set for the Maqarin dam, a Syrian-Jordanian project which highlighted the difficulties of setting up cooperation agreements over domestic water use in the area. This dam project has encountered considerable opposition from Israel because of its fear of reductions in rate of flow in the river Jordan as a consequence of increased withdrawals from the Yarmouk river.[7]

Today Jordan has to confront a water deficit, which is the result of an expanding gap between water demand by a constantly growing population, which increases at 3.6 per cent per year and a water supply that has reached its environmental and economic limits. The global amount of water required is now close to one billion cubic metres per year and goes far beyond the present water availability at some 875 million cubic metres a year. The deficit is covered through abstraction from ground water resources – with a rate of abstraction in excess of the safe yield levels – and by exploiting non-renewable water resources. In the near future Jordan will be forced to increase the use of non-conventional water resources, such as desalinated brackish water or seawater.

The consequence of this situation is that there is a very limited and declining amount of water resources available on a per capita basis. The per capita consumption will decrease from 170 cubic metres at present to 91 cubic metres by 2025. According to the World Bank classification system, which considers the minimum level of water availability per capita to be equal to 1,000 cubic metres per year, Jordan is already experiencing a situation of absolute water scarcity. The water deficit is a natural constraint on economic development and a factor for social backwardness which, in turn, could influence political stability.

Jordanian water policy

Jordan's water policy has suffered from continuous adjustments as a result of emergency situations that have arisen in the country. So far, an integrated approach to the management of water resources, which would reflect the economic, political and social dimensions of water policy has been neglected.

A primary factor which has affected the relationship between population and resources within the country has certainly been the influx of Palestinian refugees during the most active phases of the Arab-Israeli conflict. The first wave took place immediately after the creation of the state of Israel in 1948, when some 500,000 Palestinian refugees moved into Jordan. A new wave of immigration, involving about 400,000 people took place in 1967 after the loss of the West Bank. In 1991 there was a final wave of refugees after the occupation of Kuwait that came via and from Iraq. The Second Gulf War led to the eviction of around 400,000 Palestinian and Jordanian workers from the Gulf.

These continuous immigration flows into a country that, even today, only has 4.5 million inhabitants has intensified economic and social imbalances that were already there, not least because of where they settled. In fact, the flows are concentrated in the Amman-Zarqa-Wadi Sir conurbation. This urban area has expanded in a spontaneous way and without any form of urban planning, creating a very strong pressure on water resources. In addition, the concentration of population in the north of the country has penalised the south in terms of investment and development priorities.[8]

During the 1960s, Jordan developed its most significant component of the country's water infrastructure, the East Ghor Canal, as well as other projects including dams and storage basins. The aim of water policy then was to provide water for agriculture purposes. The emphasis was placed on agriculture because, apart from food production, the agricultural sector had at that time a great importance in terms of social consensus in support of the government, employment and the control of the rural population exodus. Water, where the price was kept artificially low thanks to subsidies, played the role of social stabiliser and agricultural promotion during an important phase of the transformation of the Jordanian economy.

In this context, the construction of dams and storage basins was simply designed to satisfy the consequent increase in water demand. The major water projects – financed by the United States and the international institutions were instituted at this time to improve the rural assets of the Jordan Valley. They encouraged irrigated agriculture rather than the traditional forms of rain-fed agriculture such as cereal cultivation. As a result, during this period, Jordan experienced growing imports of cereals and dependence on external funds so that the construction of its water infrastructures could be implemented.[9]

The supply side policy also created conflict between objectives concerned with water resources development and environmental protection. Technological progress made it possible to pump from deeper levels, as did declining energy costs. The exploitation of groundwater resources in Jafer, Azraq and Disi started at this time and the use of these very sensitive non-renewable water resources produced salination and deterioration of water quality, which, in turn, carried high political and social costs.

By the end of the 1970s Jordan's water policy reached its environmental and political limits. The first limit was linked to the scarcity of new sources for exploitation. The second was due to a failure of water cooperation policy with the other co-riparians of the Jordan Basin, which prevented the implementation of joint water projects.[10] The scarcity of water resources in terms of growing demand became increasingly evident, leading to the import of 'virtual water', in that it forced Jordan to buy from the global markets the products that the country was not able to produce on the basis of its water endowments.[11] Imports of strategic products, such as cereals, reduced the destabilising consequences of water stress throughout the country. As Allan has pointed out:

> The region's governments have been able to take a less than urgent approach to managing their water according to sound economic and environmental principles because there has been a ready supply of extremely cheap water available in a very effective and operational system, the world trade in food staples.[12]

At the same time, Jordan enhanced measures designed to promote productive efficiency, thanks to the application of water saving technologies in the agriculture sector. Modernisation of water systems, in the Jordan Valley, led to a remarkable reduction of the amount of water used for cultivation. The new hydro-technologies applied to the agricultural sector were introduced in the country thanks to technical assistance and economical support from the United States. These techniques can be considered neutral in terms of water balance since, as is the case with the import of cereals, they do not affect water allocations to different economic sectors and their introduction does not need any form of mediation at the political level.[13]

Meanwhile, in the decade from the middle of the 1970s to the middle of the 1980s Jordan underwent diversification of its productive economic structures. Manufacturing and services strengthened against a progressive decrease in the contribution of agriculture to Gross Domestic Product. In addition, the serious droughts of 1986 and 1991, intensified the water crisis and created a gradual growth in awareness of environmental problems in the political world and in public opinion.

The need to move from a supply-oriented policy to one oriented towards demand factors became an urgent consideration. Measures were adopted to extend the number of wastewater treatment facilities, recycling plants and desalination plants for brackish waters, as well as to increase urban and agricultural water tariffs. The justification for this was the requirement to move away from productive to allocative efficiency. The phase of big water projects and technical solutions to Jordan's water problems had been concerned with productive efficiency. Now issues of allocative efficiency came to the fore, despite the political implications and even though they jeopardised the position of the agricultural sector in terms of water allocation and undermined the consolidated privileges of strong lobbies, such as landowners.

This evolution of water policy in Jordan underlined the links between the use of environmental capital and the level of economic development. As Allan and Karshenas have pointed out, in the first stage of economic growth the use of natural resources beyond sustainable levels is necessary in order to develop the national economy and improve social welfare. Only a diversification of economic structure, linked to integration in the global economy, can generate new options for resources, such as demand management policy, allocative efficiency measures and the evolution of a form of political and social consciousness of environmental problems that, in turn, can engender 'natural resources reconstruction'.[14]

The economy of water: from productive to allocative efficiency

Water has long been considered an unlimited resource and therefore without price. In reality, it is a real economic commodity because work and means of production are necessary to extract it and to make it available at points of consumption. In addition water property rights can be acquired by public or private institutions. Furthermore, the status of economic commodities such as water has recently been enhanced as a result of private sector participation in water utilities; the introduction of regulation to guarantee water quality, which has imposed high treatment costs; and the growing competition amongst economic sectors over the use of scarce water resources.

Any discussion of water resource management must distinguish between productive and allocative efficiency. The first, also known as 'end-user efficiency', reflects technical concerns, such as, for instance, an increase in the volume and immediate availability of water by improving the delivery efficiency of irrigation systems. Allocative efficiency, on the other hand, requires water to be used selectively, in order to yield the best economic return to water. This implies price levels reflecting water scarcity and which remove all subsidy.[15] In effect, water consumers should pay the full cost – both capital cost and operating cost – of extracting, treating where necessary and delivering water. Price structures should also reflect what economists define as the long-run incremental or marginal cost, which is the cost of supplying the last unit of water demanded. The rationale for water pricing is related to the elasticity of water demand: the cheaper the water, the more it will be used. A low tariff structure increases water demand and forces the government to implement investment in water infrastructure, thereby reducing conservation and recycling initiatives.

From an historical point of view, tariff schemes in Jordan have not been sufficient to cover the cost of water service. In 1996, the Water Authority of Jordan – responsible for water and sewerage services throughout the country – together with the Jordan Valley Authority – responsible for development of the Jordan Rift Valley, including its water resources – published a new and increased fees structure.

Water prices vary regionally between Greater Amman and the rest of Jordan. The price increases proposed were higher in Greater Amman (36 per cent rise) than in all other regions (27 per cent). The present cost of water delivery is estimated at 0.780 JD/m. ($1.14) for municipal use and at 0.222 JD m. ($0.32) in the Jordan Valley. According to a World Bank analysis, the water services delivery system receives a subsidy from the government in excess of JD50 million annually ($70 million). The low price of water means that water consumption increases faster than the growth in population and forces the government to create infrastructure to meet this demand. If this pressure were not there, government could use these expenditures for long-term investment designed to improve water services.[16]

The concept of water productivity plays an essential role in the implementation of principles based on allocative efficiency. Water productivity can be calculated for each economic field and sub-field, and is equal to the production of all goods and services in a field – measured in terms of added value over time – divided by the water used in that field measured in terms of rates of flow calibrated in cubic metres. Water productivity is an indicator of the economic value of the resource when used in different production activities and it indicates the opportunity cost price, namely the value of water for alternative uses. It can be a useful instrument to evaluate policies adopted to manage water resources from the demand standpoint. The concept of opportunity cost, however, has to be modified by other considerations, such as equity measures for direct household consumption that must ensure that everyone has enough water for basic needs.

Recently in Jordan, the criterion of preferentially allocating water resources to those sectors which generate a higher contribution to Gross Domestic Product, has been imposed. The data show that water productivity in industrial activities is 40 times higher than in agricultural activities and clearly suggests the importance of diverting water away from the low-value, low-efficiency and highly subsidised irrigation sector.[17] Yet, of course, there are other essential uses, too and, if the Jordan water balance 1985 and 1987 is examined, it is possible to see how much the percentage of water resources for municipal uses has increased, from 18.2 per cent of the total water use in 1985 to 26.9 per cent in 1997. In the same period, the increase in the industrial sector rose from 3.4 per cent of the total to 4.3 per cent (Table 2). Despite a 10 per cent decrease in the quota allocated to agriculture, it is evident that this sector continued to be the greater user of water. In 1996, the water consumption in agriculture was 67 per cent of the total, although the sector accounted for only 5.4 per cent of Gross Domestic Product (Table 3).

This data demonstrates that only some of the reform objectives concerning water policy have been achieved. The cause for this resides in technological backwardness that prevents the rationalisation of resource use, as well as in the lack of political will because of powerful opposition from lobbies involved in agriculture.

Up to now, major imports of agricultural products have bridged the gap between water supply and demand without forcing the government to make difficult choices. These conditions will, however, be modified, when World Trade Organisation regulations, which will determine new potential to the global cereals market, come into force. The ending of agriculture subsidies in the main cereal exporting countries (United States and Europe) will help more efficient producers elsewhere and will change the pattern of historical advantage enjoyed by some states. The danger is that this may produce an increase in cereals price that will adversely affect cereal importing countries. If this is the case, then the winning strategy to overcome water crisis will lie in the diversification of production networks and in a deeper involvement in the globalisation process. In such circumstances, export earnings could allow Jordan to continue to import those products which need more water to produce domestically.[18]

The search for a new water strategy

Water sector management in Jordan has been characterised by short term measures, aimed at increasing water supply and by the lack of

Table 2. SECTORIAL WATER CONSUMPTION AND CONTRIBUTION TO GDP

Sectors	Water (MCM)		% of Water		GDP (JDm)		% of GDP	
	1988	1996	1988	1996	1988	1996	1988	1996
Agriculture, Hunting and Forestry	608	549	74.3	66.9	134.5	232.9	6.7	5.4
Mining and manufacturing	39	36	4.8	4.4	279.4	842.2	14.0	19.4
Service sectors	171	236	20.9	28.7	1418.7	2833.3	71.1	65.2
Others	0	0	0	0	163.5	439.3	0	0
Total	818	821	100.0	100.0	1996.1	4347.7	91.8	138.6

Source: 'Water Resources Management Policy Reforms for the Hashemite Kingdom of Jordan',
Second Regional Seminar on Policy Reform in Water Resources Management Middle East/North Africa
/Mediterranean (MENA/MED) Water Initiative, The World Bank, Amman, 8–11 May 1999.

an integrated approach to water resources planning. In an attempt to reform the water management system the Ministry of Water and Irrigation launched a new water strategy for 1995 and 1996. The new strategy stresses: improvement of water resources management, the reduction of environmental impact and the respect of inter-generational equity; protection of water resources from over-abstraction and the preservation of water quality; economic efficiency in the transport, distribution and use of water resources; and use of advanced technology to enhance resources management capacities.

There is a marked contradiction between these principles and the measures adopted by the government, which is still oriented towards expensive projects that are damaging to the environment. This is true of the Disi project, which plans a 325 km-long aqueduct, costing $625 million, in order to divert the non-renewable groundwater resources there towards Amman.[19] The aqueduct, which according to Jordan spokesmen is 'strategic and vital for the country', shows the same unproven assumptions as the *Great Manmade River*, the Libyan project for the exploitation of Saharan fossil waters. It is difficult to evaluate the environmental costs of this project which involves the pumping of non-renewable and antique fossil waters.[20] Moreover, the transfer of fossil water from Disi to the North threatens to deprive the South of its most important water reserve and will thus have a negative affect on the development of this part of the country.

One of the most important problems in managing water resources in Jordan is the reduction in unaccounted water losses between resources and consumers. This is calculated from the difference between the value of water supplied and the water tariffs paid to the government. These figures in Jordan vary between 53.8 per cent and 56.6 per cent of the value of the supplied water, compared to the international standard of 15 per cent.[21] The highest percentage of water loss is concentrated in the area of the Northeast Highlands (Governorate of Mafraq) and depends on two factors. On the one hand, there is the awareness of water as public good, an attitude which has its roots in Islamic tradition and in consequence it is considered as a free good, and on the other hand, there is the existence of a consolidated procedure of free access to water resources linked to land rental or ownership (Table 4). Land rental is extremely widely diffused mainly in the north of the country and it includes the right to pump groundwater from wells. The groundwater is exploited until salination occurs, which forces the landholder to move into new areas. This situation demonstrates the difficulty involved in modifying water policies in a cultural context where the symbolic value of the resource and the presence of informal relations based on privilege supervene over the objective of the efficient management of resources. Some authors have argued that in Jordan a form of 'rent capitalism' is developing whereby water is an instrument used by government to ensure support from specific social groups, such as landholders or the Bedouin tribes.[22]

Table 3. PERCENTAGE WATER LOSS IN JORDAN'S GOVERNORATES, 1994–8

Governorate	1994	1995	1996	1997	1998
Amman	53.55	54.41	50.30	48.53	49.45
Irbid	53.92	54.96	49.61	49.52	48.85
Zarqa	50.52	55.08	54.31	54.21	56.43
Madaba**	–	–	–	–	–
Balqa	66.48	58.85	59.60	61.20	62.07
Kerak	52.66	52.63	50.52	57.08	59.94
Tafila	40.30	42.17	42.52	44.80	43.92
Ma'an	5 0.63	50.16	56.71	65.77	67.37
Aqaba**	–	–	46.79	29.55	36.16
Mafraq	70.39	76.23	68.66	78.09	78.56
Ajloun**	–	–	57.78	59.92	60.38
Jarash**	–	–	50.15	47.37	60.06
Total	55.15	55.81	53.83	54.14	56.60*

Source: Water Authority, Yearly Report 1997; N. Barham, 'Human Impact on the Water Problem – the case of Jordan'.

In an attempt to transform water policy in Jordan, the investment programme laid down by the Ministry of Water and Irrigation now seeks to transfer infrastructure and services from the public to the private sector. The objective of the proposed private sector participation is to free up investment in the water sector by reducing the financial burden upon projects through the introduction of Build-Operate-Transfer (BOT) and Build-Operate-Own (BOO) systems. This has also meant the introduction of the management of water resources by private companies. In this connection, the French multinational *Lyonnaise des Eaux*, together with Jordan's *Montgomery Arabtech Jardaneh* (LEMA) have obtained contracts for infrastructure maintenance, tariff collection and water supply for the Amman urban area.[23]

LEMA has had to take action on unpaid tariffs and on network water losses. The aim is to eradicate privileges, which have allowed government leaders, officials and military officers to use a great amount of water for free. A very important part of the private sector strategy is to retrain Ministry of Water and Irrigation technical staff in charge of meter-reading and payment systems and training courses designed to improve efficiency have been introduced.

The contract with the French multinational is only concerned with the capital city and does not change the imbalances that continue elsewhere in the country. Even if privatisation offers new perspectives in terms of access to capital and international expertise, it is also incompatible with the informal relations, based on patronage, which have to date effected a fair allocation of water resources. Furthermore, the skeletal state of development of Jordan's financial system, together with the vulnerability of its private companies, forces the privatisation process to take place outside the national economic structure, so that it, in effect, becomes 'colonised' by major multinational water companies.[24]

Another important aspect of this modification in national water policy was the search for cooperative solutions to water problems. The Water Strategy underlines the need to defend and protect Jordan's access to shared water resources through bilateral and multilateral agreements. Special attention is paid to water and wastewater projects linked with the regional peace process. Such sensitivity towards regional cooperation also means that a positive step to protect and preserve the resources of the Jordan River Basin has been taken.

This is reflected in the Jordan-Israel peace treaty, which deals with the detailed allocation of water from the Yarmouk and the Jordan rivers, with storage and diversion dams, as well as with protection of water quality and allocation of groundwater in the Araba Valley. Israel has to provide Jordan with 50 million cubic metres of drinkable water annually and will provide 50 million cubic metres per annum more in the future, as new resources are exploited in common. Israel and Jordan are also expected to cooperate over storage and diversion facilities on the Yarmouk River. The first step as a result of this agreement will be the construction of a dam near Adasya on the Yarmouk River that will supply Jordan with 35 million cubic metres of water annually. The construction of a large de-salting plant in Haifa, which should encourage closer cooperation between the two countries is also under examination. The $200 million plant, financed by Jordan which does not have access to the Mediterranean Sea, will provide 50 million cubic metres of water annually to Israel, which, in turn, will supply Jordan with the same amount of water from Lake Tiberias. Another very important aspect of this cooperation is the link between Israeli and Jordanian computer databases in order to exchange information and manage the water crisis.

Jordan is also improving its relationship with Syria and is currently involved in negotiations concerning the division of the Yarmouk waters. The old project of Maqarin dam, now named Unity Dam, is again under discussion.

As far as regional cooperation is concerned, Jordan is participating in a working group on water, one of the five multilateral working groups created as part of the multilateral aspect of the Middle East peace negotiations in the aftermath of the Madrid Conference in 1991. The most important project resulting from these joint efforts is the implementation of a prototype desalination plant in Aqaba that was expected to provide 10 million cubic metres of desalinated water per year for the city. The project will cost between $10 million and $15 million and will start in the year 2001. Together with the desalination project, a training centre will be created where Jordanians, Israelis and Palestinians will be trained in the most advanced desalination techniques.[25] The working group has also founded a research centre in Oman which has invested $17 million to develop technical studies on the reduction of the desalination costs. The centre has been financed by the United States, Korea, Japan, the European Union, Oman and Israel. Moreover, almost $60 million have been allocated by the working group in the past three years to implement practical projects. One of them is a planning course for thirty Israeli, Jordanian and Palestinian technicians, carried out in each other's country respectively and aimed at using mobile water-quality laboratories to monitor sources of pollutants and other contaminants.

Despite the quest for answers to common problems in the Jordan basin, such as environmental conservation, quality standards and search of new sources, the joint efforts conducted by the countries of the region seem still very weak in comparison with the challenges deriving from an environment of water scarcity and power imbalance.

One of the most problematic aspects is the differential access to Jordan water between upstream and downstream countries in the Jordan Basin. The power associated with position along the river course – quite poor for Jordan – is associated with military economic and technological disparities between Israel and other co-riparian countries. To date, approaches involving conflict have prevailed over negotiation and it seems very difficult to establish goals, strategies and division of responsibilities as far as regional water resource management is concerned. As the economist, Franklin Fisher, has recently pointed out, it would be sufficient to divert the money used for military purposes to build desalination plants and to increase technological cooperation in this very sensitive sector, in order to solve the regional water problem.

Institutional problems and social resources scarcity

One of the most important aspects of water management in an arid environment is the transition from supply-side to demand-side policies. Some authors have tried to develop theoretical models to analyse transition patterns in countries with different levels of development and different levels of water resources endowment. Such an approach has the advantage that it introduces social aspects as a fundamental element in determining the adaptive capacity of a society to a situation of water scarcity. We have already cited the views of Allan and Karshenas over the links between the stages of economic development and the degradation of environmental capital. Economic development is considered the key factor in moving towards a sustainable level of water resource exploitation, but this structural change is also strictly related to institutional and social capacities able to achieve such a target.

Recently, Ohlsson pointed out that adaptation to a situation of water scarcity entails a mobilisation of social resources. This can be defined as a mix of institutional capacity for the introduction of a new set of rules regarding water use and of social ability to accept these technocratic solutions. The lack of ability for adaptation is a second order problem ('second order scarcity'), different in kind from first order problems ('first order scarcity') which are linked to natural resources.

Adaptive capacity has two components, related to structural and social concerns. Structural components depend on the intellectual capacity and level of scientific evolution of a given society. They determine the ability of the society to introduce advanced solutions into the management of the challenge of a water crisis. They can be considered partly exogenous because technological solutions can be imported from outside and can be assisted by foreign support as a consequence of a political will. Conversely, the social component of adaptive capacity is completely endogenous because it depends both on the legitimacy of the political regime and on the willingness of the population to cope with a new approach to water resource management without social disruption. In this context the dominant approach to water use, the so-called 'sanctioned discourse', plays an important role:

Sanctioned discourse is the discourse regarding what is good and acceptable practice that prevails within an institutional or a political setting at any given moment in time. Significantly this 'sanctioned discourse' forms a sort of paradigm, defining the problem on hand and the type of solutions that are acceptable.[26]

At any given time in a society, there is a political, scientific or professional leading group which allows new ideas to be introduced and dictates the content of the dominant discourse with respect to water resources. A change in water resources management towards sustainability must be associated with a new perception of water, which in turn can mobilise a new set of social resources. Supply-side strategies prevail when technological solutions allow water demand to be satisfied without arbitration, thus reducing the political cost of adjustment. The collapse of this equilibrium occurs when an ecological crisis renders the supply-side approach incapable of meeting demand. In these circumstances, a new environmental consciousness emerges, the water crisis opens a 'window of opportunity' that a new emerging elite uses to change the sanctioned discourse towards demand-side solutions. In short, if a specific social entity is able to develop a strong 'adaptive capacity' it is also able to manage the transition to a water demand management system by gradually adopting allocative efficiency measures.[27]

The theoretical approach mentioned above can be used to explain the evolution of water policy in Jordan. In the 1960s, the country adopted a supply-side policy that reached its limits as a result of increasing costs and the complexity of technological solutions. As a result, a 'first order scarcity' emerged, related to growing demand and environmental pressure on water resources.

Economic development in Jordan inevitably involves a progressive reduction in the contribution of agriculture to Gross Domestic Product while demand for resources from the domestic and industrial sectors will increase. However, this economic reality cannot influence the allocation of water resources between economic sectors because the 'sanctioned discourse' still considers agriculture as the foundation of the national economy and the government must respect elite preferences in order to maintain the political consensus. In short, in Jordan the lack of adaptive capacity to water crisis is related to a scarcity in social resources. The institutions of state and society are not strong enough to enforce awareness of environmental problems which would, in turn, lead to a new appreciation of the significance of national water resources. The symbolic value of water dominates its economic value and the Jordanian government is responsible for this attitude because:

. . . economic principles and market processes themselves are unlikely to deliver sustainable water management, without regulation and direct action by Government and its agents. Water policy can benefit from the discipline of economics, but it is no substitute for capability in political systems.[28]

The lack of law enforcement against illegal use and tolerance towards water theft demonstrates how water shortage is socially invisible in Jordan as in many Middle Eastern countries.[29] Indeed, the water problem in Jordan is a by-product of an institutional and political crisis whose features are the difficulty of introducing politically costly 'demand side management options', combined with strong social resistance towards considering technocratic solutions as both reasonable and legitimate.

Water in Jordan, as in the whole of the Middle East, has long been considered a never-ending resource – a gift from God. According to Islamic law, Muslims are partners in three elements essential for survival – water, grass and fire. This perception of water resources as a free good has influenced the pattern of water use until water emerged as a constraint to economic growth.

The appreciation of water as an economic good has led to a new approach to water resource management, involving the concept of allocative efficiency. This new approach has faced great difficulties because of the symbolic value attached to water and the strategic importance it has for the national economy. Giving a price to water, which reflects its scarcity and its use in economic sectors, guaranteeing a higher resource productivity, represents a definite change in Jordan's water policy. Much attention has been paid to protecting the water cycle through the increasing use of non-conventional sources, such as de-salting and wastewater recycling.

Although the principles of allocative efficiency can improve the management of water resources, the role of the economy is not sufficient, in itself, to alter Jordan's water situation. The cultural aspects linked to perceptions of water are still fundamental, because there are powerful obstacles to a change in social perceptions of water. This prevents the popular acceptance of principles of environmental sustainability and resource protection. It is, therefore, very important to study the behaviour of water consumers and the social dynamics of water demand management.

In this context, policy makers play an important role. They must legitimate their water strategy by introducing allocative efficiency measures at a rate that is socially and politically acceptable. Institutions must respond to the challenges generated by the water crisis, which otherwise may threaten economic development and the welfare of the population. The solution may be what some authors have called a 'new hydro-social contract' based on a common water ethic as part of a new environmental consciousness. Only fair resource distribution and an increase in social awareness of Jordan's water problem can change the outlook when water itself is becoming a factor of territorial imbalance and social inequality.

NOTES

1. H. El-Naser, 'Water resources management policy reforms for the Hashemite Kingdom of Jordan', Second Regional Seminar on Policy Reform in Water Resources Management Middle East/North Africa/Mediterranean (MENA/MED) Water Initiative, Amman, 1999.

2. *Water for the future: The West Bank and Gaza Strip, Israel and Jordan*, Washington, DC: National Academic Press, 1999.

3. Y. Bakour, J. Kolars, *The Arab Machrek: hydrologic history, problems and perspectives*. P. Rogers, P. Lydon, *Water in the Arab World*, Harvard University Press, 1994.

4. In 1997 the number of wells was 484 and 76.6 per cent of them were unlicensed. N. Barham, 'Human impact on the water problem – the case of Jordan', unpublished.

5. H. El Naser, Z. Elias, *Jordan's water sector*, United Nations Economic and Social Commission for Western Asia (ESCWA) and Centre for Environmental Health Activities (CEHA), Regional symposium on water use and conservation, 28 November–2 December 1993, Amman.

6. In Amman alone there are 1.8 million people consuming around 45 per cent of the country's 300 million cubic metres of domestic water supplies.

7. J. Trottier, 'L'eau, la Jordanie et l'entité palestinienne naissante', *Les Cahiers du Monde Arabe*, 122 (1995).

8. M. Lavergne, 'Aménagement du territoire et croissance urbaine en Jordanie: Amman et le désert jordanien', *Maghreb-Machrek*, 140 (1993).

9. E. Ferragina, 'Alcune considerazioni sulla gestione delle risorse idriche nei Paesi mediorientali: il caso della Giordania', Dept. Of Geography – Naples: University Federico II, (November 1995). E. Ferragina 'Valorisation des ressources hydriques et securité alimentaire en Jordanie', *Les Cahiers du Monde Arabe*, nos. 121–122, Centre d'Etudes et de Recherche sur le Monde Arabe Contemporaine (CERMAC), Université Catholique de Louvain (1995).

10. This is the case of the Al-Wahda Dam (Unity Dam) mentioned earlier. This was a Syro-Jordan project of the 1960s which could have partly solved the Yarmouk water storage problems during summer time. From the beginning the project was strongly opposed by Israel which led to funds being cut by the World Bank and, as a consequence, an end to the entire project. M. Shiffler, 'Sustainable development of water resources in Jordan', and G. Shapland, 'Policy options for downstream states in the Middle East', both in J. A. Allan, C. Mallat, *Water in the Middle East: legal, political and commercial implications*, London: Tauris Academic Studies, 1995.

11. Since a thousand of tons of water are needed to produce one ton of grain, the import of one ton of grain corresponds to the import of one thousand tons of water. J. A. Allan, 'The political economy of water: reason for optimism but long term caution' in J. A. Allan (ed.), *Water, peace and the Middle East: negotiating resources in the Jordan Basin*, London: Tauris Academic Studies, 1996.

12. J. A. Allan 'The Political Economy of Water: reason for Optimism but long term caution' in J. A. Allan (ed.), 1996; p.114

13. A. R. Turton, 'Water scarcity and social adaptive capacity: towards an understanding of the social dynamics of water demand management in developing

countries', MEWREW Occasional Paper, Water Issues Study Group, School of Oriental and African Studies (SOAS), 9, 1999.

14. J. A. Allan and M. Karshenas, 'Managing environment capital: the case of water in Israel, Jordan, the West Bank and Gaza, 1947–1995' in J. A. Allan (ed.), *Water peace and the Middle East: negotiating resources in the Jordan River Basin*, London: I. B. Tauris, 1996.

15. E. Ferragina, 'La gestione integrata delle risorse idriche del bacino del Giordano', *L'acqua nei paesi mediterranei. Problemi di gestione di una risorsa scarsa*, Bologna: Il Mulino, 1998.

16. El Naser (1999).

17. S. Merret, *Introduction to the Economics of Water Resources*, London: UCL Press, 1997.

18. T. Allan, *Middle East water: local and global issues*, SOAS – Water Issues Group, University of London, 1997.

19. M. Schiffler, 'Sustainable development of water resources in Jordan: ecological and economic aspects in a long-term perspective', J. A. Allan, C. Mallat, *Water in the Middle East: legal, political and commercial implications*, London: I. B. Tauris, 1995.

20. Recently Libya has announced its intention of financing half of the works and of providing the same type of pipes as those used for creating the Great Manmade River. C. Chesnot, 'Pénurie d'eau au Proche-Orient', *Le Monde Diplomatique*, February 2000.

21. These losses must include network losses, illegal connections and the destruction of water meters. The economic losses deriving from unaccounted water are enormous and could be transformed into investments in this field.

22. N. Barham, 'Human Impact on the Water Problem – The case of Jordan'.

23. Managing the demand for urban use can greatly reduce the demand of water, especially if we consider that the increase in water demand in the future will come mainly from the urban sector. LEMA has obtained the Zai treatment plant control which provides 40 per cent of the country water need. To this we add the managing of 100 wells, 4,500 km. of water network, 1,500 km. of sewers and two treatment plants for 270.000 users.

24. D. Storer, 'The potential role of privatisation in the management of water resources in the Middle East', J. A. Allan, C. Mallat (1995).

25. D. Charkasi, 'Water working group survives regional political challenge', *Jordan Times*, 20 March 2000.

26. A. R. Turton, *Water scarcity and social adaptive capacity: Towards an understanding of the social dynamics of water demand management in developing countries*, MEWREW Occasional Paper n. 9, Water Issues Study Group, School of Oriental and African Studies (SOAS), 1999.

27. Turton, op. cit., p. 10

28. J. Morris, 'Water policy: economic theory and political reality' in M. Kay, T. Franks and L. Smith (eds), *Water economics, management and demand*, London, 1997.

29. T. Allan, 'Water in international systems: a risk society analysis of regional problemsheds and global hydrologies', paper presented at the Department of Geography, Oxford University, Conference on Water Resources and Risk, March 1999.

INDEX

Index